Latecomers in the Global Economy

The past fifty years have produced examples of late developing countries, especially from East Asia, catching up with and even overtaking established economic powers. This has prompted enormous interest in the policies which have resulted in this success and the lessons which might be learned from them.

In *Latecomers in the Global Economy*, the authors address a new formulation of industrial policy for latecoming semi-industrialized countries. They argue that as national economies acquire an unprecedented degree of openness, countries which are at different stages of development increasingly compete in a common arena, but with unequal terms of competition. This book seeks to develop systematic, theoretical arguments about consistent, sustainable industrial policies for latecomers in order to offer the basis for theory and public policy.

Latecomers in the Global Economy contains contributions from some of the most esteemed international economists working in this area. It will be a valuable guide for economists and international policymakers with an interest in development issues.

Michael Storper is Professor of Regional and International Development in the School of Public Policy and Social Research at UCLA, USA. His most recent book is *Worlds of Production: the Action Frameworks of the Economy* (Harvard University Press, 1997).

Stavros B. Thomadakis is Professor of Financial Economics at the University of Athens. He is the author of several books and numerous articles on financial and industrial economics, banking and economic history.

Lena J. Tsipouri is Assistant Professor in the Department of Economic Sciences at the University of Athens, Greece. She has published widely on technological and industrial development and the management of technology.

Latecomers in the Global Economy

Edited by Michael Storper, Stavros B. Thomadakis and Lena J. Tsipouri

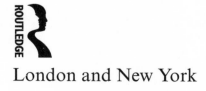

London and New York

First published 1998
by Routledge
11 New Fetter Lane, London EC4P 4EE

Simultaneously published in the USA and Canada
by Routledge
29 West 35th Street, New York, NY 10001

Typeset in Times by M Rules
Printed and bound in Great Britain by Redwood Books,
Trowbridge, Wiltshire

British Library Cataloguing in Publication Data
A catalogue record for this book is available from
the British Library

Library of Congress Cataloging in Publication Data
Latecomers in the global economy / ed., Michael Storper,
    Stavros Thomadakis, Lena Tsipouri.
        p.   cm.
    1. Industrial policy.   2. Sustainable development.
3. Competition, International.   I. Storper, Michael.
II. Thomadakis, Stavros.   III. Tsipouri, Lena, 1953–   .
HD3611.L34   1998
338.0—dc21   97–26309
                                            CIP

ISBN 0–415–14867–7

Contents

Illustrations

Contributors

Ash Amin is Professor of Geography at Durham University. His latest book is *Beyond Market and Hierarchy: Interactive Governance and Social Complexity*, coedited with Jerzy Hausner (Edward Elgar).

David Bailey is Lecturer in Industrial Economics in the Research Centre for Industrial Strategy, University of Birmingham Business School.

Christian Bellak, Department of Economics, Vienna. He has been a Research Fellow at the University of Reading (1994) and Helsinki School of Economics (1992). His main research areas are in Foreign Direct Investment and Multinational Enterprises.

John Cantwell is a Professor of International Economics at the University of Reading. He has been a Visiting Professor of Economics at the University of Rome 'La Sapienza', the University of Social Sciences, Toulouse and Rutgers University, New Jersey. His main research areas are the economics of technological change and international production.

J.R Chaponnière is a Senior Research Fellow at IREP-D/CNRS, Grenoble. He has conducted several field researches in East Asian developing countries and has extensively published on industrial policies issues.

Sandro Gaudenzi has worked on the concept of integration of European regional support mechanisms to the less favored regions and was subsequently a director for the implementation of the Community Support Framework in Ireland, Greece and Portugal.

Marc Lautier is an Assistant Professor at the University of Rouen. He has conducted several field researches in East Asian developing countries and has extensively published on industrial policies issues.

Eoin O'Malley is a Senior Research Officer in the Economics and Social Research Institute, Dublin, Ireland.

Lynn Krieger Mytelka is on leave from her positions as Professor at Carleton University (Ottawa) and CEREM/Forum, Université de Paris-X (Nanterre) and serving as Director of UNCTAD's Division on Investment, Technology and Enterprise Development in Geneva.

Christos Pitelis, Center of Financial Studies, University of Athens and Queens' College, University of Cambridge.

Michael Storper is Professor of Regional and International Development in the School of Public Policy and Social Research at UCLA, Los Angeles, USA and Professor of Human and Social Science, University of Marne-la-Vallée, France.

Roger Sugden is Professor of Industrial Economics at the University of Birmingham and Director of the Institute for Industrial Development Policy, a joint venture between the University of Birmingham and the Universita Degli Studi di Ferrara.

Morris Teubal is in the Economics Department, Hebrew University of Jerusalem, and the Industrial Development Policy Group (IDPG), Jerusalem Institute for Israel Studies, Israel.

Stavros B. Thomadakis is Professor of Financial Economics at the University of Athens. He is the author of several books and numerous articles on financial and industrial economics, banking and economic history.

Rachael Thomas was formerly a Research Associate at the Research Centre for the Industrial Strategy, University of Birmingham.

John Tomaney is lecturer in Urban and Regional Development Studies (CURDS) at Newcastle University.

Lena J. Tsipouri is Assistant Professor in the Department of Economic Sciences at the University of Athens, Greece. Her research interests are in technological change and industrial policies.

Introduction

Michael Storper, Stavros B. Thomadakis and Lena J. Tsipouri

This book addresses issues of industrial policy for *latecoming semi-industrialized countries* (LSCs). Most of the abundant literature on the subjects of industrialization, industrial policy, technological change, and the economics of development concentrates on either developed or developing countries, or focuses on a specific geographical region such as Latin America or Asia. An alternative but nonetheless important grouping of countries has been less well studied – countries that are partially industrialized and that have achieved a medium level of development. Since they share many of the strengths and weaknesses of both industrialized and developing nations, LSCs face both unique opportunities and constraints as they integrate into the world economy.

The notion of *latecomer* takes on a special meaning in an increasingly global economy. As national economies acquire an unprecedented degree of openness, countries at different stages of development find themselves competing in a common arena but under unequal terms. The traditional debate regarding the coexistence of developed and underdeveloped economies in a unifying world market must be reframed in a way which is more amenable to policy analysis, when viewed with respect to LSCs. In this context the distance and differences between pioneers and latecomers are far more limited than in the development–underdevelopment paradigm. This closer relationship between pioneers and latecomers requires a more specialized policy discussion.

Our objective is to fill this gap in the theoretical and empirical literature on industrial policy. Tackling the problem of industrial policy with respect to LSCs offers unique and powerful lessons about the possibilities for industrial development in today's world. An essential source of inspiration for the ideas presented in this book has been the *Community Support Frameworks* of the European Union, large multiperiod programs that assure massive transfer of funds to the Union's weakest regions, supporting structural adjustment in these countries so as to enable them to compete on more equal terms in the Single European Market. Politicians and policymakers have been implementing the Community Support Frameworks in an empiricist fashion, seeking guidance mainly from their regions' past experiences (often of failure) and international best practices, which are sometimes difficult to adapt to local circumstances. The chapters in this book seek to develop systematic arguments about consistent sustainable industrial policies for latecomers in order to offer the basis for positive theory, comparative perspectives, and policy specification.

The premise of this book is that LSCs have important common characteristics that make generalizations about their strategies possible. Latecomers constitute a unique class in terms of industrial development. Unlike typical developing countries, in which the lack of basic education and infrastructure present fundamental obstacles to economic progress, typical latecomers are countries that have already advanced part way to "developed" status and have at certain points of their history demonstrated high (but not sustainable) growth rates. LSCs have succeeded in generalizing education, acquired basic infrastructure, and even put together the rudiments of a national system of technology transfer and innovation. The latter is usually based on a supply–push, since they are as yet generally unable to mobilize demand and transfer knowledge into competitive manufacturing. At the same time, latecomers have inadequate productive structures, often despite massive financial transfers. LSCs also lack both industrial culture and advanced organizational skills. These factors are the main obstacles that keep them from successfully emulating the economic effectiveness of advanced countries. Discussion of these factors has often been elliptical and diffuse, precisely because no scholarly inquiry has ever focused exclusively on latecomer semi-industrialized countries. By focusing on LSCs, this book specifically defines such factors and sharpens our analytical understanding of them. Whereas traditional development thinking is rooted in the inquiry about the need to acquire "hard" factors that promote development (financial capital, skills, production techniques, specialized inputs), the inquiry focusing on latecomers has necessarily led to an examination of "soft" factors such as industrial culture, intra- and interfirm organization, cooperation, and collective goods. We shall, in particular, refer to two key concepts here: an economy based on *continuous learning*, and the *conventions,* or routines and forms of coordination needed to achieve growth through learning.

The population of LSCs is more substantial than is suggested by the dearth of scholarship on these countries. Their geographical breadth spans the countries and regions on the periphery of the European Union, including the countries of Eastern and Central Europe, and extends to several Asian economies, as well as to countries in the Latin American southern cone and Mexico. The arguments and the case studies that are presented in the book do not offer exhaustive coverage of countries. However, they reflect cases that are at once geographically widespread and similar in latecomer status so as to afford a meaningful basis for comparison. The question that immediately arises in this comparative exercise is whether country size still matters and to what extent. As the result of the process of globalization, the negotiating power of independent states has diminished, with a few exceptions where both market size and deeply rooted protectionism allow states to preserve a certain degree of negotiating power. We would argue that with the exception of China, India, and perhaps a few other highly populated countries, size matters less and less. For countries with populations in the tens of millions (and with medium per capita income), globalization acts as a catalyst for the homogenization of markets.

Globalization means increased openness of markets, and internationalization of capital flows. This makes it impossible to practice traditional industrial policy because markets cannot be closed as was once possible. Since latecomers cannot influence the constraints and conditions of globalization, other instruments of intervention need to be found. Globalization is a double-edged sword. On the one hand, it clearly creates new sets of constraints on countries through more open markets and requirements for macroeconomic performance and adjustment. These constraints are more onerous for latecomers who, by definition, suffer from lower productivity and reduced competitiveness. On the other hand, globalization does not bring about a placeless planetary economy. In many ways it is giving rise to a "re-specialization" of countries and regions, especially regarding technological competencies and *savoir-faire* related to specific functions and products. This provides an opportunity for countries to benefit substantially from participation in the global economy.

Orthodox theory proposes structural adjustment as the principal alternative to traditional industrial policy. Largely consisting of a cocktail of macroeconomic policies designed to accompany trade liberalization, monetary integration, and liberalized capital movements, structural adjustment offers solutions that address only the first of the two edges of the globalization sword, ignoring the mobilization of local competitive specificities, such as technology and know-how, trust and culture. In contrast, most of the theoretical chapters in this book argue that macroeconomic policy alone is insufficient to guide countries through the adjustment process. Moreover, a policy of implementing structural adjustment by itself may even prevent less-favored LSCs from making the transition to fully developed status, as restrictive monetary policies keep incomes from expanding. Important as it may be, macroeconomic policy has a limited role in the development process. Macroeconomic policy is fundamentally directed toward stabilization under conditions of established industrial structure; but it is not as well suited to situations where a country's position in the world division of labor is changing. Thus, while necessary for stabilization purposes, for increasing efficiency through budget-cutting, and for restoring confidence (which can even lead to positive changes in local informal rules), macroeconomic policy can never be the key to the creation of new wealth.

The new role for industrial policy is to deal with the totality of the development process, requiring coordination of micro, macro, and intermediate level policies. Consequently, the capital mobility can no longer be considered the most important prerequisite for international growth. Capital mobility is important for providing financial access in areas with a limited savings potential, but it is often related to impatient finance, which does not promote stable structures, as indicated by Stavros Thomadakis. The case studies presented here also demonstrate important limits of macroeconomic policy. Despite the implementation of a stabilization program, Ireland could not achieve accelerated development until structural intervention was introduced. Similarly, Korea and Taiwan – both typical Southeast Asian success stories – have combined macroeconomic stabilization programs with massive structural intervention. In Central Macedonia the business sector has taken the initiative of supplementing Greek macroeconomic policy with structural intervention of a highly participatory form, contributing to a record of industrial performance that surpasses that of other regions in Greece. Finally, in Central and Eastern European countries, macroeconomic policy considerations – undoubtedly correct in their isolated context – have outweighed industrial policy considerations, and this risks ultimately leading to the creation of noncompetitive local industries instead of fostering a competitive revival there.

It is the other side of the globalization process, the development of specialized technological competencies, that affords the main potential opportunity to latecomer countries. But this involves a change in status. Christian Bellak and John Cantwell stress that the accumulative, path-dependent nature of most technologies prevents latecomers from adopting infant-industry strategies. Technology standards are given for – not set by – latecomers and they must react to them by entering the global technology networks of multinational corporations. Effecting this change in status requires LSCs to foster a learning economy, wherein industrial systems and their principal agents engage in learning in order to develop specialized competitive technological competencies. Michael Storper makes this argument in Chapter 1.

The learning economy is the organization of firms that facilitates effective responses to technological change through the accumulation of know-how, continuous adaptation to new knowledge, and the pursuit of new, higher quality, more cost-effective production. The emergence of the learning economy requires investments in organizational assets at the level of both the firm and the economy. But firms are willing to carry the costs of restructuring only if profit margins allow for it and if the relevant conventions have been built up. These conditions existed, for example, in post-war Scandinavian history. The cost of continuous adaptation under uncertainty can lead to market failures. This is more pronounced in LSCs that are characterized by economic dependence, thereby leading to ever greater uncertainty. Put another way, their conventions tend to favor orientation to the short-term. Further, states have neither the funds nor the expertise to put together the elements of a learning economy through the provision of strategic public goods. The absence of organizational investments and conventions to promote transformation of generic research into productively useful results, and to enable the subsequent private appropriation of benefits from these results, is an important example of this failure. Chapter 3 by Lena Tsipouri and Sandro Gaudenzi and Chapter 5 by Morris Teubal examine this deficiency, concluding that public policy must be directed toward altering the behavioral aspects of firms rather than toward the profitability of research projects.

Many critical dimensions of coordination for learning are not assured by the market. Organizational learning is the process of generating new competencies and improving old ones. As Teubal explains, it is a social phenomenon that cannot be reduced to the individual learning processes of the members of the organization, since it requires the development of common codes for coordination and communication among the members. This leads to market failures due to both positive and negative externalities. It can also lead to conflicts between agents with different time horizons. Coordination cannot be based on short-term individual profitability; it needs to be pursued with a longer vision. Given the uncertainties that prevail in the less competitive markets of LSCs, the role of the state as a catalyst for starting and sustaining coordination becomes crucial. But this role is neither easy nor well prescribed, and more often than not massive state intervention has led to government failures substituting for earlier market failures.

In advanced countries, learning paralleled the development process. In contrast, adaptation and adjustment have been slow and fragmented in LSCs for historical reasons. Knowledge accumulation is a necessary, but not a sufficient, condition for learning and development. Learning requires coordination among a complex array of economic actors (firms, governments, labor markets, innovators) over time. Therefore, learning is a long process that can be achieved only through a distinct form of intervention, one that creates new informal rules, routines, and conventions between economic agents. It is precisely this new goal that should be the target of industrial policy. All the case studies presented in this volume indicate this in one way or another.

This focus on coordination for the purpose of learning fundamentally distinguishes LSC industrial policy from both orthodox and heterodox policy frameworks. The centrality of coordination stands in contrast to the income restraints and tight money policies that dominate standard macroeconomic policy, and the pervasiveness of capital grants in standard industrial policy. However, the primacy given to coordination-for-learning does not mean that all the standard tools of industrial policy are to be abandoned, but rather that their substantive purposes are now altered to include and give priority to coordination over time for learning.

This approach has three essential premises: that learning has collective dimensions; that the main objectives of policy should be to bring the right actors together for learning; and, most importantly, that learning has a temporal dynamic that alters the initial parameters of technological change, as well as the specific tasks in learning itself. Hence, learning involves coordination over shifting terrain, where the agents and institutions involved must be reflective about the process in which they are involved, in order to alter their own parameters over time. Successful examples, at both the macro and intermediate levels, are presented in the case studies. For example, according to Lynn Mytelka (Chapter 8), it was the Korean government's modification of its position to support widening the Chaebol sector, combined with the growth of innovative SMEs, that made the formation of an alliance between the state and industry possible. This discouraged rent-seeking and stimulated a process of continuous innovation. In Ireland, the Industrial Development Authority reviewed its policy and adapted to the behavior of multinational corporations, thus increasing the MNC contribution to local value added and generating multiplier effects. This is documented by Eoin O'Malley in Chapter 10 on Irish industrial policy, and confirmed by Ash Amin and John Tomaney's comparative analysis (Chapter 7) which finds higher contributions by multinationals to the local economy in Ireland than in either Portugal or Scotland.

If firms in LSCs are not able to adjust to global competition and external shocks by means of trajectories based on learning and adaptation, then industrial policy is reduced to a minimalist approach that seeks merely to restrain costs of production. In contrast, the expanded meaning and the special content of industrial policy as it applies to latecomers incorporates measures that enable firms to change trajectories, to adapt their qualities and outputs to new knowledge and new needs, and to carry their battle for survival and growth into a field of strategic choices. To a large extent, the same applies to government organizations, which – like firms – must learn and adjust, lest policies become rigid and ineffective. Most of the chapters in this volume, in particular Chapters 1, 3, 4, 5, and 6, shed some light on this aspect of learning for both firms and institutions, while the case studies on Ireland and Greece (Chapters 10 and 11) give both positive and negative examples of learning and adjustment. Coordination that changes parameters of action over time appears to be the only way to take LSCs from one status in the world economy to another. Consequently, coordination becomes the central component of industrial policy for latecomers.

The authors in this volume place emphasis on different aspects, levels, and forms of coordination. In some cases coordination takes the form of creating and sharing hard elements of the industrial process. For others, the foundation for a coordination-based approach is predicated on the need for soft intervention, which can rapidly improve routines and accelerate the diffusion process, leading to external economies. But regardless of the form or level, it is important to overcome barriers – seemingly inherent in LSCs – in order to achieve coordination and market sustainability. In other words, it is important to go beyond the dilemma of state or market, and to specify the forms that are most likely to succeed, identify the agents most capable of implementing cooperation, and determine transaction and governance costs. National or regional policies in Taiwan and Korea have been successful in this regard, by taking initiatives that achieve sector- or region-wide sharing of benefits. The case of the Industrial Development Authority in Ireland demonstrates that coordination can be accomplished successfully by a national administration, even in the absence of a broad coherent industrial policy. Similar elements can be found in Teubal's description of the change of routines achieved by means of well-targeted interventions in the national innovation systems in LSCs. Perhaps even more importantly, given the limitations of national policy due to government failures, particularly those intrinsic to latecomers, intermediate level collective forces and agents (corporatism) can also be mobilized to play a crucial role in LSCs. This is elaborated in Chapter 2, but concrete elements of success appear also in the case studies of Central Macedonia (Chapter 11) and the countries of Southeast Asia (Chapter 9).

The chapters in this book advance an unorthodox view of how coordination can be facilitated. Whereas much traditional literature on industrial policy centers on the effectiveness of formal institutions, rules, and incentives, that is not – in the view of the authors of the chapters that follow – the most essential part of a policy. Routines, conventions, and informal rules are now the key elements of coordination. Formal institutions and rules, while necessary, generally cannot function without these informal dimensions. Informal rules are the result of expectations that govern the responses of the actors. Conventions are the practices, routines, agreements, and associated informal or institutional forms that bind agents together through mutual expectations. Conventions are thus the (still intangible) part of informal rules that lie at the origin of decision-making on resource allocation. Behavior is the observable outcome of these conventions and rules. While informal rules and conventions are deeply rooted and very difficult to change because doing so requires the forging of new social values, individual decisions and behaviors can be changed by incentive schemes, small experiments, and dialogue. Working upward and outward, accumulated behavioral changes can gradually lead to new conventions and informal rules. Formal mechanisms are generally introduced in order to act as catalysts for change in these informal dimensions.

Mobilization of collective interests at the intermediate economic level is one of the new forms of industrial policy. This is demonstrated by the case of Central Macedonia, where local industrial federations and chambers took on behaviors of coordinated learning and thereby accumulated know-how, a characteristic that now differentiates them from corresponding organizations in other Greek regions. On the other hand, it can be argued that this is precisely what Central and Eastern European countries do not do. David Bailey, Roger Sugden, and Rachael Thomas stress in Chapter 12 that government objectives in those countries have had the common aim of making industry competitive by Western standards, hoping that indigenous industry would develop and become efficient. As multinationals could not be used to develop particular activities or industries as part of a coherent industrial strategy, indigenous industry remained weak.

This raises the question of who is to implement the policy. Institutional pluralism is a key to context-sensitivity, which is an inherent and necessary dimension of learning. Consequently, the new industrial policy can be implemented by many institutional varieties and groupings. As Teubal points out, there is no standard administrative model. Institutional diversity encompasses organizational and geographical levels: state, nonstate, collective business agents, regional, national, and others. With new tools for handling information, regional initiatives in particular can flourish within the given constraints of national environments. Various types of coalitions at different economic and geographical levels can also be built.

We know from experience that protectionist policies and macroeconomic adjustments have not succeeded in creating the external or scale economies in latecomers that would assure their sustainable development. This is due to uncertainties that lead to market failures which cannot be corrected by the state when it takes the central role. The accumulated experience of failures suggests that there is an alternative way to design industrial policy which articulates intervention in a manner that favors a climate of learning through coordination. Institutional pluralism is necessary to achieve that goal, with institutions that are autonomous, transparent, and accountable.

Clearly, the process we argue for requires agents who possess specialized capabilities to accomplish this change. They may come from the ranks of existing traditional agents who take up the challenge to transform themselves gradually to the new requirements; or they may appear in entirely new and nontraditional forms, introducing fresh modes of interaction. In the former category, the first choice might be agents who are either mature or threatened. But the likelihood of agents adapting themselves to the new needs will be enhanced when they are presented with above average opportunities to do so, for example through the allocation of the Community Support Framework funds.

On the other hand, institutional pluralism is not an absolute principle; it should not lead to an institutional free-for-all. There may be the need to set ground rules for interactions amongst institutions in order to reduce the corrosive effects of poor interactions. For example, when certain functions are decentralized to lower institutional levels, it may be necessary to establish principles for interaction, so that one institution does not simply "dump" or offload negative externalities onto another.

The state becomes a key agent in promoting private-sector learning, but because learning is a dynamic process that alters the parameters of agents' interactions over time, public institutions must be reflective, incorporating a capacity to learn themselves, and constantly adjusting their own modes of functioning. The decisive factor is that both state and nonstate agents must enjoy autonomy, while at the same time assuring transparency and accepting accountability. These requirements will differentiate the new policy approach from the earlier failures of statist formulas. In their new role, state agencies are only one part of the system; thus, the errors of an individual agent can be dampened, and problematic agents avoided or eliminated entirely, without causing the failure of the whole system.

The field of industrial policies for LSCs, as we have defined it, involves an interaction between the specificities of conditions in LSCs, their position within the world economy, and lessons that apply more generally to any industrial policy that aims at promoting sustained, high-wage economic development at the end of the twentieth century. While not calling for a complete abandonment of traditional tools of industrial policy, it calls for abandoning a certain number of them. More importantly, it requires new types of problem-solving on the part of public agencies, and very new sorts of interactions between public and private agents. The chapters that follow explore these issues in considerable detail, and we hope they will serve to crystallize a new phase of debate and practical experimentation in the field of LSC industrial policy.

Part I
Theoretical foundations

1 Industrial policy for latecomers

Products, conventions, and learning

Michael Storper[1]

INDUSTRIAL POLICY: NEITHER NATIONALIST NOR KEYNESIAN

Industrial latecomers are faced with a context in which their traditional avenues of policy to promote industrialization are no longer available. Protectionism – whether tariff-based or import-substitution-based – is more and more difficult to carry out because the emerging international trade order inhibits the latecomers from closing their markets, even selectively. Only a very few countries, such as China, have the market size that gives them real bargaining power in this domain.

At the level of domestic policy, the Keynesian–Marxian formula of balancing productivity gains and wage gains no longer provides the key to promoting virtuous circles of output and employment growth. Modern management and technology, as well as existing income-smoothing institutions, no longer tightly link growth to workers' incomes, and producers can reduce their wage costs via relocation on a global scale. The Keynesian formula of pumping up expectations as a means of generating investment and growth works to generate investment, but not full employment. For owners and investors, profitability (especially if we include appreciation of assets) has become possible without generating full employment and is no longer dependent on rates of growth that could generate full employment (Petit 1993). Even though it might be socially desirable if Marxian or Keynesian policy formulas were followed today, any nation that attempts to do so alone will be severely sanctioned by financial markets, while at the international level there is no prospect of equitable global reflation in sight.

The policy problem in the short- and medium-term, for advanced industrial nations and latecomers alike is, then, to sustain industrialization on the basis of products that do not lock them into low-wage competition. Given the impossibility of national Keynesianism, this means that they must sustain export competitiveness, and do so without simply becoming a low-wage participant in the global economy. The definition of competitiveness that we shall use here, therefore, centers on the ability of an economy to maintain stable or increasing market shares in an activity while maintaining stable or increasing standards of living for those who participate in it.[2] This poses a particular problem for latecomers. These are countries that are not fully developed – in terms of both the social institutions of the economy and technological capabilities – but that are well beyond the agro-industrial transition and where wages are already considerably higher than in the fast-growing newcomer nations. Since industrial latecomers start out with relatively low real per capita incomes, competitiveness must not only generate increasing employment, it must also steadily raise the incomes of those who are employed.

COMPETITIVENESS BASED ON LEARNING

Theories of competitiveness abound today, as do descriptive monikers for the new economy: post-industrialism, informational, knowledge-based, flexible, post-Fordist. Though each of these labels helps in understanding some dimensions of contemporary economic activity, the logic of the most advanced forms of economic competition – those capable of generating high-wage employment – can best be described as that of learning, hence the *learning economy*, which will be defined in more detail shortly.

The importance of learning can be deduced from the conditions of employment creation today in the high- and medium-wage economies, where there are three basic trends: creation of high-wage, high-skill jobs, usually in value-intensive industries or activities; creation of low-wage, low-skill jobs; and job loss. Employment losses are concentrated in manufacturing industries producing standardized outputs that are amenable to mechanization, automation, or relocation to very low-wage areas. Employment with lower wages is heavily concentrated in the consumer and retail services sector, which is the biggest sector of the whole economy; the exception is management activities in those sectors. Growth in high-wage employment is located in certain occupations, mostly those relying on intellectual labor, found in many sectors, but particularly in advanced producer and financial services, technology-intensive or design-intensive manufacturing, and consumer services with a highly customized output. The first and third of our categories have a high proportion of tradable outputs, with a highly uneven national and global locational pattern; the second category, retail and consumer services, has tradable management and input functions, but untradable final output functions; delivery must be close to the customer, thus following the distribution of population.

Location is a key dimension of employment dynamics in a number of ways. For standardized manufactures, the basic downward trend in employment is enhanced by the increasing possibility of relocation, whether to peripheral low-wage regions of advanced countries, or to low-income countries. Employment growth in this sector is occurring in a number of developing countries, most spectacularly in Southeast Asia. The technological content and transactional structure of the production systems for standardized manufactures permit easy technological transfer and long-distance linkages to core fabrication and management activities, still located mostly in the rich countries. The new competitive price structures for such goods force wages down in the developed countries for the employment that remains there (Leamer 1994).

For consumer and retail services, employment is rising as a proportion of the total in most places, but this employment has not proved capable of raising overall real incomes. At the same time that productivity improvements are applied, via increasing automation and computerization, they intersect with the same dynamics that affect standardized, routinized manufacturing activity: the increasing possibility of locational substitution due to the information revolution (e.g. the second wave of back-offices in retail services).

In contrast to these activities, the employment that could serve as a long-term motor of growth in real incomes is engaged in the production of nonstandardized, nonroutinized goods and services, especially tradables. But such activities are not easy to come by in this world, where a central logic of competition is precisely to standardize the output and routinize the production process. For latecomer countries, there is another, but temporary, way to increase real incomes: to move from simpler to more complex, but still standardized, tradable goods manufacturing. Still, this strategy is quickly confronted with downward wage competition, and further growth in incomes has to be achieved by developing export specializations in nonstandardized and nonroutinized goods and services (see, *inter alia*, Gereffi and Fonda 1992; Wade 1990; Haggard 1990).

The common way to engage in the latter, although extremely variable from sector to sector, is product-based technological learning (PBTL). Those firms, sectors, regions, and nations that can learn faster or better (higher quality or cheaper for a given quality) become competitive because their knowledge is scarce and therefore cannot be immediately imitated by new entrants or transferred, via codified and formal channels, to competitor firms, regions, or nations. The price–cost margin of such PBTL activities can rise, even while market shares increase, alleviating downward wage pressure (Dosi *et al.* 1990). In this respect, such activities are promising for high-wage areas. But the key paradox of this happy picture must not be underestimated: these activities remain immune to relocation or to substitution by competitors only insofar as latecomers are equipped to keep outrunning the powerful forces of standardization and imitation in the world economy. Once they are imitated or their outputs standardized, then there are downward wage and employment pressures. They enjoy no one-time advantage; they must become moving targets by institutionalizing learning. They must enhance product differentiation at any given moment, while constantly adapting the configuration of products and processes so as to anticipate the competition.

The PBTL economy is central to the direct objective of generating high-wage, high-skill, knowledge-intensive employment, but extends well beyond it. PBTL has propulsive effects on economies in a number of ways: technological spillover effects can widen and lengthen the wealth-producing properties of learning, while the quasi-rents earned from imperfect competition can be channeled through the producing economy in the form of wages and invest-ment incomes, and used to perpetuate advantage (Dosi *et al.* 1990).

Contemporary economic development strategies must therefore attempt to install and sustain activities embodying this propulsive dynamic as one of their central elements. In certain cases, they will become strategic, export-oriented, trade specialization sectors for an economy, the source of foreign-exchange earnings, and a key to market invasion, as affirmed by the new trade theory (for example, Krugman 1990). But the learning economy is not merely an offensive strategy; in the presence of increasingly open markets, local production can be protected in certain sectors by upgrading them con-tinuously in the conventional sense (adopting productivity and design improvements that are found in potential invader competitors), as well as by attempting to differentiate the local industry through endogenous forms of learning.

To say that the learning economy is necessary to high-wage employment generation is not to claim that it represents a complete economic strategy. All the traditional tasks also remain necessary: balancing production and con-sumption; finding the right mix between export-oriented and locally serving activity; ongoing productivity improvements; and coherent reallocation of labor. But, as we have seen, these traditional tasks of long-term economic management are by themselves no longer sufficient to generate adequate quantities of high quality employment.

Latecomers have an additional burden, which is to get from initial roles in the international division of labor, which are frequently based on low wages, to those industries or parts of industries that are based on continuous learning, or from protected local sectors to those capable of surviving in more open markets. They have to learn their ways out of the activities for which they are initially competitive, into PBTL activities. This does not imply, however, that there is any neat set of "stages" of development. Far from it: some of the most successful recent latecomers have mixed advanced, learning-based activities and traditional low-wage industries at the same time, to the benefit of the whole economy (see Gereffi and Fonda 1992; Wade 1990; Haggard 1990).

INDUSTRIAL LEARNING: THE ROLE OF CONVENTIONS

There exist extensive analyses of the organizational attributes of learning-based firms and production systems, and we shall therefore be extremely brief here. Learning implies that organizations or production systems must be relatively well equipped to move resources around in order to implement what is learned: this is what has come to be known as the "flexibility" condi-tion. Some kinds of learning necessarily involve narrow horizons of attention and high levels of focused attention of the learners within a division of labor: this is what has come to be known as the "specialization" condition. Both of these organizational attributes of learning contribute to the well-documented phenomenon of "externalization" or "quasi-externalization," by which are meant the tendency for learning-based organizations to assume the form of production networks based around an interfirm division of labor, or for (usually large) firms themselves to mimic attributes of externalization, sometimes via interfirm alliances, sometimes via the introduction of price mechanisms inside the large firm, and sometimes via increased reliance on external suppliers.[3] Networks involve many complex transactions between firms and other institutions, including labor markets and information-rich institutions such as universities, trade associations, governmental agencies, and other institutions. The precise form that such networks take in learning-based production systems varies greatly according to the industry, product market, and national–regional institutional setting.

It is to the substantive content of network transactions and their governance or regulation that we must look in order to penetrate deeper into the learning process itself, which is the object of economic policy we defined above. Unlike transactions of standardized and substitutable goods, factor inputs, and information, transactions associated with the kind of learning we are analyzing here involve the development and – perhaps even more important – the mutually consistent interpretation of information that is not fully codified, hence not fully capable of being transmitted, understood, and utilized independently of the actual agents who are developing and using it. The obvious cases are those that involve unforeseen contingencies, such as highly uncertain markets in traditional industries or movement along a technological frontier in high-technology sectors. But they go well beyond these industries. Learning of any kind – even when well planned out in the most bureaucratic innovation or research program – takes twists and turns that are impossible to predict. Moreover, every kind of production system has to cope with some form of fluctuations in markets, product design, available technology, and prices, which make difficult the full routinization of relations between firms, their environments, and employees. Many such fluctuations, if they are to be dealt with in such a way that efficiency losses or conflicts are to be avoided, involve less-than-bureaucratic procedures and adjustment mechanisms, which vary greatly from place to place precisely because they are highly embedded in not-fully-formalized rules and practices.

There are two levels of this relational quality of transactions. In the first, personal contacts, knowledge of the other, and reputation are the basis of the relation, and they represent something like assets that the parties "own" due to these personal investments. In many other cases, however, transactions are not so completely idiosyncratic; they do have dimensions that can be reproduced or imitated by other agents. But transaction is, by definition, mutual; so only those agents who are equipped to enter into the kind of relation that has come to be accepted as the norm for the particular learning process at hand (by the parties with whom they will transact) can do so. They are so equipped when they possess faculties permitting them to take in, interpret, and use information in a way that is consistent with the other transacting party, where this is not fully codified or standardized. Such faculties are, essentially, *conventions* that coordinate these productive agents. Most conventions are a kind of half-way house between fully personalized and idiosyncratic relations and fully depersonalized, easy to imitate relations (although even the latter do have conventional foundations, not natural or behaviorally universal foundations).[4]

Conventional or relational transactions (henceforth C-R) affect many dimensions of production systems, but the nature and functions of such conventions differ from industry to industry, according to the type of product, the economic fluctuations associated with its markets and production processes, and the type of learning that is possible. C-R transactions may be found in at least five principal domains:

1 interfirm "hard" transactions, as in buyer–seller relations that involve market imperfections;
2 interfirm "soft" transactions, as in the sharing or diffusion of nontraded information about the environment or about learning;
3 hard and soft intrafirm relations, as the bases for the functioning of large firms that are "internally externalized" in the way we noted above;
4 factor markets, especially labor markets, that involve skills that are not entirely substitutable on an interindustry or interregional basis, i.e. where there are industry- or region-specific dimensions to workers' skills; and
5 economy–formal institution relationships, where universities, governments, industry associations, and firms are able to communicate and coordinate their interactions only by using channels with a strong conventional/relational content.

Note that, in this analysis, the learning economy and its conventional/relational foundations is not based on a stark contrast between hierarchies and markets, but rather on the notion that all advanced, learning-based forms of economic activity involve complex transactional structures that, in turn, have a high conventional/relational content.

Learning economies as coherent systems

For any given set of products/technologies/markets, and any given set of actors, the various conventions and relations have to fit together. They must be *coherent*, not only so that what is produced embodies endogenous learning, but also so that the resulting product passes external tests of competitiveness by being sold at prices and quantities sufficient to reproduce the system.

The unit of accounting of such coherence is ultimately the product – whether it be intermediate or final – for it is the product that must pass the external test. There are several organizational subdivisions of the economy that correspond to production types, just as there are coherent levels of the division of labor other than the final output sector.[5] Some are "smaller" than, i.e. upstream of, the final output sector, such as capital goods industries; others are "bigger" than final output sectors, in that they are essential to a number of such sectors but have wide competencies: these are Perrouxian technological spaces. There are, in other words, a number of different organizational subdivisions of the modern economy that define systems in which sets of conventions and relations must be mutually coherent for economically viable learning to take place. What follows is a heuristic typology of four basic kinds of production, based on the kinds of interactions each involves around the tasks of technology or knowledge development (Storper and Salais 1997).

The first kind of production grows out of artisanal industry, and consists often of nondurable consumer goods heavily affected by fashion and design. It faces markets that are highly uncertain, due to ongoing product redesign and differentiation, resulting in a low scale of production. Innovation itself consists of applying specialized talent or knowledge to ongoing product differentiation. Critical here is the existence of a community of specialists who redesign the product, on very short time horizons, by deploying their tacit and customary knowledge of the product's qualities and possible dimensions. This is a highly "interpersonal" community, based on traditional acquired skills, where constant communication between members of the community is necessary to carry out knowledge development. Interaction between the producers and the users of technologies is essential to innovation; an example of this is the equipment maker who adapts for the final producer in order to accommodate the rapidly evolving final output. Typically, such communities are concentrated in particular geographical areas where informal processes of communication are central to their successful operation.

A modern-day version of this interpersonal community of innovators can be found in parts of high-technology industries, which is the second production type. Typically, high-technology industries are based on the organized application of R&D and scientific knowledge to technological change. Their products often involve large-scale technological systems that require a great deal of planning. This is a much more formal process than in the "interpersonal" worlds referred to above. These formal processes rely on forms of communication that can be stretched over large distances because they are carried out at regular intervals in a planned fashion (through meetings, congresses, and private sector projects with long planning horizons, where communication involves highly codified and hence standardized, nonculture-dependent, scientific language). This corresponds to large-firm corporate networks in high technology today. But what is often overlooked is that these networks are tied, for some of their key cutting-edge technology inputs, into precisely the kinds of interpersonal communities alluded to above. Many of the core components of their large-scale research and development projects cannot be planned; there is technological uncertainty. This uncertainty requires scientific and technical personnel to be able to interact informally, in unplanned and uncodifiable ways. The large-scale technology-based industries often have, at their cores, geographically concentrated interpersonal communities of innovators, even though their other innovative activities are highly planned and not highly localized.

A third kind of product corresponds to our image of mass production. Where economies of scale and long production runs dominate, products are typically made by large oligopolistic firms. Such firms are capable of operating production systems at national and international scale, distributing parts and components and assembly plants across the landscape, and coordinating the whole, as in the automobile industry. Nonetheless, even in these industries, context is key to whether competitive learning occurs. Japanese, German, and American automobile companies, for example, have historically drawn heavily from the results of public and private national R&D strengths in their respective countries. Their core technology development activities are also highly centered on particular regions. These big firms have access to localized contexts characterized by dense information flows that have been built up over long periods of time, including many flows that are internal to the firm but dependent on the system of relations among these units, and between them and their external environments.

The fourth type is that part of mass production that has been transformed into "lean production" in recent years. The stability of these industries' markets has declined, and to survive they must combine the cost control associated with scale and long production runs with the capacity to have a wide mix of products and frequent change in products. They must be flexible mass producers. Lean production usually relies on a just-in-time system for parts delivery and quality control. Just-in-time is not only a way to deliver inputs, however; it is also a way to structure information flows that helps producers incrementally alter and refine their products.

For each of these kinds of products, there are conventions that permit learning and competitiveness in all the domains described above. The policy problem is to build the set of conventions appropriate to the potential learning-based specializations of the economy at hand. For latecomers, there is a transition problem that consists of getting from their existing products to higher-value-added learning-based product niches.

LATECOMER ROLES IN THE GLOBAL ECONOMY

There is no automatic correspondence between internationalization of markets and deterritorialization of productive activity. The core technology- and knowledge-intensive outputs of the world economy continue to be produced in relatively few places on the globe, from whence they are traded (Storper 1992). Moreover, the major world trading economies manifest *increasing* trade specializations, in spite of their similar income levels, due to increases in both intra-industry specialization and trade, and final output specializations (Dosi *et al*. 1990). Such activities are also increasingly inserted into networks of relationships with other territorialized cores and with the deterritorialized (routine production) activities of their production and marketing systems, giving rise to globalized-localized systems of production (sometimes now called "glocalized" in contrast to the incorrect image of placelessness associated with the term "globalization"). One of the major agents of this process is the multinational firm that taps into territorialized technological competencies and gives them worldwide effect.

There is both continuity and change in the international division of labor. The post-war development of global commodity chains continues on a world scale. This development takes the form of territorial division of multinational production systems into core areas (those where technological knowledge mastery, i.e. advanced learning, takes place), routine production regions (branch-plant regions for certain components and assembly, and market-serving assembly), and excluded regions (those who do not partake of international production circuits in an important way)

Most low-wage industrializing countries – such as Sri Lanka, Indonesia, Turkey, or the Philippines – are routine production sites with respect to the global economy. They are in some ways more vulnerable than they were in the post-war "core–periphery" configuration. In that system, cores and peripheries had standard center–hinterland relationships, whether at the national or international level. Such clear, hierarchical, structured roles within production systems and as whole economies no longer exist (Veltz 1996). Routine production areas are, in most cases, simple production locations which do not require any wider relations to "core" investing economies. The extreme manifestation of this is that in some industries, especially those with low fixed capital requirements, there is a "roving" division of labor, with companies alighting in a country or region for just a few years and then moving on as soon as wages rise above the global minimum. This has been happening in certain areas of Southeast Asia and Central America in recent years. In general, the developmental possibilities afforded by branch-plant development are more limited than ever. It remains fundamentally vulnerable to changes in markets and technology if export-oriented; it remains fundamentally subject to local income constraints if oriented toward domestic markets; and in neither case is it a creator of markets and technologies. Thus, while the expansion of mass production on a global level continues apace, and generates spectacular growth effects at certain times in particular developing regions, it cannot, taken alone, serve as a vehicle of true development.

In other cases, branch plants involve a certain amount of technological and skill upgrading, and the state plays a significant role in determining the extent to which this is the case. Brazil and Mexico are intermediate cases, where what remains of post-war import-substitution strategies and existing capital-goods production leads to some upgrading (with the notable exception of most of the Mexican *maquiladora* border industries).

A third group of countries interacts with the global economy in a different way. The long-term driving force in their regional and national development success (defined as growth with proportionately increasing real per capita incomes) is the progressive improvement of their technological capabilities, while combining this with productivity advantages. These countries have all sustained the development process, and are moving toward the point of absolute technological advantage in certain areas, on a par with the advanced nations. In some, this occurs primarily through foreign direct investment on the part of transnational firms (e.g. Singapore); in others it occurs through locally owned large firms (Korea) or locally owned small to medium-sized enterprises (Hong Kong, Taiwan) (Gereffi and Fonda 1992). Nations that pursue such learning-based activities have an entirely different territorial relationship to the global economy from the other two groups of countries cited above. Paradoxically, their favorable relationship through exporting exists because their learning process is highly "contained" within firms or networks of firms, actors, and institutions; learning is contingent on scarce and territorially specific knowledge and practices. The examples of these countries suggest that there are possibilities for latecomers.

The most ambiguous position is held by middle-income countries that are not leaders in export-centered development, including nations such as Greece or Ireland in the EU, as well as some of the nations of Eastern Europe. While logically they should be poised to reap the same advantages from the world system that have been enjoyed by the successful latecomers of South and East Asia, the question is whether they can construct the conventional and relational contexts that would allow them to follow such an intersectoral and intrasectoral learning process.

MAKING COHERENT CONVENTIONS FOR LEARNING

Policy in a learning economy ideally would support the development of packages of conventions and relations in coherent product-based subdivisions of the economy. Because these conventions and relations must be developed according to such subdivisions, policy must have strategic content; because such conventions and relations must be mutually coherent, policy's task is to support the development of groups of conventions that give the actors involved an efficient common context for proceeding with a given kind of learning.

A major problem for development strategies now poses itself: where appropriate conventions cannot be constructed, it is unlikely that any economic development program, no matter how brilliantly executed around the traded dimensions of the economy, will be successful.

Two trajectories, not one

It used to be thought that economic development could be forced via technology policy. In developed countries, especially in post-war continental European countries, most such policies were mission-oriented: they undertook large-scale technology development programs leading to a specific kind of final output such as petrochemicals, airplanes, or computers. The United States adopted a military version of these policies in order to wage the Cold War. These policies are very expensive, have long latency periods, and suffer from high failure rates, such failure being largely technological for military projects and both technological and economic for civilian projects (Ergas 1996). They also have produced brilliant successes, such as Airbus or French high-speed trains. Brazil succeeded via such a policy with the civilian branch of its aircraft industry, Embraer, but did not succeed with its computer industry (Schmitz and Cassiolato 1992). Success tends to come in industries where basic knowledge is already fairly mature and the product is a large-scale technical ensemble with very high barriers to entry. Mission-oriented technology policies do not appear to work for basic technological components (microelectronics), final outputs with rapid learning curves (computers), or complex capital goods (machine tools). They do not even work for low-tech but highly differentiated products (the French *plan textile* failed). The learning economy is thus only partially adapted to mission-oriented policies.

The object of policy in the learning economy must not be simply to install hardware and the skills required to operate it, but to set a nation or region on a learning-based technological trajectory in particular technological-economic spaces (ensembles of activities characterized by direct and indirect linkages). The task is complex, designed to keep the region moving from one point in a trajectory to another.

But just as learning is the outcome of nontraded as well as traded linkages, so policy must focus not only on technological trajectories *per se*. A national or regional economy must also construct and continue reconstructing the conventions – frameworks of action that facilitate economic coordination and communication – that enable it to turn one-time skills and given stocks of hardware into effective technological trajectories. The challenge of the global learning economy to territorial economies, then, is to establish and maintain not one economic dynamic, but two. The first is the technological trajectory, entailing mastery of specific spaces in the economy characterized by specific technological spillovers and complementarities (Dosi *et al.* 1990). The second is the trajectory of conventions or untraded interdependencies that build the capacities for ongoing collective action in regions and nations so as to permit ongoing transformations of hardware into technological trajectories.

Latecomer economies, however, cannot be expected to do this in the same fashion as fully developed economies. Inventing the leading edge in a sector will be most difficult for them. But a realistic equivalent of the learning economy for them is one of adaptation. Rapid mastery of the latest technologies and techniques and the capacity to do so on an ongoing basis is a reasonable starting point for their participation in the learning economy – a sort of learning-based diffusion process.

BUILDING CONVENTIONS: TALK, PRECEDENT, AND CONFIDENCE

It is probably no accident that considerable recent research reveals the cardinal importance of so-called soft factors such as civic culture (Putnam 1992; Doeringer and Terkla 1990) in the performance of democratic institutions, but few venture any policy-oriented recommendations on how the lack of such a culture could be addressed. Very unorthodox policy strategies are needed in order to break out of the dilemmas posed by lack of an appropriate culture. Two of these may be labeled, respectively, "talk" and "confidence."

Relations and conventions are recursive outcomes of precedents that act as guides to action. The problem is that if such precedents do not exist or are not adequate to the kind of learning system that is to be created, deliberate institutions to create them are hindered by the circularity identified above. A learning system is a complex organizational structure with many different actors engaging in innumerable transactions. Hence, many different conventions and types of relations must be built, based on precedents that are effectively indivisible, if the learning system is to work. In the face of such indivisibilities, the magic wand of information that is supposed to illuminate real preferences and interests does not work.

Institutions consist of persistent and connected sets of rules, formal and informal, that prescribe behavioral roles, constrain activity, and shape expectations. For this reason, institutions cannot be reduced to specific organizations, although the latter may be important in the generation of expectations, preferences, and rules. Common to both public and nonpublic institutions, to formal and nonformal institutions, is that they have to give order to expectations and allow actors to coordinate under conditions of uncertainty. In terms of a production system, they have to do this so that coordination is economically successful. This means that there is a circular relation between conventions and institutions. Institutions have a strong effect, by generating regularity and precedent, in the formation of conventions that people employ to cope with the persistent and pervasive uncertainty of their interactions with other people in the economy. But by the same token, formal organized institutions can function successfully only if the rules, procedures, incentives, and sanctions they establish are integrated into the conventions that guide people's behavior. Even coercion is ultimately a convention, in that if people do not take sanctions seriously, it is unlikely that the institution will be able to coerce for long. More commonly, who cannot think of ways in which the common, taken-for-granted ("conventional") wisdom of a large segment of the population causes it to interact in ways that render formal rules inefficacious, from the formal econom to paradoxical and unanticipated effects of economic regulation in land, capital, and industrial markets? In these cases, we can say that formal institutions are not fully consistent with the conventions of the populations they are meant to affect. Successful formal institutions, then, have a hard organizational side and a "soft" conventional foundation.

Policies intended to create or sustain the learning economy would involve a relationship between public, formal institutions and conventions or relations that are neither fully public nor fully formal. There is a circularity here: formal public institutions, in creating or sustaining worlds of learning, must in effect create or sustain the conventions and relations of the latter. In turn, those formal public institutions can only assist in world-making if the people in both institutions – the learning production system and the formal public institution – are coordinated by conventions consistent with that project. This kind of endless circularity cannot be gotten around by any traditional notion such as incentive, compulsion, or formal rule.

The circular relation between public institutions and the institutionalized learning economy requires that the parties to public institutions somehow be convinced of the utility of having a public institution support the conventions and relations that make up the learning economy. They must share a convention of the utility of the public institution in some specific domain, before it can even get started. *Talk* between the parties may be one approach. Much has been said about the difference between institutions that function via a combination of loyalty and voice, versus those that rely on exit for adjustment and structure (Hirschman 1970). Talk is upstream of voice, in that there is no institution yet existing in which the channels for voice among loyal parties are already established.

Talk refers to communicative interaction, designed not simply to transmit information and relay preferences, but to achieve mutual understanding.[6] In the case of prospective learning, information from other experiences (where learning has worked; on evolutions in product markets; on suggested potentials for the parties at hand, given their current resources and skills) can be valuable as a stimulus, even though it cannot be represented as experimental and therefore automatically useful or valid in other circumstances. Such information can be used as the valid pretext for talk.

An immediate objection is that if there is no tradition of communication, or worse, if there is distrust or antipathy, what is the possible basis for talk? The objection is important: it is probably difficult to stimulate talk, precisely because talk is not free in that it takes time and effort, and payoffs are not evident, especially if the history of relations is bad or the economic culture is organized by conventions that do not encourage learning relationships (Hirschman 1970). On the other hand, talk is cheap and the risks are relatively low. Public institutions thus certainly have a possibility of getting low-cost talk going.

Precedents that underpin conventions or relations inherently involve confidence, without which single events would be just that, and would have no impact on future expectations. Insofar as conventions and relations involve expectations about how others will interact in situations that involve some uncertainty, such confidence involves a measure of vulnerability: it is necessary for interacting agents to place themselves in a position where, should the other not follow precedent, they will be subject to a real loss. To have confidence in what others will do is, in this sense, to trust them – not in the moral sense, but in the sense of making oneself vulnerable on the basis of confidence in the precedent (Lorenz and Lazaric 1997). But how can such confidence be established so as to bring relation and convention into being where they do not exist, or worse, where there are histories of mistrust, broken promises, antagonisms?

Talk may involve the parties in getting the ball rolling on a learning project, but it does not establish confidence in the specific sense that generates precedent and convention. Bribery through special material incentives, such as subsidies, provided by a public institution to private actors is likely to work only as long as the incentives last; if each actor calculates that others are motivated only by special incentives, then a convention based on incentives is established, and with it the possibility of lock-in to subsidy. Therefore, it would be better to offer some sort of reinsurance (Sabel 1993), a safety net (at least partial) for failure, revealing the efficacy of talk increasing the propensity of agents to entrust confidence. Moreover, if the intention of a policy is to establish learning conventions that are not dependent on permanent subsidies, other approaches will have to be tried, or incentives will have to be slowly replaced with confidence in other, unsubsidized precedents.

One method of creating confidence in a sea of nonconfidence is, of course, bureaucracy. It has been found, in economic policymaking, that certain projects are amenable to isolation from the overall economic culture, by internalizing them within hierarchical bureaucracies. The military is the model. Defense procurement in the USA, or major indivisible high-technology projects such as the French TGV, are carried out by quasi-military bureaucracies with strong financial incentives and command-and-control authority. This instills a certain form of confidence, and the bureaucracies can function like well-oiled machines as they carry out their technological tasks. But internalization is not a solution for much of the learning economy, precisely because of the open-endedness and high degree of risk inherent in much learning; nobody is willing to pay to internalize it, and the technological character of the product does not permit near-monopoly. Some other method of building confidence must be used.

Small, repeated, experimental interactions may be useful for this purpose. Small interactions are important because they enable policy to cope with the dispersed nature of learning economies, which tend to involve many different, organizationally separate agents. This becomes rapidly unmanageable as a policy problem. Experiments, as a policy device, mean setting the parties to work in limited relations that facilitate learning, and then attempting to build up in complexity. This does not mean trying to prove the utility of any general, abstract solution. Most importantly, such experiments must proceed as if confidence existed. In other words, the small experiments build on the communicative understanding that comes from talk, asking the parties to interact by suspending their fears and doubts.

The likelihood of getting the parties to act as if confidence existed, as the first step toward establishing real precedents, should logically rise with the degree of knowledge they have about each other. Depth is one dimension: how much the parties know about each other in a specific domain; but breadth is another: how much they know about each other in general, through collateral forms of information. Depth has a complicated geography, in that in some cases professional interactions have channels involving strong long-distance relations and weak local ones; but this is more valid for rare professions or for highly formalized ones. Breadth has a strong localist dimension: we are more likely to have information on someone's reputation, and to be able to validate it by interpreting it against a context with which we are intimately familiar, in a local context. There is thus some relationship between localness and mutual knowledge that should allow parties to act as if confidence existed, as a first step toward generating precedent. The use of a combination of depth and breadth in talk as a way of generating confidence, while not the province of the locality, is in some cases more likely to succeed when geographically localized, although this is not a hard and fast rule.[7]

THE NEW HETERODOX POLICY PARADIGM

There are many intricate dimensions of talk and confidence-building as vehicles for creating precedent, relation, and convention. Who should talk? What should they talk about? What techniques should be used to facilitate such talk? What small relations should be attempted first? What kind of assurance should be offered to get the parties to suspend skepticism? It is impossible to give a complete response here, because the answers will vary both according to the kind of world that talk is designed to get started, and according to the starting point of the parties. This section offers a modest initial examination of the subject.

Recently, analysis of economic performance of industrial systems – variously termed industrial districts, flexible specialization, lean manufacturing, post-Fordist production, or even the learning economy – has prompted inquiry into policies and institutions that could be used to institute such systems. A new heterodox policy framework has emerged, largely based on the experiences of successful sectors and regions.[8]

The new framework has many versions which share a number of features. One common feature is that they favor policies that are context-sensitive, meaning that they are interested in the embeddedness of industrial practices in specific contexts and regions, and hence "bottom-up." They also tend to focus on production systems rather than on firms. Key words include: networks, flexibility, decentralization, cooperation, research and development, human capital, technopoles, training. The policies are heterodox because of the kinds of public goods they would provide. In standard public goods theory, market failures sometimes occur and when they do, public goods can be provided to rectify them. Such public goods must have economy-wide application, that is, they must be as generic as possible. The new theory also calls for policy to produce public goods, but allows that these goods may be specific to technological spaces: it is their developmental properties (evolution along trajectories through learning) that ultimately generalize their benefits, via spillovers and complementarities, to the wider economy and society.

We may summarize the varying ingredients of this cocktail, as follows:[9]

- *Networking*   The most widely shared element of the policy framework is to promote networking among firms. It is held that new forms of economic competition involve high levels of vertical disintegration and that there are extensive market failures in information exchange between firms. It follows that interestablishment and interfirm relations and networks need to be supported to enhance their efficiency.

- *Promoting technology transfer*   It is widely accepted that the rates at which technologies are absorbed by firms vary widely from place to place, especially when the economic base is composed mostly of small and medium-sized firms. As a result, publicly funded innovation and technology transfer centers are becoming favored as a means to enhance the adoption of new technologies, as well as to stimulate convergence in user–producer relations, so that incremental innovation can proceed more rapidly.

- *Local labor markets: training and focusing institutions*   In industries with high levels of industry-specific or region-specific skills, but also with high levels of local labor market flexibility, there can be strong negative externalities: producers will not want to invest in adequate levels of labor training for fear of losing workers once they are trained. Moreover, in the face of rapid change in labor skills, no single employer will have the wherewithal to effect the change in skill supply, and lack of coordination may lead to a downward competitive spiral. Under these conditions, public institutions that provide for labor training particularly applicable to the industry or region, that promote strategic changes in the direction of training, and that help workers to secure jobs in the face of flexibility in specific, regionally concentrated sectors, can attenuate the effects of market failure.

- *Infant industry and getting a start: precompetitive R&D and stimulating markets*   Infant industries can be based on new and experimental kinds of products. In these industries, the probability of generating new products is high, but product configurations have not yet settled onto an identifiable technological trajectory. High levels of risk and uncertainty exist for producers in these nascent sectors. The collective effect of waiting, however, may create a vicious circle, where everyone waits for everyone else, and the overall rate of development is thereby retarded. By the same token, regions that could successfully develop a new industry may find that a delayed start (especially when another region has moved ahead of them) locks them permanently out of a promising niche in the new industry. There are potential benefits to getting an early start, in contrast to this common free-rider problem. Industries, firms, regions, and nations that get ahead early often retain a leading position for quite some time, and in the early years there can be significant superprofits to new products. As a result, industry-specific, precompetitive R&D policies, and other policies to stimulate regional or national (often public) markets for risky new technology products, may be called for, in addition to networking and technology transfer centers.

- *Entrepreneurship, especially for small firms* Good ideas become reality only when potential entrepreneurs enjoy the conditions that permit them to establish and sustain a business. The conditions favoring firm formation include such traditional hard factors as access to capital markets, and soft factors as cultural images of the entrepreneur and sanctions to failure. They also include such conditions as access to information, locational sites, rules on hiring and firing labor, and access to potential customers in other firms. Entrepreneurship policies are designed, variously, to help potential entrepreneurs overcome these difficulties, although in practice the majority of them consist of loan programs for small firms.

- *Service centers* In the many successful Italian industrial districts, the practice of assisting existing firms in a series of concrete ways has emerged as a key method for establishing public support for those communities of producers. Industry service centers are particularly devoted to spreading the costs for certain kinds of resources that single firms cannot afford for themselves alone, including systematic market research, foreign marketing, technology research, and, in some cases, technology sharing and on-line electronic networking facilities. In Italian regions, especially Modena, major industrial estates for small firms have been created, where state-of-the-art flexible configurations of space are made available to firms at below-market cost, not only permitting them to modernize their facilities, but also permitting them to remain together, thus enhancing communication and networking. Service centers have also been involved in the promotion of regional brand names (something like *appellation controlée* for wine, but now applied to the market identities of other kinds of products), so as to enhance their nonsubstitutability in national and international markets.

The dangers of orthodoxy

As with any attempt to create a policy formula based on a complex analysis of economic reality, the emerging paradigm runs the danger of missing its target. An example from an earlier period with a different policy framework may help to illustrate this point. In the 1950s and 1960s, a theoretical analysis of industrial complexes was used as the theoretical justification for growth pole strategies in many countries. The results were impressive at the national level in certain cases (e.g. French industrial planning in the late 1950s), but were almost total failures at the regional level in all places. Later, growth pole policies failed at the national level in most developing countries.

These failures were not simply due to changes in external environment; there were errors in the way in which growth pole theory was turned into a formula for policy. Growth poles, a notion invented by François Perroux, were defined as economic spaces (sets of dense input–output relations, where stimulating downstream activities would reverberate upstream through a multiplier effect). Perroux was very clear that his intention was to identify economic spaces and not territorial spaces; he actually wanted to break up old regional economies in France in favor of national economic integration, to be achieved through national economic planning. Growth pole policies, however, transformed these economic spaces into territorial spaces by assuming that input–output linkages could be contained within national or regional spaces. This worked, to some extent, at the national level, when markets were protected, as was the case in post-war France and in developing countries using import substitution regulations. It failed utterly at the regional level, however, because many such input–output relations are not relations of proximity; in other words, installing a downstream activity does not induce upstream development in the same territory. Policymakers took a theory and applied it in a technically flawed manner, with sometimes disastrous results.

Another more important flaw was substantive rather than technical. Growth pole policies often ignored the heart and soul of the growth pole theory. Even more clearly than Perroux, development economists (especially the ECLA School and the Brazilians) understood that the core of any development process was the mastery of technology (Furtado 1963; Prebisch 1982; Hirschman 1958). Policymakers nonetheless implemented growth poles as if they were merely complexes of input–output relations, somehow assuming that the technological level of a region or a nation could be raised by providing the hardware. This turned out not to be true: one-time advantages most often did not turn into long-term learning.

This example of growth pole policy gone awry can be complemented with another, "hardware without development," where the absence of collective order and coordination makes hardware prone to failure. In the 1970s, Italy increased the autonomy of the regional governments. They were endowed with a wide range of powers to promote economic development, though not much direct power in the matter of industrial policy. Over the same period, the *cassa per il Mezzogiorno* was quite active in installing a variety of public goods and private investments in the southern regions. This was followed by a massive infusion of resources from the structural funds of the EEC. There has never been a more ideal testing ground for the possibility of promoting regional development in an underdeveloped region: national and international funding and institutional decentralization within a wealthy, constitutionally stable country, where other regions in the same country experienced impressive, internationally competitive economic growth during those decades. The fate of both the regional governments and the economies of the southern regions is indicative of the problem. Putnam (1992) studied the regional governments from 1970 to 1990, showing that those in the south had all performed poorly in their mission, while those in the north performed well. The absence of what he calls a "civic culture," and what we are more precisely calling a set of virtuous conventions of economic coordination, makes almost any effort at creating formal institutions or of applying investments doomed to failure. Mistrust, fear, the retreat to particularistic social groupings such as natural family or Mafia family, impede the formation of such conventions, no matter how high the investment level or how wide the institutional powers. We can easily see analogous phenomena in certain regions in latecomer countries.

By way of contrast, accounts of successful East Asian development and the Japanology literature (for a developed-country context) make repeated references to confidence-building and loyalty-building rules inside firms and in firm–firm relations, and even refer to "relation-specific assets" (Asanuma 1991; Aoki 1990; Dore 1987; Gambetta 1988; Gereffi and Fonda 1992). These conventions, by which firms establish relationships to markets, are specific and particularly effective at sustaining learning because of the ways in which they maintain interfirm coordination over time. Another subject in the Asian development literature is the relationship between financial institutions and productive firms. Although these relationships vary greatly among countries and industries, the constant factor is the confidence in saving that is established throughout the economy, and the practices of financial institutions in keeping interest rates down, coupled with the arm's-length relationship of firms to investors, allowing dividends to be low and retained earnings high. These, too, are conventions that join the parties to these arrangements, not explicit or formal rules. Other examples can be found in the system of labor relations, as in the convention of loyalty in return for hierarchy in large Japanese firms and in their subcontracting relationships. It is in these detailed webs of precedents and expectations, and the specific content they give to interdependencies in the production system, that different pathways of learning and competitiveness may be sought.

From framework to formula: the danger

In order to transform the new paradigm into effective policy, both technical and substantive reductionisms must be avoided. Substantively, just as the means to establishing growth poles was not input–output relations but technological mastery, so the heterodox framework is not essentially about small firms, networking, localism, or flexibility *per se*; it is rather about adaptive technological learning in a territorial context. The proper goals of such policies depend upon the nature of the product:

1 for traditional or small-scale intermediate products this means ongoing adaptation of products and processes, especially through product differentiation or moves up the price-quality curve so as to respond to the ongoing and inevitable entry by competitors, whether large firms or other regional systems; and

2 for scale-intensive or new technology products, this entails movement along
   the technological frontier, where that frontier is unknown or unknowable.

The substantive thrust of an industrial policy for LSCs must be geared to
these substantive goals, as specified in light of particular products and their
conventions. The new policies are only means to these ends. As theory now
becomes packaged into policy, a real danger exists that such policies will
become detached from the substantive content and necessary process of
building convention, and instead devolve into mechanical formulas and self-
referential content.

STRATEGIC CONSIDERATIONS FOR LATECOMERS

Starting points: strategic assessment

It has long been standard practice in formulating industrial policy to carry
out strategic assessments of local, regional, or national possibilities (depending on the policy's target). The idea is to eliminate unreasonable goals by
assessing the existing state of factors such as technological levels, labor markets, infrastructure, and market structure. In practice, such analyses vary
greatly in quality, and unfortunately there is a high propensity for error, especially excessive optimism (since the assessments are usually paid for by
agencies with a vested interest in being in the policy business). Critics of
industrial policy claim that this is inherent in such policies, but such skepticism is unwarranted, since there are also examples of excellent strategic
assessments having led to wise decisions (e.g. the TGV in France; numerical
controls in the USA; MITI on semiconductor machinery)·
   Simplifying, we can say that, in the 1960s, it was possible for many
European countries to carry out strategic assessment based on a standard
factor input-cost method. An assessment was essentially an evaluation of
the requirements and costs to bring into existence an industry to serve a
national or regional market at something close to world best practice. In the
context of rapid world economic expansion, especially in Europe, the main
consideration for efficiency was simply to assess whether the industry could
find a market that would enable it to enjoy optimal scale economies, and in
that context to implement state-of-the-art production technology. Oftentimes,
filière (commodity chain) analysis was applied to maximize the local content
of the target industry in the national or regional space (Salomon 1985).
   The demands placed on strategic assessment in the context of the learning economy have become vastly more complex than they were during this
earlier period, but the techniques of assessment have not caught up. It
would no longer be possible, for example, to use the same method that the
French employed to plan Fos-sur-Mer today, because world capacity in virtually every major sector is much closer to saturation, and there is no
comfortable time lag during which policy can simply copy the best of what

is being done elsewhere. The Brazilians learned this with their market protection law for computers; although it has had some considerable positive effects, it has absolutely failed to encourage competitive computer-making, leaving Brazil generations behind (Schmitz and Cassiolato 1992). Any strategic assessment carried out today must have as its goal moving from an existing point (the state of the economy, region, or sector in question) to somehow catching up to a moving target (changing technology, markets, and institutions), while recognizing that the target will continue to move even as the policy is implemented.

The product as the central unit of assessment

Strategic assessment has characteristically been organized around industry or sectoral lines, evaluating the feasibility of establishing, say, a computer industry or a shipbuilding industry. The advent of the learning economy means that standard sectoral-*filière* assessments are no longer adequate to the task. Most of the output of our economies is composed of intermediate goods, and social and spatial divisions of labor create all manner of organizational clusters in the economy that do not correspond to final output sectors, or even to the grand (and now crude) distinctions between consumer and producer goods. Some of the most significant such clusters have to do with generic intermediate products that go to very different final output sectors; they also have to do with products that have little concrete resemblance but have parallel or convergent technological trajectories, or technological complementarities.

Consequently, the principal unit of assessment must shift to the product, or to a technological space of products, defined by spillovers and complementarities. Products are the objects in which learning is embodied and submitted to the test of markets. Thus, the basis of assessment becomes product technology and the potential for product-based technological learning. This does not mean that traditional sectoral analysis is ignored. Success in a given product generally depends on the existence of a production system that extends upstream and downstream of that product in a *filière*, or spills over to complementary technological spaces; but this is, from an industrial policy perspective, an empirical question, not an a priori goal – a tactic rather than a purpose.[10]

Strategic assessment has to include evaluation of future scenarios, to which talk and confidence-building are to be applied as means to establishing precedents. But assessments cannot be left entirely to the experts. By definition, the talk to which we refer in the previous section can have no hope of setting conventions and relations into motion if it is a mere pretext for ratifying assessments already made by technocrats. It is likely that talk will reveal information to which technocrats otherwise have no access. Further, not relying exclusively on experts is the key to avoiding the circularity problem, where those who talk are only talking about something that has already been decided by the technocrats.

Developmental starting points

Countries and regions have different starting points: the size of the market; current endowments of technology, infrastructure, and knowledge; the generic image of the country or region; underlying relationships between groups, especially between organized interests; the existing stock of firms and interlinkages between them; the nature and effectiveness of public administration; and so on. Two standard approaches to starting points can be viewed with extreme caution in light of the analysis advanced here.

The first approach is to differentiate among grand categories of starting points. The principal categories of countries and regions would include:

- large, wealthy, and technologically endowed;
- small, wealthy, and technologically endowed;
- large, semi-industrialized latecomers;
- small, semi-industrialized latecomers ("less favored" in the current EU jargon); and
- poor, non-industrialized.

These categories have some descriptive utility, but they do not lead anywhere in particular with respect to strategies for product-based technological learning. Their principal categories – size and technology endowments – are most relevant to large, capital- and technology-intensive industries, but even there, many small rich countries have apparently broken the size rule (Holland with Philips, Sweden with Ericsson), and many big countries have failed in spite of it (France with Thomson and Bull). These classifications are instructive, but only up to a point.

The second and preferable approach is to distinguish cases according to broad categories of products. For products with low barriers to entry – mostly certain products in the interpersonal or market worlds – the experiences of Italy and Germany may be guides. In the Italian case, traditional skills were deployed in interpersonal industries, to serve a national market in the 1950s and early 1960s. That market was large and relatively fragmented. Smaller countries do not have such big markets, however, and virtually all countries are more open to import competition today than was Italy in the early 1950s. The lesson is that such industries are likely to flourish only where at least one of the following three conditions are met:

1 skills are good enough or highly focused enough that they can contribute something unique to the world market;
2 skills can serve a local or national market that is not being satisfied by imports, or can do so in a way that passes the indifference test: higher local prices are compensated by better tailoring to local demand (but with open markets and media, the knife-edge is sharper and sharper);
3 innovative institutional arrangements, such as specification subcontracting, are used to link local producers to clients in a way that builds their skills and responsibilities.

For industries with high barriers to entry, whether because of traditional scale concerns or because of high investment in technology, the choice is a very stark one: either go all the way with a major technology policy designed to cover a technological space (e.g. Airbus, the Japanese semiconductor policy, US military procurement), or target particular subsectors with potential for developing spillovers. In such cases, and regardless of country size, it is likely that large multinational partners will be necessary and that substantial commitments of local resources over long periods of time will be required. The only strategies likely to succeed in the case of targeting subsectors are those where technological branching points are at hand, and where the risk is taken to develop along one branch rather than another. Examples might include specific models of high-definition television or systems for transmitting mobile telephone calls.

The optimistic note for this strategic assessment process is that there is rarely a single world best practice for any group of products. Entrants can define products and practices, and they can trace out developmental pathways that continue to redefine such products and practices. Another approach to strategic assessment is to establish a set of norms for countries – categorical standards against which starting points can be compared. This leads to developmental recipes, using criteria such as capital institutions, technological infrastructure, political and administrative institutions, and entrepreneurship. However, such an approach is flawed in two respects. First there is the fact that, among successful countries and regions, there exists great diversity in terms of products, and hence also in terms of accompanying economic conventions, practices, and institutions. Successful countries do not all follow the same rules with respect to provision of capital, training of the workforce, public administration, entrepreneurship, and so on. Even within given sectors, there is an abundance of different successful models. It is a gross oversimplification, except at the most abstract level (e.g. honest versus corrupt public administration; schooling versus no schooling) to try to reduce the development process to a single set of general goals with respect to different starting points.

The second problem with developmental recipes is that ending points will also differ by country or region, according to the specialization of the learning economy to be created, and the worlds of production they embody. Ending points are determined by assessing what kind of identities and capacities for action and coordination among the participants in the production system are to be created.

FOCUSING ON THE OBJECTIVE

The dual trajectories of technology and conventions as elements of economic development policy are, admittedly, much more complex objects of policy than is the norm. And the policy goal suggested in this chapter – that middle-income latecomer countries must necessarily develop some propulsive activities that have enough endogenous absolute advantages to command world market shares – is both more difficult and demanding than the goal of import substitution and national Keynesianism. This agenda is not proposed as the single goal or the sole means of economic or regional policy today, but rather as a necessary component of such policies, without which there is no "motor" for the rest of the national economy under current global constraints. There are many other policy tasks and means to implement policies that have also to be thoroughly considered for latecomer economies. This is especially true with respect to external constraints, improving the set of international rules (for production, trade, and capital flows), and internal strategies (income redistribution, social policy, and overall rationalization of economic institutions).

The institutions of the new economy incorporate a complex circular relationship between specific, convention-bound, and learning-oriented production systems that are themselves institutions, and a variety of formal organized institutions, notably firms, public governmental institutions, universities, unions, and trade associations. Any policy framework that involves the creation of public institutions to build or sustain the institution of the learning economy has to be based on ways to cut into this circle, and must reject the traditional logic of "public = institution" versus "private = noninstitution."

Strategic assessment has a technical dimension, which is the determination of what kinds of products are susceptible to being mastered in the economy at hand, where mastery is defined as ongoing competitive technological learning. There is a complex interaction between the product as a technology – a knowledge field – and its associated process technology, for just as products evolve through learning, so do processes, and both have dynamic parallels and complementarities that spill over their boundaries at a given moment. So the technical part of strategic assessment involves two interrelated forms of learning-based evolution.

However, strategic assessment is not only a technocratic task. Learning depends on the conventions that define the collective identities of the actors in the production system by giving them access to a common context of coordination. Without this context, learning will fail, no matter how good the hardware is. The context cannot be produced by plans, nor bought by subsidies; in order to know whether the strategy is possible, it has to be known whether there is any reason to expect actors to go along. The circular relationship described here can be penetrated only by talk, which is a necessary component of strategic assessment.

The second step is the definition of the capacities for action and identities of actors that are associated with the type of product to be assisted by policy. Each product involves conventions, which coordinate interfirm relations, product markets, labor markets, and so on. These are the substantive goals, the specific (and differentiated) end points of policy. They, too, can be defined only through the difficult and clumsy exercise of talk, in concert with analysis.

The third step is the implementation of specific versions of economic policies whose content is defined by a combination of technical assessment and social process, especially talk. The substantive method of policies is not to attempt the construction of learning-based worlds of production from whole cloth, but rather to try to create precedents that build confidence and hence make possible the deepening and widening of conventions. Small experiments are one practical way in which to proceed.

Only at the end of this long and "soft" process can the need for further formal institution-building be realistically assessed and practically undertaken, the latter on the basis of confidence, precedent (and hopefully success in learning), and consequently emerging collective identities. Other dimensions of formal institutions have not been considered in this analysis (e.g. macro-competition rules, banking, education). They too require links to the substantive concerns elaborated here. For example, education policies in different countries favor very different kinds of economic action and lead to different routes of specialization. Some decisions about institutional structures at these levels can be taken with respect to strictly generic concerns (universal values of the society, inputs to any kind of modern economic activity); but a surprising number involve more concrete visions of the particular kind of productive economy and collective action that is desired. Here we have merely laid out the fragments of this way of thinking about the problem – the problem of constructing coherent conventions and frameworks of action so as to permit latecomers to participate in the learning economy.

NOTES

1 Certain parts of this paper draw from an earlier paper entitled "Institutions of the Learning Economy" (Storper 1996); and Section IV draws from a paper entitled "Territorial development in the global learning economy," *Review of International Political Economy*, 1995.
2 This is the definition developed by the Berkeley Roundtable on the International Economy, for the US Competitiveness Council. See, for example, Tyson 1987.
3 See the articles in the special edition of *Research Policy*, 1991, edited by C. De Bresson and R. Walker, especially that of Lundvall.
4 For a detailed analysis of convention, see Storper and Salais 1997.
5 On the division of labor, see Sayer and Walker 1992.
6 Lundvall date, relies partially on Habermas 1976.
7 I deal with this in greater detail in Storper 1995.
8 There is now a vast literature on this framework, too voluminous to cite here.
9 Some of what follows is drawn from work carried out jointly with Allen Scott. See: Storper and Scott 1995.
10 In this respect, while there is much of interest in Porter 1990, the "diamond" framework it advances is too mechanical, a sort of "one-size-fits-all" policy package.

REFERENCES

Aoki, M. (1990) "Toward an economic model of the Japanese firm," *Journal of Economic Literature* 28: 1–27.

Asanuma, B. (1991) "Manufacturer–supplier relationships and the concept of relation-specific skill," *Journal of the Japanese and International Economies* 3: 1–30.

Doeringer, P. and Terkla, D. (1990) "How intangible factors contribute to economic development," *World Development* 18: 1295–1308.

Dore, R. (1987) *Flexible Rigidities*, Stanford: Stanford University Press.

Dosi, G., Pavitt, K., and Soete, L. (1990) *The Economics of Technical Change and International Trade*, New York: New York University Press.

Ergas, H. (forthcoming) "The failures of mission-oriented technology policies," in P. Bianchi and M. Quere (eds) *Systems of Innovation at the National and Local Levels*, Amsterdam: Kluwer.

Furtado, C. (1963) *Formacao Economica do Brasil*, Brasilia: Universidade de Brasilia.

Gambetta, D. (ed.) (1988) *Trust*, Oxford: Basil Blackwell.

Gereffi, G. and Fonda, S. (1992) "Regional paths of development," *Annual Review of Sociology* 18: 419–448.

Habermas, J. (1976) *Connaissance et Interêt* (original in German, 1968), Paris: Gallimard.

Haggard, S. (1990) *Pathways from the Periphery: The Politics of Growth in the Newly Industrializing Countries*, Ithaca, NY: Cornell University Press.

Hirschman, A. (1958) *The Strategy of Economic Development*, New Haven: Yale University Press.

——(1970) *Exit, Voice and Loyalty: Responses to Decline in Firms, Organizations, and States*, Cambridge, MA: Harvard University Press.

Krugman, P. (1990) *Rethinking International Trade*, Cambridge, MA: MIT Press.

Leamer, E. (1994) "Third World imports and the unskilled in the West," UCLA Conference on the World Trading System after the Uruguay Round, Los Angeles: UCLA Center for International Relations.

Lorenz, E. and Lazaric, N. (1997) "Trust, norm and convention," in E. Lorenz and N. Lazaric (eds) *Trust*, London: Edward Elgar.

Petit, P. (1993) "Are full employment policies passé?," Paper presented to the annual meeting of the American Economics Association, Anaheim, California.

Porter, M. (1990) *The Competitive Advantage of Nations*, London: Macmillan.

Prebisch, R. (1982) *La Obra de Prebisch en CEPAL*, Mexico: Fondo de Cultura Economica.

Putnam, R. (1992) *Making Democracy Work*, Princeton, NJ: Princeton University Press.

Sabel, C. (1993) "Constitutional ordering in historical context," in F. Scharpf (ed.) *Games in Hierarchies and Networks*, Boulder, CO: Westview Press.

Salomon, J. J. (1985) "Le Gaulois, le cowboy, et le samourai," Report to the Ministry of Industry and Research, Paris.

Sayer, A. and Walker, R. (1992) *The New Social Economy*, Oxford: Basil Blackwell.

Schmitz, H. and Cassiolato, J. (eds) (1992) *High Tech for Industrial Development: Lessons from the Brazilian Experience in Electronics and Automation*, London: Routledge.

Storper, M. (1992) "The limits to globalization: technology districts and international trade," *Economic Geography* 68, 1: 273–305.

——(1995a) "Territorial development in the global learning economy," *Review of International Political Economy* 2, 3: 394–424 (summer).

——(1995b) "Regional technology coalitions: an essential dimension of national technology policy," *Research Policy* 24: 895–911.

——(1996) "Institutions of the learning economy," in B.A. Lundvall and D. Foray (eds) *Employment and Growth in the Knowledge-Based Economy*, Paris: OECD.

Storper, M. and Salais, R. (1997) *Worlds of Production: The Action Frameworks of the Economy*, Cambridge, MA: Harvard University Press.

Storper, M. and Scott, A. J. (1995) "The wealth of regions," *Futures* 27, 5: 505–526.

Tyson, L. (1987) *Creating Advantage: Strategic Policy for National Competitiveness*, Berkeley: BRIE.

Veltz, P. (1996) *Mondialisation, Villes, et Territoires: L'Economie de l'Archipel*, Paris: Presses Universitaires de France.

Wade, R. (1990) *Governing the Market: Economic Theory and the Role of Government in East Asian Industrialization*, Princeton, NJ: Princeton University Press.

2 Globalization tendencies relevant for latecomers

Some conceptual issues

Christian Bellak and John Cantwell

INTRODUCTION

Although integration led to the convergence of income levels across Europe, some countries, here termed as *latecomers* (LCs), are still lagging behind. The globalization of the economic and political environment puts new pressures on these countries as they try to catch up with the technologically leading European nations. This chapter attempts to answer the questions of how the globalization process turns constraints into opportunities, and whether the inability of these countries to pursue protectionist policies creates a new set of constraints. We concentrate our arguments on those factors that shape an LC's competitiveness and determine the rate of catching up. These include: innovation, technology, trade and foreign direct investment (FDI), size and resource endowments, and institutional factors. In the globalized environment, these factors are increasingly interlinked. Given that the European LCs are relatively small, the role of size and its relationship to development figures prominently in our analysis.

Factors in the globalization process that are exclusively relevant for LCs may be difficult to define, not only since globalization affects almost every part of economic life, but also because the notion of the latecomer does not imply a sharp definition. LCs occupy a position between highly developed and less developed countries (LDCs). For this reason, some of the issues that we address will also be relevant to more developed countries and to LDCs. This hybrid position also implies that some aspects of globalization may enhance the rate at which LCs catch up, while others may impede it. However, we conclude that LCs are more likely to benefit from the globalization process and be confronted with increased opportunities to catch up, than they are to be harmed by it and fall further behind.

This chapter begins with a description of globalization trends, by identifying the characteristics of LCs and explaining how they are affected by the process of globalization. This is followed by a discussion of the importance of country size on the development of a country, and how size corresponds to the degree of openness. In particular, we ask whether there are lessons that can be learned from the globalization strategies of newly industrialized countries (NICs) and other highly developed small countries. The next section looks at the roles that technology and innovation play in linking globalization and development.[1] Following these purely economic questions, we turn to a public choice issue when we argue that traditional processes of public policy formulation, both formal and informal, will have to change in globalized economies in order to improve organizational efficiency and flexibility in the economy. In examining the impact that globalization exerts on corporatism – in other words, the bargaining relationship between labor, business, and the state – we ask whether there is a need to change existing corporatist arrangements. We also explore how corporatism is linked to *industrial policy* (IP). In the final section, we present the policy implications for latecomer industrial policy.

GLOBALIZATION TRENDS

In the 1980s and early 1990s the degree of international competition increased sharply with three main consequences:

- *a widening process*, as more countries acquired a significant share of world trade, NICs for example;
- *a deepening process*, manifested by a higher degree of integration (EU, NAFTA), particularly among advanced economies and within regional groups; and
- *an intertwining process*, as evidenced by the emergence of so-called new forms of international involvement (contractual agreements, networks, strategic alliances) in addition to traditional FDI.

Together, these developments constitute the phenomenon of *globalization*. Involving markets for goods, services, capital, and labor, globalization

> refers to the multiplicity of linkages and interconnections between the states and societies which make up the present world system . . . it also implies an intensification on the levels of interaction, interconnectedness or *interdependence* between the states and societies which constitute the world community.
>
> (McGrew and Lewis 1992: 23, quoted in Dunning 1994b: 23)

Later on we will see that corporate activities in general, and international production in particular, normally tend to be organized regionally instead of globally (Cantwell 1994a: 319). Multinational corporations (MNCs) stand at the forefront of the economic arena of globalization and internationalization, while national governments as well as inter- and supranational bodies are the main players in the political arena.

A quantitative assessment of the globalization phenomenon is presented in Table 2.1 (see also UNCTAD 1996a). However, even these figures underestimate the extent of international production, since FDI is measured at historical values (Cantwell and Bellak 1994).[2] The following subsection

Table 2.1 Worldwide FDI and selected economic indicators, 1992 and growth rates for 1981–1985, 1986–1990, 1991, and 1992

Indicator	Value at current prices 1992 ($bn)	Annual growth rate (%)			
		1981– 1985[a]	1986– 1990[a]	1991	1992
FDI outflows	0.171	3	24	–17	–11
FDI outward stock	2.125[b]	5	11	10	6
Sales of foreign affiliates of TNCs[c]	4.800[d]	2[e]	15	–13	–
Current gross domestic product at factor cost	23.300	2	9	4	5
Gross domestic investment	5.120	0.4	10	4	5
Exports of goods and non-factor services	4.500[d]	–0.2	13	3	–
Royalty and fees receipts	0.37	0.1	19	8	5

Source: UNCTAD-DTCI 1994: 20
a Compounded growth rate estimates, based on a semi-logarithmic regression equation
b 1993
c TNCs . . . Transnational Companies; Estimated by extrapolating the worldwide sales of foreign affiliates of TNCs from Germany, Japan and the United States on the basis of the relative importance of these countries in worldwide outward FDI stock.
d 1991
e 1982–1985

assesses the nature of international competition and highlights some quantitative measures of globalization.

International trade

International trade still is the main path to integration at the global level (e.g. WTO) as well as at the regional level (e.g. NAFTA, FTAA). Its nature has changed dramatically and a good deal of change was brought about by MNCs.

* Today, about one-third of total trade is free trade, one-third is managed trade, and between 30 and 40 percent is intrafirm trade by MNCs (and up to 60 to 70 percent in the case of intangible assets such as technology and organizational skills; see UNCTAD-DTCI 1994; Dunning 1994c).
* International trade patterns are increasingly shifting regionally as intra-industry trade replaces traditional trade based on resources and comparative advantage in some industries.
* Intraregional exports are increasing their share in total exports in regions with liberalization and deepening integration and are thus growing faster than interregional trade.[3]
* MNCs account for an ever increasing share of world trade. For example, domestic and foreign MNCs are responsible for up to 80 percent of British exports in some years, while in Asia MNCs account for up to 70 percent of trade (Parry 1990: 112).

Depending on the definition of MNC-related trade, MNCs may account for as little as 33 percent (intrafirm trade), or as much as 80 percent (parent company trade) of total trade (based on US 1982 figures). It would go beyond the scope of this chapter to describe quantitative trade developments in general, hence only two characteristics related to MNCs are highlighted:

- World exports of goods and nonfactor services in 1995 amounted to about $4.7 trillion, $3 trillion excluding estimated intrafirm trade (at current prices).
- Some 80 percent of international payments for royalties and fees (as a measure of transfer of technology via MNCs) are undertaken on an intrafirm basis.

Foreign direct investment

FDI has shaped trade flows and domestic economic activities alike. The motives for FDI are numerous and can be grouped into five categories: resource-seeking (natural as well as created), efficiency-seeking (production cost, location), strategic-asset-seeking (strategic alliances, mergers, acquisitions), market-seeking (localization of activities, distribution), and agglomeration-seeking. International competition through FDI increased considerably during the merger and acquisition waves of the 1980s and 1990s, leading to an increase in intra-industry and intrabloc FDI, and causing international concentration in many industries to rise.

Table 2.2 The role of FDI in world economic activity, 1913, 1960, 1975, 1980, 1985, and 1991

Item	1913	1960	1975	1980	1985	1991
World FDI stock as a share of world output	9.0[a]	4.4	4.5	4.8	6.4	8.5
World FDI inflows as a share of world output	–	0.3	0.3	0.5	0.5	0.7
World FDI inflows as a share of world gross fixed capital formation	–	1.1	1.4	2.0	1.8	3.5
World sales of foreign affiliates as a share of world exports	–	84[b]	97[c]	99[d]	99[d]	122

Source: UNCTAD-DTCI 1994: 130
a Estimate
b 1967 based on United States figures
c Based on United and Japanese figures
d 1982 based on German, Japanese, and United States data

Again, a few selected figures provide a picture of the relative importance of FDI:

- Table 2.2 illustrates the role of FDI in the process of globalization by presenting the main monetary indicators of FDI in relation to other measures of economic activity (GDP, investment). In 1995, FDI reached a level comparable to that of international trade, with FDI book value of $2.7 trillion, MNC turnover of $6 trillion, and world trade of $4.7 trillion. Given the many caveats related to FDI figures in particular (Cantwell 1992a; Bellak 1998), these figures should be treated as trend indicators rather than as absolute figures.

- Services comprise the largest share of the outward FDI stock in the five major investor countries (France, Germany, Japan, UK, and US), ranging from 46 to 66 percent.
- Outward FDI flows from the five major home countries account for about two-thirds of worldwide outflows. A comparison of FDI stocks reveals that for Japan, Germany, US, and UK, the constant-value share of outward investment in domestic capital stocks was 12.8 percent in 1990, while on a historical-cost basis it was only 8.0 percent (Cantwell and Bellak 1994; Bellak and Cantwell 1996).
- These countries account for about 60 to 70 percent of worldwide FDI stocks. The worldwide FDI stock – a proxy for the productive capacity of MNCs outside their home countries – continued to increase, reaching an estimated $2.7 trillion measured at historical values at the end of 1995.

Multinational enterprises

MNCs are the main economic players in the globalization process, but judgment of their role in development is split into two camps. On one side are the nationalists, emphasizing that the global orientation of MNCs and their independence from national identifications leaves traditional paradigms of the coincidence of nationality of firms and states meaningless: "For internationally dispersed companies the nationality of ownership does not coincide with the nationality of output" (Thomsen and Nicolaides 1990: 4). The question of "corporate citizenship" (OECD 1991) becomes particularly crucial when we turn to IP matters. Firms migrate and thus the nationality of a national government's bargaining partner – the MNC – may change, affecting, inter alia, the corporatist structure of the country in question. The other camp argues that for most MNCs the home base continues to be the most important center, especially from the viewpoint of the determinants of technological competence (Cantwell 1989, 1992b, Pearce 1989). Even where firms change the location of their headquarters for legal or tax reasons – and it does not happen often – the original home base remains crucial to MNCs' productive operations.

The numbers concerning MNCs are impressive (Table 2.3), but again should be treated with caution:

- In the mid-1990s there were about 38,000 parent firms with 260,000 foreign affiliates worldwide (UNCTAD 1996a: 9).

Table 2.3 World FDI stock and estimated employment in transnational corporations, 1975, 1985, 1990, and 1992 (millions of dollars and millions of employees)

Item	1975	1985	1990	1992
Outward FDI stock	282	674	1,649	1,932
Estimated employment in TNCs	40	65	70	73[a]
Employment in parent companies at home	–	43	44	44[a]
Employment in foreign affiliates	–	22	26	29[a]
Developed countries	–	15	17	17[a]
Developing countries	–	7	9	12[a]
China	–	–	3	6
Memorandum:				
Employment in United States TNCs	26[b]	25	25	–
Of which:				
Employment in foreign affiliates	7	6	7	–

Source: UNCTAD-DTCI 1994: 175
a Preliminary estimate
b 1977

- MNCs accounted for 73 million employees at home and abroad, constituting 10 percent of paid employment in nonagricultural activities worldwide. Even more employment is indirectly attributable to MNCs through suppliers, distributors, and the like.
- Sales by MNCs reached $6 trillion, exceeding trade in goods and nonfactor services.
- "The world's largest 100 TNCs (not including those in banking and finance) ranked by foreign assets, had about 3.4 trillion USD in global assets in 1992, of which about 1.3 trillion USD were held outside their respective home countries. These firms are estimated to account for about one-third of the combined outward FDI of their countries of origin" (UNCTAD-DTCI 1994: 5, see also UNCTAD 1996a: 29).
- Employment at home and abroad is estimated to be about twelve million (UNCTAD 1996a: 29).
- The fact that "90 percent of parent firms are based in developed countries" (UNCTAD-DTCI 1994: 3) means that a major part of the globe is actually excluded from globalization.

To summarize, the intensification and improvement of the international division of labor by new technologies and new forms of enterprise organization is both expanding the global economy and increasing its interdependence. In this globalized environment, each LC must find its niche of specific competence, considered in combination with general location factors, in order to be able to catch up with the leading economies.

COUNTRY SIZE, RESOURCES, AND GLOBALIZATION

Because European LCs are small countries, they are more strongly affected by globalization than large countries, and hence follow a different development path. Orthodox theories of the impact of country size refer to the development potential of an economy and the discretion of national policy (see Bellak 1994a). A small nation is usually assumed to have a large share of trade in GDP, and yet to account for a small share of world trade. Smallness is seen primarily as a constraint for development in economic terms, with the exception of the specialization pressure.

A *small home market* is a constraint to exploit fully economies of scale, leading to firm size below minimum efficient technological scale. Because there are few suppliers, competition is restricted in many industries. Since a small domestic market provides little incentive to innovate, small countries generally do not generate major technologies; they are, rather, flexible adapters to structural change abroad. Small, highly developed European countries are increasingly squeezed between emerging new competitors like NICs, and large countries that spend large amounts on R&D in key industries like telecommunications.

A *shortage of natural resources* is also seen as a constraint of small countries. Yet, in higher developed countries natural resources are no longer crucial factors of production compared to created resources. Further, contrary to the implicit assumption that resources are equally distributed over the globe, many of them are concentrated in a few locations (e.g. certain minerals in small African countries, tourist sites in Switzerland and Austria).

Disadvantages from the *small size of firms* in small countries are evident: 80 percent of the top 100 MNCs and of the 200 largest companies in Europe are based in large countries (calculated from Commission of the European Communities 1994: 90 and UNCTAD-DTCI 1994: 8). Small firms follow supplier-oriented or dependent strategies, implying a low degree of geographical diversification of sales, not least because of disadvantages in market-specific product differentiation. They tend to be specialized niche suppliers, hence exhibiting little product diversification. Their ownership advantages are confined to a few niches where they can achieve price-setter positions. Consequently, both their market power and their scope for foreign operations (exports and FDI) are less than for large firms.

The *trade dependence* of small countries did not matter for classical economists, provided that trade was completely free. In a world of market distortions such as tariffs, size *does* matter, while in a world of fully integrated nations size *does not* matter. Trade dependence involves several issues:

1 small countries are price takers in international markets acting under externally given terms of trade;
2 their exports are not well diversified (geographically as well as structurally); and

3 the total volume of trade (exports and imports) is higher than in large countries, because exporting is a strategy to exploit scale economies and importing is necessary to overcome the natural-resource shortage and lack of some investment-good industries.

As a consequence of trade dependence, small countries are more vulnerable to protectionist policies adopted by large countries. This is of particular concern since exporting is positively related to economic development and growth (Hosono 1995).

Small countries face a *restructuring process* that differs from that of large countries:

> in large economies where there is a greater number of industries, it is more likely that the consequences of structural change "average out": when employment opportunities decrease somewhere in the economy, there will probably be new ones emerging somewhere else. With more specialized industrial structures, small open economies are more vulnerable to restructuring which may not "average out" to the same degree as in the bigger economies.
>
> (Landesmann and Vartianinen 1992: 212f.)

It is thus likely that restructuring in small countries will be slower than in large countries due to the relatively large social impact.

Two other small-country features have macroeconomic ramifications. First, a high degree of *corporatism* (discussed further below) influences macrolevel performance such as income distribution, which may accelerate or impede structural adaptation on the microlevel. Second, dependence on other countries reduces and limits *discretion in national policy* as structural change and exchange-rate movements affect demand and supply conditions in the small open economy.

The influence of country size on development must not be overestimated. If we allow for more openness than just trade – for example, integration and foreign direct investment – then the constraints of smallness and the role of size lose their significance further. Several mechanisms combine to lead to a relative convergence of small and large countries, even when large differences persist in absolute terms.

Both small and large countries are increasingly trade dependent. The increased importance of created resources, accompanied by a decreasing reliance on natural resources, eliminates the small-country resource constraint in most industries. There are few reasons to assume that small countries will not be able to create the same relative resources per capita as large countries. Further, size and resource abundance are not exclusively related to one another, as Cantwell's (1997) division of countries into groups according to these attributes makes clear. One finds resource abundance amongst both large countries (Brazil, Canada, US) and small countries (Indonesia, Malaysia, Philippines, Sweden), just as one finds both small

(Belgium, Hong Kong, Netherlands, Singapore) and large (Argentina, South Korea, UK) resource-scarce countries. Clearly, resource-abundance is a secondary issue to size.

These factors imply that small countries are not a homogenous group. Although they have a small home market in common, the importance of size has diminished, replaced by the increased importance of resource creation and internationalization of competitive advantage derived from specialization. This suggests an array of potential development paths for inward FDI and domestic industry across the spectrum of country size and resource endowment, as illustrated in Table 2.4 from Cantwell 1997.

Table 2.4 Potential development paths for inward direct investment, and their association with local industrialization across different types of country

Categorization of national development	Link between domestic development and the growth of foreign involvement	Type of new foreign firm
Resource-abundant	Related diversification (for example, from mining), downstream processing (for example, metal processing, wood products, oil-related chemicals, agribusiness), with some other upgrading of industry in large countries (see below)	Firms from resource-rich countries Firms from resource-scarce newly industrialized countries
Resource-scarce large countries (with broader range of local competence and skills)	Industrial upgrading and export growth (as wages rise following productivity growth), and extension of local infrastructure	Manufacturing firms, in new areas Construction and local service firms
Large countries (lacking the capability for sustained export expansion)	Slower expansion of an essentially similar industrial structure	Local market-seeking manufacturing firms
Resource-scarce small countries	Shift away from simpler manufacturing activity to some industrial upgrading, but more towards a greater service-orientation	Newly industrialized country firms relocating activity International service groups

Source: Cantwell 1997: 171

Globalization and development strategy

Historically, the strategies followed by LCs regarding the globalization or internationalization of their economies have been diverse and cannot easily be generalized (Doherty and McDevitt 1991). However, based on the experience of other small countries, there seems to be widespread consensus that we observe a positive relationship between the growth and internationalization of an economy, especially with respect to trade and technology transfer. We argue that there is a definite and increasing connection between development and globalization, but that the effects may be either positive or negative. It is important to view globalization not merely as a financial phenomenon but also as a real phenomenon.

There are multiple paths by which internationalization can lead to growth, especially since the positive relationship between growth and increased openness in international transactions (trade and FDI) runs in both directions. Increased globalization implies that the inward-oriented strategies of the past, although not protectionist, must now be supplemented by strategic alliances in order to accomplish structural change and to exploit technological, organizational, and other forms of competitive advantage.

LCs have followed a variety of strategies for increasing their openness to trade, foreign investment, and the acquisition of foreign technology. The developed small countries in Europe, like their larger counterparts, were quick to open their trade as a first step towards integration into the world economy after the Second World War. Various free trade agreements and other institutions were set up in order to promote exports. Two small countries, Ireland and Austria, also relied heavily on inward FDI. Outward FDI by small countries was a strategy that gained momentum only in the 1980s, initially by Sweden and later by Finland and Austria. Switzerland and The Netherlands are exceptions, having exhibited an above average outward FDI stock compared to their size (Bellak 1994b).

Parry (1990) emphasizes the many different roles FDI plays in a country's development by helping to overcome certain bottlenecks. Depending on its financing, FDI shaped the exports, technology, and know-how of the host countries, emphasizing one or another characteristic of the bundle of activities transferred via FDI. Countries have succeeded to a varying degree to influence the kind of FDI that is complementary to their activities, and thus most beneficial to their welfare (see also Ernst and O'Connor 1989; Ozawa 1992; Hosono 1995).

The result of a recent study (Borensztein *et al.* 1995: 3) emphasizes the crucial role of human capital and suggests that

> FDI is in fact an important vehicle for the transfer of technology contributing to growth in larger measure than domestic investment. . . . However our empirical results imply that FDI is more productive than domestic investment only when the host country has a minimum threshold stock of human capital.

The experience of the high-performing East Asian economies was similar, although there the process was strongly organized and directed by governments that created institutions, implemented policies to attract inward investment, and employed varying degrees of openness. Felix (1994) warns about the difficulty of transferring the Asian experience to other regions, and cautions against placing too much stress on the role of FDI in development as compared to the roles of government policy, flexible capital markets, and other factors. A World Bank report (1993) describes the East Asian approach as having been based on export-push and technology-input-via-inward-investments strategies, which helped to enhance economic efficiency and subsequently increased the growth of output and employment. With regard to inward investment, it should be noted that today some industries are less footloose than one might think, and contrary to many historical experiences, spillovers seemed to be positive in these countries (World Bank 1993: 303). Basic factors of production like "the locationally specific elements of the technological structures and collective skills that are embodied in national organizations" are still immobile and, as such, are "tied to the traditions of local educational and training systems, organizational methods, operating customs, business and institutional practices, company exchange arrangements and so forth" (Cantwell 1994a: 323).

The positive relationship between development and globalization should not, however, be overstated. A negative relationship may be established in two cases. First, increased competition through imports or inward FDI may destroy domestic industries, or dynamic interaction among foreign, open domestic, and sheltered domestic sectors may be absent. European LCs are, however, in a position where such effects are not very relevant. Since their level of development and their infrastructure are already quite advanced, they should be able to absorb certain external shocks from a globalized environment. Only in LCs where the gap between the domestic and international economy is too large to gain from inward FDI and openness in trade would foreign MNCs act as "islands," isolated from the rest of the economy, leading to a situation where the country would lose income from the reduction of tariffs. The second case occurs when entry barriers to foreign markets are too high to overcome (Krugman 1993). In this context, entry barriers should not be understood to be limited to tariff and nontariff trade barriers, but foremost to include new forms of enterprise organization, in other words, the emergence of global networks. These create new types of strategic entry barriers which not only affect costs in the short run, but also affect the long-run development potential of firms or regions. These barriers play a crucial role in the innovation process.

INNOVATION AND THE ROLE OF STRATEGIC ALLIANCES

Modern growth theory establishes a positive relationship between technology and productivity growth. The stylized facts suggest that "before World War I and after World War II, activities of innovation/creative imitation occurred at a higher rate in 'late-comers'" (Dosi *et al.* 1994: 14). This catching up was possible only through increased integration into the world economy. "Successful latecomers have combined heavy imports of technology with strong expansion of indigenous efforts devoted to technical change. Imports of technology and autonomous innovative efforts are not alternative but complementary activities" (Dosi *et al.* 1994: 20). As Cantwell (1992b) argues, much depends on the initial competence of indigenous firms. This is particularly relevant for LCs with a weak industrial base. Table 2.5 shows the relationship between the form of technological competence, the stage of development, and the national course of inward FDI.

Table 2.5 Technological accumulation and the national course of inward direct investment

	Stages of national development		
	(1)	*(2)*	*(3)*
Form of technological competence of leading indigenous firms	Basic engineering skills, complementary organizational routines and structures	More sophisticated engineering practices, basic scientific knowledge, more complex organizational methods	More science-based, advanced engineering, organizational structures reflect needs of coordination
Type of inward direct investment	Early resource- or market-seeking investment	More advanced resource-oriented or market-targeted investment	Research-related investment and integration into international networks
Industrial course of inward direct investment	Resource based (extractive TNCs or backward vertical integration) and simple manufacturing	More forward processing of resources, wider local market-oriented and export-platform manufacturing	More sophisticated manufacturing systems, international integration of investment

Source: Cantwell 1997: 166

The following subsections explore the role of innovation and strategic alliances in greater detail. Technology is used here to describe the characteristics of production systems as a whole, thus encompassing all aspects of the organization of production. This broad usage of technology conforms with the evolutionary theoretical view which examines technology creation and innovation as a path-dependent corporate learning process. It is exactly this cumulative nature of technology in the international context that is relevant for LCs with respect to strategic alliances and global networks – the two forms of integration into the global economy that we examine next.

Strategic alliances

Empirical evidence on technology alliances shows that LCs are ranked last compared to other EC countries, whether the criterion is EC–US alliances, EC–Japanese alliances, Intra-EC alliances, R&D expenditures as a share of GDP, or share of OECD high-tech exports (Hagedoorn and Narula 1994: Table 2). In principle, the deepening of the globalization process opens new channels for LCs to participate in strategic alliances and reap some benefits from network firm structures. The increasing specialization of countries and the intensified international division of labor imply that a country's development depends crucially on its participation in the global production system.

It is widely acknowledged that technology consists of two elements – public knowledge and tacit capability – that can be used productively only with one another. The public element is usually a generic technology (e.g. biotechnology, information technology, microelectronics) that is potentially applicable in almost all other industries, be it manufacturing or services. The public element has some characteristics of a public good, in that it may create positive externalities when put on the market. Market failure is limited by the fact that its diffusion depends on the tacit capabilities. Cantwell (1992b: 33) states that "technological competence does not leak out or dissipate easily" in some fields, and for this reason interfirm exchanges of knowledge actually tend to be greater in R&D-intensive industries (Cantwell 1994b: 11). Thus, contrary to the standard view, the public element can be exposed to the market if its use requires a costly learning process by other firms.

It is often maintained that LCs should actively involve their firms in strategic alliances with foreign partners in order to create technological spillovers and to adapt their economies quickly to the globalized environment. Strategic alliances are to be preferred to the import of technology in the long run, since they avoid external technological dependence. For example, Sachwald (1995: 23) emphasizes the "role of cooperative agreements as a way of jumping over barriers to entry, through the provision of complementary resources and learning opportunities." In this view, strategic alliances are accelerators of change within firms' strategies in a quickly changing environment, rather than a means to cope with increasing transaction costs. Other motivations for strategic alliances by LCs – in addition to those related to ownership and control – include sharing high R&D costs and gaining access to scarce pools of qualified personnel and knowledge; these latter are crucial for mastering the convergence between major technologies, but are not available in-house (Ernst and O'Connor 1989: 25).

In the case of innovation as the main source of growth, this view must be adapted to LCs, since the complementarity of the public and tacit elements of technology has two important implications with regard to strategic alliances in this field. First, a strategic alliance in technology creation is most likely to be successful when it incorporates a complementary learning process that ultimately leads to the creation of tacit capabilities to operationalize the new technology. But the problem for LCs arises when their firms do not meet the necessary preconditions of a level of technological development that make them attractive partners for foreign firms. Those firms in LCs that are capable of developing or providing such tacit elements would profit from such alliances, but they may be hard to identify. Thus, the ironic second implication: the increasing importance of strategic alliances means that "producers in smaller countries now face even higher barriers to entry in such industries if they want to develop beyond 'dependent' exporting; they have little to offer by way of an entry ticket to the two-way partnership" (Stopford and Strange 1991: 93). An example of such an industry might be semiconductors. Thus, in some stages of value-added activities, strategic alliances between LC firms and foreign firms will undoubtedly arise, such as marketing and distribution. Yet, in the crucial stage, namely innovation–technology creation, strategic alliances will be difficult to establish, all the more so where global networks dominate, the subject to which we now turn.

Global networks

MNCs have established regional and global networks coordinating their innovatory activities, partly through internal technology flows, partly through strategic alliances. These networks rely on intra- and interfirm linkages, representing varying degrees of integration and specialization. Thus, "'networks' are not only a support of transactions, but more fundamental strategic structures that allow the incorporation of actors into chains in which the costs and gains from integration are the essential economic factor" (Veltz 1991: 202). Contrary to the orthodox transaction cost view, the new techno-economic paradigm and adaptation to global change are the main forces behind the formation of networks, which consequently become "exclusive clubs of insiders." Economizing on innovation rather than economizing on cost creates the competitive advantage of such networks.

Networks exert two distinct effects on outsider firms and countries. First, they create entry barriers through information advantages (asymmetries) *vis-à-vis* outsiders, thus increasing the gap in technological innovation. For example, "software and telecommunication networks are two areas where the search for competitive advantage may lead to standards which tend to lock out alternative systems" (Ernst and O'Connor 1989: 24).

Second, and more importantly with respect to LCs, these international networks tend to favor advanced and highly developed firms and regions. Even a cost advantage such as low wages, or a reduction in transportation costs, will not open the door for LCs, since innovation is usually created in high-wage regions and centers. This poses a threat to LCs, which have already lost important production capacity as low-cost locations, since

> reducing transportation cost has two effects: it facilitates locating production where it is cheapest, but it also facilitates concentration of production

in one location so as to realize economies of scale. And when production is concentrated, it may pay to concentrate it at the location with higher costs but better access [to resources].

(Krugman 1993: 96)

This is even true for innovatory activities, which depend crucially on the quality of the labor force.

Apart from the immediate spatial consequences of the new international division of labor (see Veltz 1991), "there is some evidence that the creation by TNCs of international networks to support their own technological innovation may help to reinforce existing patterns of national specialization" (Cantwell 1994b: 18). This points to a "lock-in" scenario for LCs, since they are not on the map of "existing patterns of specialization" – at least with respect for innovatory activities – in the increasingly intrafirm international division of labor. Inward FDI as well as strategic alliances will tend to concentrate in comparatively advantaged industries and in comparatively advantaged locations, a mix that excludes most parts of LCs for lack of either or both preconditions.

In general, as assembly subcontracting has become more automated, it has required more skilled operators as well as a pool of skilled technicians to maintain, repair and troubleshoot the automated equipment. The increased skill intensity, infrastructure intensity (higher energy consumption, e.g.), and engineering intensity of subcontract assembly strongly suggests that only a relatively few NIEs which possess an abundance of those 'factors' are likely to be major participants in assembly subcontracting for more technology-intensive products in the future.

(Ernst and O'Connor 1989: 85)

The implication of this is, once again, a paradoxical situation in which it is difficult for LCs to enter such networks since they would have to provide beforehand what they actually seek to gain from such a network. This is something of a "vicious development cycle" argument, not only for LC firms, but for LCs in general, resulting from the fact that "centers of only intermediate significance, however can be subject to the erosion of local technological capacity as international economic integration increases, in part through the changing locational decisions of TNCs" (Cantwell 1994b: 25, quoting from Cantwell and Dunning 1991). It is this interaction between the firm and country level that may aggravate the problem for LCs to enter global innovation networks. We address the policy conclusions of this on p 72 (see also UNCTAD 1996b: Ch. IV).

CORPORATISM AND GLOBALIZATION

Globalization creates the need for greater flexibility, with respect to both firms and government policies, as the economic environment changes rapidly. In such an environment, stable conditions in some fields may provide the necessary room for flexible actions by the government, trade unions, and MNCs in other fields. Corporatism, defined as the degree of interest intermediation between private interest groups (trade unions, employers associations, business interest associations, and the state) is affected in many ways by globalization (see Grant 1992; Bellak 1995). It may in turn enhance economic stability and increase the organizational flexibility of the economy as a whole; or it may slow down restructuring and change.

Table 2.6 International comparison of degree of macrocorporatism

Schmitter	*Lehmbruch*	*Schmidt*
Strong		
Austria	Austria	Austria
Norway	Sweden	Norway
Denmark	Norway	Sweden
Finland	Netherlands	Switzerland
Sweden		
Medium		
Netherlands	Belgium	Belgium
Belgium	West Germany	Denmark
West Germany	Denmark	Finland
Switzerland	Finland	West Germany
	Switzerland (borderline)	Netherlands
Weak		
Canada	United Kingdom	Canada
Ireland	Italy	France
United States		Italy
France		United Kingdom
United Kingdom		United States
Pluralism		
	United States	
	Canada	

Source: Williamson 1989: 150
Note: the measures used in the three studies differ, and the ranking was modified by
   Williamson.

There is some empirical evidence regarding different types of corporatism in European LCs (see e.g. Barreto 1992; Kritsantonis 1992). Various studies point to a close correlation between corporatism and country size. Table 2.6 summarizes the results of important studies, all using different measures. From this, Williamson concludes that

corporatism appears to be most developed in the smaller polities, and much weaker in the larger ones. *Size may not, however, be the key variable.* It may, for example be that in smaller countries there is less socioeconomic differentiation, and that it is this that allows for a more unified and centralized macro-structure of interest group polities.

(Williamson 1989: 151, emphasis added)

Not included in the table is a major international investor, namely Japan. That country is characterized by a dual- or semicorporatist structure, where labor interests are organized on the microlevel of the firm, while capital's interests are represented and centralized in the highest levels of the ministerial bureaucracy, that is, MITI.

Whether corporatism and economic performance are positively related, as Table 2.6 indirectly suggests, is also subject to heavy debate. Therborn argues "that other factors such as the aims of the labor movement, elite attitudes to unemployment and market conditions can have evident and significant repercussions on wage increases" (quoted in Williamson 1989: 153). Although it has not yet been established that there exists a positive relationship between corporatism and economic performance, one might still ask if it can be a model for small LCs to improve their economic performance.

With respect to globalization and development, two issues in particular dominate the microlevel discussion: first, the impact of MNCs as the main bargaining partners on the level and structure of corporatism; and second, the impact of corporatism on restructuring and technological innovation (resource allocation).[4]

MNCs as bargaining partners

MNCs generally press for closer economic integration and international freedom of movement of production factors, as, for example, in the EU. Bargaining at the firm level is becoming more widespread, particularly among large MNCs. Three main reasons account for this development:

- Because the competitive positions of large MNCs are becoming increasingly varied, their objectives, and consequently both the bargaining process and outcomes, also differ increasingly.
- Traditional bargaining systems are too inflexible to account for these changes.
- The qualitative increase in globalization (i.e. the increasing interrelatedness of firms via networks) prompts regional strategies of MNCs that might well go beyond the borders of countries, and hence beyond the national bargaining system.

We develop these points further through the use of several illustrative descriptions, all but one taken from the UNCTAD-DTCI *World Investment Report 1994*.

Example 1: [The integrated international production] . . . form of organizing production has implications for industrial relations systems, as can be seen from trends in those regions. . . . As a result of the creation of the Single Market and following a wave of acquisitions, mergers and alliances, large TNCs operating in the European Union have created integrated management structures at a pan-European level, distinct from their formerly national organizational divisions. The new structures indicate a tendency for developing firm-specific employment-systems or "organization-based" arrangements for dealing with industrial relations.

(UNCTAD-DTCI 1994: 270)

The MNC thus replaces traditional bargaining structures by its international hierarchy as the level of bargaining. It is the manner in which countries are connected via firms that leads to a change in the organizational principles and governance structures (Bellak 1995). We advance several propositions on the effects of this process:

1 The high degree of centralization in collective bargaining may be threatened by large MNCs as they bargain on a more decentralized level.

Example 2: Bargaining at the level of the enterprise or plant. Transnational corporations from the United States, used to bargaining at the level of the enterprise or plant, contributed to this practice in a number of Western European countries, although generally in the form of supplementary bargaining within the framework of multi-employer, industry-wide agreements. Bargaining at the level of the individual plant or enterprise brings a number of advantages to employers. . . . However, in those countries in which collective negotiations are firmly established, TNC managers seem to play an active role in the actions and policies of employers' associations. This occurs, for example, in Belgium where collective agreements achieved through federated bargaining are not only legally binding, but can be imposed on nonparticipants.

(UNCTAD-DTCI 1994: 266)

2 The bargaining relationships themselves are usually long term and durable, and thus may be challenged by specific relocations of capital, and by capital flexibility in general. The increasing need for flexibility and rapid change under globalization might therefore be a threat to corporatist arrangements.

3 Where currently the interests of individual firms are collectively represented through pressure groups (lobbies), they are more likely to be represented at the individual level in the future, at least in the case of large MNCs with independent strategies.

Example 3: This development transcends the established industry and sectoral frameworks for collective bargaining in Europe and reinforces the trend towards a decentralization of bargaining to the company or plant level, especially, as traditional structures of industry (or multi-employer bargaining) are unable to encompass the growing interfirm diversity of industrial relations outcomes. The impact on the national industrial relations system can be seen in the United Kingdom, but is also significant in other European countries where TNCs negotiate their own agreements, e.g. the Netherlands, or where TNCs are quite active in bargaining at the company level as a supplement to sectoral agreements, e.g. in France, Italy, Spain and Sweden. . . . The number of TNCs that have adopted such arrangements is not large; but given their size, they may play an important role of determining the future of multi-employer bargaining in that region. The establishment of voluntary company councils at the European level is an indication of the current trend.

(UNCTAD-DTCI 1994: 270)

Example 4: Moreover, the shift to complex integration strategies, particularly evident among large TNCs in Europe, has been associated with the emergence of company-based industrial relations structures that are likely to have some impact on established industry-wide patterns of collective bargaining.

(UNCTAD-DTCI 1994: 272)

Example 5: However, there has been, particularly over the past decade, a tendency for management to take up certain employment issues in the context of human resource management, thus removing them from the domain of collective industrial relations. The expanding influence of TNCs over domestic economic activity is accompanied by perceptible changes in industrial relations practices, both within TNCs and in industrial relations in general.

(UNCTAD-DTCI 1994: xxv)

4 The traditional tripartite mechanism (i.e. intermediation between interest groups of labor, capital, and the state) cannot simply be transferred to a supranational level, because there is no state-like organization with which to bargain.

5 The organization of one or more interest groups into associations whose delegates have the authority to engage in negotiations on behalf of their members is even more unlikely on a consensus basis in an internationalized environment on a supranational level with a large number of divergent interests.

Example 6: But compared to the paradigmatic national political systems of the firm, interest representation around and within the Community was always much more 'pluralist' than it was corporatist.

(Streeck and Schmitter 1991: 136)

The implications are that large, important MNCs are likely to have room for discretion, be exempted from certain regulations, and be able to play national governments off against one another in order to gain concessions (Bellak 1997).[5] All of which leads us to the second issue, namely the role of corporatism for industrial restructuring and change.

Corporatism, restructuring, and technological innovation

Unlike the evidence on the macrolevel, where there is widespread consensus that corporatism is positively related to growth, equality, and employment, the evidence on the microlevel is mixed. We distinguish between two schools of thought, one arguing that the impact of corporatism on restructuring is positive, and the other that it is negative.[6] It should be emphasized that these schools have in mind a certain type of macrocorporatism, and not corporatism *per se*. Later we propose changes in order for this type of corporatism to be effective in a globalized environment.

The first school establishes a positive relationship between corporatism, restructuring, and innovation. This view is of particular interest to small LCs, since not only do they need substantial restructuring to catch up, but also the entire process will be concentrated in a few industries (see the discussion on p 47). The argument for this positive view goes as follows: the danger of crisis during the process of industrial restructuring may enhance the possibility of some corporatist agreement between the tripartite interest groups in order to socially absorb the negative externalities arising in this process. With regard to small LCs, the problem is aggravated by global competition in the form of exchange-rate and other international price movements. The main contribution of corporatism lies in its role to provide institutions that "can promote stability and structure in economic decision making by reducing uncertainty and by providing game rules for organized interests or associations" (Henley and Tsakalotos 1993: 43). Macroeconomic policy management is committed to general welfare, and information flows are optimized, hence transaction costs from imperfect information, inflexibility in decision-making, or organizational inefficiencies are reduced.

The second school argues that corporatism may constitute a serious impediment to innovation, restructuring, and internationalization. Despite the fact that the arguments stem mainly from empirical observation in small, high-income European countries, this approach is also relevant for the LCs: first, they do not wish to replicate past failures, and second, a critical view of corporatism might lead LCs to possible improvements. Conclusions like the following are typical of this view:

> the process of structural adjustment has . . . been hampered by an industrial policy which favored large capital-intensive enterprises rather than small businesses, as well as by high and growing wage differentials which kept capital and labor too long in marginal production.
>
> (Guger and Polt 1994: 156 on Austria)

The central aspect of this view is the selective nature of policy measures in corporatist systems that parallel, and either accelerate or decelerate, structural change.

"'Regulatory capture,' a situation where the administration of industrial policy, say, is 'captured' by organized groups to serve their own interests, is a distinct possibility" (Henley and Tsakalotos 1993: 130). This is especially true for LCs with a large nationalized sector, or with structure-preserving IP measures which tend to survive once they have been introduced. Again, globalization pressures increase the possibility that certain groups will try to follow defensive strategies, thus opting for protecting certain regions or industries. Corporatism may even tend to create "log-rolling," where social partners exchange one specific protection against another. In this view, IP is decelerative and protectionist, and therefore macrocorporatist policies are to be preferred to IP, since they guarantee stability.

Both schools find some support empirically. LCs should consequently try to maximize benefits over costs when reshaping their corporate systems. In particular, two immediate conclusions can be drawn from our discussion about the role of corporatism in LCs in the process of catching up:

1 *The new corporatist arrangements in LCs will be based increasingly on the micro- rather than the macrolevel.* Typical corporatist systems are generally thought of as being macro-oriented by relying on a centralized wage bargaining structure at their core. The economic and political processes of LCs shaped by globalization tend to reduce the capacity of macrocorporatism, which will largely be confined to incomes and distribution policy. Microcorporatism will be strengthened as a means of resource allocation and as a way of improving competitiveness via the lowering of international productivity differentials. Microcorporatism can be understood as a flexible coordinated system of interest intermediation that requires a high-skilled, flexible, and motivated workforce (Henley and Tsakalotos 1993), which in turn leads to a new role for education policy (as discussed in the final section of this chapter). This may result in an improved coordination of structural change, and a higher motivation of labor to accept the diffusion of new technologies and innovation and to participate in the gains from restructuring, consequently leading to higher growth. Thus, the need by LCs for higher flexibility in a globalized environment can be met by putting emphasis on microcorporatism, and at the same time trying not to destroy overall bargaining structures. Henley and Tsakalotos (1993: 137) stress that the former may even have positive feedbacks on the latter. Such measures will also have a positive impact on income distribution – an issue we have identified earlier as a crucial policy field in the growth process of LCs.

2 *The shift from macro- towards microcorporatism requires an upgrading of the role of industrial policy in LCs.* Traditionally, IP was seen as a second-order priority to the macrocorporatist wage-bargaining, in order to respond to price competition in international markets. IPs in corporatist countries are characterized as indirect policies, since they were introduced mainly via labor market policy. As Landesmann (1992: 245) points out, the reason is that "industrial policies are designed to be specific, i.e. directed towards particular industries, firms, regions, groups . . . rather than general." The implementation of IP therefore has distributional consequences

and is not judged equally, like macropolicies that are designed to increase general welfare. Since incomes policy loses some of its instruments in a globalized environment, and technology becomes the crucial factor of growth, there is a need to redirect government policies toward a stronger IP. The role of IP must therefore be shifted toward direct IPs – foremost technology policy – and at least be placed on equal footing with incomes policy. One precondition to achieve this goal is an understanding of IP as a means to increase general national welfare, replacing institutionalized group lobbying (primarily by labor). The new role of direct industrial policies in LCs meets well with the introduction of more microcorporatist features that we discuss in our first conclusion below.

The case for and constraints to national industrial policy in LCs is discussed in the next section.

OPPORTUNITIES AND CONSTRAINTS

Before proceeding with a discussion and evaluation of industrial policy appropriate to LCs, we summarize the main conclusions of our examination of LCs and globalization thus far. How these results translate into opportunities and constraints for LCs is summarized in Table 2.7. Our summary is organized around four questions that correspond to the main issues discussed in this chapter. The most striking general finding is that globalization presents LCs with both constraints and opportunities, suggesting that industrial policy does not just matter, it is critical in the determination of whether LCs will catch up or fall further behind. The final section concentrates on how these opportunities can be strengthened and how the constraints may be limited or reduced by industrial policy in LCs.

How important is size for the development of an LC?

The smallness of European LCs is relevant because it leads to certain constraints. These become increasingly irrelevant, the more an LC is integrated into the world economy, which also creates different and new constraints, especially in the IP-making process and with respect to sovereignty. The more important issue here is the resource-abundance of a country (created as well as natural) which clearly affects large and small countries.

How are globalization and LC development linked?

Countries usually host only part of a production process that is international in scope. In order to grow, LC firms have to specialize in competitive segments and enter the global scene in order to exploit their specialization in goods and services. The increasing specialization of countries and the intensified international division of labor imply that an LC's development depends

Table 2.7 Opportunities and constraints for latecomers from globalization

Characteristics of LCs encounter . . .	. . . globalization trends and become . . .	. . . either opportunities . . .	. . . or constraints.
1. Short history of rapid industrial development	regional integration (macro level)	1. Growth (via trade and enhanced technology diffusion), "bottleneck function of FDI" and inward-looking market development 2. Increased technology transfer and cross-border cooperation (strategic alliances) through international programs 3. Opening of Eastern Europe creates the possibility of acting as a gate to East and South (attract services, holding companies) and to relocate certain activities to neighboring countries (and they are future markets).	1. New international competition from other areas (e.g. Eastern European countries as future EU-members) leads to a speeding-up of structural transformation in industries where LCs have been successful in the past. The "latecomer-squeeze" creates more pressure to attract *new* investment in order to replace FDI that were traditionally directed towards LCs (esp. Ireland, Portugal). 2. R&D is increasingly transferred from the public domain to the private (Ernst and O'Connor 1989), since MNCs are on the forefront of technological development and internalize their R&D. This prevents quick technology acquisition and absorption by LCs, because there is no external market for technology. 3. Positive effects of trade which accelerate growth and technological learning are only temporary in the initial phase and tend to level off since restructuring and relocation are speeding up.
2. Weak foundation of industrial structures (technology) and weak human resource base	increasingly footloose industries and regional concentrated value-added activities	1. Utilized positive spill-over effects from inward FDI and strategic alliances 2. Increasing service-intensity, where role of information technology is crucial and entry barriers are not suitable for Eastern Europe, because of high-quality standards and high wage sensitivity.	1. Key firm activities are increasingly concerned in certain highly developed locations (Pearce 1989, Cantwell 1989) and the growing inputs create high entry barriers in many industries. 2. Small size of LCs implies that a small country usually has only one (or very few) industries where the path of industrialization may be transformed from an inward-substituting to an export-led growth. This restricts the option for the catching-up process considerably especially if these industries are not typical growth-sectors.

<table>
<tr>
<td></td>
<td></td>
<td>3. The transformation from resource-based towards a technology-driven strategy, based on experience accumulated earlier might be difficult if the LC's industries are not at a certain level of development. Especially the small LCs do not have many manufacturing industries, hence catching up via this route can only be part of the strategy.</td>
</tr>
<tr>
<td>3. Limited subcontracting networks</td>
<td>integrated production and increased inter-firm cooperation, global networks (micro level), strategic (technology) alliances</td>
<td>1. Participation in international clusters or networks on the end of production and services in segments, which are not suitable for Eastern Europe, because of high-quality standards and high wage sensitivity.
2. Specializing in certain activities of clusters which comprise all activities of production and services of certain good/service, and which favor the most efficient location by optimizing the international division of labor.
3. Developing segments of higher quality inputs for export to foreign firms.
4. Attracting foreign MNCs in order to build up a supplier-industry based on small and medium-sized firms.

1. Heavy competition from advanced small countries as subcontractors
2. High entry barriers in assembly and subcontracting as they are no longer – as in many Asian NIEs – differentiation strategies, since they do not lead to technology transfer on a sufficient scale to stimulate endogenous innovation.
3. Higher degree of specialization of (also large) countries implies that they have to specialize even more (but: see also opportunities from specialization and integration).</td>
</tr>
<tr>
<td>4. Basic infrastructure (tangible)</td>
<td>state-led competition for FDI; large investments necessary; increasing specialization of large countries</td>
<td>1. Compete with other countries in immaterial infrastructure
2. LCs might profit from new wave of relocation strategies with low labor cost of lean-production industries (e.g. Mexico from automobile industry)
3. Engage in outward FDI and increase future income earning capacity

1. Development of immaterial infrastructure as high as in developed countries is necessary in order to compete actively with other states for FDI. Many of the crucial improvements in the (immaterial) infrastructure take a long time (education etc.) and thus might not be achieved with sufficient speed.</td>
</tr>
</table>

Table 2.7 Opportunities and constraints for latecomers from globalization – *contd*

Characteristics of LCs encounter . . .	. . . globalization trends and become . . .	. . . either opportunities . . .	. . . or constraints.
		4. "Latecomers can take advantage of the effects of the broad diffusion of the ideas behind the original concept" (Stopford and Strange 1991, p.73). This means it can be advantageous not to be at the forefront of (technological) development. The East Asian countries, for example, have relied heavily on imitation before switching to indigenous research and development. The European LCs must be at the forefront of technology, i.e. enter the global networks directly. There is no time for a (costly) waiting and imitation process, otherwise they will be overtaken by "second tier" LCs.	2. Gap between existing and required infrastructure may be too large, especially the development of immaterial infrastructure takes a long time. In the short run, inward FDI must match the infrastructure of the LC, but in the long run it is vice versa! Globalization increases the likelihood of changes in the global environment, which require a constant adjustment of the LCs infrastructure to be compatible with production/services which might be located in their territory. 3. Increasing cost-awareness of advanced countries
5. Organisational deficiencies on a national and international level	role of lobbying for a share in international orders and contracts; change of corporatist structure	1. New exports in areas of specialization and new routes of order acquisition ("managed competition") 2. Emergence of more efficient regulations of the process and outcomes of globalization (Directive on M&A, Directive on Works Councils, competition rules and industrial policy competencies in the Treaty of Maastricht) 3. Due to smallness, chances for development of a microcorporatist structure is high in order to compensate loss of macro-corporatist functions.	1. Traditional principles of interest intermediation maybe too inflexible to meet the increasingly related industrial policy measures (e.g. wage bargaining, flexibility of working hours). Since organizations are difficult to transform this might result in failure to keep pace with requirements of firms and deter potential inward investors. 2. Potential orders are not acquired because of the lack of experience in international bidding.

crucially on its participation in the global production system. However, it is increasingly difficult for LCs to enter the crucial stages of the production system (for example, the innovation stage) where economic growth is mainly generated. In this respect, the extent of indigenous technological capability influences the gains from globalization, as shown above. Thus, building an infrastructure that promotes inward FDI and strategic alliances, particularly in the innovation and technology creation processes, is a necessary condition for LCs to catch up.

Which globalization tendencies are particularly relevant for LCs?

Generally, the development of an LC is linked to its globalization. Several globalization tendencies were identified that are particularly relevant for LCs:

* global network structures of MNCs which create the main innovations and technologies, yet are difficult to enter;
* competition among countries for inward FDI;
* the increasing mobility of firms, and the speed of relocations;
* the increasing necessity for governments to provide a competitive infrastructure to "log-on" to international networks and enable domestic firms to enter strategic alliances;
* increased regional integration in both real and monetary terms, particularly in newly developing areas like Eastern Europe and Asia;
* the danger of long-term dependence on technology provided by foreign MNCs;
* increased competitive pressures on existing industries which accelerate the process of restructuring;
* a positive link between openness – as manifested by exports and FDI – and economic development, as exhibited by innovation and growth.

Given certain fundamental conditions, this new form of participation by LCs in the global network may lead to enhanced technology acquisition and development. If the preconditions are not met, however, it may lead to a vicious cycle of low growth for LCs.

How does globalization affect the process of industrial policy formulation in LCs?

Globalization demands flexibility of both regulations and implementation. MNCs play a crucial role, as the bargaining process between them, labor, and the state is increasingly transferred to the level of industries and firms, thus creating specific rather than general policy measures and outcomes. Globalization also affects income distribution within and between countries. Centralized bargaining may be more likely to achieve consensus at the macrolevel, but at the same time it may negatively affect the international competitiveness of certain industries at the intermediate and microlevel. Thus, effective utilization of appropriate corporatist structures becomes essential to ensure broad acceptance of IP measures, especially with regard to technology policy. In particular, LCs will need to substitute microcorporatist structures for some existing macrocorporalist arrangements.

INDUSTRIAL POLICY

The fact that LCs face increasingly high barriers due to globalization does not imply that catching up becomes impossible; rather, it is more difficult to achieve. How this process may be enhanced by industrial policy, and where IP strategies may fail, is the subject of this final section. We first examine the various theoretical arguments for IP and then explore its specific application to LCs.

Theoretical arguments for industrial policy

The theoretical basis for IP can be grouped into two major schools: *orthodox* and *modern*. The main arguments of each, as well as the measures they propose, are briefly outlined here. The orthodox view is based on market failure which causes social returns to exceed private returns, thus requiring intervention. This argument is widely applied to education and technology. The goals of technology policy measures that are derived from it are to provide public goods such as basic research (carried out by public institutions such as universities), and to internalize external benefits that otherwise lead to underinvestment, for example, the infant-industry argument. Consequently, a market for technology is established in the form of a patent system on the national and international level, and basic R&D is subsidized or publicly provided.[7]

There are several modern theoretical approaches: regional and structural theories, modern growth theory, evolutionary theory, and strategic trade theory. They are rooted in different kinds of market imperfections, addressing both the distributional consequences for nations, and the effects on the allocation of production factors and the resulting externalities in the growth process. *Regional approaches* focus on spatial aspects of the international mobility of production factors; these include growth poles and export-base approaches. According to the former, innovations lead to regionally concentrated development and growth, which can be supported by IP measures fostering agglomeration and firm size ("picking the winners"). The export-base approach assumes that only export sectors contribute to an increase in regional net income (local production for domestic markets is considered to be a redistribution of income). Consequently, IP measures should subsidize export sectors.

The *structural adaptation approach* assigns two roles to IP: first, the internalization of positive externalities arising in the process of economic growth (see modern growth theory below); and second, the internalization or "social smoothing" of negative external effects arising in the growth process. These latter may take the form of international or other exogenous economic shocks that affect certain industries or regions, through relocation of production, breakdown of markets, and financial speculation. While the first role demands accelerative IP measures, the second requires decelerative IP measures.

The *evolutionary approach* uses knowledge (broadly defined as being incorporated in physical capital, human capital, and in innovations) as the endogenous variable that explains growth in modern growth theory. Contrary to the orthodox externalities argument, this approach maintains that the "return that firms capture even on the basic R&D they perform is enough to encourage them to conduct such research, alongside the development of their tacit capability in production" (Cantwell 1995: 69). The purpose of IP is to facilitate the creation of tacit capabilities in those firms that lack them by providing institutions for training and research. In other words, the evolutionary approach addresses *institutional* rather than *market* failure. Since innovation itself depends on R&D, the channeling of private resources into R&D by public institutions becomes crucial. IP has two functions in this context: first, it supports public R&D, acting as a catalyst rather than replacing missing private endeavors (Cantwell 1995); second, IP must direct public education and public knowledge creation to flexible multipurpose skills (e.g. computer sciences, communication, languages, social capabilities). In some ways, these skills are more easily provided through formal education and training systems than are "traditional manufacturing skills [which] primarily require . . . extensive 'learning by doing'" (Ernst and O'Connor 1989: 24).

The *strategic trade approach* is also based on modern growth theory, which assumes the existence of increasing scale economies, differentiated products, and high entry barriers. Dynamic economies of scale arise from learning processes over time and depend on quantity supplied. This implies that firm growth depends on being first in a new market, that is, the notion of first-mover advantages. Industrial policy measures are related to the economic rents that arise in these imperfect markets:

- *rent creation* by subsidizing domestic growth sectors directly or indirectly; and
- *rent shifting* by protecting firms' market shares domestically and internationally.

Principal policy instruments include: tariffs, export subsidies, limit-pricing strategies (entry-deterring prices that are subsidized by the government), risk-sharing financing, and promotion of FDI.

The effects of the policy measures advocated by the various approaches overlap, as every measure has spatial, structural, and institutional consequences. Globalization affects the theoretical arguments in two ways (Bellak 1997a): first, it involves the loss of national sovereignty, since some IPs are shifted to supranational entities (e.g. competition policy in the EU); second, the bargaining power of national governments is weakened. There are three reasons for this reduction in bargaining power:

- the relocation and restructuring potential of large MNCs;
- the shift of R&D from the public to the private sector (MNCs, global networks);
- the liberalization and re- or deregulation processes that accompany increasing international integration.

Having outlined the theoretical arguments for IP, we turn finally to its specific application to the case of LCs. We examine both feasible strategies and constraining conditions for pursuing IP on a national level. These measures are interrelated, and different combinations will be appropriate to the various LCs. We begin with two arguments against traditional IP, and then proceed to the new role for IP in a globalized environment.

Industrial policy for LCs

Latecomer growth depends mainly on the technological path that LCs follow. The nature of technology as consisting of two complementary elements, public and tacit, implies that IP measures need not essentially be directed towards the malfunctioning of markets as contended in the traditional theoretical view. An exception is the argument put forward by Landesmann and Vartianinen, who conclude that

> in countries which have to close a 'technological gap' . . . the necessary initial outlay on training and infrastructure is simply too large to be undertaken by the private sector. The same could still be true for economies which are small relative to the large businesses operating internationally in certain industries and with which domestic firms have to compete.
>
> (Landesmann and Vartianinen 1992: 220)

Of course, the economies they refer to fit our definition of LCs. For small European LCs this implies that the basic research and education system must be financed by the state, which should compensate for this market failure due to relative size differentials.

At the same time, neither leapfrogging (i.e. catching up through development of next-generation technologies) nor the establishment of infant industries are feasible strategies for LCs. Again, the cumulative path-dependent nature of most technologies prevents LCs from taking this route successfully. Technological standards are given for, not set by, LCs, and they must react to them by entering the global technology networks of MNCs. Facilitating this process is exactly the new role of IP, in its regional, structural, evolutionary, and strategic dimensions.

The regional dimension of IP lies in the global networks of MNCs which direct their activities to high-income agglomerations, and thus tend to reinforce national and regional patterns of specialization. MNCs get their affiliates "to specialize because they want to tap into the locally specific stream of innovation in each center" (Cantwell 1995: 70). It is thus difficult for LCs to attract such subsidiaries, and the danger of a widening gap exists. The low-growth–low-cost strategies of the past must be abandoned and substituted by growth policies.

> In doing so, nation states also thereby have the authority to bargain with MNCs to ensure that a "fair" share of the returns on investments is retained locally. A strong micro-corporatist structure will support this process. However, the scope for nation states to behave in this fashion is now diminished if the country wishes to participate in the international integration of activity being organized by MNCs elsewhere. Even if the strategy succeeds, it is likely to reduce local dynamism.
>
> (Cantwell 1997: 13)

On the microlevel, IP has to provide the tangible and intangible infrastructure to upgrade local firms' capabilities and innovativeness to enable them to absorb and use skills and knowledge efficiently (e.g. technology diffusion programs). Such measures are necessary but not sufficient conditions for LC firms to use new technologies and enter strategic alliances, enabling them to surpass the entry barriers and become part of the global networks. This process must be paralleled on the macro- and intermediate levels with the creation and development of national systems of innovation; these are networks of institutions between the private and public sectors that support the initiation, modification, and diffusion of new technologies.

The specific measures to achieve these goals are based on evolutionary theory as outlined below. Herein lies an important connection to corporatism: successful pursuit of these goals depends crucially on the backing of the necessary measures by the social partners. First, some of the institutions of a national innovation system will be financed and organized by employer and labor organizations, and as such will have competence and information advantages the government may depend on. A national system of innovation cannot exist outside or independently of a corporatist agreement between the social partners and the state; even more, it must become a functioning corporatism. Second, globalization and technology oriented IP will lead to substantial structural changes in precisely those LCs that are experiencing high social costs from adjustment. The redirection of IP away from mainly decelerating measures towards accelerative innovation policy affords a number of structural measures that may help to sustain this transition, both politically and economically.

Generally, the gains from growth industries will more than compensate for the losses in declining industries. Yet, this may not be the case in small countries, as we have shown, and a social corporatist structure may be advantageous. Moreover, the distributional consequences might be enormous, and IP may have to accommodate income distribution measures during the growth process. Incomes policy will also gain importance in growing economies, for two reasons. First, it remains the main policy instrument on the national level when exchange-rate adjustments are not possible. Second – and here is another link to corporatism – incomes policy will have to adjust to the new imperative of globalization, that being the shift in the bargaining process from the macro- or intermediate level to the firm level. A strong microcorporatist structure may prevent excessive wage claims by single firms' employees and ensure growth- and inflation-oriented wage increases (like a public good), to the benefit of the general welfare and stability.

Smaller European LCs do not have the capacity to follow a strategy that focuses exclusively on industrialization. As a result, IP measures to promote a shift towards services have been proposed frequently. The argument rests on the general observation that highly developed countries earn most of their GDP from services, and on the fact that manufacturing in LCs is constantly under pressure from other, low-cost locations. This argument has great appeal, in particular with respect to the issue of compensating for dying industries. It must, however, be treated carefully. Service economies may be based on services *per se* (e.g. tourism, wholesale trade, financial and social services) or they may be based on an increase in the service intensity of their economy. Concentrating on the former may turn out to be a low-wage–low-growth strategy, especially if the services consist of simple data-processing activities, where European LCs probably lost a promising niche to countries like India and other NICs a decade ago. The strategy of increasing service intensity is relevant for LCs, since it involves the technological upgrading of production, as the manufacturing base shifts towards more services. Moreover, such a strategy represents the restructuring of mature traditional industries, rather than artificially implementing new ones. The services we have in mind include: engineering, architectural services, construction management, database services, technical testing, and analysis services. Cantwell (1993: 208) maintains that "in Europe the Eastern European countries (along with Portugal and Greece) will prove relatively more attractive locations for the siting of affiliates responsible for simpler types of services, such as construction and transport and communication facilities." Simple services might, however, be quite footloose and short term because they can easily and quickly be relocated when local wages rise. On the other hand, producer services are more location-specific. This is a further strong argument to introduce IP measures that increase the service intensity of the manufacturing sector (also termed tertiarization of industry) rather than to promote the service sector itself.

In emphasizing the regional and structural dimensions of industrial policies in LCs, we have frequently touched upon issues of innovation and technology without being very precise. Previously, we theoretically identified an institutional market failure on the basis that innovation is the main source of growth. This failure can be overcome by IP: "By supporting education and training, governments help to lower the costs and facilitate the creation of tacit capability" (Cantwell 1995: 69). This increases the likelihood that local firms in LCs will profit from the knowledge and appropriate more fully the potential returns on their private research. The building of local institutions and their coordination becomes the main policy arena, rather than state-supported R&D. Another conclusion from the evolutionary approach is to facilitate local intercompany networks for cross-licensing and other schemes for the mutual enhancement of technological development. This measure will also lead to a regional spread of innovation networks towards LCs, if MNCs consider LCs an attractive location. One promising possibility in this respect is the building of "clusters [as a] form of national specialization, determined largely by created resources and the countries' historical experiences" (Bellak 1995: 96), with the institutional background provided mainly by the state. This creates economies of agglomeration and may attract complementary inward FDI. In addition, the globalization of technological innovation in LCs "tends to reinforce patterns of development or systems of innovation that are peculiar to their country" (Cantwell 1995: 70). Combining both arguments, we conclude that the long-term objective of LC industrial policy should be to support national clusters of firms institutionally, since these networks are in turn strengthened by the globalization process.

Strategic trade policy acts mainly to protect local industries. Although European LCs will profit from such policies, at least in the short term, they will be able to influence these policies only marginally to their advantages. The other side of the coin is the barriers such policies create in interbloc competition, which might limit the growth of certain LC industries in EU markets (the global welfare loss from protectionism not being taken into account).

In summary, the efficiency of IP and room for national discretion are limited by the globalization process on both the micro- and macrolevel. But a case can be made for a new type of national IP that focuses on institution-building. The ongoing process of integration, globalization, and internationalization must not be used as an excuse by LC governments for not having a national IP strategy; rather it must lead to an immediate and substantial revision of current IP strategies. In particular, the new paradigms require a multiple-path strategy, replacing the stepwise strategy from inward- to outward-looking policies that might have succeeded in the past. According to the classifications used in Table 2.5, European LCs are somewhere between the second and third stage of national development. The fact that they are part of the Single Market implies that there are no barriers for inward FDI and strategic alliances. LCs should try to attract the type of inward investment that best fits their industrial structure. Inward FDI and strategic alliances in technology will tend to enhance technological accumulation in LCs if it leads to increased competition or spillover effects that can be absorbed, and if it leads to a restructuring of existing industries. How best to attract this complementary investment is, however, a difficult task. IP also has a vital marketing role, by supplying material and intangible infrastructure that disseminates information about the LCs as industrial locations. On the other hand, policies such as direct subsidies are becoming increasingly less feasible due to the increased emphasis on competition policy in the EU.

CONCLUSION

Globalization may be a factor in overcoming latecomer status and a mechanism to closing the gap between LCs and small advanced countries (SACs). But a minimum level of development, in terms of the globalization and integration of the LCs and their firms, seems to be a necessary though not sufficient condition for catching up via exporting, FDI, strategic alliances, and technological accumulation. The higher the level of globalization, the greater the opportunity to pursue a multiple-strategy approach to national IPs, utilizing different inward- and outward-oriented IP strategies at the same time. This in turn increases the chances for success, since it is unlikely that a single IP strategy can cope with the multidimensional determinants of growth.

Yet, as we demonstrated throughout the chapter, and as clearly illustrated in Table 2.7, this positive view must be qualified by several arguments that support the notion of globalization as a constraint. Thus, the ability of LCs to benefit from globalization will, to an extent, depend on how well they adjust to the given international economic environment, meeting the preconditions of externally given forces of globalization. The prospect of LCs enduring in their latecomer status, prevented from catching up by global competition, is the less likely, but not impossible scenario, especially if the process is supported by accelerating IP measures. LCs cannot avoid integrating the role of MNCs into their development strategies, even if this option may have been available to others in the past. However, there are still different forms of MNC involvement in local development, depending in part on the path taken. Eastern European countries are clearly in a second-tier position to LCs, rather than direct competitors. And small developing countries whose latecomer status is even more extreme, are much more likely to be locked-in to the existing international division of labor as a result of globalization, at least for the foreseeable future.

NOTES

1 This question is also addressed by Lundvall (1994).
2 This leads to a bias, especially when FDI is compared to other economic indicators at constant or current values as well as when countries' FDI positions are compared.
3 The rate of real growth of intraregional exports between 1986 and 1991 was 4 percent for Western Europe, 9.7 percent in Asia, and negative 6.1 percent in North America.
4 Two issues are also increasingly discussed at the macrolevel. The first is the changing relationship between income distribution and growth (Chang 1994). The closer the social partners are involved in government policies, the more efficiently the problem of income distribution will be solved. The second issue relates to the

appropriate stabilization policy. The higher the degree of integration, the more important incomes policy will be as a stabilizer, replacing exchange-rate policy (in the single currency scenario) as a price–cost adjustment in global competition.
5 See van Liemt, 1992 for an assessment of the social consequences of company relocation.
6 Landesmann and Vartianinen (1992) present theoretical arguments on the relationship between corporatism and accumulation.
7 Cross-border market failure, outlined by Dunning (1994b), is mainly a case for inter- and supranational IP, and hence not treated here in greater detail.

REFERENCES

Barreto, J. (1992) "Portugal: industrial relations under democracy," in A. Ferner and R. Hyman (eds) *Industrial Relations in the New Europe*, Oxford: Basil Blackwell.
Bellak, C. (1994a) "Small nations reconsidered," Paper presented at the SMOPEC Workshop, Vienna, Mimeographed.
—— (1994b) "Outsiders' response to EC'92 – evidence from Austria," *Multinational Business Review* fall: 40–43.
—— (1995) "Multinational enterprises and industrial policy," in B. Unger and F. V. Waarden (eds) *Convergence or Divergence*, Aldershot: Avebury: 80–107.
—— (1997) "Reeling in the transnationals," *New Economy* 1: 17–21.
—— (1998) "The measurement of foreign direct investment: a critical review," Vienna, forthcoming in *The International Trade Journal*.
Bellak, C. and Cantwell, J. A. (1996) "FDI – How much is it worth?," *Transnational Corporations* 5, 5: 85–97.
Borensztein, E., DeGregorio, J., and Lee, J. (1995) "How does foreign direct investment affect economic growth?," NBER Working Papers, No. 5057, Cambridge, MA.
Cantwell, J. A. (1989) *Technological Innovation and Multinational Corporations*, Oxford: Basil Blackwell.
—— (1992a) "The methodological problems raised by the collection of foreign direct investment data," *Scandinavian International Business Review* 1, 1: 86–102.
—— (1992b) "Innovation and technological competitiveness," in P. J. Buckley and M. Casson (eds) *Multinational Enterprises in the World Economy*, Aldershot: Edward Elgar.
—— (1993) "The contribution of recent foreign direct investment in services to a changing international division of labour," *Development and International Cooperation* 9, 17: 193–222.
—— (1994a) "The relationship between international trade and international production," in D. Greenaway and L. Alan Winters (eds) *Surveys in International Trade*, Oxford: Basil Blackwell.
—— (1994b) "Introduction," in J. A. Cantwell (ed.) *Transnational Corporations and Innovatory Activities*, London: Routledge.
—— (1995) "Innovation in a global world," *New Economy* 2, 2: 66–70.
—— (1997) "Globalization and development in Africa," in J. H. Dunning and K. A. Hamdani (eds) *The New Globalism and Developing Countries*, Tokyo *et al.*, UN University Press, pp. 155–179.
Cantwell, J. A. and Bellak, C. (1994) "Measuring the importance of international production: the re-estimation of foreign direct investment at current values," University of Reading Discussion Papers in International Investment and Business Studies, No. 192, Reading.
Cantwell, J. A. and Bellak, C. (forthcoming), "How important is foreign direct investment?," *Oxford Bulletin of Economics and Statistics*.

Cantwell, J. A. and Dunning, J. H. (1991) "Multinationals, technology and the competitiveness of European industries," *Aussenwirtschaft*, 46, 1: 45–65.

Chang, R. (1994) "Income inequality and economic growth: evidence and recent theories," *Federal Reserve Bank of Atlanta Economic Review* 79, 4: 1–10.

Commission of the European Communities (1994) *EC Panorama*, Brussels.

Doherty, O. and McDevitt, J. (1991) "Globalisation and the small less advanced member states," Synthesis report, Vol. 19, Irish Science and Technology Agency, National S&T Policy Unit, Dublin.

Dosi, G., Freeman, C., and Fabiani, S. (1994) "The process of economic development: introducing some stylized facts and theories on technologies, firms and institutions," *Industrial and Corporate Change* 3, 1: 1–45.

Dunning, J. H. (1994a) "Globalization: the challenge for national economic regimes," University of Reading Discussion Papers in International Investment and Business Studies, No. 186, Reading.

—— (1994b) "Globalization, economic restructuring and development," University of Reading Discussion Papers in International Investment and Business Studies, No. 187, Reading.

—— (1994c) "Revaluating the benefits of foreign direct investment," University of Reading Discussion Papers in International Investment and Business Studies, No. 188, Reading.

Ernst, D. and O'Connor, D. (1989) "Technology and global competition: the challenge for newly industrializing economies," *Development Centre Studies*, Paris: OECD.

Felix, D. (1994) "Industrial development in east Asia: what are the lessons for Latin America?," UNCTAD Discussion Paper, No. 84, Geneva.

Grant, W. (1992) "Economic globalisation, stateless firms and international governance," Working paper, No. 105, Department of Politics and International Studies, University of Warwick.

Guger, A. and Polt, W. (1994) "Corporatism and incomes policy in Austria – experiences and perspectives," in R. Dore, R. Boyer, and Z. Mars (eds) *The Return to Incomes Policy*, London: Pinter.

Hagedoorn, J. and Narula, R. (1994) "Choosing models of governance for strategic technology partnering: international and sectoral differences," EIBA proceedings, Warsaw, 105–129.

Henley, A. and Tsakalotos, E. (1993) *Corporatism and Economic Performance*, Aldershot: Edward Elgar.

Hollingsworth, J. R., Schmitter, Ph. C., and Streeck, W. (1994) *Governing Capitalist Economies: Performance and Control of Sectors*, New York: Oxford University Press.

Hosono, A. (1995) "The 'East Asian miracle' and Latin America," *EXIM Review* 14, 2: 117–145.

Kritsantonis, N. D. (1992) Greece: "From state authoritarianism to modernization," in A. Ferner, and R. Hyman (eds) *Industrial Relations in the New Europe*, Oxford: Basil Blackwell.

Krugman, P. (1993) *Geography and Trade*, 4th ed. Cambridge, MA: MIT Press.

Kyrkilis, D. and Pantelidis, P. (1992) "Effects of foreign direct investment on trade flows: the case of Greece," *Rivista Internazionale Di Scienze Economiche Commerciali* 39, 4: 365–373.

Landesmann, M. (1992) "Industrial policies and social corporatism," in J. Pekkarinen, M. Pohjolaa, and B. Rowthorn (eds) *Social Corporatism: A Superior Economic System?*, Oxford: Clarendon Press.

Landesmann, M. and Vartianinen, J. (1992) "Social corporatism and industrial policy," in J. Pekkarinen, M. Pohjolaa, and B. Rowthorn (eds) *Social Corporatism: A Superior Economic System?*, Oxford: Clarendon Press.

Lundvall, B. A. (1994) "Innovation policy and the learning economy." Paper presented at the International Seminar on Policies for Technological Development, organized by CIDE, Mexico.

OECD (1991) *Globalization, Corporate Citizenship and Industrial Policy*, DSTI.IIND 91, 38, Paris.

Ozawa, T. (1992) "Foreign direct investment and development," *Transnational Corporations* 1, 1: 27–54.

Parry, T. G. (1990) "The role of foreign capital in east Asian industrialization, growth and development," in H. Hughes (ed.) *Achieving Industrialization in East Asia*, Cambridge: Cambridge University Press.

Pearce, R. (1989) *The Internationalisation of Research and Development by Multinational Enterprises*, New York: St Martin's Press.

Sachwald, F. (1995) "Cooperative agreements and the theory of the firm: focussing on barriers to change," EMOT workshop paper, University of Reading, Reading.

Stopford, J. M. and Strange, S., with Henley, J. S. (1991) *Rival States, Rival Firms: Competition for World Market Shares*, Cambridge: Cambridge University Press.

Streeck, W. and Schmitter, Ph. C. (1991) "From national corporatism to transnational pluralism: organized interests in the single European market," *Politics & Society* 19, 2: 133–164.

Thomsen, S. and Nicolaides, P. (1990) "Foreign direct investment: 1992 and global markets," RIIA discussion papers 28, London.

UN (1992) *World Investment Report 1992: Transnational Corporations as Engines of Growth*, New York: United Nations.

UNCTAD-DTCI (1992) *World Investment Directory*, Volumes I–IV, New York and Geneva: United Nations.

—— (1994) *World Investment Report 1994: Transnational Corporations, Employment and the Workplace*, New York and Geneva: United Nations.

—— (1996a) *World Investment Report 1996:* Geneva: United Nations.

—— (1996b) *New Technologies and Technological Capability-building at the Enterprise Level: Some Policy Implications*, New York and Geneva: United Nations.

van Liemt, G. (1992) (ed.) *Industry On the Move: Causes and Consequences of International Relocation in the Manufacturing Industry*, Geneva: ILO.

Veltz, P. (1991) "New models of production organisation and trends in spatial development," in G. Benko and M. Dunford (eds) *Industrial Change and Regional Development: The Transformation of New Industrial Spaces*, London and New York: Belhaven Press.

Williamson, P. J. (1989) *Corporatism in Perspective*, London: Sage.

World Bank (1993) *The East Asian Miracle – Economic Growth and Public Policy*, Oxford: Oxford University Press.

3 Principles of an operational industrial policy for latecomers

Failures of analogy, strategies, and degrees of freedom

Lena J. Tsipouri and Sandro Gaudenzi

INTRODUCTION

This chapter traces the implications for new industrial policies of the theoretical approach toward latecomers economies[1] (LCs), found in the two previous contributions in this volume:

- Storper's theoretical argumentation suggesting that the only alternative for LCs is to adopt learning approaches since they can no longer compete via low wages, and
- the argument of Bellak and Cantwell that globalization does open windows of opportunities, even if under very competitive terms.

We suggest that this new body of theory has significant implications for industrial policy instruments in latecoming countries. In previous analyses and policy-making, local characteristics mattered less and analogies from advanced countries could easily be drawn. But if our analysis is correct, traditional support mechanisms prove insufficient because they can affect long-term growth only if they are complemented by the necessary accompanying measures that enable them to penetrate the behavior of relevant agents. We argue that the industrial culture, which is determinant for the economic system, is not an exogenous variable and may be influenced in the medium term by specifically designed tools. Our objective is thus precisely to identify these tools, some of them being of general validity, others requiring case by case tailoring.[2]

In this chapter we reject the idea of any linearity in either economic development or the process of technological change. Empirically, the rule in the past was that industrial policy in LCs was shaped by an imitation of successful actions in advanced countries, to the extent that this was permitted by available resources. In line with neoclassical orthodoxy, only financial constraints prevented latecomers from an allocation of resources that was as efficient as that of core economies. Thus, industrial policy for less favored regions and developing countries has been traditionally built upon state support for infrastructure, subsidies for productive investment, and only later, following the seminal works of Theodore Schultz (1981) and Nelson and

Winter (1982), on human resources and technology development respectively. The common target of all these instruments was directly or indirectly to improve the return on investment so that individual projects would become more profitable and materialize[3]

Methodologically, we argue that reproducing measures proven elsewhere may be not only insufficient, but wrong, because the technocratic approach does not take into account differences in the environment. Borrowing elements from recent theories on path dependence, institutional change (North 1990), and the specificities of national or regional innovation systems (Nelson 1993), one can contest the mechanistic approach which offers prescriptions without regard to the environment in which they are being applied. Empirically also, the literature on convergence and divergence demonstrates that even when financial support is available, catch-up does not automatically occur (Fagerberg *et al.* 1994).

In most cases, this system of supporting investment in infrastructure and production proved insufficient even though it is capable of increasing the number of start-ups and expanding productive investment. This is because capital incentives by themselves at best produce fragmented successful investments which generate employment and wealth to the extent to which they are subsidized, but they are incapable of triggering sustainable growth. Externalities, which help the growth process in advanced economies, are the result of interaction, which is itself based on behavior, social conventions, and deeper cultural links which are different in latecomers than in core countries. From different sides emerges the idea that there is a need to build "a conventions trajectory" next to the hard one (Storper 1993), which is the equivalent of what Doringer and Streeten (1990) consider the need to build upon intangible sources of growth.

The cornerstone of our approach is the importance of going beyond formal rules to include the soft elements of development, notably informal rules with emphasis on conventions and path dependence. We attempt to identify how and to what extent trajectories can be modified and accelerated by policy intervention. Following North's definitions (1990: 39–41, 93, 104), institutions are made up of formal rules (constitutions, statute, regulations), informal constraints (conventions, norms of behavior, and self-imposed codes of conduct), and their enforcement characteristics. Informal constraints thus arise to coordinate repeated human interactions and to extend, elaborate, and modify formal rules, socially sanctioned norms of behavior, and internally enforced standards of conduct. Conventions are an important subset of informal constraints; they represent "rules that have never been consciously designed and that are in everyone's interest to keep."[4] Path dependence explains why history matters, based on a transactions costs approach; history would not matter if transaction costs were zero, but in the real world the process by which we arrive at today's institutions is relevant and constrains future choices. Our conceptual framework is completed by the term "social capability," used here to reflect a country's ability to utilize a technological gap and to catch up in relation to technology leaders (Abramovitz 1994). Consequently, a central issue of this chapter becomes the improvement of the social capabilities of latecomers.

Our point of departure is that latecomers share certain inherent characteristics that differentiate them from both developed and developing countries. These include: development of basic infrastructure, although it is usually neither fully utilized nor very effectively managed; a manufacturing base that is competitive under certain conditions;[5] the rudiments of a national research system; and generalized education. But at the same time, LCs' social capabilities are not fully developed because the organizational and institutional factors that have to accompany the technological system do not correspond to their educational and technological achievements. Explanations include conventions reflecting risk aversion, lack of trust in both local producers and the public sector, and limited access to relevant information sources. Using the previous terminology of the technical change literature, the problems seem to lie in the diffusion process, inhibited by social rather than economic elements.

When this first stage of introducing social capabilities is attained, industrial policy can become more ambitious, go beyond individual profitability, and use tools that target a rapid change in industrial culture. Such tools exist and the challenges for a new industrial policy is to identify them; in this way latecomers could find an optimal strategy, determined both by the globalization process and by their own path dependence. Latecomers did not restructure in time to reap the benefits of liberalization, not least because they were unable or unwilling to bear the cost.[6] They are now confronted with a situation where they cannot influence economic power, the role of the multinational enterprises, productive systems, and strategic alliances.[7] Even though windows of opportunity continue to open to all latecomers equally, and the globalization process would require a uniform pattern of reaction in each country, additional limitations or opportunities are imposed by each country's own path dependence which determines how and to what extent local agents react (or do not react) to any technocratic set of measures. Different propensities to collaborate locally, to develop trust (among firms or between individual enterprises and the state), and to accept formal rules (tax evasion is mentioned as only one example) figure in what specific policies need to consider, while formulating a new range of instruments that may be effective in one latecomer and not at all in another.

Our effort here is to identify common needs and to introduce further analysis needed to adapt these principles to each country. Thus, we first discuss the limits and inadequacies of the established tools of intervention by stressing the new embeddedness of industrial policy. Then we turn to the boundaries imposed by the common characteristics of latecomers; this means that some (but not all) elements of strategy are shared by all countries considered. Finally, we try to suggest areas and issues where each country needs to design its own intervention, leaving much room for maneuver within common overall directions. This is dictated by path dependency and the resulting need to transfer best practices in a way that respects the background of each country. The common denominator is that while up until now industrial funds were used in a reactive rather than strategic manner, in the future a clear strategy composed of both general and country-specific principles is needed.

THE LIMITS OF THE ESTABLISHED TOOLS OF INDUSTRIAL INTERVENTION: FAILURES OF ANALOGY

Efficiency in orthodox theory is based upon free market equilibria, with intervention justified only to correct market failures. Removal of barriers to entry and exit and restrictions against collusive practices were among the first policy measures suggested by economists and are now well established. Further in-depth examination of market failures later led to more active policies, which either offered generalized support for a variety of new investments in the form of grants, subsidized loans, or tax allowances, or which applied selective, specific, and targeted interventions. We call this packet of measures the established tools of industrial intervention.

The selective approaches usually related to:

- *size*: supporting small and medium-sized enterprises, thus helping them to compete with their larger rivals on more equal terms;
- *sector*: supporting entrants in new technological fields to encourage them to face high preparadigmatic uncertainty, or assisting firms in declining sectors to facilitate restructuring efforts;[8]
- *dynamics*: supporting winners who are expected to contribute to social welfare through increased employment or exports, or losers who might harm the overall level of demand through collective dismissals; or finally
- *ownership*: supporting either foreign direct investment (FDI) which attracts new capital, skills, and organizational techniques, or local investment which is free of mobility risks.

But whether generalized or selective, the element common to all established tools is that they are directed toward the profitability of individual projects, expecting spillovers to be generated automatically. It is precisely this *failure of analogy* between countries at different stages of development that we wish to question.

Generalized support for investment is a typical instrument used very widely in advanced, latecoming, and developing countries. Generalized support initially addressed the acquisition of machinery and was later extended, particularly in advanced and latecoming countries, to research skills creation. Improved industrial competitiveness was expected to follow enhanced support (both direct and indirect) of R&D, as well as increased emphasis on intrafirm training and continuous education. A nondiscriminatory subsidy policy is particularly appropriate when a country has underutilized resources. In the best of all possible cases, such policies can influence entrepreneurial decision-making by diminishing amortization periods and increasing returns on investment; but given the lock-in situations and path dependencies inherent in LCs, spillovers are unlikely to occur. Horizontal nonselective measures can be unevenly distributed because business functions are distributed unevenly across firms of different sizes and industries, and because successful firms self-select for participation in programs (OECD 1993). In some cases, generalized support measures were taken up selectively by specific sectors, driving those countries to international specialization; but these cases are the exception rather than the rule, and other conditions related to diffusion practices were equally fulfilled. It would be of interest to identify the conditions that led those few cases to differentiate themselves from the norm.

Selective approaches follow more sophisticated thinking, yet their logic is not basically different. In mainstream economics, support for small and medium-size companies originates from the need to eliminate market failures which give an advantage to larger firms able to distort competition through their economic power. Consequently, most industrial innovation and even training policies in developed countries are small-firm oriented. In such cases, the state agrees to share the risk, in particular with regard to support for innovation, employment, and training. Countries succeed thus in maintaining a basis of small dynamic firms, adapting to new market developments faster than their larger competitors who are locked into the need to amortize massive investments. A particular case of such support that led to collective efficiency is the Third Italy case, where local conventions allowed for a positive reaction to regional initiatives and intense interaction among supported and nonsupported firms. Similarly, clusters are observed in developed countries (Porter 1991) where long-term interaction between big and small companies created unique situations of specialization. Even developing countries benefit from this increased small-firm support, although the driving force in LCs is related to initial low cost or protection rather than learning. (This reflects our interpretation of Rabelotti 1995 and Humphrey 1995.)

Conditions in latecoming economies are totally different. Small and medium-size companies are concentrated in traditional sectors and do not benefit from innovative margins as do dynamic, new technology-based firms in core regions. Small firms in latecomers are in the majority too small (below 50 employees) to benefit substantially from economies of scale, and their survival originates from legal or natural protectionism rather than from flexibility.[9] At the same time, small firms lose the low-cost advantage that would allow linkages to be created around increased international demand resulting from low prices. Failure of analogy is caused by the different nature of such firms, so that some of the support for small companies in less favored countries (LFCs) is equivalent to the support for losers in more dynamic economies.

The Japanese success, followed by Korea and Taiwan, has triggered a fashion for *sectoral intervention*, whereby the state supports specific industries.

Much of the literature in the 1970s saw sectoral support as an instrument for creating synergies and positive externalities; in particular, many latecoming and developing countries saw new technology sectors as an opportunity to leapfrog.[10] But sectoral policies, fashionable in the late 1970s and early 1980s, were based on assumptions about induced linkages that did not materialize in the case of imitators.

Empirical evidence from LFCs led to a demystification of the issue there. And while promoting strategic sectors is possible, particularly with the criterion of substantial rent, the new trade theories suggest that even in the most advanced countries strategic sectors cannot be identified with any confidence (Krugman 1986). Porter helped to broaden the debate by describing the dynamics of clusters rather than sectors, but there is not yet any widely accepted methodology for identifying selection criteria. Here, there is limited transferability because of time constraints, since it takes generations for clusters to form, while intervention tools are at best medium-term oriented.

Differentiation according to the dynamics of firms may reflect either political priorities or social considerations. In some cases, restructuring can help to regain international competitiveness through capacity reduction, automation, and a shift of emphasis from price to quality competition. This applies to countries where skills and interaction (see social capabilities) prevail and create this dynamism, as evidenced by the textile sector in Europe, and in Italy in particular. But more often, supporting losers becomes a "red cross"-type of policy, imposed as the result of social considerations rather than for reasons of industrial competitiveness, and consequently aggravating the vicious circles in the endangered sectors. Such a policy does not, because it cannot, aim at reintegrating companies in an internationally competitive environment. In latecomers, where constantly eroding labor cost advantages fail to be replaced by quality standards, the salvation operation takes on a social protection dimension only. This is not to argue for a policy that facilitates exit, but rather that where "losers policies" are required, they should be part of a social budget (as an alternative to unemployment allowances) and not an industrial one.

Supporting winners, on the other hand, is justified by the assumption that they constitute successful enterprises that do not possess the necessary means to grow as rapidly as their organization and market situation would permit. The main form of this intervention, most notably during the 1960s, was identifying and assisting firms with potential to compete in international markets, thus focusing on large, national champions. In these cases, company size is promoted by encouraging mergers, other permissive policies, and through the provision of funds at privileged terms. There is now widespread recognition that these policies have been a failure, among other reasons because of the very nature of the problem of picking winners and the near exclusive focus on size (Pitelis 1994). Recently, more modest "picking winners" policies have emerged; against generalized support for start-ups, it has been proposed to look for winners in businesses between three and five years old and with at least 20 employees (Storey 1994).[11] Such a policy has been broadly adopted in EU LCs in an effort to manage structural funds better. "Business plan" approaches by investment project are applied and are expected to be more promising than the generalized approaches. But in that sense they constitute control mechanisms rather than selection of winners with wider spillover expectations, and are at the edge of being generalized rather than selective in nature. Winners grow, but because of their origin and nature they are unlikely to influence macroeconomic evolution. The absence of transferability is explained merely by size.

Support for FDI follows the same rationale as generalized national support. Macroeconomic arguments, rather than industrial structure considerations, are marshaled in support of inward investment: employment creation, balance of payment effects, and tax opportunities. More often than not, latecomers see their multinational investment concentrated in routine production that does not affect prevailing international specialization patterns. This situation is different from recent tendencies to apply criteria for assuring the "richness" of foreign investments in developmental terms, as analyzed by Ash Amin in Chapter 7 of this book.

We conclude this section by suggesting that all types of established tools can be applied to LCs, but given their industrial structure, standard tools are insufficient to produce more than isolated successes. Supporting small and medium-size companies is likely to result in their survival but not in their international competitiveness, as long as they lack the characteristic common background suggested to be the source of successful flexible specialization (Schmitz 1995); supporting FDI will benefit macroeconomic rather than structural aggregates; and policies targeted at picking winners, even moderate versions, will act as a control mechanism for efficient allocation of aid but will not guarantee social benefits. This type of aid is capable of sustaining individual profitability in those European LCs that have the financial resources to apply such measures, selectively benefiting many firms that are then able to distinguish themselves, or at least survive. These three types of support constitute the core of the hard measures to support industrial competitiveness, but they do not insure linkages, spillovers, and diffusion.

DEADLOCKS IN THE NATIONAL INNOVATION SYSTEMS OF LATECOMERS

The concept of the "vicious circle" is prominent in the economic development literature as a source of persistent underdevelopment. We argue that if we systematically pursue the origins of the failures of analogy suggested under the various measures in the preceding section, we can identify "deadlocks" shared by all latecoming economies.

The limitations of the established tools of industrial policy were first realized in advanced countries where social capabilities permit a faster transition and more easily lead to collective efficiency. New approaches emerged from the recent body of literature on evolutionary economics, innovation system theory, and industrial organization. In the 1990s, successful industrial policies are characterized by increased flexibility and innovative responses, adaptation to new organizational patterns such as lean production, and reorganization and improvement of training. Some countries are moving towards adopting a more strategic policy approach, attempting to assist firms to improve their business performance by focusing on market failures (upgrading skills, diffusing new techniques, supplying information), while trying to ameliorate the overall framework conditions for business competitiveness (technology, training, quality, finance, business regulation, and corporate law) (OECD 1993: 14). Such measures lead to agglomeration economies and accelerate the accommodation of technological change.

Large countries promote their relative strengths in leading-edge clusters, while in the Nordic countries public policy takes special responsibility for education, training, and the generation of technological and organizational competencies. In addition, since the many small and medium-size companies have very limited capacity for strategic planning, and experience great difficulties in keeping abreast of the rapid development of technology and management principles, new forms of public coordination had to be considered, such as dialogue-oriented policy models (Gjerding *et al.* 1992) and encouraging keener competition.

In spite of the fact that these elements of industrial policy were rapidly transferred to latecomers, the difficulties of transferability remain. Even when these new principles are followed, in practice the support offered in LCs does not diffuse at the same pace, and, as a consequence, additional intervention is needed in order to enhance spillovers that are otherwise generated automatically in countries where interactive learning is rooted. This is because the entities in which path-dependent technological learning is embedded are subject to substantial behavioral inertia. In essence, the path dependency of organizational and behavioral change may well reinforce each other. At an aggregate level, country-wide institutions, jointly with typical organizational patterns and interactive norms, become forms of externalities that shape and reproduce specific behavioral patterns (Dosi 1992).

We need to examine more thoroughly why diffusion is not as rapid in latecomers. Some enterprises are successful when measured by international standards while not assuming the role of growth engine for local suppliers or clients. Still others react to the incentives to increase their research and technological performance while failing to become leading edge. But the majority of companies do not even participate in the incentives programs available, although they persistently complain about the lack of financial resources. These remarks lead us to identify three types of deadlocks common to all latecomers that act as barriers to the successful implementation of modern industrial policy interventions: anti-agglomeration, failure to engage in ongoing learning, and ineffective technology transfer. Although encountered to different degrees, in our view they constitute important determinants of strategic possibilities, which we will elaborate in more detail.

Uncertainty and anti-agglomeration

The most important deadlock is the one inhibiting spillover of success and the exploitation of externalities. LFCs suffer from an inherent *anti-agglomeration effect* which can be explained as the effort of national champions to reduce uncertainty by seeking rents outside their own environment. Companies, especially at initial stages of success, renounce local linkages that would lead to agglomeration economies. Their main concern is to reduce uncertainties arising from local conventions. Thus, they react to local market propensities for poor quality control, limited service provision, lack of respect for timely deliveries, and other similar features by purchasing equipment and raw materials in more advanced markets, often at higher costs than for locally available supplies. They also target export markets as offering better prices and growth opportunities.[12] In other words, successful companies in LFCs tend to collaborate with local firms less than their counterparts in industrially mature regions because the LC winners find themselves operating differently and using different conventions than other agents in their environment. Consequently, they are willing to pay a premium in order to assure a better working environment.[13] This is the price they pay for being ahead. They very rapidly integrate into global networks,[14] but by that very process, and as a consequence of the growing distance between them and their local environment, they produce an anti-agglomeration effect.

At the same time, local firms tend not to approach these technological leaders. From the point of view of small and medium-size companies, there are major risks in cooperating with other local companies, whatever their size. Partly because they operate in sectors with low appropriability potential, partly because the enforcement of competition rules is insufficient, and partly because they lack the necessary reserves to act strategically, these enterprises fear that by cooperating they may be treated unfairly by their partners, lose potential benefits or even their autonomy. Uncertainty for them takes a different form and meaning and relates to survival.

Thus, although justified by microeconomic considerations, the situation impedes the growth of a linkage-based local development process. The inevitable result is industrial dualism instead of flexible specialization. This model explains why entrepreneurial rents are possible (as they have been empirically identified) in LFCs, in particular when some kind of legal, natural, or technological monopolistic power gives them an initial impetus: they are the result of firms grasping this initial quasi-protection and creating a successful trajectory of their own. But this capabilities gap leads to reduced spillover benefits, at least to the extent that it fails to trigger the creation of clusters or flexibly specialized supply chains around leading firms.

Even where these national champions continue to grow and increase their rents so that uncertainty is reduced and cost considerations drive them back to their local environment, it can be argued that they will try to organize vertically rather than create supply chains. New threats in the global market, increased uncertainties, and rent reductions, like those that have triggered disintegrating effects in developed countries, might temporarily increase linkages with local productive forces as an alternative to an overall reduction of their scope of activities. To put it bluntly: the only thing that industrial policy based on the imitation of best practices in core countries can do is to help improve the organization of a limited number of firms – those that have a chance to participate in world trade – but imposed linkages will be difficult.

Alternatively, one can argue that what matters finally is organization. In a sense this thesis proposes that organization is another factor to be considered alongside patterns of innovation and diffusion as explanatory variables for economic divergence (Dosi 1992). Organization is defined here in its broadest sense, regarding all forms of organization of economic activities: the internal organization of firms (managerial models), relation among them (virtual or extended enterprises, flexible production or sales decisions), and relations to their environments (labor markets, financial institutions, government regulations). There is thus a strong correlation between the degree of modernization of national markets (which also determines transaction costs) and the average organizational efficiency of the indigenous agents. What is called imperfect competition in international trade results in differences of efficiency that are not independent of the origin of the agents. The most efficient agents enjoy rents resulting from their better organization which allows them to influence prices and the behavior of other agents, despite formal competition rules. Industrial and trade policies in advanced countries recognize this potential and try to reinforce the situation of rent, to the benefit of their agents, in order to increase national welfare and despite the GATT/ITO regulations.

Reversing this argument, one can assume that agents in latecomers are less efficient (and those who are efficient are not locally rooted), creating a *negative rent situation* (whose origins are organizational) both for them and for their environment in international markets. Globalization is imposed on top of this negative rent situation. Large, advanced countries set the rules regarding the pace of competition, while small and rich countries with competitive industrial structures are in a position to react through increased specialization, with all the benefits and dangers related to it (Perez and Soete, 1988). But latecomers are really worse off; they have neither locally rooted champions, nor the tradition of organizational networking by small and medium-size companies. Their growth based on peripheral Fordism is challenged not only by cheaper labor in emerging developing countries, but, more importantly, by the new models of industrial organization in advanced countries. They require a new approach that takes this evolution and their own organizational deficiencies (as opposed to capital or skill shortages) into consideration.

Finally, the nature of global change must be considered. As the information society integrates economic activities globally, particularly with regard to the organization of industrial applications rather than technical achievements, and as a cyber-culture emerges slowly but steadily, even in small and medium-size enterprises, location advantages are likely to diminish gradually while interregional complementarities will become easier to achieve. Even small and less successful companies will find it easy to network globally, this time not in order to pay a premium for reducing uncertainty, but rather to access complementary knowledge and skills with low transaction costs. When this occurs, the argument for localization of benefits will gradually lose its validity.

Current incentives lead to occasional but not persistent and interactive learning

The second deadlock we address is the inability of many medium-size companies to become internationally competitive in niche markets or to capture the national market. The research capability that LCs possess is concentrated in research institutions rather than enterprises. Only recently, and timidly, have efforts to support downstream activities of diffusion and technology transfer been adopted.

In core countries, public policies directed at stimulating industrial technological change have shifted over time from the largely uncoordinated "science policies" and "industrial policies" of the 1960s, to the more integrated "innovation policies" of the 1970s, and then to the collaborative precompetitive research-based "technology policies" of the 1980s. These changes were accompanied by increasing collaboration between government departments involved in the formulation and implementation of science and technology policies. In Europe, they have led to increased emphasis on the stimulation of innovation for small and medium-size companies, a growing focus on stimulating the creation and growth of new technology-based firms, and the introduction of national technology policies involving major programs of collaborative precompetitive research in information technology (Rothwell and Dodgson 1992). These policies have been widely imitated by latecomers who have gradually adopted the OECD guidelines for:

* increased participation of the industry itself in R&D spending,
* reduction of core funding and increase in cofunded research at public laboratories, and
* introduction of peer review and strategic sectoral programs.[15]

Following the model of advanced countries, and recognizing the role that adaptation to technological change plays in industrial competitiveness, many latecomers, led by the small, less favored regions of the European Union, have substantially increased resources devoted to R&D. However, evaluation of these measures does not confirm their contribution to industrial regeneration. Research results, even when leading to industrial innovations, indicate that they may be technically successful but their performance in the market remains modest (CEC 1991; Tsipouri and Xanthakis 1993). Firms do not have access to the necessary complementary assets, like competitive production structures, distribution channels, financial resources, or strong appropriability regimes to market their new knowledge profitably (Teece 1986). Barriers imposed by the framework conditions of the economy, the local financial system, human skills, and the generic country image do not allow for rapid or massive exploitation of innovative results that would lead to changes of scale. Thus, even if they are innovative, LC firms are bound to limit themselves to moderate ambitions.

Although these policies are relevant in LCs, they do not have the same impact as they do in advanced countries. Latecomers benefit from technology policy only to a limited extent, where the impact is concentrated in highly skilled research teams. Sometimes an additional benefit lies in facilitating the repatriation of diaspora scientists because of increased local opportunities. Firms rarely reap benefits from the exploitation of innovations with global ambitions. The improvement of the local R&D system benefits mainly the research process itself, not industry. According to Dunning (1994), ownership of R&D becomes increasingly concentrated while its location becomes more dispersed. The increased subcontracting of research in latecoming countries and the Third World is only a reaction of firms to the rapid improvement of skills and attainment of high levels of competence, while costs remain significantly lower than in advanced countries. Therefore, increased research activity is not equivalent to increased technological change in industry.

Empirical evidence from Greece corroborates this (Tsipouri and Xanthakis 1994). Studying 600 innovations with technically feasible solutions in the Greek manufacturing sector, it was found that the impacts of technology policies were better explained by, instead of the classical distinctions, *product/process/organization* and *radical/marginal*, two different classifications:

- *fragmented/persistent*
- *degree of relevance*, measured *ex post*.

The former suggested that a considerable number of the Greek innovations studied were promising but not integrated into a technological trajectory resulting from company strategy. In particular, the innovations of small and medium-size companies that were subsidized by specific public schemes proved that, although they were in many cases adopted by the production process and improved competitiveness for a limited period of time, no follow-up was designed by the companies themselves. Consequently, the marginal competitive advantage was very quickly eroded. This is precisely the opposite of the insight emanating from the literature on national innovation systems in advanced countries, notably that innovation is interactive and collective, and that firms do not innovate in isolation.

Analysis based on the second classification was even more disappointing, where relevance was defined as positively affecting company results (employment, turnover, exports, or profit).[16] Only 5 percent of the innovations studied were relevant, about 50 percent were irrelevant, and 45 percent were not even introduced in the production process.

This combination of technically feasible but either less relevant or sporadic innovations explains why increased input in technological subsidization does not change the overall competitiveness of local industry. Companies do not react to incentives in order to improve their know-how and change their competitive position; instead, they see technology support as a means to:

- *access cash*: a number of factors (dysfunctionalities or dislike of the banking system, uncertainty about exchange rates, underdeveloped stock markets) make companies in LFCs more dependent on any type of subsidy, thus reducing additionality.[17]
- *change scale*, rather than to upgrade: the dream of growing rich, because of a very original idea (preferably overnight) is more pronounced in latecomers; thus, R&D loses the features worked out by the evolutionary theory and, in the strategy of a company, it becomes almost exogenous once again.
- *increase reputation* and capture value indirectly by being designated an R&D-intensive company. Firms dependent upon public procurement or entering the stock market are particularly apt to follow such a strategy.

Thus, innovation policy in LCs loses much of the justification that shifted it to the center of policy-making in advanced countries. By definition, it cannot be science-based or pursue radical innovations that change the evolution of whole industries, because of the existing structure of the manufacturing sector. But, as long as it is used in isolated projects, neither can it be expected to create new entrepreneurial spirits willing to change strategies and select new directions while accepting the risks and merits of constantly extending the variety of options.

The argument that increased research does not automatically lead to industrial competitiveness in latecomers may, to some extent, be applied to education and training as well. Recognition of the importance of the role of human capital has channeled an enormous amount of structural funds to all types of education in small, less favored European countries. There is no doubt that this contributed to the substantial upgrading of human capital in the last decade, but it is not clear to what extent this new knowledge was really incorporated in the production process. The most important among the explanations for this limited return to human capital enhancement is the difficulty in identifying the needs of the economy and subsequent tailoring of curricula accordingly. The poor performance of the supply of human capital highlights the need for a careful consideration of whether the allocation of substantial levels of scarce national resources to broad-based educational output is indeed optimal (Daniels 1993).

The technology transfer process

Thus far, we have focused on the more modern sector of the economy, because it is mainly the restructured, more successful firms that we expect to react first to industrial policies, overcome existing barriers, and become the nuclei of agglomeration effects and persistent innovation. But the local economy in LCs is predominantly composed of traditional small and medium-size companies that continue to dominate the industrial fabric. For them, R&D, training, and dense interrelations are not on the agenda. All evaluations of research, training, or investment subsidy instruments persistently conclude that these firms are much less likely to react to the incentives offered, perhaps excepting those that are immediately threatened.

It may be argued that the traditional sector is bound to disappear in the medium or long term, as its competitiveness is gradually eroded. But the firms that comprise this sector can also be viewed as the source of new entrants to the competitive system. They represent a pool of purely motivated and trained entrepreneurs, some of whom may succeed in transforming themselves into competitive medium-size firms of global scope, if the right guidance can be provided. For them it is important to find at least modest means to accommodate mature technological tools.

Diffusion of know-how and accommodation of generic technological change is faster in advanced countries than in latecomers. Technology transfer there is a process initiated by market mechanisms, either because profit expectations are high enough to initiate the process or because of greater competitive pressures. Capabilities within firms are such that at least established tools are rapidly adopted and partly operated by internal skills, and do not necessarily require external upgrading or replacement of personnel. This is especially true for information-processing and management tools.

However, in latecomers a virtual dichotomy appears between companies that adopt new tools and those that are overcome by events. We know by now that technology transfer is of equal importance to the leading role R&D played in the past. And the single most important determinant for successful technology transfer projects is the human factor.

THE STRATEGIC PRINCIPLES

The theoretical arguments and identification of deficiencies elucidated in previous sections now need to be transformed into an operational strategy for latecomers. The ultimate – and perhaps too ambitious – objective is to design and employ incentives that not only influence direct profitability, but also *transform the business culture* in the latecomer. Further, this must be accomplished in a reasonable time horizon, using, wherever possible, subsidies as leverage for changing conventions and for creating a collective background. Conceiving such a medium-term strategy is a more difficult and delicate task than designing a plan for an encompassing, long-term restructuring, which would use all available means for a narrow set of directions.

This should not be interpreted as advocating an end to research support. Academic research remains important, but more for educational purposes than for stimulating innovation. Industrial policy itself has to concentrate on the creation of linkages and the technology transfer process. The real need to be recognized is to change the informal rules dictating how to deal with technological and organizational knowledge. It goes without saying that in order to avoid idle capacities (the usual bottlenecks to development), three dimensions should grow in parallel:

- technological/organizational knowledge,
- informal rules, and
- institutional assets.

As a consequence, policy should be aimed at strengthening capabilities in those lagging behind, inducing them to catch up, and not at reinforcing the leaders.

The ideas suggested here may be interpreted as ways of increasing social capabilities so that they become adequate to absorb more advanced technologies that will enable latecomers to catch up. But since the institutional and human capital components of social capabilities develop only slowly, the pace of their development limits the strength of technological potentiality (Abramovitz 1986). Increasing social capabilities may then be a matter of promoting the desirable cultural changes without creating counter forces.

The proposed strategy has a single aim: to create the conditions for individual firms to evolve into parts of a learning process. The systems-of-innovation approach sees the overall innovation performance of an economy as depending not so much on how specific organizations perform, but on how they interact with each other as elements of a collective system of knowledge creation and use. Individual firms rather than public agencies are the targets of policy. The latter can only play a supporting role; they do not create wealth by themselves (Nelson 1993). On the other hand, firms in less favored regions are clearly the weakest part of the chain, as the organizations that have to face uncertainties,[18] whereas universities and research centers are quicker to adapt, although they are also subject to the process of changing conventions.

Credibility is the single most important principle for such a strategy. Determination of a medium-term time horizon is a prerequisite for starting to change conventions. The selection mechanisms are particularly important; these stand in sharp contrast to mainstream economic thinking, wherein policymakers (consultants or government officials) are deemed incapable of identifying opportunities, and the state is expected to limit its activities to horizontal interventions while allowing entrepreneurs to select opportunities based on market mechanisms. At the same time, empirical analysis reveals substantial market imperfections in less favored economies, and opportunities are not grasped for several reasons.[19] The anti-agglomeration tendencies mentioned above are only one example, while Porter, in his analysis of the

Portuguese economy, cites other reasons why firms do not cooperate and the state needs to play a catalytic role, including an absence of confidence among competitors and a failure to realize dynamic externalities. The challenge for designing a medium-term strategy is to eliminate market failures while at the same time avoiding the creation of government failures.

Clearly, the strategy will have to take into account disparate cultural factors. This will require policies that are flexible and determined on a case by case basis. But regardless of its specific form, the strategy should contain the following elements:

1 Incentives for small companies with efficient built-in control mechanisms; support for inward investment, technology, and education; all complemented by a new set of measures with a *vision of broader change*.

2 The new policy can work only if it manages to *achieve consensus* between productive agents and the public authorities: any ambitious targeting synergies have to be based on the full consensus between industrial companies as the agents implementing entrepreneurial decisions, public infrastructure, and the state. This intervention can materialize only when public and private benefits coexist. Consensus is one of the concepts that is theoretically supported by everybody, but which quickly results in conflict or resignation in reality. Consensus may mean that particular firms agree to carry costs like training, even though it may, under certain circumstances, benefit potential competitors; that trade unions agree to changes in job descriptions and work profiles; and that the state diminishes its intervention in areas where agents can act alone. For public authorities it may mean that they finance activities that not only do not win votes, but whose results do not materialize during their term in office. Creating consensus is a most difficult task, and it has to spread over several layers of hierarchy. Agreement among members of government, national or sectoral industrial federations, and unions are insufficient. Transforming agreement at the top into consensus at the bottom is more difficult than it appears to be. Local conventions must be taken into consideration in order to form permanent alliances capable of surviving *ad hoc* blows and deeply rooted differences.

3 Since the new policy is bound to be based initially on a precarious equilibrium, and any failure will discredit its advocates, selected measures need to have *direct applicability* to avoid resistance to change. The need for direct applicability is likely to lead to the selection of small systems where intervention can be very rapid and effective, but where spillovers are lower; at the same time, direct applicability renders policymakers vulnerable to criticism for favoritism. Direct applicability does not alter the medium-term strategy of the new policy. Once initial success is achieved, the policy can become more ambitious, using the pilots as models reinforcing the process of change. As it proceeds, the need for direct applicability will be gradually reduced.

4 Finally, *avoiding government failures* is also part of the strategy design. The capabilities of the public sector, generally very weak in latecomers, are likely to be overestimated in a wave of initial enthusiasm.[20] Government failures can be avoided in part if the consensus policy works so well that other social partners enter the game and use their capabilities. The design of the new policy should not require from state agencies much more than they can reasonably offer; demanding nothing more will fail to evoke change, while requiring too much will lead to failure. This lesson applies to all layers of hierarchy. Political authorities alone cannot trigger a change of conventions; some inefficient bureaucracies and frustrated bureaucrats will need to become allies at a certain point in time. Unfortunately, it is the policy that will need to adapt to the existing public service and not vice versa.

These are the principles we believe each country has to respect. How each specifically responds to the deadlocks it confronts will depend on its environment and history. In the following section we offer several suggestions.

ORGANIZING PATH-DEPENDENT INTERVENTION

How should one proceed when announcing a new industrial policy? Respecting strategies is insufficient, since, as we have argued in the previous sections, path dependencies need to be explicitly considered in each case. A multistage approach seems inevitable. To start with, current financial incentives should not be abolished because this would probably increase mistrust, but they should be complemented in a way that channels them toward structures with a higher likelihood of above-average success. Only then can they gradually diminish. Any government has to start with pilots; the more that confidence is built, the more one can become ambitious. But over time the emphasis should shift away from individual investment and toward behavior.

Some ideas are suggested here as examples, influenced by European pathways. Although they may appear technical, it seems important to suggest operational action plans, while keeping in mind that these are examples of specific situations only; they should not be taken as guidelines that end up reducing the context of the whole theory to specific measures.

Path-dependent intervention would use existing direct instruments in areas where consensus can be achieved, direct applicability is identified, and the government is in a position to play such a role. We thus analyze three areas of intervention that correspond to the deadlocks we have identified earlier:

• opportunities determined by the evolution of global trends, selecting those that fit the existing industry structure and reinforcing the national component of international productive systems in these particular areas (elements of other systems may continue to restructure, but this will be supported by the existing instruments of traditional policy);

- increasing the number of agents who are willing to become persistent, in other words agents who are likely to go beyond their financial expectations and become part of a learning system;
- facilitating less aggressive firms in their accommodation of generic tools.

In the first case, the state aims at reinforcing linkages where above-average yields attract the elements of the system and give them the incentive to collaborate. In the second area, individual agents or small consortia are addressed, whereby the state adopts new rules aimed to reinforce persistence rather than scientific merit or institutional competence. The latter deals with the change of culture at the less competitive and less adaption oriented firms.

It emerges that our approach deals with three types of firms: those strong enough (and large enough) to generate spillovers in regards to their organizational skills, competencies, and competitive performance; firms of all sizes mature enough to become part of a learning system; and finally, new entrants, with potential to renew the industrial fabric. New entrants to the system may be new technology based firms, a phenomenon that is well documented in the literature regarding advanced countries. In most LCs the number of start-ups is low because of high uncertainty and the rejection of failures, the latter being a convention that increases as the level of development diminishes. But even in those countries where there is a relatively high birth rate of new firms – particularly in software, multimedia, telecommunications applications, and automation – they tend to disappear quickly or to remain very small in size. The reasons for that can be related to windows of opportunities, the maturity of technologies (Soete and Perez 1988), and increased concentration as standards mature (Utterback and Suarez 1993). There are also limitations of human resources, even where skills exist, because experienced people do not wish to enter small, unknown firms, especially in their first years. Thus, the often suggested strategies of changing the industrial fabric through massive support to new technology based firms is limited by local informal constraints. R&D and innovation policies are necessary (in the way that physical infrastructure is necessary), but they are unable to contribute to ambitious plans of industrial reform beyond providing generalized aid to help the renewal process. Thus, attracting the creation of new competitive firms will have to rely partly on the transformation of the behavior of traditional entrepreneurs.

Each of these three areas – overlapping with the three populations of firms – are discussed in the following sections.

Reinforcing national components of international productive systems

The absence of natural networking in LCs requires a substitute in the form of strategic networking. The first problem to solve in providing additional support for selected productive systems is the selection process itself. We see three possible ways for doing that: "objectivization" of criteria, "subjective" preselection, and private-sector network creation. In each case, local circumstances will suggest which one (or which combination) is best suited.

The first approach is to *objectivize criteria ex ante*, selecting among clusters (if they exist) or manufacturing subsectors, using proxies to indicate which selected areas of intervention have the greatest likelihood of generating multiplication effects in the regional economy. Such proxies are commonly used, including export shares, local value added, indirect employment effects, and other more sophisticated variables based upon input–output calculations.[21] Success is most likely where clusters are already formed and well defined. Another advantage is that this approach is not likely to be subject to charges of favoritism. Nonetheless, this approach suffers from two important shortcomings: first, data are not available at the level of productive systems; and second, the top-down design of this method, wherein public welfare is the only selection criterion and entrepreneurial expectations are not taken into consideration, seriously diminishes the likelihood of success.

The second approach uses a *political preselection* of areas of intervention based on extensive knowledge of the country's abilities and potential. Following the initial subjective basis for deciding on the variety of cases to be considered, other objective criteria can also be applied, but in an *ex post* rather than *ex ante* fashion. These might include issues of at-risk sectors, market and other opportunities, potential for network formation, and the projected characteristics of potential clusters and industrial districts. According to our definition of latecomers, structural problems are already well analyzed (or they can rapidly be evaluated) so the identification of a number of areas, where additional intervention may be expected to lead to public welfare, should not be difficult. What is more relevant in this approach is collaboration with potential investors. This model attempts to reconcile private and public welfare to the greatest extent possible. However, this does not eliminate the danger of being accused of using arbitrary selection procedures; the vulnerability of this approach lies in the *subjective* preselection, whereby policymakers may be accused both of favoritism and of not trying to maximize the multiplication effects of public intervention. A certain culture of central programming and effective government is necessary in this case.

The third selection concept relies on *private-sector network* creation. This would require calls for proposals for network creation, well-defined scope and selection criteria. In this case, private interests are given the lead, and the methodologies to bring them to a common denominator are no more objective than the preselection in the approach described above. Although this model would yield the highest benefits to the private sector, it is unlikely that it would be effective in changing conventions, since the networks formed would follow their own behavioral rules, adapting the intervention to their conventions rather than creating new ones.

Typically, of the three approaches described, none can be shown to be the uniquely best method for operationalizing network promotion in LCs.

Portugal had the analytical tools to enable it to adopt the first approach. Third Italy (referring to earlier stages when it could be considered a late-comer) was able very successfully to adopt the second. While Greece – following indecision between the second and the third – opted for the latter. But several indicative policy criteria may facilitate the design. These can include:

Potential for adaptation through networking

Networks are selected when agents are either in high-tech sectors facing new opportunities because of growing markets, or in declining strongly competitive areas where the threat of bankruptcy makes them more collaborative. Threatened agents and those facing new opportunities are the first populations to be addressed.[22] The appraisal of opportunities for growth or survival is shared between policymakers, technology providers, and investors, while action is undertaken with the aim of breaking vicious circles (conventions) and trying to exploit conjectural elements that trigger virtuous circles. The initial selection of pilot projects is a special responsibility, since massive failure would only reinforce the very conventions the new policy is trying to modify. For this reason, agents in pilot projects should be carefully selected on the assumption that they have valid reasons for participating in a process of changing conventions.

Credible coordinating structures

Various forms of governance have proved to work successfully in market-driven clusters and agglomerations, while at the same time similar forms (in particular centrally planned activities) did not succeed with carefully designed state intervention (Humphrey 1995). The credibility of the coordinating structure becomes an important element for consensus. Whether winners become key clients, infrastructure plays a coordinating role, or clubs of companies promote actions under their auspices, it is important that the administration/management has the full confidence of both investors and the state.

Alternative structures of governance

The pilot structure is expected to form an initial experiment to be replicated in other areas (geographical or economic). For this reason, pilot networks with a variety of governing structures should be adopted in the first selection round in order to identify the most successful structure; this can then form the basis for transferability. Ideally, over time, the state can channel a rising share of the intervention into selected productive systems, thus providing a widening basis for change in the systems with the highest likelihood of success.

Catalysis

According to orthodox economic thinking, where consensus can be created and a potential for adaptation through networking is appreciated, alliances should arise automatically through market forces. This is precisely where path-dependent intervention is justified; in contrast to the nonagglomeration syndrome, effective intervention here provides a "seal of approval," on behalf of individual agents, sectoral and regional organizations, and the state, all acting against traditional uncertainties. The intervention is additional to the market (in a Hirschmannian sense it is there to amplify market messages) and will act as a catalyst, stimulating a reaction and then withdrawing.

Reinforcing persistent learning

The idea of *persistent learning* corresponds to mature firms that demonstrate a willingness to react to market pressures and incentives. The competitiveness of small enterprises depends on the role and abilities of the owner/manager, intangible investment (monitoring technology, training, and organization), tangible investment, and strategic capabilities. Being interactive and collective helps firms to increase their competence, specialization, and market position.

But not all firms are willing to act as members of productive systems. We have identified a deeply rooted convention in latecomers that is related to a very peculiar version of the "collaboration and competition" principle: while competition is less fierce, collaboration is also less appreciated, and despite the fact that relations with local competitors seldom take the form of battles for survival, mistrust among them is high.

In such cases the state must design its policy by taking into consideration these seemingly contradictory tendencies of the targeted firms. This applies to research, development, transfer of new technology, and training incentives, but not to direct investment subsidies or to generic application of new technology. A clear distinction is made here between technology transfer, defined as the adoption and adaptation of technology created and proven elsewhere (in a research laboratory, in another company, or in another country) with which we deal here, and the transfer of generic tools, mature and standardized, with which we deal in the next section.

Experience in developed countries and latecomers alike shows that many firms are able to benefit repeatedly from the same schemes, because they become experts in filing grant applications and they see these incentives as additional revenue opportunities. This finding has led state agencies to envisage the attraction of new clientele as an important target of their policy. On the other hand, empirical evidence from the patent literature suggests that when a firm becomes more than an occasional inventor, its economic performance becomes above average; this can be easily explained by the fact that this is the best way to incorporate such firms into the learning economy.

Here again, though, we have a case where conventions in latecomers are totally different from those in developed countries. The continuous reappearance of the same firms in the list of research, technology transfer, and innovation grant winners is better explained by their disposition to rely on state support for part of their revenue (or perhaps to finance their hobby activities) than by their transformation into persistent learners. While successful schemes in Germany, France, and Italy see repetition as an indicator of persistence, the same behavior in latecomers raises suspicions of abuse and often leads to political decisions to exclude repeat beneficiaries from a variety of similar incentives.[23]

More analysis is required from the public administration of industrial policy in latecomers to address conventions. The choices are not easy and the capabilities of the public service may not be sufficient to play an efficient hands-on role. But two directions need to be followed:

- to strengthen the position of persistent (rent-seeking) learners, and
- to encourage new (possibly occasional) entrants to the population of firms applying for technology incentives.

Policy instruments that reinforce learning should permit the awarding of research grants to repeat winners, while being cautious not to turn these incentives into a form of revenue generation. Companies applying for additional support should be subject to strict criteria of market success in previous projects, but incentives should then be more generous where such success and growth can be demonstrated. Support should be offered for ambitious technology creation or adaptation, related to new products, new processes in core competencies, and state-of-the-art management models. Technological risk and aggressive growth considerations should be the underlying principles of this policy. In general, this support should be given to initiatives that demonstrate at least one of the following criteria:

- direct applicability for firms that are closer to market success, in particular in the international market;
- the application of specific criteria, such as the share of sales from new products and the variety of new alternatives examined;
- the creation of trust in the monitoring procedure established by the public; and finally
- the design of measures that are open, which are clearly not intended to simply "pick winners," and where all firms are eligible but none can become permanent beneficiaries.

Transplanting generic technological tools

We noted earlier that traditional industry in latecomers is characterized by a reluctance to experiment and reward new technology, even when it matures. There is a not unimportant number of companies reluctant to proceed with any kind of collaboration, in particular those enjoying conditions of a relatively stable environment.[24] No incentives are strong enough to move them towards a voluntary effort to change their behavior and overcome their mistrust, which, more often than not, extends to the public sector. A considerable share of these companies refuses even to apply for state grants, which they do not consider worthwhile; instead, these incentives are perceived as being bureaucratic, slow, and ultimately dangerous, since they may drive companies to undertake financial obligations while the state itself retards subsidies payments or changes the rules of the game without prior notice. While financial arguments provide one valid reason for this reluctance, the sociology of development has also identified many others.

Intervention in such cases can be based on the idea that people can sometimes learn on the job. When caught in positions of continuously deteriorating competitiveness, traditional small-firm entrepreneurs in latecomers cannot believe that change is possible and thus do not concentrate their efforts on it. Change seems too big a step and too big a risk for them. The challenge for intervention in this case is to diminish the magnitude of change and allow them gradually to experiment with it at low risk. The idea is that once they become part of the system of learning, they will naturally recognize the potential benefits and eventually overcome their initial reluctance. Thus, incentives for small technology transfer experimentation emerge as a necessary instrument.

This approach is quite different from the one we described in the previous section, where we spoke of persistent new technology adoption, because it does not refer to core technologies but to generic tools of wider use. Examples include: electronic office support, quality control procedures, modest management techniques, and rudimentary automation. These represent transplantation instruments that have already become well established elsewhere, and where reluctance of use can be overcome through experimentation. Change can then diffuse, not only in the pioneering companies, but also in their environment as cultural aversion diminishes. Cultural transplants are thus achieved against the expectations and almost against the will of the agents involved. Such adaptations may begin in fragmented fashion, but they are more likely to become persistent.

Again, the key question is how to operationalize this change. While one can reasonably argue that this is a matter of education and training, both the lack of efficiency of the local training system and the resistance of the target population suggest that one cannot rely on it. Thus, a focused selection of activities and technologies becomes necessary, and though again path dependent, we suggest two criteria to be used, consistent with previous argumentation:

- *generic character*, which yields two advantages:
    1 receivers are likely to have heard of their use and merit elsewhere, and
    2 even where immediate applicability is not obvious, entrepreneurs are more

likely to believe that the investment in learning is worthwhile because such broad technologies and activities may well be transferable to future activities;

- *simplicity*, which is related to maturity and standardization: since applicants are likely to doubt the benefits and resist the introduction of the new tools, it is likely that it will be easier to attract them to use simple and standardized products or processes, rather than those that need increased training.

CONCLUSIONS

This chapter has tried to identify guideposts for the reorientation of industrial policies for latecomers, based on the assumption that the ultimate goal of any policy is to improve social capabilities which determine the ability of LCs to catch up technologically. Empirical evidence shows that economic agents in LCs react differently to policies and incentives than their counterparts in the developed world. This failure of comparability reduces the possibility of effectively reproducing the forms of industrial support used elsewhere and leads us to suggest that improvement of social capabilities requires going beyond profitability to changing the behavior and informal rules of economic agents. In addition, this view suggests that several forms of intervention that are carried out under industrial policy labels are, in fact, social or educational policies and should be considered as such.

Latecomers, characterized by an improved level of basic infrastructure, generalized education, and the rudiments of an RTD system, still encounter, to some extent, three main deadlocks that inhibit spillovers from individual industrial successes: notably, a tendency to avoid agglomeration effects, the inability to turn individual projects into persistent learning processes, and a reluctance to engage in untargeted learning. Consequently, the strategic element of the new policy suggested is precisely to eliminate – or, less ambitiously, to reduce – these deadlocks, and in this way improve social capabilities.

The translation of these strategic principles into practical forms of intervention is path dependent. We suggest some orientation, criteria, and the direction of analysis that should be followed on a case by case basis. How they will be implemented depends then on the abilities of each country. Learning occurs as a result of business strategies or even incidentally, as in the case of adaptation to new technology.

Consensus is of crucial importance to the success of this type of effort, suggesting that it is necessary to achieve broader acceptance, where political and business powers cooperate with the aim of spending public funds efficiently. For the business sector, globalization threats lead them to cooperate more than in the past. This could allow a transformation from short-term reactions to longer-term planning, and an enlargement of economic horizons that diminishes not only the danger of corporatism but also the danger of change of political power. For the political sector and the public administration, things are less homogeneous. In the best case, the political sector feels globalization threats in similar manner to the business world. In less mature political systems, the complexity of the public administration makes it vulnerable to sliding back to established formal rules if any change occurs. Consensus is the only means to guarantee continuity, as it is unlikely that all relevant agents change spontaneously. In such a consensual context it will be more feasible to adopt transparent and accountable policy instruments.

NOTES

1 In the EU jargon these countries are also called less favoured countries (LFCs), a term used hereafter as synonymous to LCs
2 Neoclassical theory considers industrial culture as totally exogenous, since output and productivity are only a function of capital and labor, while in many sociological analyses industrial culture is also considered as a determinant of the inability of the system to adopt rational organization (Boecke). Finally, at the economic policy level it is often argued that efficient public measures are not taken up by local agents in latecomers or developing countries because of the industrial culture, thus being used as an alibi to explain inertia.
3 The need to increase the return on investment artificially may be justified either by the low yield achieved as compared to foreign competitors because of inadequate industrial structures and infrastructures (trade theories), or by the need to amplify the market messages compared to those in more advanced countries (Hirschman 1958).
4 In this regard, North refers explicitly to earlier work of Sugden (1986).
5 Most often these constraints are related to a certain degree of protectionism, or, when internationally competitive, to a still favorable wage structure.
6 Contrast this with the Scandinavian countries and Austria in the first two post-war decades where, due to social conventions, the private sector carried the restructuring.
7 Very large economies with centralized power like China are obviously still the exception.
8 The market failure arises in this case by pressures in international trade: the lower prices of new entrants are a result not of better allocative efficiency, but of a political (path-dependent) choice of a lower welfare that results in cost reduction. Companies in threatened sectors thus pay for the general level of prosperity, in terms of education, health care and workers' rights. The state is then disposed to support local companies to restructure in order to meet with this challenge, which often proves impossible, independently of how high and long term grants can be.
9 One important element of natural protectionism is market size, and as latecomers grow their markets become more attractive and thus competitive pressures increase as a function of GDP.
10 The particular case of software, which needs low physical investment and high skills, was the most typical area where all latecomers and developing countries believed they could become key international players.
11 This suggestion operated in the context of an effort to shift from start-up support to firms that can already prove a dynamic track record, although not aiming at substantial market shares.
12 Price here is meant in the most complete sense. Export prices may be subject to higher competitive pressures, but risks are lower, since they are usually covered by bank guarantees, and in many LCs they are further supported by export subsidies.

13 Although there is as yet no systematic empirical evidence in this respect, discussions with leading industrialists in Greece have confirmed their willingness to pay this premium because the quality controlled supplies and better price conditions allow them to apply a more ambitious strategy themselves. In only one case was the issue raised that this may be linked to the old argument of tax evasion through false invoicing rather than security premia.

14 In a case study of technology management in Greece we found in a randomly selected sample of 40 successful companies that 19 were globally networked, high-skills companies. A similar study in the UK, where the sample included major multinationals, found only 10 out of 25 globally networked, high-skills companies (Dankbaar and Cannell forthcoming).

15 The less favored regions of the EU have adopted operational programs responding to these needs in order to receive the Community Support Frameworks, and several Latin American countries have also followed this example. More recently, Eastern and Central European countries adopting Phare-supported R&D policies have followed suit.

16 An arbitrary measure of 20 percent compared to the pre-innovation situation was selected in this particular case.

17 Although these schemes always require cofinance, it is common knowledge that it is the exception rather than the rule that companies contribute new cash to these activities; instead they charge existing personnel, equipment, and travel expenses to the project. Public authorities have to accept this mode of behavior, since otherwise there would be very limited take up of the suggested schemes.

18 The other elements of the local innovation system work with rules and conventions closer to those of the learning economy. The success with which selected research teams in European LFCs work with the major European companies is only one proof of how quickly the system in latecomers can adapt if uncertainties are eliminated.

19 The size of the local market is one of the main sources of market imperfections.

20 The exception of Ireland might be worth mentioning here. Path dependence in this case distinguishes this country from other latecomers, as it can entrust its government with more powers and ambitions. When the first draft of this chapter was written, the major success of Ireland leading it to overcome the threshold of a conversion country was not achieved; but this fact only corroborates what we argued earlier.

21 Porter (1991) used this method in Portugal, taking relative export shares into account.

22 This approach is very different from the "loser support" policy, since its objective is not saving employment but changing (the word restructuring is avoided intentionally) firms in order to regain international competitiveness.

23 In a new jargon these firms can be called "usual suspects."

24 In theory, such a stable environment cannot last, a fact that current practice is coming to appreciate, even if precariously.

REFERENCES

Abramovitz, M. (1986) "Catching up, forging ahead, and falling behind," *Journal of Economic History* 46, 2: 385–406.

—— (1994) "The origins of postwar catch-up and convergence boom," in J. Fagerberg, B. Verspagen, and N. von Tunzelman (eds) *The Dynamics of Technology, Trade and Growth*, Aldershot: Edward Elgar.

CEC (1991) *Evaluation of the Effects of the EC Framework Programme for Research and Technological Development on Economic and Social Cohesion in the Community*, Evaluations and Reviews, Brussels.

CIRCA (1993) *The Consequences of the Community Support Frameworks for RTD in Ireland, Portugal and Greece*, A report to the Commission of the European Union, Brussels, Mimeographed.

Daniels, P. (1993) "Research and development, human capital and trade performance in technology-intensive manufactures: A cross country analysis," *Research Policy* 22: 207–241.

Dankbaar, B. and Cannell, W. (forthcoming) *Technology Management and Public Policy in the European Union*, Oxford and New York: Office for Official Publications of the European Communities and Oxford University Press.

Doeringer, P. B. and Streeten, P. P. (1990) "How economic institutions affect economic performance in industrialized countries: Lessons for development," *World Development* 18, 9: 1249–53.

Dosi, G. (1992) "Industrial organisation, competitiveness and growth," *Révue d'Economie Industrielle* 59: 27–43.

Dunning, J. H. (1994) "Multinational enterprises and the globalization of inventory capacity," *Research Policy* 23: 67–88.

Fagerberg, J., Verspagen, B., and von Tunzelman, N. (eds) (1994) *The Dynamics of Technology, Trade and Growth*, Aldershot: Edward Elgar.

Gjerding, A. N., Johnson, B., Kallehauge, L., Lundvall, B., and Madsen, P. T. (1992) *The Productivity Mystery*, Copenhagen: DJOF Publishing.

Hirschman, A. O. (1958) *The Strategy of Economic Development*, New Haven: Yale University Press.

Humphrey, J. (1995) "Industrial reorganisation and developing countries: from models to trajectories," *World Development* 23, 1: 149–162.

Katz, M. L. and Shapiro, C. (1994) "Systems competition and network effects," *Journal of Economic Perspectives* 8, 2: 93–115.

Krugman, P. R. (1986) *Strategic Trade Policy and the New International Economics*, Cambridge, MA: MIT Press.

Lundvall, B. (1994) "Innovation policy and the learning economy," Paper presented at the International Seminar on Policies for Technological Development organised by CIDE, Mexico.

Nelson, R. R. (1993) *National Innovation Systems*, New York: Oxford University Press.

Nelson, R. and Winter, S. (1982) *An Evolutionary Theory of Economic Change*, Boston: Harvard University Press.

North, D. C. (1990) *Institutions, Institutional Change and Economic Performance*, Cambridge: Cambridge University Press.

OECD (1993) *Industrial Policy in OECD Countries*, Annual review 1993, Paris: OECD.

Perez, C. and Soete, L. (1988) "Bridging the technological gap: barriers to entry and windows of opportunity", in G. Dosi *et al. Technical Change and Economic Theory*, London: Pinter.

Pitelis, C. (1994) "Industrial strategy: for Britain in Europe in the world," *Journal of Economic Studies* 21, 5: 2–92.

Porter, M. (1991) *The Competitive Advantage of Nations*, London: Macmillan.

Rabelotti, R. (1995) "Is there an 'Industrial District Model'? Footware districts in Italy and Mexico compared," *World Development* 23, 1: 29–41.

Rothwell, R. and Dodgson, M. (1992) "European technology policy evolution: convergence towards SMEs and regional technology transfer," *Technovation* 12, 4: 223–238.

Schmitz, H. (1995) "Small shoemakers and Fordist giants: Tale of a supercluster," *World Development* 23, 1: 9–28.

Schultz, T. W. (1981) *Investing in People*, Berkeley, CA and London: University of California Press.

Storey, D. (1994) *Understanding the Small Business Sector*, London: Routledge.
Storper, M. (1993) "Territorial development in the global learning economy: the challenge to developing countries," Paper presented in the conference "Globalização, Fragmentação e Reforma Urbana," October 26–29, 1993, Itamontes, Minas Gerais, Brazil, Mimeographed.
Sugden, R. (1986) *The Economics of Rights, Co-operation and Welfare*, Oxford: Basil Blackwell.
Teece, D. (1986) "Profiting from technological innovation: implications for integration, collaboration, licensing and public policy," *Research Policy* 15: 285–305.
Thorelli, H. B. (1986), "Networks: between markets and hierarchies," *Strategic Management Journal* 7: 37–51.
Tsipouri, L. and Xanthakis, M. (1994) "Investigation of successful and unsuccessful innovations in Greek manufacturing" (in Greek), Athens: STRIDE Program Report to the General Secretariat For Research and Technology, Mimeographed.
—— (1993) "The impact of EU RTD policy on Greek RTD policy," a report to the Commission of the EU, Mimeographed.
Utterback, J. and Suarez, F. F. (1993) "Innovation, competition and industry structure," *Research Policy* 22: 1–21.

Part II
Policies, instruments and agents

4 Coordinated industrialization

Institutional agendas for less favored countries

Stavros B. Thomadakis

INTRODUCTION

This chapter examines the design and execution of industrial policy in those less favored countries (LFCs) that participate in regional macroeconomic coordination and free trade associations. Concerns regarding the industrialization of less favored regions that belong to the European Union have motivated interest in industrial policy in LFCs. But the subject has wider importance, since LFCs around the world participate in an increasingly liberal international economic order where free trade, liberalized financial markets, and capital movements impose severe constraints on domestic policies.

The definition of LFCs employed in this chapter includes countries that are semi-industrialized, a status that denotes both progress toward industrialization and the existence of obstacles to sustaining that progress to the point of convergence with fully industrialized economies. Their past progress usually includes some experience with industrialization policies from which positive and negative lessons can be drawn. Consequently, the important issues in this chapter revolve around the *renewal of industrial policy* in order to overcome the obstacles that prevent LFCs from progressing to a pathway of convergence with highly industrialized ones. LFCs also have in place basic institutions of policymaking and economic regulation; therefore, the issue of renewed industrial policy involves not so much issues of institutional design *per se*, as reform of the institutional environment and of its enrichment with new capabilities.

Several important questions elaborate the basic theme:

- What institutional arrangements can foster industrialization, and how can they be established?
- Are these institutional arrangements expected to arise spontaneously in the extant economic formation of LFCs, or should they be explicitly designed as an output of policy?
- How can the lessons of past experiments, both successes and failures, be turned into "assets" in the process of formulating and implementing industrialization agendas?

- What mix of political accountability and regulatory flexibility can be realistically sought in state-related agents and institutions of industrialization in LFCs, given the particularities of political culture and relative economic backwardness?

We begin our analysis by recognizing that internationalization creates competitive pressures on LFCs. The modes of adjustment by industrial firms, collective entities, and governments in LFCs are classified into two broad groups, depending on whether they are defensive or strategic in character. This is followed by an examination of the causes underlying short-termist behaviors, and identification of hurdles that must be overcome for strategic behaviors to take root. In the third section, an institutional agenda for continued industrialization in LFCs is identified, based on a series of analytical requirements. The fundamental principle of that agenda is a reformed, decentralized, and flexible mode of public intervention whose main goal is to enable the internalization of strategic externalities. In the final section we focus on the relation of finance and continued industrialization. In the context of increasing market liberalization, prudential regulation of markets, supply of pluralistic institutional financial services, and utilization of flexible financial instruments are all seen as necessary components of LFC strategy.

LFCS AND INTERNATIONAL COMPETITION: MODES OF ADJUSTMENT OF INTEGRATING ECONOMIES

Less favored countries participating in regional macroeconomic coordination and free trade associations are, by definition, the more backward partners in those groupings. LFCs are admissible into regional groupings with more advanced economies, while nevertheless being relatively backward with respect to these economies. More frequently than not, the degree of industrialization attained by LFCs has been crafted in the context of protectionist trade policies, administered credit policies, and other forms of domestic regulatory interventions.[1] Thus, the task of furthering industrialization in the context of open economy policies, trade and financial liberalization, and free-market constrained macroeconomic policy presents a new challenge.

The backwardness of semi-industrialized countries relative to their more advanced partners makes itself felt in at least three ways. First, they exhibit *lower average productivity*. Second, this lower productivity is due, in part, to a *lower level of industrialization*, meaning a lower share of the manufacturing sector in national economic activity, relative technological backwardness, and more labor-intensive production methods. Third, they lack social capital in the form of "soft" infrastructures that normally enhance the return on capital. Under these conditions, a fundamental question arises: does free trade combined with financial liberalization and macroeconomic coordination impede further industrialization by "locking in" the specificities and existing comparative advantages and disadvantages of more backward regions? Does this set of policies also thereby lock in LFC backwardness itself?

Let us consider a stylized story. The opening up of trade generates a new type of competition in manufacturing. Competition does not create equal pressures upon unequally qualified partners. Instead, pressure is disproportionately felt by firms and infrastructure in LFCs because of their lower average productivity and quality. An unlimited variety of reactive tactics can then be mounted by enterprises. These can usefully be classified into three categories: atomistic reactions, collective business reactions, and government-coordinated reactions. Within each category we distinguish between two basic types of measures with fundamentally different implications for economic adjustment of LFCs:

- measures that are forward looking and strategic, and thus capable of generating new prospects and new strength to face competition;
- measures that are purely defensive and reactive, and thus incapable of creating conditions to better withstand new bouts of intense international competition.

This distinction centers on the viability of different adjustment strategies. Purely defensive adjustments ultimately exhaust themselves. Strategic adjustments are capable of creating new prospects, albeit never with certainty. Since the distinction between defensive and strategic types of adjustment can be applied to all three of our categories, it follows that the analysis of the character of adjustment should not be limited to the firm, but must be extended to collective business and government reactions to competitive pressure as well.

Atomistic reactions by enterprises

Defensive atomistic reactions to increased international competition often involve cost-cutting by means of wage restraints, lower quality inputs, increased tax evasion, and attempts to delay or directly violate financial obligations. Each of these tactics can produce immediate relief for the firm that has come under competitive pressure. Most of them also imply that the firm employing them gives up some potential asset that might prove useful in the future. Thus, a reduction in input quality will eventually contribute to deeper loss of competitive advantage. Wage cuts may mean the loss of loyalty and skills of the more mobile and valued employees, who may seek jobs elsewhere. Increased tax evasion will force the firm to avoid a multiplicity of useful contacts with public authorities. Breaking financial promises creates the risk of creditor response, and will, in any case, tarnish the firm's future ability to raise capital through a negative reputation effect. Raising prices, another possible atomistic reaction to the erosion of profitability from international competition, is a rather unlikely choice, unless there is some element of business coordination, as we shall examine below.

Forward-looking strategies can also be delineated within the category of atomistic reactions. These might include a redesign of process and product, reorganization of the firm so as to obtain more cohesion and flexibility, penetrating new market niches, and, most importantly, enhancing the ability to learn and to transform learning into action and into market access. All of these are examples of actions that involve the deployment of a strategic stance towards competition, and of a longer-term perspective of firm survival and growth.

Compared to forward-looking strategies, purely defensive reactions appear not only limited but also counterproductive. They may contradict the firm's attempts to reorganize its activities and its links to input and output markets. Thus, pure cost-cutting without parallel reorganization is simply a short-term reaction that may have negative effects on the long-term prospects of a firm.[2]

In effect, the ability of any firm to rise above defensive policies and pursue more strategic adjustment will depend on a number of *intrafirm* factors, some of them predictable. The size of the firm's capital will become an important factor in the sense that reorganization and strategic reaction usually require time and some risk-taking. A more amply capitalized firm is normally much better able to undertake strategic adjustment. In this respect then, both the initial size of capital (and of the firm), and the channels of access to outside capital that can support the process of adjustment become important. The quality of the firm's human resources is another source of influence. Flexibility of human skills is important to adjustment. Organizational flexibility, such as the ease of dissolving a firm and forming another, can also play a role in the ability of entrepreneurial interests to reshape themselves. Lastly, the quality of the firm as organization, its ability to learn collectively and to pursue adjustments in tandem with learning, is of prime importance.[3]

Collective business reactions

Let us now consider the category of collective business reactions. Under certain conditions a collective reaction to a competitive crisis can take the form of sectoral coordination. In this case, firms might attempt to increase product prices if they can enforce a common price policy. This type of reaction, however, becomes highly unlikely where free trade prevails and import competition is active. A policy of wage cuts could also be sectorally, or even intersectorally, designed and enforced, assuming that collective bargaining arrangements are available. Finally, various types of pressure could be brought to bear upon government to undertake its own measures (discussed below) for the relief of crisis-stricken sectors. This array of alternatives describes the basic defensive modes available for collective action in face of a competitive crisis.

Alternatively, a variety of forms of interfirm cooperation or networking can be envisaged, representing modes of strategic collective action that provide long-term boosts to sectors, subsectors, or even intersectoral groupings (see Best 1990, especially Chapters 8–9). Two fundamental types of action will be distinguished here in order to focus the discussion. The first includes forms of cooperation that improve *efficiency in the use of existing resources* by either enforcing a certain degree of division of labor, or by securing economies of scale in parts of the production and distribution process. Examples include: exchange of information about markets for inputs and outputs; common undertakings *vis-à-vis* suppliers of important inputs; schemes for mutual assistance in export markets; and pre-established specializations in the design of products or in the manufacture of certain components of products. All of these may be considered as a first stage of networking among firms in one or more sectors. These forms of networking are relatively easy to secure in the sense that they depend on individual firms' desires to maximize the utilization of resources that have been already committed as the result of individual decisions by the respective firms. Yet, such arrangements are not always forthcoming in the context of LFCs. An important question therefore concerns the type of institutional arrangements that encourage cooperative solutions to use existing resources. This is a matter to which we return below.

A second and more advanced type of cooperation involves undertaking collective investment for cost reduction, product improvement, increasing productivity, and ameliorating market access. Collective investments can range over a wide variety of possibilities, choices, and activities. Frequent examples are: common training centers for specialized personnel; purchasing and marketing cooperatives; common technical research centers; mutual guarantee financing schemes; trading companies; and export promotion schemes. Compared to coordinating actions over already committed resources, collective investments must overcome obstacles of a higher order of magnitude in order to be feasible. Such investments require an agreement on project definition among all parties to a collective undertaking; they require sharing rules about the costs and benefits of the investment. They also require mutually acceptable monitoring arrangements regarding continued performance or discontinuation of the project. These tasks can be quite complex, and this complexity may prohibit their realization. Again, institutional arrangements are critical to the design and enforcement of rules for sharing collective investments. Another important question focuses on whether there are optimal groupings of firms for the conception, design, and realization of collective investments.

Government coordinated reactions

Let us finally consider the category of government-coordinated actions relating to competitive adjustment. Again the dichotomy between short-term defensive and strategic actions can be represented with clarity. The former are usually those taken under the pressure of an unfolding crisis, or under lobbying pressure by business and other social groups for immediate protection. These actions are, of course, mediated by the political environment and circumstance. The stability of a government, which depends on the size and coherence of its parliamentary majority, may make it more or less prone to yield to such pressures. The approach of elections may also influence government decisions to offer short-term relief to sectors affected by competitive pressure. Also, the fiscal position of the government at the time of competitive adjustment can be influential, since surpluses make it much easier to provide short-term relief than pre-existing deficits allow.

A fundamental aspect of short-term defensive action by government is that it can use the tool of income redistribution to support those agents whose returns diminish under competitive pressure. This action may be completely justifiable on short-term grounds, but it always runs the risk of becoming a permanent feature of government-sponsored redistribution, long after the period of adjustment to any exogenous competitive shock has passed. In this case, a bona fide program of temporary relief can turn into a politically sanctioned entitlement. The knowledge that this possibility exists, in turn engenders rent-seeking behaviors on the part of potential recipients under the guise of crisis relief. Consequently, the appearance of political demands for protection will, on balance, outrun the true necessity. Subsidies, income supports, and tax forgiveness offered for special purposes, are various tools that may mask the provision of rents. Equally, they could be tools used for strategic action. Whether they represent one or the other depends on other aspects of policy, which ensure its strategic character. The tendency for industrial policies intended to grant temporary protection to be frozen into entitlement schemes represents a policy life cycle that is the exact opposite of policy-learning. Instead of shifting supports from proven failures to prospective successes, policy freezes in favor of failures and perpetuates their existence.

Strategic action taken by government must necessarily seek to serve the goal of supporting the formulation and consistent implementation of strategic actions at the two other levels of decision-making – the atomistic actions of firms and the collective actions of business groups. Government action must therefore involve both the production of strategic public goods, and the supply of "framework arrangements" that facilitate more desegregated strategic actions to be undertaken by others. In essence, these two categories of activity run parallel to the classic agenda of traditional development theory which prescribed that governments should provide infrastructure and should correct market failures. The context of the present discussion is, of course, much more specific than that of traditional development theory. Nevertheless, this discussion can be informed by insights that development theory has supplied, including the incidence of so-called government failures.[4]

A crucial aspect of government capabilities in the context of macroeconomic coordination is that the degree of freedom of policy action is highly reduced relative to that available to the state as viewed by earlier development theorists. Explicit commitments to macroeconomic coordination, such as those undertaken by national governments in the European Union, for example, rule out the use of large fiscal deficits, exchange-rate devaluations, and a whole series of subsidies, as tools of domestic policy. Furthermore, with intercountry capital mobility, government policies are continuously subjected to market discipline in the form of actual or potential pressure on the balance of payments, and on domestic financial markets. Thus, the context of strategic policies for industrialization of LFCs in integrating economies is necessarily one of parsimonious resource commitments on the part of the public sector, and of linkages between private and public action that will be stable, efficient, and relatively error-free in the utilization of scarce resources, public or private. In fact, as compared to the traditional vision of the state in development theory, our specific context involves much less emphasis on the use of the state to generate savings directly for investment, and much more emphasis on the use of the state to generate *coordination among agents* who make saving and investment decisions in the national economy.

HURDLES TO STRATEGIC ACTIVITIES: THE FUNDAMENTALS OF SHORT-TERMIST BEHAVIOR IN LFCs

A critical policy question is how to effect the transformation from a regime of short-term defensive reactions to a pattern of strategic actions. Short-termism in the broadest sense is a syndrome affecting all actors in an economy: firms, business associations, labor unions, and government. A policy that places LFCs on a sustained path of industrialization must overcome short-termism at many levels simultaneously. Stated differently, it is necessary to engender an entire cluster of social actors to switch from short-termist to strategic behaviors. The important point is not simply how each type of actor can be individually and separately lured into strategic action, but rather how they can collectively switch to strategic action, taking into account interdependencies and mutual reinforcements, positive or negative. Strategic action is a process that involves considerable externalities, and these can be internalized only by movement that is sufficiently collective.

Before discussing the externalities of strategic behavior, a few typological observations must be borne in mind. It is, of course, difficult and risky to offer accurate general characterizations of LFCs and their industrial structures. Yet, some simplifications are necessary in order to proceed. We present three stylized facts: first, LFCs tend to be price-takers in world markets; second, industrial structures in LFCs involve a much lower presence of "world class" firms, or even of "region class" firms, compared to their more advanced partners; and third, LFCs are also "technology-takers," that is, strong importers of technology that normally comes embodied in capital goods, or in prearranged production processes.

These plausible generalizations have important implications for the analysis of strategic behaviors. On the one hand, they imply that economic agents in LFCs must build their strategies using building blocks that are determined by others. The perennial problem of the latecomer is that it must succeed in a world where first movers have already established many parameters like prices, technologies, major markets, and networks of large corporations serving these markets. On the other hand, our generalizations also imply that average economic agents in LFCs are unable to mount individual strategic responses because they are too small, too weak, and incapable of asserting substantial control on their environment. Finally, this inherent weakness of LFC firms is manifested in relatively shallow value-added chains, both in an intrafirm sense and in the sense that entire economies may lack vertical depth. Uncertainty and unpredictability of outcomes is then a fundamental obstacle to strategic action. The basic condition for the feasibility of strategic response is therefore a combination of agents that can sufficiently control their environment and that can impose a modicum of predictability on the effects of various courses of action.[5] The important questions are self-evident: What are the best ways to obtain such combinations? What is the role of government in fostering them? And what institutional arrangements can support, sustain, and enable them to flourish?

The externalities of strategic action are both positive and negative, with regard to individual firms. Positive externalities arise from strategic complementarity. When a firm undertakes an innovation, for example, its success will be dependent on other firms' parallel initiatives. Cases in point are: the upgrading of inputs and of their delivery pattern by supplier firms; the availability of technical expertise for service and repair of new equipment; the supply of qualified personnel for required new tasks; and the availability of marketing outlets into new markets. Strong world-class firms in leading industrialized countries may be able to marshal a good portion of these resources and functions on an in-house basis, thereby internalizing the externality, and subjecting the combination of strategic inputs to hierarchical coordination. Weaker firms in LFCs will, as a rule, be much more dependent on extrafirm cooperation for securing the same effects. Interfirm coordination mechanisms are then required. This coordination may be forthcoming through markets. However, classic problems of market failure make necessary the emergence of extramarket coordination, especially in LFCs.[6]

Market failures that are due to captivity and free-rider problems are quite valid and frequent in the business environment of LFCs. This is precisely due to the weakness of the average firm, the shallowness of the value-added chains represented by firms, and the unavailability of codes of business ethics that cover long-lived transactional chains (as opposed to easily finalized and rapidly concluded transactions). The problem of captivity arises precisely from strategic complementarities. When one agent precedes others in tying up resources in uses that require complementary action from other agents, it risks becoming the captive of others. Lacking a pre-existing agreement or other restraining means, other agents are tempted to extract from the prime mover most of its profit, as compensation for undertaking the complementary action.[7] Clearly this is a disincentive for becoming a prime mover, and such a disincentive can prove costly in the case of LFCs, which need prime movers badly.

The problem of free riding is a well-known externality, whereby the benefits from a certain good (or service) are not fully captured by the good's owner or purchaser, but can be diffused to other users who do not bear the initial costs of purchase or investment. In the case of LFCs this can be a common problem regarding infrastructure investments. Well-accepted public goods in the form of roads, ports, and telecommunication lines fall clearly in the purview of public investment initiatives. They share the basic characteristic that they involve large immobile investments whose services are easily diffused. However, not only so-called hard infrastructures are involved; "soft" aspects of infrastructure are not normally found in the traditional arsenal of public investments, but their importance is heightened in the context of present conditions in LFCs. A fundamental example is skilled personnel. Externalities related to personnel arise not from fixity and immobility, as in the case of hard infrastructures, but from quite the reverse: high mobility. The risk of a highly trained individual moving to another firm leads to underinvestment in skills, or, secondarily, to a definition of skills in ways that are not transferable to other firms without substantial additional costs. In world-class firms the second alternative is far more easily attainable than in weak LFC firms. Hence, underinvestment in skills, which is a general tendency of private firms, is expected to appear as an even stronger tendency in LFC firms.

Externalities associated with the emergence or suppression of strategic behaviors are not only firm-to-firm problems: they can also be found in firm-to-government relationships. For example, firms that undertake immobile investments under a favorable tax regime may later be subjected to a change in tax treatment by a subsequently elected government. This is again a problem of captivity, whose possible emergence may discourage private investment. On the other hand, governments may also suffer from being captive to private firms. For example, in the construction of public works, private contractors sometimes require *ex-post* increases in compensation to complete a project, exploiting the government's prior commitments to its constituents to furnish a particular project, and also the government's inability, due to rules of public accountability, to allow prior disbursements to go to waste.

At first glance then, strategic action is riddled with externalities, and its realization is often impeded by the absence of appropriate institutional arrangements that enable both the internalization of externalities, and the stabilization of mutual commitments over time. In that sense, short-termism is not so much characteristic of the ideology of economic agents, but rather a manifestation of their inability to overcome obstacles to strategic action. There are other sources of short-termist impulses as well. Important systemic causes of anti-strategic behaviors in LFCs can spring from politics and financial markets.

Authoritative writers on government and government failure suggest that democratic politics, the need to win elections, and the shortness of elected terms endow political decision-makers with short-term horizons and strong time preferences.[8] This view has found its way into a great variety of theoretical work on the behavior of governments and the content of policies.[9] Of course, advanced industrial democracies have also long had institutional arrangements that protect and promote public policies of a long-term character. Examples range from tax allowances for investment to special credit institutions to finance long-term assets. Needless to say, many of these institutions have been subject to waves of negative political sentiment, such as the trend to market liberalization of the last decade. Still, they have been instrumental in embedding incentives for long-term action in democratic political systems.

An important question is whether political short-termism extends to public policies in LFCs, and whether it has different effects than in more advanced countries. This question can be further subdivided: first, are institutional arrangements that support long-term resource commitments less available in LFCs? and second, are demands for political short-termist type actions more intense in LFCs? Casual observation suggests that the answer to the first question is negative, while the second is more likely to be positive. Institutional arrangements have not been absent in LFCs, at least at the central level of public policy. Institutions to support long-term economic initiative certainly have been active in LFCs, although serious differences are apparent regarding their success. These range from investment incentive laws to tax credits to development agencies (e.g. the Irish IDA), to development funds or banks (e.g. the Italian Cassa per il Mezzogiorno or the Greek ETVA). On the other hand, it is precisely the international competitive pressures that have descended on the LFCs that stimulate additional social demands for short-termist type actions to be undertaken by their political classes. Economic crisis evokes demands for relief, and relief requires, at first pass, redistributive action. However, if relief is excessive so that it magnifies macroeconomic imbalances, the requirements of macroeconomic coordination trigger stabilization countermeasures, which are frequently equally short-termist. Thus, a cycle of short-termist actions and reactions may set in.

Financial markets, the other important source underlying short-termism takes many forms, depending on the influence and role of financial intermediaries, government controls on credit, and freedom of international capital flows. The most significant recent trend has been financial liberalization, and the increasing role of arm's-length markets for the placement and trading of instruments issued by firms, i.e. direct markets for money instruments, bonds, shares, or derivatives based thereon (see OECD 1995). These markets regulate capital values and supply discipline to firms by rewarding or penalizing their performance through price adjustments. They therefore improve the allocation and utilization of investable funds. This proposition has been at the foundation of theoretical and political initiatives for financial market liberalization in both developed and developing economies.[10]

One critique leveled at financial systems organized around arm's-length markets is that they may induce short-termism in the managers of firms, since market investors are interested in current stock price achievements rather than future gains. The highly competitive character of successful financial markets undoubtedly guarantees an efficient current valuation of a firm, but at the same time it may be a disadvantage to firms if only a few individual investors are able to recognize and evaluate a firm's strategic action, or have the patience to wait out the results. In that case, the "impatience of finance" will dissuade decision-makers from undertaking strategic action, as this may, in fact, harm their standing with opinion-makers in the financial community. The converse of this argument is that strategic action is more compatible with "patient finance," external funding provided by an intermediary capable of separating the evaluation of users from the particular needs and perceptions of the primary suppliers of finance. Banks, venture capitalists, and a host of other financial institutions usually do this.

In summary then, the factors that engender short-termism in economic behaviors in LFCs include inabilities to internalize externalities, political behaviors in response to crisis, and competitive investor behavior in arm's-length markets with limited information. The relative intensity of each category of causes may vary in each case. Any attempts to overcome short-termism and enhance strategic behavior must address all categories if they are to be generic. It is clear that a great deal of weight must be placed on institutional arrangements, in the political, economic, and regulatory spheres. The arguments put forth here answer the first question we posed at the outset: institutional arrangements promoting industrialization will not arise spontaneously, but require intervention in order to survive against the forces that promote short-term behavior.

ON THE INSTITUTIONAL AGENDA FOR SUSTAINED INDUSTRIALIZATION

Two sets of factors prevent the application of generalized institutional formulae to groups of countries, or even to different regions within a country: cultural variations and historical differences. Culture embraces traditions of trust and structures of cooperation among individuals. History refers to collective experiences of both progress and crisis. Culture and history are deep influences on basic forms of human socialization: relations between the individual and the state, and with correlate forms of authority. The variation in these forms is vast. The peculiarities of history and culture determine the type and sophistication of institutional arrangements that emerge from below, from civil society, as well as the success or failure of institutions that are implemented from above, by elites controlling the state. Hence, meaningful institutional agendas can only include a set of minimum requirements and some likely examples of how they could be made to work in desirable fashion.

Countries such as LFCs emerge with an array of institutional arrangements that were designed to support their earlier phase of partial industrialization, but which may not be appropriate for the next phase of sustained industrialization. Reevaluation of existing institutions is, therefore, a primary requirement, with the goal of revamping or replacing arrangements that are no longer suitable. The transition to sustained industrialization generally entails five different shifts in focus, each with important implications for institutions:

1 The new phase of industrialization will be undertaken under much more open economic conditions, requiring ventures with potential to quickly become internationally competitive. Inevitably, product quality, innovative capability, productive flexibility, and technological content become more important parameters than in the early phase of industrialization, which occurred in protected national markets.

2 Traditional tools of national trade-cum-industrial policy, such as tariff protection, export subsidies, and competitive devaluations of the national currency, are ruled out through LFC's membership in international arrangements for free trade and macroeconomic coordination.

3 Early industrialization is highly dependent on the supply of hard infrastructures. Continued industrialization increasingly depends on other types of collective goods (e.g. training, information, expertise, insurance) which are more specialized, less tangible, and have a higher service content.

4 Early industrialization is akin to colonization of an empty, or sparsely utilized, space. Sustained industrialization must be weaved into already occupied spaces, and must therefore take account of existing assets, values, and capabilities. This implies an inevitable "situated" character to policy.

5 Early industrialization produces populations of active industrial firms capable of economic calculus and administrative action; sustained industrialization increases the feasibility of substituting purely private ventures by public–private or cooperative–private ventures.

These lines of change describe the terrain of new or modified institutional arrangements: Macroeconomic tools must be phased out in favor of intermediate or microeconomic tools; national market information must be supplemented by international market-monitoring; local information about existing capabilities must be embodied in policies; and a diversity of collective initiatives must be allowed to replace existing public ones. At the same time, tackling the systemic causes of short-termism in industrial enterprises, namely political and financial market biases, must supplement the institutional agenda.

We turn first to the political prerequisites. Sustained industrialization must become an active part of the political discourse in LFCs. Giving priority to goals of macroeconomic stability and market liberalization is a common component of the political agenda that advanced partners have successfully diffused to LFCs. Thus, for example, the overwhelming political priority of economic and monetary union in the European Union generates a political discourse centered on the need to attain and safeguard monetary stability. This relegates industrialization to a secondary role, whereas it should be a major goal in the specific circumstances of LFCs, precisely as a complement to the Union-wide emphasis on monetary stability. Furthermore, policies of macroeconomic stabilization are often couched in neoliberal conceptions of the need to limit government influence, privatize parts of the public sector, and give more freedom to markets. These conceptions may be correct in recognizing government failure, but their ideological orientation is clearly tilted against recognition of market failures, even though the latter are prime obstacles to sustained industrialization. Realistic political formulations designed to promote industrialization in LFCs should be thoughtful and selective, rather than cultivate the falsehood that markets alone will automatically foster industrialization.

The public structures that implement policy, as well as readjust it in response to new information and changing circumstances, are of central importance. Once the goal of industrialization has been legitimized by its insertion in political discourse, effective and flexible implementation require a degree of political autonomy for policymakers in order to overcome the short-termist political bias. As development economist Pranab Bardhan has aptly put it:

> it is not so much authoritarianism per se which makes a difference, but the extent of insulation (or 'relative autonomy') that the decision-makers can organize against the ravages of short-run pork-barrel politics. Authoritarianism is neither necessary nor sufficient for this insulation. The difficult political challenge . . . is to construct a durable coalition of modernizing interests under freer and wider participation.
>
> (Bardhan 1990: 5)

Autonomy of decision-makers in a democratic polity implies a mixture of independence and accountability. A much touted current example of institutional autonomy is the independence of central banks. Inasmuch as sustained industrialization is as important a goal as monetary stability for LFCs, one can argue for comparable institutional autonomy of an industrial development authority. Just as the autonomous central bank is charged with safeguarding the stability of money, the industrial development authority's autonomy could be constituted around the goal of safeguarding the level, quality, and requisite returns of public investment in hard or soft infrastructures, strategic collective ventures, and innovation schemes.

The analogy between central banks and industrial development authorities is limited by issues of scale and information. The mission of a central bank is organized around an item that is, by construction, transacted on a national scale: national money. The mission of an industrial development authority should be organized around transactions with significant specificities at the subnational level (regional, local, and sectoral). As we have already argued, these specificities arise from externalities appearing in smaller-than-national contexts, local information about existing assets and capabilities, and local or sectoral policy successes and failures. It may be cumbersome and very costly for a national authority to collect and assess such information, whereas more decentralized structures could prove far more efficient. The appreciation of this point is evident in assessments derived from more advanced industrial economies; for example, a lesson from German experience suggests that, "successful structural policies are often those adopted by institutions small enough to develop an intimate understanding of the microeconomics of regional development but large enough – and with the necessary political legitimacy – to act upon them" (Amin and Tomaney 1995b: 309).

In more industrialized countries, the industrial ethic is an accepted and unifying element of social culture. But LFCs probably need a mixed system to attain the required combination of local information efficiency and political legitimacy. Decentralized institutional entities, enjoying common principles but different tools, could be organized under the umbrella of a national industrial development authority, along the lines of the corporate structure of a holding company. This type of arrangement would allow both variety in the forms of intervention, and unifying principles. Furthermore, although strategic initiatives may have mainly local or regional character, positive externalities may indeed arise from cooperation across regions, or even across countries. Part of the mandate for the umbrella organization, therefore, should be the promotion of coordinated schemes that extend beyond local or regional boundaries.

Primary industrial policy interventions will consist of the supply of coordination services. The main purpose of these services will be to exploit positive and overcome negative externalities. Further, policy will largely take the form of projects involving programs of commitments, collective investments, and so forth. Consequently, several important principles should inform the institutional structure with regard to *project origination* and *project design* on the one hand, and *project implementation* on the other.

Project origination should rarely be rooted in the public authority, but must, with increasing emphasis, emanate from interested firms or social groups. For example, a firm proposing a program of measures with collective benefit may require help in seeking commitments from other potential program beneficiaries. The ability of interested parties to initiate projects is essential, both for access to local information and for local legitimization.

Project design must seek to internalize as many of the external effects as possible. This requires authorities to seek out optimal combinations of program participants, as well as desirable implementation tools. These tools may consist simply of trust-building measures among a small group of firms so that fears of capture may be allayed; they may take the form of a coordinated program of modernizing adjustments in a large group of firms; or finally, they may involve a collective investment with narrow, wide, or even transnational externalities. The design must always generate interest on the part of initial participants to continue their participation. One important tool for establishing credible commitments can be to require initial resource commitments by participants. Efficient project design is one that allows the parties involved to switch collectively to strategic decision-making, and which facilitates the maximization of benefits from these decisions.

Project implementation must include not only monitoring the execution of commonly agreed decisions, but also, and more importantly, monitoring the achievements of these decisions. A basic flaw of many industrial policy interventions, such as investment subsidies, is that they fail to assess their own effectiveness because they lack the capacity for *ex-post* observation of performance.[11] This capability must be contractually enforced, and can be further strengthened by making pecuniary public assistance contingent on performance. Continued monitoring is beneficial both in promoting policy flexibility (i.e. the ability to correct, adjust, and fine tune policy), and in facilitating coordination among participants. The latter is essential because groups of nominally independent firms will and must maintain some competition between them.[12] Hence, centrifugal tendencies will naturally arise. A mix of cooperation and competition is a desideratum for genuine and successful industrial districts precisely because it keeps alive both the ability of latecoming firms to enter cooperative arrangements, and because it is also more likely to maintain active incentives for innovation.[13] Yet, the mix is frequently unstable and may require external (policy) energies in order to remain in operation.[14] Free riding is a problem that will typically develop during the implementation of strategic initiatives; for example, the incentive to cheat upon previously concluded agreements is a fundamental feature of opportunistic behavior.

Ex-post monitoring does not have to be associated solely with regulatory intent. It can become the basis of additional supply-side interventions. So-called soft follow-up policy measures, including training, one-stop shopping for enterprises, and general "after-care" support, have been identified as important elements of policy in North European less favored regions (Amin and Tomaney 1995a: 214–217). Monitoring must be fashioned to furnish a foundation for such supply-side activities on the part of public authorities. If this is achieved, firms will more likely comply voluntarily with the information requirements imposed upon them for successful monitoring.

A major advantage of a decentralized institutional network that can effect policies at the intermediate and microeconomic levels is that it can engender a movement towards a more developmentalist culture of industrialization at the local political and governmental level. Decentralized networks can also more effectively deal with negative externalities, such as microenvironmental issues. They may become hubs for the devolution of various collective actions that seek coordinated responses to a range of social and economic problems, as, for example, those associated with unemployment and social exclusion, environmental protection, continuing education, or the organization of social support networks. In short, a successful decentralized public authority, with a broad mandate for promoting industrial transformation using a pluralistic set of instruments, can itself become the source of positive social externalities.

THE FINANCIAL SYSTEM AND SUSTAINED INDUSTRIALIZATION

Financial market liberalization has become a dominant policy goal in most semi-industrialized countries. In the preliberalization era, finance was broadly used to coordinate industrial policy in these countries.[15] The advantages of liberalized financial markets are many: a more differentiated supply of financial products to savers with rising incomes; a better allocation of finance to alternative investment uses; and a disciplining function on firms' managers towards constant optimization of performance. Financial market liberalization expands the role of arm's-length financial markets. But its disadvantage is to impose short-term horizons on decision-makers, who are pushed to maximize current value rather than undertake initiatives with long gestation periods. This is what we earlier called the effect of *impatient finance*. Strategic investment may be harmed by impatient finance for two reasons. First, it is based on complex calculations, contingent on outcomes outside the immediate control of the firm. Complexity and wide-ranging uncertainty are not well suited to the evaluative capabilities of competitive arm's-length markets, which normally function with standardized devices for collecting and interpreting information. Second, strategic initiatives often involve confidential information that must remain private for competitive reasons and cannot, therefore, be broadcast in open financial markets. Both these reasons suggest that strategic initiatives are especially conducive to information asymmetries between entrepreneurs and investors. Information asymmetries are known to be a fundamental cause of divergence of market outcomes from efficient equilibria (see Stiglitz and Weiss 1981).

Traditional systems of financial control, as used in most industrializing countries, were systems that could supply *patient finance*. Practically all were based on indirect financing via intermediaries, commercial or development banks, and other more specialized credit institutions. Institutional finance attempted to attain three goals in controlled credit environments:

1 concentrate sufficiently in preferred sectors so as to achieve an emergence of strategic complementarities from parallel actions of many firms;
2 spread the risk from many long bets, so as not to endanger the capital base of financing institutions (which were typically large); and
3 tailor financing terms, such as grace periods, maturities, and collaterals, to the specific needs of preferred strategic projects or sectors.

Inasmuch as credit control systems were coincident with credit rationing, they carried a fundamental flaw as well. Rationing can be based on multiple criteria. Under stress and where political short-termism permeates credit rationing schemes, a system of patient finance can degenerate into a system of clientelistic finance. Ultimately, this degeneration can lead to a worse distribution of risks, threaten the capital base of institutions, and render the entire system unsound and unsustainable. In several countries, the impulse for financial liberalization has arisen from such tendencies.[16]

Patient finance for the benefit of sustained LFC industrialization must be designed within a mixed system that attempts to combine the advantages and limit the disadvantages of earlier designs. It would seem undesirable, for example, to suggest a new generation of publicly owned financial institutions that would engage in development banking. Instead, a more decentralized solution should be pursued, one that combines market discipline with an ability to finance high-risk strategic ventures. Such a general formulation of objectives opens up a wide range of conjecture, but can draw only limited insights from recorded experience. In this spirit, an initial proposition can be made. A public interventionist authority, such as the one posited in the previous section, *should not* be endowed with great financial powers.[17] The main financing source for strategic ventures of firms should be rooted either in the self-finance of enterprises, or in finance supplied by autonomous institutions that are ultimately subject to market discipline. Naturally, channels for diffusion of information between an industrial development agency and designated financial institutions should also be part of the scheme. Yet, if the power of project-planning and the power of finance remain basically separated, this will protect the integrity of both processes through a system of "checks and balances." It is nevertheless clear that just as networking at the level of firms can internalize externalities, so also networking of specialized financial institutions, with each other and with the public interventionist authority, can produce analogous effects with respect to informational and risk-sharing externalities.

The experience of advanced industrial countries indicates that a sufficient variety of institutional forms and instruments has been generated within developed financial systems; clearly, this variety enables the use or adaptation of some of these institutions and instruments as prototypes for industrial finance in semi-industrialized countries. At the risk of being eclectic, one can focus on two examples that appear to offer new possibilities for LFCs: venture capital and mutual guarantee schemes. The former is an institutional form of finance particularly suited to risky initiatives and to developmental possibilities of innovative firms. The mutual guarantee scheme is an institutional form of a cooperative nature, particularly suited to cooperative ventures and to collective self-monitoring among its participants. Both these specialized institutional forms can be adapted to local conditions, while at the same time integrating into the broader financial system.

Possible models for specific techniques and instruments of finance might include those developed for project finance, which usually involve complex financing programs of several clients who are simultaneously involved in the execution of a large project. These complex financing schemes represent non-market coordinated arrangements that solve strategic financing problems that would prove insuperable in open markets. Finally, even within the context of arm's-length financial markets, more complex instruments are also available for the finance of strategic initiatives, high-risk ventures, or innovation programs. The most common example is the set of convertible securities, offering a large and flexible arsenal of potential instruments for industrial finance.[18] The design of a convertible instrument can enable the supplier of finance to reap future benefits contingent on the success of the strategic investment, while at the same time provide the receiver of finance with an incentive to maximize effort for its success.

A rudimentary agenda for public policy initiatives in the area of financial systems that appears compatible with the goals of continued industrialization should embrace several notions:

1 Given the general trend towards market liberalization, emphasis should be placed on prudential regulation of markets and financial institutions. Adequate regulation can ensure that the former remain free from pricing distortions, as far as possible, and that the latter remain sound, in terms of capital base and ability to withstand risks. A financial system that is itself well protected against risks should be able to better provide patient finance.

2 Within the context of liberalization, policy should underwrite and encourage institutional pluralism on the one hand, and a differentiation of instruments on the other. Pluralism implies that possibilities for specialization of institutions and for the customizing of instruments will become abundant at the start of the process of reindustrialization, and that there will be ample space for social learning through practice in the area of financial relations.

3 The design and maintenance of channels of information between public authorities charged with industrialization initiatives and financial institutions specializing in development finance is a necessary policy for the

reduction of information asymmetry that, if left untreated, will create financial disadvantage for strategic initiatives.

CONCLUSION

The basic tenet of this chapter is that sustained industrialization in LFCs will not arise spontaneously from market forces, especially in the context of trade liberalization and macroeconomic coordination with more advanced industrial partners. It requires policy intervention of a new type. The fundamental goal of policy intervention must be to engender strategic behavior among business, labor, and government actors. The institutional agenda for sustained industrialization in LFCs must fashion tools capable of supplying coordination with flexibility, in order to support that behavior. The ability to learn via monitoring and adjustment, and the enforcement of market discipline via the mechanisms of institutional finance are indispensable ingredients to renewed industrial policy. Policy parameters must nevertheless be situated in a great variety of ways, given national or regional specificities of culture and history. The study of these specificities, and the ability to learn from the example of the experience of industrialized countries, constitute tasks for further policy research.

The success of social forces in LFCs in overcoming short-termist behaviors must be understood as an outcome of mutual reinforcements between firms, governments, and other social organizations. Coordinated action can produce results whose scale will surpass by far the sum of results from particularistic and isolated efforts. Hence, the construction of strategic consensus among social forces is not only a condition that makes long-term initiatives compatible with a democratic order; it is also a necessity for economic and industrial development and for increasing social welfare in LFCs.

NOTES

1 See Gereffi 1990 for a comparative overview of the policies and processes of industrialization in middle-income countries in Latin America and East Asia.
2 The distinction here is reminiscent of a distinction arising in recent literature about "performance firms" versus "cost-cutting" or "price-sensitive firms." The former are those that seek competitive advantage from product quality, innovation, and new market creation. A fundamental question is how can an existing or new firm be nudged towards the model of the "performance firm" in the context of LFCs. See Mytelka 1991.
3 Interfirm factors can make a substantial difference in the enhancement of intrafirm factor effects. These are discussed further below. On the learning quality of organizations see M. Teubal's contribution in this volume (Chapter 5).
4 See Krueger 1995 for a comprehensive review of the concepts of market and government failure, and its contextual significance in the evolution of development thinking.
5 The core of this idea goes back to Gerschenkron's views of backwardness and of how it can be overcome; see Gerschenkron 1962. The important role of combination of agents in latecomers is obvious throughout the experiences of successful

late development. It is also obvious, however, that combinations can take a great variety of forms, ranging from the Korean chaebols to the networks of small firms in the "Third Italy."

6 Examples of nonmarket coordination among firms abound in highly industrialized countries of course. Besides the common references to the "Third Italy," see Lorenz 1991 for an interesting example in France.

7 For a classic exposition of this problem see Williamson 1975. In Williamson's view, this problem is a major incentive for vertical integration. In LFCs, however, vertical integration may be a costly alternative because of the lack of capital, lack of expertise to manage large organizations, and chiefly because it may represent an inflexible solution that disallows easy exit from the cooperative arrangement at a later point in time.

8 A detailed essay on the analysis of government and market failures is offered in Wolf 1988. See especially Chapter 3 where the time structure of political rewards is discussed in the context of democratic politics.

9 The recognition of short political horizons is inherent, for example, in two very separate strands of literature. On one hand, political cycle analysis has been theoretically developed after the seminal contribution of Nordhaus 1975, basically pertaining to democracies and electoral processes. For an example of empirical work related to industrialized democracies along that line see Soh 1986. On the other hand, the converse side of the argument seems to imply that long-term horizons and strategic state action are more compatible with political authoritarianism of some type. Thus, considerable literature is devoted to the notion that the "developmentalist state" is also an autocratic state, as witnessed by East Asian examples and experiences. See Deyo 1987 and Cheng 1990 for expositions on the political character of the regimes in Korea and Taiwan.

10 At the origin of the drive for financial liberalization in developing countries is the famous presentation and critique of "financial repression" in McKinnon 1973 and Shaw 1973. For a review of issues, debates, and political dimensions of financial liberalization in industrializing economies see Haggard and Lee (1993).

11 The implementation of Greek investment incentive laws, which provide most of the subsidy up front, has had that serious flaw for the last decade. As soon as it is certified that the subsidized investment is in place, the public authority withdraws from the process. As a result, no one knows the measurable effect of the incentive schemes.

12 The fundamental nature of the firm's activities in the rich conception of "New Competition" offered by M. Best, consists precisely of a mix of competition and cooperation, which can be achieved by self-initiatives of firms in a sector or an industrial district. See Best 1990, especially Chapter. 9. In LFCs, and wherever the culture of cooperation is weak, flexible policy can furnish a ground for such outcomes.

13 The process of innovation itself can optimally contain elements of both cooperation and competition. See Jorde and Teece 1990.

14 In a simple but attractive example, Krugman (1995) shows how a manufacturing sector may be faced with two equilibria, where one internalizes externalities and the other does not. The presumption here is that more effort is required to achieve the solution of equilibrium-cum-externalities, and that this effort should be at the basis of policy intervention.

15 See, for example, the series of country studies for Latin America and East Asia in Haggard, Lee, and Maxfield 1993. See also Halikias 1978 for a detailed exposition of credit controls in Greece.

16 On the transition from credit controls to financial liberalization, see several interesting case studies: Cheng 1993 for Taiwan; Hutchcroft 1993 for the Philippines; Hastings 1993 for Chile; and Maxfield 1993 for Mexico.

17 Pure public goods are of course excluded from this proposition.
18 Classic instruments of this type are warrants (a type of option to buy shares in the future) and convertible bonds. Both instruments include contractual terms of conversion into equity. However, one can imagine several variations of these simple instruments.

REFERENCES

Amin, A. and Tomaney, J. (1995a) "The regional development potential of inward investment in the less favoured regions of the European Community," in A. Amin and J. Tomaney (eds) *Behind the Myth of the European Union*, London: Routledge.
—— (1995b) "A framework for cohesion," in A. Amin and J. Tomaney (eds) *Behind the Myth of the European Union*, London: Routledge.
Bardhan, P. (1990) "Symposium on the state and economic development," *Journal of Economic Perspectives* 4, 3: 3–7.
Best, M. (1990) *The New Competition*, Cambridge, MA: Harvard University Press.
Cheng, T. (1990) "Political regimes and development strategies: South Korea and Taiwan," in G. Gereffi and D. L. Wyman (eds) *Manufacturing Miracles: Paths of Industrialization in Latin America and East Asia*, Princeton, NJ: Princeton University Press.
—— (1993) "Guarding the commanding heights: the state as banker in Taiwan," in S. Haggard, C. Lee, and S. Maxfield (eds) *The Politics of Finance in Developing Countries*, Ithaca, NY: Cornell University Press.
Deyo, F. (1987) "State and labor: modes of political exclusion in East Asian development," in F. Deyo (ed.) *The Political Economy of New Asian Industrialism*, Ithaca, NY: Cornell University Press.
Gereffi, G. (1990) "Paths of industrialization: an overview," in G. Gereffi and D. L. Wyman (eds) *Manufacturing Miracles: Paths of Industrialization in Latin America and East Asia*, Princeton, NJ: Princeton University Press.
Gerschenkron, A. (1962) *Economic Backwardness in Historical Perspective*, Cambridge, MA: Harvard University Press.
Haggard, S. and Lee, C. H. (1993) "The political dimension of finance in economic development," in S. Haggard, C.H. Lee, and S. Maxfield (eds) *The Politics of Finance in Developing Countries*, Ithaca, NY: Cornell University Press.
Halikias, D. (1978) *Money and Credit in a Developing Economy: The Case of Greece*, New York: New York University Press.
Hastings, L. (1993) "Regulatory revenge: the politics of free market financial reforms in Chile," in S. Haggard, C.H. Lee, and S. Maxfield (eds) *The Politics of Finance in Developing Countries*, Ithaca, NY: Cornell University Press.
Hutchcroft, P. D. (1993) "Selective squander: the politics of preferential credit allocation in the Philippines," in S. Haggard, C.H. Lee, and S. Maxfield (eds) *The Politics of Finance in Developing Countries*, Ithaca, NY: Cornell University Press.
Jorde, T. M. and Teece, D. J. (1990) "Innovation and cooperation: implications for competition and antitrust," *Journal of Economic Perspectives* 4, 3: 75–96.
Krueger, A. O. (1995) *Political Economy and Policy Reform in Developing Countries*, Cambridge, MA: MIT Press.
Krugman, P. (1995) *Development, Geography, and Economic Theory*, Cambridge, MA: MIT Press.
Lorenz, E. H. (1991) "Neither friends nor strangers: informal networks of subcontracting in French industry," in G. Thompson, J. Frances, R. Levasic, and J. Mitchell (eds) *Markets, Hierarchies and Networks,* London: Sage.
McKinnon, R. (1973) *Money and Capital in Economic Development*, Washington, DC: Brookings Institution.

Maxfield, S. (1993) "The politics of Mexican financial policy," in S. Haggard, C.H. Lee, and S. Maxfield (eds) *The Politics of Finance in Developing Countries*, Ithaca, NY: Cornell University Press.

Mytelka, L. (1991) *Strategic Partnerships and the World Economy,* London: Pinter.

Nordhaus, W. (1975) "The political business cycle", *Review of Economic Studies* April: 169–190.

OECD (1995) *The New Financial Landscape*, Paris: OECD.

Ostrom, E., Schroeder, L., and Wynne, S. (1993) *Institutional Incentives and Sustainable Development: Infrastructure Policies in Perspective*, Boulder, CO: Westview Press.

Shaw, E. S. (1973) *Financial Deepening in Economic Development*, Oxford: Oxford University Press.

Soh, B. H. (1986) "Political business cycles in industrialized democratic countries," *Kyklos* 39: 31–46.

Stiglitz, J. (1989) "Financial markets and development," *Oxford Review of Economic Policy* 5, 4: 55–68.

Stiglitz, J. and Weiss, A. (1981) "Credit rationing in markets with imperfect information," *American Economic Review* 71, 3: 393–410.

Williamson, O. (1975) *Markets and Hierarchies: Analysis and Antitrust Implications*, New York: Free Press.

Wolf Jr., C. (1988) *Markets or Governments*, Cambridge, MA: MIT Press.

5 Implications of organizational learning for horizontal technology policies

An exploratory study

Morris Teubal[1]

EVOLUTIONARY HTP FRAMEWORK: A SUMMARY OF EXISTING RESEARCH

Horizontal technology policies (HTP) have been widely used to promote innovation and technical change. Until recently, however, there has been almost no attempt to conceptualize such policies and contrast them with other types of industrial and technological policy. One explanation for this omission follows from the need to explicitly use the tenets of evolutionary theory when dealing with an HTP framework. Under a neoclassical perspective, the contours of the real world are supposed to be relatively well known, including the nature and location of market failure, and little can be said for a distinct family of horizontal technology and industrial support programs.

Making use of evolutionary principles in technology policy is not easy, as Metcalfe demonstrated in his survey of neoclassical and evolutionary theories of technology policy. First, there are no absolute welfare criteria, since innovation almost inevitably leads to gainers and losers, and "while the former may in principle be able to compensate the latter . . . there is no obvious reason why this compensation should take place" (Metcalfe 1993: 5). Second, it is almost impossible to create a formal theoretical structure for technology policy without substantial preliminary ground work. This is particularly true because of the need to explicitly consider complex learning processes, the multiplicity of selection mechanisms, and the coevolution of technology with policy and institutions. Moreover, such an emerging framework will for a long time very likely involve appreciative theory and computer simulations rather than formal theory.

HTP is a category of technology policy whose objective is to promote technological development *per se*, and associated management and organizational routines, irrespective of industrial branch or technological area. It is, in principle, applicable to a variety of activities, such as: enterprise R&D; technology transfer, absorption, and diffusion; and technological infrastructure (on the latter, see Teubal *et al.* 1996). These are termed "socially desirable technological activities." The specific activities that a country chooses to implement depend on national strategic considerations involving the internal and external environment. HTPs are being increasingly adopted by both advanced countries and NICs in response to the new opportunities and threats opened up by the technology revolution and by the processes of liberalization and globalization. They complement the more specific and well-known (although controversial) selective and vertical polices aimed at individual sectors and technologies.

The Mark 1 HTP Framework

An HTP framework based on evolutionary principles was initially developed and presented in Teubal (1996). Called the Mark 1 HTP Framework (or simply Mark 1), the structure developed is broad enough to be applicable in some measure to both NICs and advanced countries. Mark 1 focuses on market friendly policies involving *project-based* incentives (e.g. R&D project-based grants) rather than incentives based on larger activity aggregates (e.g. tax-based incentives for annual R&D expenditures).

The analysis in Mark 1 is conducted within a *learning-to-innovate* framework, with emphasis on collective learning, search, and market-building. The central outcome is a technology policy cycle that largely mirrors the standard product life cycle, with distinct infant, growth, and mature phases. In this context, proactive generation of a critical mass of projects for efficient learning and diffusion of innovation routines becomes the aim of the infant phase, while the mature phase of the policy focuses on policy restructuring, including drastic reductions in the support of routine projects and enhanced support of more complex types of innovation.

Finally, the HTP framework emphasizes the importance of three additional factors: a neutrality component for incentives in the infant phase; increasing selectivity through time; and building policy capabilities for efficient policy design and implementation. Explicit recognition of the fundamental uncertainty surrounding innovation and the impacts of government policy on the one hand, and the lack of those policy capabilities that are required early in the implementation phase on the other, make HTPs good candidates for implementation by NICs and European latecomer countries (LCs).

The technology policy cycle and its infant phase[2]

The Mark 1 technology policy cycle is illustrated in Tables 5.1 and 5.2, which show the main features of the infant (or experimental) and mature phases of an "ideal," firm-based, R&D and innovation promotion policy, one that seems to capture the context of both NICs and European LCs wishing to promote technology and innovation.[3] Each phase has specific objectives and targets (column 1); a specific set of obstacles, market failures, and policy constraints (column 2); and a policy approach and set of policy components (column 3). The differences in objectives and targets are central: during

Table 5.1 Technology policy cycle – the infant stage

Objective/Targets	Obstacles, Market Failures and Policy Constraints	Policy Approach and Policy Components
• Widespread Endogenization of the R&D process • Collective, Multidisciplinary and Cumulative Learning Process • Achieving "critical mass" of projects • Developing Policy Capabilities • Defining the specifies of firm-based incentives	• Lack of good R&D projects • Pervasive market failures • Absence of R&D (and search) routine at firms • Underdeveloped R&D consultancy/advisory services and financial services markets • Partially inadequate institutional framework • Inadequate governmental approach and policy capabilities	• Learning approach: government agency becoming an N3 network entrepreneur; generating relevant project taxonomies; modification of policy experience • Massive and flexible support • Mix between finance monetary incentives and institutional market building policies • Predominance of neutrality in incentives finance • Proactive policies (project generation) • Investments in new policy capabilities (training; staff work, etc.)

Source: Teubal 1996

Table 5.2 Technology policy cycle – the mature stage

Objective/Targets	Obstacles, Market Failures and Policy Constraints	Policy Approach and Policy Components
Objective: • Restructuring of policy Target: • Reduced support for ("new" category of) routine projects • Stimulating shift to "complex" R&D • Supporting new classes of sophisticated technological effort (e.g. precompetitive, cooperative projects)	• Budget constraint • Political constraints (e.g. political clout of large firms) • Inadequate capabilities to identify relevant market failures and associated R&D project categories • Scarcity of R&D personnel • High transaction costs • Obstacles, market failures and constraints associated with new types of R&D (Infant Stage)	• More Selectivity and less Universality in incentives • new categories of projects

Source: Teubal 1996

the infant stage, the objective is to pave the way for widespread endogenization of the R&D process in the economy, first and foremost by assuring a collective, cumulative, and multidisciplinary learning process in R&D (which in turn might require the execution of at least a critical mass of good R&D projects). The objective of the mature phase is to restructure the R&D promotion policy, both in terms of reduced support for routine R&D and in terms of encouraging firms to undertake more complex projects that entail both higher risks and higher expected returns.[4] The assumptions underlying this view of the mature phase objectives are that take-off and endogenization of the R&D process has already taken place as a result of successful policies at the infant stage, a set of routine projects emerged, learning has to some extent been exhausted, and significant improvements in appropriability have reduced the gap between social and private profitability. Notice also that a policy objective at the infant stage is development of policy capabilities in order to be able to undertake the restructuring required at the later phase while increasingly applying selective rather than neutral criteria of support.

A significant difference between the two phases relates to policy constraints facing decision-makers. Under an ideal scheme such as the one described here, a real budget constraint does not exist at the infant stage since there is a generalized absence of good projects and of associated search and management-organizational routines. Thus, essentially any good project must receive government support (note that the criteria for "goodness" must be absolute rather than relative, while remaining both flexible and general). This is not the case in the mature phase, where a constant flow of privately profitable projects continuously emerges from the system, creating an excess demand for government funds (at infant stage levels of support) and an effective budget constraint. However, at this later phase the political clout of large firms may hinder restructuring of support toward higher risk and novel types of projects and activities (such as precompetitive, collaborative consortia rather than single-firm product/process development). Reduction in support for routine projects, of course, is a result of the fact that while pervasive market failures characterize the infant stage, these are localized only within particular groups of projects at the mature phase; projects requiring support tend to be sophisticated, large and altogether different, requiring additional routines within firms. Correspondingly, enhanced selectivity, as well as specific criteria and policy instruments appropriate to different classes of projects, should replace the largely massive and neutral support during the infant stage.

Objectives of the chapter

There are important connections between technology policy and organizational learning to be developed in the form of a successor to the Mark 1 framework. Despite its clear focus, attractiveness, and proved applicability, numerous possibilities for improvement and fuller development of Mark 1 exist. Two factors have not been adequately taken into account:

- the process of *organizational learning* (as distinct from individual learning) and,
- the emergence, through time, of a variety of *innovation promotion schemes* which goes beyond that associated with increased selectivity of incentives.

In fact, Mark 1 is a peculiar mixture between a learning approach to policy at the infant phase and a traditional market failure approach at the mature phase. The objective of this chapter is to integrate both into a fuller evolutionary HTP framework which will be termed Mark 2.

There are many concrete policy implications of Mark 2, in particular for European LCs. These include: an increased emphasis on the infant phase of policy and on the associated learning approach to be adopted; further specification of the types of market failure that policymakers should identify; and the need for and possible configurations of variety within mature phase promotion schemes. The chapter concludes with some more general implications of the HTP framework from an evolutionary standpoint, including links to other frameworks for technology policy, both neoclassical and other recently emerging European frameworks.

Needless to say, this chapter will not solve all of the problems with Mark 1. A major gap relates to the emerging literature on firm competencies – an important strand in current evolutionary work. While our framework tells a story of accumulated experience with innovation and associated innovation routines, it does not explicitly consider accumulation processes for specific innovation-related competencies. An implicit assumption in this chapter is that these other competencies accumulate from "doing and learning about innovation;" that they are embodied in scientists, engineers, and other specialists, as well as in innovation-related routines and organizational capabilities; and that they may be, to some extent, influenced by policy. Consequently, this chapter neither traces the building of specific technological and techno-economic competencies, nor does it explore the mutual relationships between these competencies and organizational capabilities.

APPROACHES TO ORGANIZATIONAL LEARNING

In what follows, we will review some of the characteristic features of learning-to-innovate by firms and with organizational learning more generally. The survey does not cover strands in the literature dealing with creating and sustaining enterprise competitive advantage; for example, neither Porter's analysis of competitive forces nor the literature on strategic conflict are included (see Porter 1980; Shapiro 1989; Teece *et al.* 1994).

The section begins by surveying differences between individual and organizational learning. This is followed by a summary of characteristics of a *learning organization*. A case history of experience-based learning-to-innovate by an electronics firm is presented, focusing on the functional areas involved. It analyzes "learning about," in particular the importance of marketing and the linking of technology to needs. This study of intrafirm spillovers does not include a specific analysis of the introduction of new management methods and organizational routines. It does, however, emphasize new knowledge on innovation that could lead to new management methods and routines within the organization. Its purpose is to emphasize the distinction between accumulation of experience and fully-fledged organizational learning.

Two additional perspectives on organizational learning are then briefly surveyed. The first involves the notion of firm routine (Nelson and Winter 1982) or organizational and managerial processes (Teece *et al.* 1994). These are illustrated by a brief history of the introduction of innovation-related routines and processes for a traditional castings firm. The second and last perspective summarized briefly considers the notion of core capabilities and the notion of a firm's distinct, dynamic capabilities following the resource-based theory of the firm.[5]

The nature of organizational learning

Marengo (1994) states that

> *Organizational knowledge* is neither presupposed nor can it be derived from the available information but emerges as a property of the learning system and is shaped by the interaction among the various learning processes which constitute the organization. . . . *Organizational learning* is the process of generation of new competencies and improvement of the old ones. It is a social phenomenon and cannot be reduced to the individual learning processes of the members of the organization. It requires the development of common codes for coordination and communication among the parts of the learning process; and the generation of such codes is shaped by the hierarchical structure.
>
> (Marengo 1994)

A number of distinctive features characterize organizational learning, which is a multiagent type of learning. These include:

1 *rules*, in which the process is embodied, and which may be evaluated, selected, added, modified, and discarded;
2 *coordination* of the goals and learning processes of many individuals;
3 a *mechanism to reduce conflict* due to different representations of the environment across individuals; and
4 the *cumulative and path dependent* nature of the process. Because new competencies can be acquired only by building upon existing ones, the process is difficult and slow, and its final outcome remains highly uncertain, being dependent both on individual learning processes and on the organizational structure.

These characteristics of organizational learning make it very different from individual learning. They build upon the notion of *routine* (or *rule*) analyzed by Nelson and Winter (1982). It is clear that a number of higher level routines and mechanisms are required side by side with operational routines. To the coordination and conflict reducing mechanisms noted above should be added the importance of tacit knowledge in organizations, as well as the fact that effective incorporation of new knowledge into an organization frequently requires making use of numerous skills distributed across the individuals of an organization (Senker and Senker 1994). Besides coordination of learning, this also involves coordination of actions and behavior. All of this suggests the enormous variety of potential structures, mechanisms, and outcomes of organizational learning among firms.

Strata (1989) contributed additional insights with his characterization of firms and organizations as giant networks of interconnected nodes where changes to improve performance in one part can negatively affect performance in other parts of the organization. Therefore, decisions based on a local level (which is often the only information available) can be counterproductive for the system as a whole. There are constraints on the ability to understand what is actually going on in complex organizations. According to Strata, experimental studies confirm that decision-makers consistently misjudge complex systems with multiple feedback processes and delays. However, tools to analyze and design complex electronic systems have been used to perform the same functions in complex organization systems. By using these tools and computers, Strata stresses, we can simulate organizational behavior and show how the structure and policies of companies may generate undesirable performance that is often blamed on the external environment.[6]

Strata argues that organizational learning occurs through shared insights, knowledge, and mental models. An important implication is that the organization can learn only as fast as the slowest link learns, and that change is blocked unless all major decision-makers learn together. Further, he explains that while learning depends on memory, organizational memory depends on institutional mechanisms such as policies, strategies, and explicit models. Organizations cannot rely on only the memories of individuals because of risks and also because of job mobility. A major challenge is to discover new management tools and methods to accelerate organizational learning and the processes subsumed under it, such as attaining shared goals, building consensus for change, and facilitating the change process. Systems thinking, and particularly system dynamics, are powerful tools to facilitate both individual and organizational learning. Vision exercises and the process of corporate planning may, according to Strata, significantly trigger organizational change and associated management innovations (as discussed further below).

Building a learning organization

Related to organizational learning is the notion of a learning organization. Garvin (1993) argues that continuous improvement is the key for survival and that this requires a commitment to learning. He begins by noting that most scholars view organizational learning as a process that unfolds over time and link it with knowledge acquisition and improved performance. Howeve., analysts differ over the relative importance of specific attributes, as expressed in the following two questions: first, are new ways of thinking sufficient, or must changes in behavior also be included?, and second, is learning as information processing sufficient, or are the generation of shared insights, organizational routines, and memory of equal importance?

"A learning organization is an organization skilled at creating, acquiring and transferring knowledge and skilled at modifying its behavior to reflect new knowledge and insights" (Marengo 1994). Whatever their source, ideas are the trigger for organizational improvement, but without accompanying changes in the way that work gets done, only the potential for improvement exists. For example, TQM (Total Quality Management) is taught at many business schools, yet the number using it to guide their own decision-making is very small. Similarly, GM had little success (with a few exceptions) in revamping its manufacturing practices even though its managers are experts in lean manufacturing, just-in-time production, and the requirements for improved quality of work life. Organizations that do pass the definition of a learning organization (Honda, Corning, and GE) have been adept at translating new knowledge into new ways of operating. These companies actively manage the learning process to ensure that it occurs by design rather than by chance. Distinctive practices and policies that are responsible for their success constitute the building blocks of a learning organization.

Garvin identifies five building blocks of learning organizations:

1 systematic problem-solving;
2 experimentation with new approaches;
3 learning from own experience and past history;
4 learning from the experiences and practices of others; and
5 transferring knowledge quickly and efficiently throughout the organization.

Garvin proceeds to specify each one of these while making extensive reference to actual cases, particularly in the US. He also specifies a number of mechanisms, such as incentive schemes, and organizational routines associated with these building blocks.

The transition toward a learning organization is not automatic nor does it involve a single stage or phase. Rather, it is useful to consider it as involving three overlapping stages: cognitive, behavioral, and implementation. First, members are exposed to new ideas, thereby expanding their knowledge and motivating them to think differently. The second stage is when they begin to internalize their insights and behave differently. In the third stage, behavioral changes lead to measurable performance improvements. Conditions for arriving at the cognitive phase in the transition toward a learning organization include: the formulation of strategic plans; analysis of customer needs; assessments of current work systems; and product innovation.[7]

Garvin's description of the transition towards a learning organization illustrates what immediate steps government agencies can take in order to implement an HTP effectively, consistent with a Mark 2 viewpoint (see below). Note that a paradox may arise, with government policy aimed at producing such changes within recipient agents of the business sector while the agencies in charge are starved of up-to-date talent and/or resources to transform themselves effectively into learning organizations. One objective of the policy should be to assure that this metamorphosis effectively takes place. This may be the best way to build policy capabilities and to assure both policy restructuring and diversification (as discussed in the following section) on the one hand, and timely and efficient policy follow-up on the other.[8]

"Learning about" and intrafirm spillovers

This section summarizes a detailed case study of the innovation history of Elscint, an Israeli company specializing in diagnostic nuclear medicine instrumentation, during its first decade of existence (see Teubal 1982, 1987b: chapters 6 and 8). The objective was to understand the process of accretion of innovation capabilities in what was then the flagship of Israel's private-sector, R&D performing enterprises. During the 1970s, the company was involved in R&D, production, and marketing of various classes of instruments, particularly nuclear scanners and gamma cameras. In these (and closely related) areas the firm undertook nine R&D projects involving five product classes (see Table 5.3). Two projects were successive generations of the nuclear scanner (projects 2 and 3 of product class II); and four projects were successive generations of the gamma camera (projects 1, 6, 8, and 9 of product class I). The firm's first project represented a dead end and was not followed by other product generations despite sales that more or less covered R&D costs. The second was a technological failure, an early gamma camera that did not directly benefit subsequent projects, in part due to a lack of marketing. (This failure, however, was instrumental in arriving at an appropriate R&D strategy for the second generation of this product, project 6, appearing in year 6.)

Despite these initial setbacks, the firm continued developing, producing, and selling nuclear medicine instrumentation. The firm's third project was the first generation nuclear scanner, which at least qualified as a nonfailure in that significant sales were attained, with a sales-to-R&D ratio of about four.[9] This project generated numerous spillovers which benefited subsequent projects, both the second generation nuclear scanner (project 6) and, indirectly, the second generation of the gamma camera. Qualitative evidence confirms the presumption that with the second nuclear scanner the firm clearly *learned*

Table 5.3 R&D profitability of the case firm's projects

Project (i)	Product		Base year	$\rho'=\rho_i/\rho_3$
1	I		1	0.35
2	II	first generation	1	0.00
3	III	first generation	2	1.00
4	III	second generation	3	1.85
5	IV		4	2.89
6	II	second generation	5	0.33
7	V		6	0.19
8	II	third generation	6	1.06
9	II	fourth generation	9	1.79[b]

Notes:
a No significance attaches to the absolute values of these ratios. Their usefulness lies in showing the variation of project profitability within and across products.
b Underestimate.

about numerous functional areas associated with subsequent innovations both within and beyond the product class. This is what we term *intrafirm spillovers*. The effect was an increase in the profitability of these latter projects. This is why we state that the first generation of the nuclear scanner also had strong indirect profitability.

Figure 5.1 describes direct project profitability (linked to the sales-to-R&D ratio) on the vertical axes and the year within the decade studied. It also indicates the nature of the intrafirm project spillovers connecting the various projects: R&D, reputation (R); useful knowledge obtained from marketing and user feedback (M); and a line effect (L). These are the learning-about items that connected the projects comprising Elscint's innovation activities. They are the functional areas where innovation was learned, and in which new managerial and organizational routines were most likely to have been established (as noted, the case study did not focus on the process of setting or changing routines).

More specifically, the contribution of the nuclear scanner projects to subsequent firm innovation activity followed largely from some of the more successful features of the product. This included the video display processor and associated minicomputer attached to the instrument, which considerably enhanced the speed, quality, and variety of diagnoses achieved. (These features eliminated dependence on the central hospital computer, thereby also enabling the penetration of new markets niches, e.g. private doctors.) This project and resultant product first earned Elscint its valuable reputation with respect to potential customers, competitors, and partners such as General Electric. It undoubtedly bolstered future sales of subsequent instruments, including gamma cameras. The R&D associated with the video display processor contributed enormously to the development of a similar attachment to the more sophisticated gamma cameras, and the fact that scanners were already offered by the firm enabled it to sell its first cameras more easily

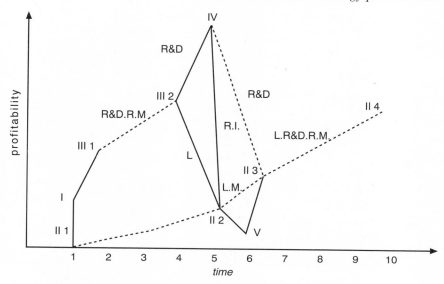

Figure 5.1 Project profitability and spillovers

two to three years later (line effect). Needless to say, the first and second scanners provided an enormous amount of information on user needs that was extremely useful in designing cameras.

This process exemplifies the nature of intrafirm spillovers that early projects can create. Many of these involve learning-to-innovate – a process that generates a fund of intangibles that directly and functionally benefit subsequent innovation, and enhance its profitability. Three observations are relevant here. First, some intangibles, such as reputation effects, are also assets accumulated in the wake of early projects and should most probably not be considered learning as such. Second, a measurable share of indirect profitability (see below) may be attributable to physical infrastructure developed during early projects that served subsequent projects.[10] These also should not be counted as learning, although they may be partly considered as investments facilitating either future knowledge creation or effective knowledge utilization. Third, there are no specific descriptions of any organizational change in Elscint that most probably accompanied the innovation activities during this period. These might have included, for example, the introduction of new innovation management rules and procedures that might have enabled the above effects to be as strong as they in fact seemed to be. Such mechanisms would have several effects: to systematize, codify, and routinize the processes of acquisition of knowledge in the functional areas mentioned above; to maintain such knowledge within the organization for future use (thus becoming the memory of the organization); and to effectively enable the utilization of such knowledge in the future.[11]

Table 5.4 Direct and indirect profitability (Elscint Projects)

	Assumption	
	(1)	*(2)*
Profitability of products III first generation		
1 Direct ($\pi' = \pi/\rho_3$)	0.16	0.25
2 Total: direct plus second generation profitability[a]		
attributable to first generation ($\Pi' = \Pi/\rho_3$)	0.30	0.63
Profitability of product II-related projects[b]		
3 Direct ($\pi' = \pi/\rho_3$)	0.17	0.24
4 Total: direct plus fourth generation profitability		
attributable to prior project 8[b] ($\Pi' = \Pi/\rho_3$)	0.24	0.46
Indirect profitability as percentage of total		
Product III, (line 2 – line 1)/line 2	46	61
Product II, (line 4 – line 3)/line 2	30	44

Notes:
a For the definition of probability and for the specific assumptions of columns (1) and (2), see
   Teubal 1982.
b Comprises the second and third product II projects IV. The base year was arbitrarily set at
   the base year of the latest of the projects in the set, the third product II project.

Table 5.4 shows two discrete estimates of indirect profitability, which for practical purposes will be taken as essentially reflecting the economic value of this learning. These estimates are expressed as the percentage increase in operating profits per unit of fixed costs of innovation. The estimates are extremely conservative, for example a real interest rate of 10 percent was used for discounting future project sales to the base period (note, however, that the estimates are *ex-post*, so no allowance for risk is taken). The last two lines show the measure of indirect profitability as a share of total project profitability. Given the conservative assumptions made, it ranges from 29 percent to 60 percent, depending on the segment of spillovers analyzed and on other assumptions.

Government grants for R&D were a critical condition facilitating the process of learning-to-innovate. Israel's successful horizontal technology policy was also instrumental in stimulating numerous other firms such as Elscint. However, many questions remain unanswered. For example, what share of spillovers and value were due to the timely introduction of new management routines appropriate to innovation? Could the value of learning be increased by a more systematic managerial focus on learning than the one actually followed by Elscint? How does the value of learning-to-innovate depend on firms' strategies with respect to a dynamic environment, and on their awareness of the importance of becoming learning organizations? The following section addresses these questions. Note that the difference between experience with innovation and experience leading to the successful introduction of new managerial and organizational routines relates to difference between learning on the one hand, and learning-to-learn on the other. My argument is that the objective of technology policy should be the stimulation of new routines or, more generally, the creation of innovation-related *organizational capital* within the business sector; a critical aspect of such a policy will be the promotion of learning to learn with respect to innovation.

Routines and organizational and management processes

The behavioral theory of the firm and evolutionary economics recognize that organizational rules or routines are crucial components of the organization of a firm, and that they are both enabled by and induced by organizational learning.[12] Nelson and Winter (1982) and subsequent authors define routines as:

- largely *tacit heuristic rules* of behavior embodied in the organization and management of the firm, comprising part of its organizational competencies;
- *rigid and informationally encapsulated* from changes (within a range) in the environment;
- the loci of *collective memory* of the organization, so that routines do not depend on particular individuals for implementation;
- enabling *continued and automatic activity*, as, for example, innovation routines that enable firms to undertake innovations continuously rather than preparing for each undertaking as a distinct once-and-for-all activity.

Most routines are, to some extent, informationally encapsulated, which will continue despite discrete changes in the environment. Nelson and Winter also recognize the role of *search and change routines* for changing an operational routine once changes in the environment make the latter inefficient or irrelevant.

Teece and associates introduced the term "organizational and management processes" to encompass the strict definition of both routine and other broader processes whose existence would comprise the organizational capital of a firm. Critical elements or components of these processes are related to coordination and integration functions within the enterprise, as well as with learning. Moreover, a critical capability of an enterprise is that of reconfiguring or restructuring its organization and activity (discussed below).

The notion of organizational routine enables us to formulate the target of technology-innovation policy as involving not only the promotion of learning-to-innovate, as exemplified in the Elscint case study, but also the adoption of innovation routines or innovation management routines within the population of target firms. While some learning-to-innovate will always result from experience with innovation, it is not enough, given the dynamic environment that forces firms to be continually involved in innovation for survival and growth. Therefore, an explicit effort should be made to build upon innovation experience by expending effort and resources to embody such learning into new organizational competencies or routines. The following case study is an example of this approach.

Case study: Fundición Imperial[13]

This case considers a small family-owned firm involved in traditional technologies in an outlying area of southern Chile (the Concepción area). It provides a healthy contrast to the larger complex organizations treated by Strata. In the description that follows, context is extremely important and the focus is on the gradual introduction of new organizational routines associated with innovation as the result of two factors: strategic planning by the company, and government incentives to private innovation. (The incentives were introduced as part of FONTEC, Chile's first broad horizontal technology policy program directed to the business enterprise sector.)

Fundición Imperial was a traditional castings firm involved in the production of small rudders (less than 2 meters), originally from bronze, and a number of other products (some based on the casting of other materials). Competitors were other local firms based on the same artisanal principles sustaining Fundicion Imperial until the early 1990s. (Apparently, competition from imports was felt only for larger rudders, a field dominated by large foreign firms.) The firm had not undertaken any technological development projects until the FONTEC project of 1993.

During 1991–1992 the firm became aware of quality problems in its traditional bronze rudders. They asked the Faculty of Engineering at the University of Concepción to identify the causes, whether the problems arose from the alloy used, the design, or the materials involved. Simultaneously, a number of tenders for rudders were received from firms in Peru and elsewhere, to which the firm could not answer owing to the enormous uncertainty in the quality of its rudders. These problems, lost opportunities, and a potential threat of enhanced competition from imports, led the firm to formulate a multipronged strategic plan in 1992, one of its components being technological development. The plan also involved the purchase of equipment that enhanced the range of products that the firm could produce (electric furnaces that substituted for oil furnaces), and the training of one or two people in marketing and promotion.

Discussions with various government agencies and an industry association helped to identify the problem as the alloy used rather than defective quality control procedures.[14] As a result, the firm instituted an R&D project that led to a shift from bronze castings to a bronze-aluminum-nickel alloy. The firm had considered commissioning the work externally, but it rapidly felt the need for in-house capabilities in the new castings. Technology in this area (and especially for small rudders) is not codified and cannot be bought nor be readily imitated; it almost has to be reproduced within the firm from scratch, although elements of the knowledge could be brought from outside. (In fact, the firm hired a consultant who spent time in Germany learning about the technology as applied to larger rudders.) The requirements are very difficult to reproduce, so a perfect recipe must be arrived at in order to produce high and consistent quality.

The objectives of the government-approved FONTEC innovation project were three-fold: first, to design appropriate rudders for the company; second, to find an optimum alloy for these rudders; and third, to test and experiment in order to get a consistent product. Eleven individuals worked on the project, nine of them directly, seven of whom were from the firm. FONTEC's contribution was multipronged:

1 it stimulated the firm to initiate its first technological development project earlier than it otherwise would have done;
2 it significantly shortened lead times from 2–3 years to 8 months;
3 it significantly enhanced the quality of the results and the learning process involved;
4 it generated new R&D routines and a great deal of motivation within the firm to undertake innovation, since it demonstrated that this activity leads to results; and
5 use of the FONTEC logotype is expected to help future commercialization of rudders (a reputation effect of sorts).

Interviewees were explicit about the learning processes induced by the project. These included innovation-related work procedures (e.g. how to experiment); how to work in teams; and how to motivate people. Motivation increased over time once the experiments yielded results (demonstrating the critical nature of a particular chemical composition for consistent outcomes), and the firm became aware that this was a critical aspect of the management of innovation. A major issue was the characteristics of the team leader in charge of the innovation project. The individuals interviewed stated emphatically that R&D had not previously been established as a routine in the company, and that they (and SMEs more generally) would not normally have entered this activity without external help. Moreover, some elements of the innovation routines relevant for the company were not only novel, but contradicted pre-existing routines prevailing in the firm. Among these was testing and wide experimentation with new materials, which, from a purely operational viewpoint, seemed wasteful of materials. Central features of the new routines absorbed by the firm included being careful and systematic, and there were routines for selecting project participants, particularly the optimal combination of practically-oriented and theoretically-oriented people in innovation projects.

A no less important routine developed in connection with the project concerned use of external consultants (the metallurgical consultant). This was extremely important for the firm and a general objective for SMEs in many contexts and countries – those that seem to have a generalized lack of confidence on these sources of information and knowledge.

It is worth noting that while the contribution of technology policy to the technological development of the company and to its adoption of innovation routines may have been critical, it depended on a previously developed strategic reorientation undertaken by the firm itself. This involved not only innovation but a number of additional activities and investments as well, for example new equipment purchases, and the development of marketing and promotional capabilities. The firm believes that much more can be done to help introduce R&D and innovation within SMEs. Specifically, FONTEC could better explain what R&D is all about and how the promotion fund works. This could expose non-R&D performing firms to the nature of experimentation, analysis, evaluation, and selection of development alternatives. It should also demonstrate how development goals may eventually be achieved, as well as the importance of adopting a new set of organizational routines associated with innovation.

The distinct capabilities of a firm

The centrality of innovation in management[15]

The centrality of organizational competencies in general, and routines in particular, is also put forward by Strata (1989), who saw US industrial restructuring problems of the late 1980s as being associated with a lack of management innovation, rather than due to deficiencies in product and process innovation *per se*. Good and innovative management would seem to be both necessary and sufficient for a firm's competitive advantage. Strata illustrates how *management innovation* (i.e. introduction of new management methods, routines, and techniques) can correct for technological deficiencies while enabling firms to adapt successfully to dynamic and changing environments. Using Japanese auto-makers as an example, and drawing on the experiences of his own company, Analogue Devices, Strata concludes that American firms lag behind in the management innovation required to take full advantage of their technology leadership.

According to Strata, during the early years of Japanese industry, small Japanese auto-makers, especially Toyota, triumphed over their giant US competitors not with product innovation, superior manufacturing technology, or greater capital investment per employee. They succeeded by means of management innovation that turned presumed disadvantages (lower production volumes and smaller lot sizes) into advantages (shorter manufacturing cycles, lower inventories, and eventually, higher quality and lower costs).

New technology for management, as for engineering, comes in the form of new knowledge, tools, and methods. Strata began to search for new technologies and ideas that would change, if not revolutionize, the way Analogue Devices was managed. He learned about the work of Jay Forrester and Peter Senge, who applied system dynamics and feedback theory to the analysis and design of complex social systems. An MIT project entitled "New

Management Style Project" focused on using system dynamics to improve our understanding of complex organizations. Strata claims to have successfully applied these new methodologies in Analogue Devices to spur the introduction of new management tools and methods.

Dynamic resource-based theories

Teece and associates (Teece, Pisano, and Shuen 1994; Teece and Pisano 1994) developed a dynamic version of the so-called resource-based theory of the firm (Hamel and Prahalad 1994). These theories focus on the strategic capabilities that are specific to a firm, define it, and provide it with sustainable competitive advantage. While the conceptual development of the theory is not yet complete, it is clear that management and organizational capabilities (organizational capital) are an important – although not exclusive – part of such distinct capabilities. Technological capabilities *per se* are certainly not enough, since some can be accessed via the market, and those that cannot need additional functional and managerial capabilities in order to be effectively utilized to generate profits and growth.

Distinct and strategic capabilities should be honed to user needs, are unique to the firm, and are difficult to replicate. They are embedded in the organization, so that low-powered incentives to individuals coupled with rewards at the group level may elicit strong commitment and effort from employees. They include timely responsiveness to threats and opportunities, implying rapid and flexible product innovation. This last feature highlights the key role played by strategic management and organizational processes associated with the adaptation, coordination, redeployment, and reconfiguration of internal skills, resources, and competencies (including those to access external skills, resources, and competencies). Reconfiguration – such as a shift from the Fordist, mass-production type of organization to niche- and product-differentiated markets – requires surveillance and a willingness to adopt best practice. This capability to change and learn is itself learned.

Distinct, strategic capabilities include not only management skills (as Strata would seem to imply) but more conventional resources or business assets, such as specialized plant and equipment, difficult-to-trade knowledge assets, some of the assets complementary to such knowledge assets, and reputational and relational assets.

Organizational learning: concluding comments

This survey of models of accumulation of innovation-related capabilities has identified at least three types of capabilities that might be stimulated by horizontal technology policies. These are:

1 *simple experience accumulation*: know-how and partial know-why without building specific organizational capital;

2 *establishment of innovation management routines* in combinations with innovation experience: learning to learn about innovation and building organizational capital in the field, without significant distinct and strategic capabilities; and
3 the generation of *distinct and strategic capabilities* in firms with both innovation experience and a measure of organizational capital associated with innovation.

This tripartite classification will be useful in differentiating HTP promotion schemes. It should be recognized that numerous subcategories may be found, as, for example, in alternative functional areas.

HTP IN THE MATURE PHASE: FROM MARK 1 TO MARK 2

Previous work on Mark 1 HTP viewed the restructuring of technology policy at the mature phase as involving enhanced selectivity of incentives. Still insufficient emphasis was given to an equally important process, namely the diversification of promotion schemes or tools. The latter should always be considered within an evolutionary perspective on technology policy, especially since technologies and technology regimes show considerable variety.

Enhanced selectivity of incentives is associated with three factors:

- the initial situation, specifically both the allocation of market failure and its impact;
- a stylized view of the dynamics of market failure through time; and
- increased knowledge of such failures.

The dynamics of market failure involves at least four elements, all of them related to learning:

1 the elimination of market failure in certain types of innovation that have become routine (e.g. routine product and process improvements in the main business lines of large firms having access to international capital markets);[16]
2 the emergence of new market failures, such as those pertaining to complex projects;
3 new types of socially desirable technological activity, such as generic R&D undertaken cooperatively; and
4 economically relevant indivisible projects emerging from the infant technology policy phase.

The implication of these characteristics of dynamic market failure is that some incentives must decline and even be eliminated, while others should be enhanced. The outcome is diversification of promotion schemes based on a measure of differential innovation incentives.

Mark 1 assumed that market failures at the infant policy phase were pervasive and that there was fundamental uncertainty about their strength and extent. This corresponds to the situation of NICs, with initially scant or fragmentary innovative activity, suddenly facing a process of liberalization, globalization, and a technological revolution (Teubal 1996).[17] Over time, however, a less uniformly distributed pattern of market failure is expected, as well as enhanced knowledge about them. This necessarily leads to both less universality and more selectivity, in other words, greater diversity of promotion schemes.[18] Moreover, the more knowledge policymakers have regarding the nature, scope, and location of various market failures, the more diversified incentive schemes will likely be.[19]

Combining the learning-to-innovate and market failure perspectives

The Mark 1 framework combines a learning-to-innovate focus at the infant policy phase with a more traditional market failure focus at the mature phase. The former calls for massive project support, both to correct existing market failures and in order to achieve a critical mass of projects for efficient learning, meaning collective learning, since there are ample opportunities for learning-from-others and eventual R&D endogenization (i.e. firms will undertake a dominant share of the activity without or with drastically reduced government support). This is why policy at the infant phase involves much more than incentives.

In contrast to the emphasis on infant phase learning, the Mark 1 mature phase policy emphasizes restructuring guided by the identification of market failure for particular categories of innovation, in other words, pairs of elements defined both by firm and by innovation characteristics. While it is true that such a pattern of market failure is the outcome of (infant phase) learning, there is no explicit account of learning as such at the mature phase.[20] Nor is there any discussion of the extent of diffusion of related innovation management routines, the assumption being that a dominant segment of innovative activity has been routinized. Incorporation of these processes pertaining to learning and organizational change into the mature phase of HTP is both needed and has significant variety-enhancing implications for promotion schemes.

An organizational learning perspective to HTP has potential policy implications that differ from those of Mark 1. For example, the emergence of complex project opportunities during the mature phase might conceivably occur in two distinct situations: first, within firms having undergone a real metamorphosis in their management of innovation routines; and second, in firms that have not undergone such changes. In the former group, the bottleneck preventing implementation of complex projects would be closer to a traditional market failure that could then be dealt with by incentives. On the other hand, provision of incentives to the latter group may not be enough, since additional measures would have to be taken to promote organizational learning, either because this is a requirement for successful implementation of this new type of socially desirable project, or because the adoption of more sophisticated innovation routines for complex projects should be a mature phase policy objective in itself (see policy concatenation below).[21]

Organizational learning versus individual learning

Adopting an incomplete "organizational learning approach to technology policy" has additional implications that become apparent once it is recognized that Mark 1 implicitly equates organizational learning with individual learning or with the simple experience model of accumulating innovation capabilities. Under a learning perspective that focuses on the individual rather than on the organization, learning by individual agents is more easily identified with routinization of a large share of projects and with the associated possibility of undertaking routine innovations on a continuous basis. The absence of a specific microeconomic analysis of what constitutes learning in organizations leads to a simplistic dichotomous view of organizational capabilities (i.e. capabilities either exist or not). Thus, under this perspective, the emergence of complex projects can be adequately treated by new incentives schemes rather than by packages involving both incentives and other inducements to organizational learning.

The Mark 1 perspective implies that firms in the HTP mature phase (as described above) will have learned by having introduced the necessary innovation management routines. The possibility of having to learn again, or having to introduce additional routines or management techniques in the mature phase, is ignored, as are the organizational needs of different types of firms (and types of innovative activity) for undertaking a *continuous* process of restructuring and innovation. Moreover, overemphasis of the cognitive aspect of the learning process (which an individual learning perspective imposes) leads to the assumption of rapid diffusion of a single set of innovation management routines. Recall that Garver identified at least two other stages in organizational learning: a behavioral stage, and an implementation (or organizational change) stage leading to performance improvements. Thus, diffusion could be easier for individuals than for multiperson organizations. Since Mark 1 was predicated on the former, it is an inappropriate model, in particular for mature phase policies (i.e. it allows only a restricted variety of promotion schemes in this phase).

Market failure in adopting innovation management routines

An increased focus on the organization and management of innovation and technical change (rather than on innovation *per se*) leads to a corresponding shift away from analysis that exclusively focuses on identifying market failure in innovation, and toward analysis that primarily addresses market failure in the adoption of innovation management routines and capabilities. In other words, learning-to-innovate is replaced by learning-to-learn as the object of study and policy, a change that is relevant for both the infant and mature phases of HTP. This shift requires both static and dynamic assessment of innovation-related capabilities and organizational routines at the firm level. A wide range of firm types needs to be considered, including well-established and newly established firms, as well as potential entrants (particularly in new and high-tech fields).[22]

At the infant phase, such an assessment would not change the basic objective of assembling a critical mass of innovation projects to induce collective learning. However, it would lead to a set of categories of firms where adoption of appropriate innovation management routines could make a significant contribution to innovation and to its endogenization through time. A clear distinction should be made between firms characterized by both types of market failure (implying that incentives are not enough) and those characterized exclusively by the traditional market failure in innovation (where incentives would suffice).

The shift in focus at the mature phase could be even more dramatic, ranging from innovation itself to deficiencies and disparities in organization and management processes connected with innovation, and even to distinct dynamic capabilities. Despite the widespread diffusion of simpler types of innovation management routines and techniques (at least those adapted to routine product-process improvement) among the target population in the mature phase, this proposed refocusing is justified under our conceptual framework because there are likely to be significant differences among firms in the underlying level and pattern of management routines and capabilities, and in firms' preparedness for the future challenges facing the business sector. The assessment and categorization effort should attempt to map this state of affairs.[23]

Variety in promotion schemes

Our analysis suggests that promotion efforts developed under an organizational learning approach to innovation policy will be more diversified than those arising out of the traditional market failure focus. This can be visualized as follows:

categories of firms, innovations,
and organizational routines[24]
↓

market failure configurations
↓

promotion efforts

The basic idea is that the set of categories is richer under an organizational learning approach than Mark 1 allowed for, since our approach now involves three rather than two elements (organizational routines being added to firms and innovations), and hence a larger set of variables. Additional patterns of market failure might appear, some based on innovation exclusively, others on both innovation and innovation routines, and so on. Consequently, this will likely lead to a broader set of promotion possibilities. Tables 5.5a and 5.5b describe some of the variables or components pertaining to the first and third sets of this relationship.

Table 5.5a Classification of firm, innovation, and routine characteristics

Traditional firm characteristics (employment, sales, R&D, etc.)
Sector, technology and technology regime associated with the firm
Scope and structure of innovative activities (e.g. minor product improvements, complex projects, etc.)
Innovation management routines (structure and sophistication)
Variables associated with firm strategy (e.g. existence or nonexistence of an explicit strategy)

Table 5.5b Possible elements of promotion schemes

incentives
information provision and transfer of nonproprietary experience from other firms
support in adopting new innovation management routines (a package with several elements)
stimulating use of external advisory and consultancy services
providing advice on intellectual property rights
stimulating collaboration (various measures)
coordination among various innovation projects belonging to a certain area or cluster
promoting exchange of information among firms and between firms and other institutions
support for broad types of "search"
collaborative forward-looking orientations

Thus, we have defined the basic structure of the Mark 2 paradigm, details of which are considered in the following section. Needless to say, while our focus has been on diversification of promotion schemes at the mature phase of the policy, the analysis is also applicable to the earlier infant phase of HTP. If enough information were available at the initiation of program implementation, a number of alternative possibilities could be offered then, and strict neutrality in incentives would not be warranted at the infant phase. However, our general presumption is that due to experience and other information gathered during program implementation, the degree of selectivity and the extent of variety will tend to increase through time.

MARK 2: IMPLICATIONS FOR POLICY IMPLEMENTATION

Table 5.6 HTP aspects and components influenced by the Mark 2 framework

---

Policy objectives
Importance of a learning perspective
Nature of market failures and role of market failure analysis
Mature phase restructuring and diversification
Search and other information gathering activities
Strategic and policy design dimensions
Policy capabilities

The emphasis on organizational learning in this chapter has a number of implications for HTP, as listed in Table 5.6. Some of these have already been dealt with in the previous section, and others were mentioned elsewhere in a more fragmentary way. The discussion that follows refers to four examples of government programs that support innovation and technological activities:

1 Israel's grants to support enterprise R&D in industry;
2 Chile's program of technological modernization, especially R&D by private sector enterprises;
3 The Teaching Company Scheme (TCS) in the UK which promotes technology transfer and training of company personnel at universities; and
4 West Germany's support of R&D personnel in SMEs during the late 1970s and 1980s.

All of these programs are, broadly speaking, horizontal, since they stress technological development activity across sectors and technologies. Israel's program was initiated in 1969 and today involves disbursements of approximately 250 million dollars annually. The core of the program continues to be the 50 percent subsidy of R&D costs that dates back to its inception. Chile's FONTEC program began in 1992 and has led to cumulated disbursements of approximately 30 million dollars during the first three years of operation. Although this represents a promising beginning for a developing country where previously very little R&D was performed in the business sector, it is probably too early to claim that R&D has been endogenized (as in the case of Israel) or even routinized in the economy. Moreover, diffusion of innovation within the business sector is still quite limited.

The UK's TCS program is considered a successful government program involving relatively few resources. Joint supervision of students – who work at enterprises (especially SMEs) and are supposed to be employed in senior management positions – is shared by a university professor and company managers. The program pays both the students and the academic supervisor. The objective is to increase SME access to knowledge generated at universities. The fourth example, the German program, was designed to promote R&D and innovation within SMEs. Incentives were not given to projects, as in the previous three cases, but instead were extended to R&D personnel. The program began in the late 1970s and was terminated in 1989. While its utilization by the relevant SME population was high, and R&D matching significant (estimated at 0.6), evaluations pointed to limited impacts on the initiation of nonroutine R&D involved in generating new product lines.[25]

Policy objectives and targets

In addition to Mark 1's HTP objectives and targets,[26] the Mark 2 framework incorporates a set of specific targets that should more explicitly include: first, business sector adoption of new organizational routines pertaining to innovation; and second, diversification of promotion schemes and paving the way for *policy follow-up* in the mature phase of the program.

In this regard, Chile's FONTEC program and the UK's TCS program come closest to the objective of specifically focusing on and searching out new innovation-related organizational routines. Chile's more recent program manifests an awareness of the importance of establishing objectives that go beyond simply promoting R&D. This seems also to be the case with TCS, since although technology transfer and industry-based training are the program's main objectives, TCS explicitly incorporates at least one organizational aspect – forging lasting partnerships between academia and business. However, it is not clear what weight is given to this objective, nor how the articulation of such an objective ultimately affects adoption of new innovation routines.[27]

The nature and scope of the learning approach to policy

Mark 2 stresses the importance of adopting a learning approach to HTP beyond that adopted for Mark 1. This expresses itself in a number of senses:

- greater emphasis on adoption and diffusion of new innovation management routines, representing a more profound type of learning (learning-to-learn) than that flowing simply from innovation experience;
- this perspective on learning should also be applicable to the mature phase of the policy cycle, with objectives that also include inducing *collective organizational learning*. In a dynamic world, new innovation management routines should continuously be considered for adoption. This includes more sophisticated activities and processes that may be covered by the program or could be the subject of a follow-up program;[28]
- Increased complexity in the taxonomies of beneficiary firms requires much more data, information, and case study work by policymakers (see Conclusion below).

The Israeli HTP program is a good example of *de facto* adoption of a learning perspective during its infant phase (in the 1970s), and failure to adopt – at least until the last eight years – a dynamic learning approach during the mature phase. The enormous growth of firms performing in-house R&D activities during the first decade of the program (most of them being new technology-based entrants) provides at least indirect evidence that strong collective learning occurred. Israel's small and compact features generated conditions for the rapid diffusion to potential new entrepreneurs of the informal, nonproprietary information and experience associated with managing innovation. To a certain extent the opposite was true during the second decade (the 1980s), despite the fact that diffusion of R&D and R&D experience continued. Very little restructuring of promotion schemes took place, despite several failed attempts to diversify incentives and tap additional (tax-based) sources of finance. More specifically, incentives to large firms generally continued to be undifferentiated from those of small firms; nor was there any other real program diversification. Both factors are indicative of a gradual weakening of the learning approach and objective so well represented in the previous phase.[29] This conclusion is even more convincing once we recognize that a strategic deficiency arose in connection with cooperative projects on generic R&D (these were not specifically promoted until 1993). It is therefore doubtful that Israel's mature phase reflected even Mark 1 (let alone Mark 2).[30]

The references consulted regarding the German program do not contain sufficient information concerning adoption of a learning approach to policy. One possibility is that a learning perspective was not adequately embodied in policy implementation, despite the wide diffusion of the incentives offered by the program. One *a priori* reason is that these incentives were not project based, a fact that probably reduces the possibility of collective learning derived from the experiences of the individual companies. A complementary reason is that the program apparently did not sufficiently induce firms to undertake more significant types of R&D associated with new products (Meyer-Kramer 1990). This view has been, at least indirectly, confirmed by official OECD reports (quoted in Teubal 1996). It might be that a more explicit focus on inducing adoption of new innovation management routines within more traditional SME organizational frameworks would have generated a better profile and an improved structure to the additional innovative activity supported.

The nature of market failures and role of market failure analysis

The policy objective of achieving rapid growth of innovation, together with endogenization of significant portions of this activity, requires explicit consideration of market failure in the adoption and diffusion of innovation management routines rather than exclusively focusing on innovation. Naturally, in some cases firms with innovation routines face a traditional market failure in innovation that can be solved by appropriate incentives. But in the general case, especially at the infant phase but also in the mature phase, it is essential to consider this organizational, and more fundamental, type of market failure. In such cases, the policy response might involve not only (greater) incentives, but also additional effort at promoting learning and diffusion of the new routines. While the Mark 1 framework considered this more or less explicitly, it was limited to the infant phase. Moreover, as already explained, it emphasized learning-to-innovate rather than explicit incorporation of the new knowledge into new organizational capital.

An important aspect of policy is to establish the role of market failure in technology policy. Clearly, a notion of market failure that is equivalent to imperfect markets is not only useless but a contradiction in terms (Metcalfe 1993 and personal communication). A relevant notion, however, could be constructed by focusing on the *market mechanism* and its contribution in generating those socially desirable activities in which it has a comparative advantage over other mechanisms (see Teubal forthcoming). In this context it is possible to talk about market failure in innovation and in the adoption and diffusion of innovation management routines.[31]

Having said that, we should be aware that market failure analysis is only possible at the tactical level of policy (Lall and Teubal 1996). It is not applicable to *strategic* decisions involving significant coordination and interactions among its various components. These decisions include priorities for HTP programs (as well as vertical decisions such as the targeting of sectors, clusters, regions, and technologies). Thus a decision to initiate an HTP program supporting enterprise R&D at a particular time is a *strategic* decision – it cannot be arrived at by market failure analysis. However, given implementation of such a program, market failure analysis is important in order to restructure incentives and to diversify promotion schemes.[32]

Mature phase restructuring and diversification

The Israeli promotion scheme was characterized by delayed restructuring in the 1980s and diversification that occurred only in the 1990s. While some of the programs – for example those directed at engineers and scientists recently arriving from the former Soviet Union – seem to have been useful, extensive diversification of promotion schemes probably has not occurred *within* the main grants to R&D programs. (There are exceptions, such as the royalties fund which has *de facto* reduced the effective subsidy to large firms by assuring repayment according to a formula on sales.[33] But these exceptions probably confirm the main presumption rather than contradict it.)

The Chilean program shows signs of attempting a significant degree of diversification and integration with other preexistent schemes. This is extremely important for the second four-year term of the policy implemented in that country. It is obviously too early to assess to what extent these efforts will succeed in the future, although there seems to be a clear awareness of the need to restructure and diversify.

Search and information-gathering activities

It should be clear by now, particularly given the variety of promotion schemes required under Mark 2, that intense search and information-gathering activities are needed to implement a bona fide learning perspective to policy at both infant and mature phases. Case studies of individual enterprises can play an important role, given the importance of uncovering alternative configurations of innovation management routines. These configurations will then play an important role in identifying the various combinations of firm, innovation, and organizational routines on which a diversification of policy should based.[34] Both case study work and surveys should be used for understanding the nature, sources, and channels of the collective learning process triggered by the government agency in charge of the HTP.[35]

Policy capabilities

An important institutional underpinning of Mark 2 is building an explicit component for government learning and capability development into the policy framework. This is clearly more important than had appeared in the design of Mark 1, the reason being that policy redesign, restructuring, and diversification is a continuous process, while the Mark 1 perspective was that it takes place at discrete moments along the technology policy cycle.[36]

The conditions for building a learning organization drawn by Garvin seem to be an appropriate way to start thinking about these issues. Presumably, few of these were explicitly implemented in the Israeli case (despite the fact that learning by government did take place in the initial phase of the policy), particularly during the decade of the 1980s. No routines existed to monitor systematically what similar programs were doing abroad; and no awareness existed of the need to generate some redundancy in order to learn. Moreover, operational pressures on the limited staff of the Office of the Chief Scientist (in the Ministry of Trade and Industry), which were increasing year by year, continuously constrained the possibility of initiating such a process.

No information really exists on these issues concerning the UK and German programs, although one good sign in this respect has been that evaluations have been undertaken. However important these may be, they in themselves are not sufficient for the continuous adaptation of the program. Therefore, the extent and speed by which the government agencies involved were transformed toward becoming learning organizations is not clear.[37]

CONCLUSION

The horizontal technology policy framework presented in previous work and further extended in this chapter is significantly different from neoclassical analysis of technology policy (see Metcalfe 1993; and Teubal 1996, concluding section). This is despite the fact that the proposed framework still makes use (in a restricted sense and at a tactical level exclusively) of market failure analysis and maintains an important (although not exclusive) role to financial incentives. The proposed framework is distinct on three main grounds: its emphasis on collective learning and on organizational changes and their diffusion through time; the explicit recognition given to partial ignorance of policymakers, for example in connection with the location of market failure; and the consequent need for governments to learn and to build policy capabilities while recognizing the existence of a technology policy cycle.

A no less important source of difference between the postulated HTP framework and the neoclassical perspective lies in the recognition of the importance of the strategic and design underpinnings to the implementation of policy, an element completely absent from the neoclassical perspective. There is an overall underawareness of the importance of these functions and elements. Surveying the German experience with technology policy evaluations, F. Meyer-Kramer (1995) argues that most of these were either of the accompanying (real time) and monitoring type, or *ex post* analyses. There has been a dearth of *ex ante* and strategic evaluations.[38] Meyer-Kramer also claims that evaluations have begun late and that these have caused late entry into new areas of policy.[39]

The framework may also contribute to explaining patterns of technology policy through time. Meyer-Kramer notes a shift from evaluations concerning broad programs supporting R&D with broad terms of reference and an emphasis on SMEs, to larger scale and technology-specific programs (e.g. in information technology, biotechnology, etc.). While this is not in itself a statement about the structure of the technology policy portfolio, it might bear a significant relationship to a trend from horizontal programs supporting R&D and diffusion on the one hand, to more specific programs involving both greater variety and greater selectivity on the other. This chapter provides support for such a trend in policies through time, given its dynamic focus and its emphasis on a learning and organizational change and on policy follow-up. However, the trend favoring variety and selectivity in government programs (which has yet to be substantiated with empirical evidence) may have been affected by other factors beyond the dynamics of learning about innovation and technology in the business sector (including the dynamics of government learning about these processes). These would include the emergence and diffusion of a set of generic technologies in the last 15 years, possible effects of budget constraints on national programs, and the perceived effects of enhanced international competition on EC programs.[40]

Two final comments on future work conclude this chapter: first, it is important to integrate qualitatively and conceptually the notion of horizontal technology policies within a wider framework that also allows for other types of policies (both vertical and semi-horizontal, policies toward basic research, standard setting, regulation, and intellectual property, etc.). This should be an exercise in appreciative theory. A second type of work is to flesh out the details of the Mark 2 HTP framework in order to clarify basic concepts and processes. This is extremely important but requires access to nonpublished information and to knowledgeable policy decision-makers and enlightened entrepreneurs. The rewards from such an undertaking, however, may be great, since the exercise will enable a more successful application of the already promising HTP framework of analysis to real world problems.

NOTES

1 I have greatly benefited from discussions with J. Fageberg, M. Hobday, and S. Metcalfe on the general subject matter of this chapter. Seminars given at ECLA (Chile), Institute of Economic Research (University of Buenos Aires, Faculty of Economics), Summer School on Industrial Economics (Cargese), SPRU (University of Sussex), NUPI (Oslo), PREST (Manchester University), and Roskilde University (Denmark) have been helpful in consolidating the issues raised here, as were comments from A. Diaz, J. Katz, J. Olivera, and P. Swann.

2 This section has been taken from Teubal 1996. Numerous aspects of context pertaining to NICs and applicable to European latecomer countries can be found in this article (and to some extent in Teubal forthcoming).

3 I should mention here that promotion of innovation and technological development in these economies requires a variety of programs, including horizontal programs of the type described here.

4 The diversification of Elscint, an Israeli medical diagnostic instrumentation firm active in the nuclear medicine area, to the computerized tomography area during the late 1970s was significantly stimulated by a new support program at the Office of the Chief Scientist (OCS) of the Ministry of Industry and Trade (The National Projects Program). This scheme substantially increased the monetary incentives to complex, multidisciplinary R&D programs. CAT scanner R&D is more complex and multidisciplinary than that involved in nuclear medicine. Part of the difference in scope and complexity of innovation is reflected in product price: while gamma cameras were priced at that time between 50 and 100 thousand dollars per system (depending on the specific configuration ordered), CAT scanners were priced at a minimum of half a million dollars.

5 For an interesting analysis of some of the connections between the resource-based theory of the firm and technology policy see, Wegloop 1996.

6 An additional function of system dynamics is as a training tool. Thus, by explicitly modeling how the organization works or should work, we create a precise language with which to share our understanding. This is both a mechanism for convergence on a shared model and also a mechanism for transmitting the organization's stored experience and knowledge to younger, less experienced managers.

7 Garvin mentions that "learning is difficult when employees are harassed and rushed – it tends to be driven out by the pressures of the moment. Only if top management explicitly frees up employees' time for the purpose does learning occur with any frequency" (Garvin 1993). This supports the evolutionary perspective that creativity and variety require redundancy (Metcalfe 1993)

8 The objective of building policy capabilities has been integrated into the infant stage of Mark 1 (see Table 5.1). Mark 2 should go beyond this and deal also with associated institutional underpinnings. The capabilities emerging from "learning government agencies" would not only facilitate restructuring policy at the mature phase, they could also better tackle the strategic dimension of HTP as well as the policy design aspects arising at this phase, as discussed further below (see also Teubal forthcoming, Lall and Teubal 1996).

9   In Table 5.3 the Greek letter rho (ρ) indicates the ratio between the real discounted value of sales flowing from a project to the real value of the R&D invested in it. Rho prime (ρ') is rho normalized for the first generation of the nuclear scanner, the first nonfailure of the firm (project 3, first generation of product III). Figure 5.1 and Table 5.4 use a profitability measure π that is the ratio of the real value of operating profits to the real value of the fixed costs of the innovation (R&D plus other fixed costs, where a fixed proportion between R&D and non-R&D costs is assumed across innovations). This profitability measure is linearly related to the rhos, given the assumptions made. For further clarifications see Teubal 1982.

10 We have been unable to make a breakdown of project R&D costs between infrastructural elements, on the one hand, and other specific project components on the other.

11 This case study was prepared partly during the 1970s as a follow-up of a broader study of the Israeli biomedical electronic instrumentation sector (Teubal *et al*. 1996), and partly during the early 1980s prior to the appearance of Nelson and Winter's book (1982). This explains the insufficient awareness at the time of the importance of organizational routines. Note that not all case studies need to ignore routines and in fact these are beginning to be recorded.

12 For Nelson and Winter (1982) the firm is a collection of routines.

13 The summary follows Teubal 1994.

14 Discussions were held with representatives of several government agencies, including Corfo and Sercotech, and with the Comite Metalmecanico 8th Region. Corfo is a powerful government agency whose functions are similar to those of a ministry of industry, national development bank, and public enterprise holding company. Sercotech is an SME-promoting agency. The Comite Metalmecanico 8th Region is an industry association that was formed at the time to help jobbers collectively in the area whose subcontracting work had ended.

15 The following subsection closely follows Strata 1989.

16 This may be the outcome of the exhaustion of learning potential and of other factors.

17 Peter Swann has pointed out that it can be formally proved that a situation of complete uncertainty, such as that described at the initiation of the infant HTP phase, leads to a neutral incentives scheme.

18 This may take the form of a trend rather than a once-and-for-all increase in policy diversity.

19 Where market failure was not pervasive initially, but localized in specific and well-known pockets of firms and innovative activity, the tendency toward increased selectivity and diversity of promotion schemes need not be so strong, since selectivity would exist at the outset of the program. If this is combined with a dynamic environment involving drastic restructuring of market failure and with increased uncertainty about their specific location, then there would be an even weaker trend toward increased selectivity and diversification, if at all.

20 There is no discussion of a critical mass of complex projects to trigger a new type of collective learning. Moreover, the analysis is cast as if the relevant market failures in projects are not related to externalities from learning but from other factors such as indivisibilities and uncertainty.

21 This also raises issues of how to redefine the mature phase of HTP. Under Mark 1 it is connected to emergence of a dominant group of routine projects that might generally be thought of as involving minor product and process improvements. Our current attempt at reformulating the HTP framework to more fully incorporate organizational learning will mean that it would be more appropriate to characterize the mature policy phase as one involving a sufficiently large number of firms having adopted adequate innovation management routines and

techniques. Additional conceptual work is clearly required in regards to this issue.

22 Assessment of potential entrants should be linked to policies promoting entrepreneurship by identifying both traditional market failures (e.g. capital market imperfections) and ways to provide would-be entrepreneurs with sufficient management skills to establish and run new technology-based firms (start-ups).

23 Direct identification of these differences is also likely to be feasible due to experience with the program's infant phase (provided other explicit intellectual and knowledge acquisition efforts by policymakers are undertaken). Note that this organizational learning focus on innovation policy has, to some extent, been adopted within the Innovation Management Techniques program of the 4th Framework Program in Europe (see European Commission 1995). A firm may be rational in not adopting modern innovation management routines, given the fixed costs associated with adoption, and the externalities that adoption by one company generates to other companies willing to follow suit. Thus, the policymaker is correct in targeting such modern methods, since he would consider the overall collective learning process rather than that of any individual firm.

24 The terms innovation and organizational routines are used to include routines, organizational and management processes, and dynamic (strategic) capabilities associated with innovation.

25 For the Israeli program see Teubal 1987a, 1993; for the UK TCS see Senker and Senker 1994; and for the German program see Meyer-Kramer 1990, 1995. Information on the Chilean program is contained in a report written for the Chilean government (see Teubal 1994).

26 These involve growth of innovative activity and collective learning in the infant phase, and activity endogenization and policy-restructuring in the mature phase of HTP.

27 The objective of the program evaluation focused not directly on learning and adoption of new routines, but rather on quantifiable benefits and on how these varied according to factors such as type of firm, nature of academic input, etc. The interpretation of some of the results was occasionally cast in more evolutionary terms, but this seemed not to be systematic.

28 Generally speaking, the terminal stock of organizational capital should also be included in the benefits of the HTP program.

29 One cause of this trend was, undoubtedly, the inflationary environment in Israel during part of the 1980s.

30 This strategic deficiency in itself was a reflection of the failure to adopt a learning approach in the mature phase, since it is one result of the absence of formal and systematic evaluations of technology policy programs. A program evaluation is a means of gathering information about program efficiency and performance and a means of evaluating strategic options. For support of this statement, see Meyer-Kramer 1995. Israel's high-tech successes in the 1990s were fueled by a number of factors including a new technology promotion program that stimulated venture capital. This operated separately from the main program mentioned in the text.

31 The context of the proposed market mechanism failure would not be one of economic equilibrium. Moreover, the background "social needs" concept would have to emerge from a collective prioritization process reflecting the articulation of national objectives (both economic and noneconomic).

32 An example is the analysis of additionality of R&D support programs. Extensive discussion of this point and other related issues can be found in Lall and Teubal 1996.

33 In these and in other cases, however, many programs would have been undertaken by the enterprises even without government support.

34 Case study work should therefore not only emphasize the effects of policy support on the cognitive aspects of the firm's learning (e.g. knowledge that links marketing to R&D is critical for instrument innovations), but also the mechanisms of incorporation of this learning into new organizational and management routines (behavioral and implementation aspects).

35 There seems to be a chronic underevaluation of the importance of case study work for policy. This derives not only from high relative cost, but also from a misunderstanding of the central role they can play in policy implementation and design. This role goes through the better conceptualization of the relevant policy processes and the policy issues that this form of knowledge acquisition permits policymakers to address.

36 The accumulated set of changes to Mark 1 bear a certain similarity to the fluidization of the rigid last stage of the classical product life cycle (for the "classical" product life cycle see Utterback and Abernathy 1975).

37 The Chilean program, by virtue of being a newer one, has been more aware since its beginning of the need to learn from others. It remains to be seen whether the government agency in charge will become a fully-fledged learning organization – but the opportunity is there.

38 This is also Israel's case. No explicit, objective, and independent evaluation has been undertaken since the inception of the program in the late 1960s. The resultant information gap has contributed to delayed implementation of the above-mentioned precompetitive, collaborative R&D scheme. It was implemented only in 1993. For additional information on the process leading to it see Justman *et al.* 1993.

39 While Meyer-Kramer's conceptual technology policy framework is not explicitly evolutionary, it does emphasize the importance of strategic and program design dimensions. These are termed "program diagnosis" and "program definition" respectively. They are clearly differentiated from program implementation, but they allow positive feedback effects from implementation that are relevant for follow-up and experimental programs.

40 For a discussion of trends in technology policy, particularly within the European Community, see Sharp and Pavitt 1993. These authors emphasize the shift from sectoral policies favoring national champions in sunset industries in the 1960s and 1970s, to support of, first, sunrise technologies (e.g. the UK's Alvey program supporting information technologies), and, second, broadly based support of science, technological infrastructure, and programs raising the awareness of technology and improving education, training, and market information. This chapter is not concerned directly with this trend, which also has a lot to do with the emergence of technology policy as the main component of industrial policy. Rather, it is concerned with the structure of the new activities, in particular the relative importance of horizontal, semi-horizontal (e.g. support of information technology across all sectors), and vertical policies; neutrality versus selectivity; and trends in the variety of promotion schemes. It is clear that these dimensions of a technology policy portfolio require much more specific information than is usually available in general surveys of policy and policy trends.

REFERENCES

European Commission (1995) *Green Paper on Innovation*, Brussels–Luxembourg: EGKS-EG-EAG.

Garvin, D. (1993) "Building a learning organization," *Harvard Business Review* July/August: 78–91.

Hamel, G. and Prahalad, C. K. (1994) *Competing For the Future*, Boston: Harvard University Press.

Justman, M. and Teubal, M. (1986) "Innovation policy in an open economy: a normative framework to strategic and tactical issues," *Research Policy* 15: 121–138.

Justman, M., Teubal, M., and Zuscovitch, E. (1993) *Technological Infrastructure Policy for Renewed Growth* (in Hebrew), Industrial Development Policy Group, Jerusalem, Israel: The Jerusalem Institute.

Lall, S. and Teubal, M. (1996) "A framework for market stimulating industrial and technology policy," in progress.

Marengo, L. (1994) "Structure, competence and learning in an adaptive model of the firm," typescript.

Metcalfe, S. (1993) "The economic foundations of technology policy: Equilibrium and evolutionary perspectives," Discussion paper 95, School of Economic Studies, University of Manchester.

Meyer-Kramer, F. (1990) "The determinants of investment in R&D and the role of public policies: An evaluation," in E. Deiaco, E. Hornell, and G. Vickery (eds) *Technology and Investment. Crucial Issues for the 1990s*, London: Pinter.

—— (1995) "Technology policy evaluation in Germany," *International Journal of Technology Management* 10, 4–6: 601–621.

Nelson, R. and Winter, S. (1982) *An Evolutionary Theory of Economic Change*, Boston: Harvard University Press.

Porter, M. E. (1980) *Competitive Strategy*, New York: Free Press.

Senker, P. and Senker, J. (1994) "Transferring knowledge and expertise from universities to industry: Britain's teaching company scheme," *New Technology, Work and Employment* 9, 2: 81–92.

Shapiro, C. (1989) "The theory of business strategy," *Rand Journal of Economics* spring.

Sharp, M. and Pavitt, K. (1993) "Technology policy in the 1990s: Old trends and new realities," *Journal of Common Market Studies* 31, 2: 129–151.

Stiglitz, J. (1988) "Learning to learn: localized learning and technological progress," in P. Dasgupta and P. Stoneman (eds) *Economic Policy and Technological Development*.

Strata, R. (1989) "Organizational learning – the key to management innovation," *Sloan Management Review* spring: 63–74.

Teece, D. and Pisano, G. (1994) "The dynamic capabilities of firm: An introduction," in D. Teece, G. Pisano, A. and Schuen (1994) "Dynamic capabilities and strategic management," CCC working paper No. 90–8, Center For Research in Management, University of California at Berkeley.

Teece, D., Pisano, G., and Schuen, A. (1994) "Dynamic capabilities and strategic management," CCC working paper No. 90–8, Center For Research in Management, University of California at Berkeley.

Teubal, M. (1982) "The R&D performance through time of a young, high-technology firm: Methodology and illustration," *Research Policy* 11: 333–346.

—— (1987a) "Neutrality in science policy: the case of sophisticated industrial technology in Israel," in M. Teubal (ed.) *Innovation Performance, Learning and Government Policy*, Wisconsin: Wisconsin University Press.

—— (ed.) (1987b) *Innovation Performance, Learning and Government Policy*, Wisconsin: Wisconsin University Press.

—— (1993) "The innovation system of Israel: description, analysis and outstanding issues," in R. Nelson (ed.) *National Systems of Innovation*, Oxford: Oxford University Press.

—— (1994) "Towards an evaluation of Chile's FONTEC and FONDEF programs," typescript.

—— (1996) "R&D and technology policy at NIC's as learning processes," *World Development* May.

—— (1997) "A catalytic and evolutionary approach to horizontal technology policies," *Research Policy* 25: 1161–1188.

Teubal, M., Foray, D., Justman, M., and Zuscovitch, E. (1996) *Technological Infrastructure Policy: An International Perspective*, Dordrecht, Boston and London: Kluwer Academic Publishers.

Utterback, J. and Abernathy, W. (1975) "A dynamic model of process and product innovation," *Omega*: 639–56.

Wegloop, P. (1996) "Integration, firm strategy and government policy: why and how they should be linked," Ph.D. Thesis, The University of Roskilde, Department of Social Sciences.

6 Industrial policy, competitive strategy, and networks of small and medium-sized firms

Theoretical issues and implications for less favored countries

Christos Pitelis[1]

ABSTRACT

The aims of this chapter are:

1 to propose the idea that industrial policies inspired by the mainstream neoclassical ideas of industrial organization may be incompatible with firms' competitive strategies inspired by the same perspective;
2 to examine ways through which the incompatibility can be removed *within* the framework of neoclassical theorizing;
3 to examine alternative ways through which industrial policy and competitive strategy can be compatible; and
4 to compare these alternatives by examining their compatibility with a sustainable national strategy for development.

Theories of the state and national strategy are discussed. The chapter concludes by supporting an industrial strategy favoring clusters of small and medium-sized enterprises. This is argued to have implications for an industrial strategy for less favored countries (LFCs).

INTRODUCTION

This chapter has two methods of achieving the four aims set out above. First, it assesses the extent to which industrial strategy and competitive strategy are compatible, and examines possible ways through which compatibility can be achieved in theory and in practice. Second, the chapter provides a conceptual framework that delineates the choices to be made between alternative types of compatible industrial and competitive strategies. The chapter begins with some definitional issues pointing to a possible inconsistency between textbook industrial policy/strategy and competitive strategy; we critically evaluate existing theoretical methods of dealing with this inconsistency. In the following section we argue that existing approaches are not embedded within a general conceptual framework that allows for compatibility between industrial strategy and national strategy. An inescapable precondition for the derivation of such a framework is an analysis of the role of the state in market economies and, in particular, its objectives and constraints. Such an analysis provides the conceptual basis for solving the potential inconsistency puzzle between national, industrial, and competitive strategy. The last section compares the compatibility of two specific strategies or limiting cases, favoring large size and networks of small firms respectively. We argue that the latter is more in line with national strategy as derived in the previous section. This is argued to have implications for the industrial strategy of LFCs.

INDUSTRIAL, COMPETITIVE, AND NATIONAL STRATEGIES

Etymologically, the world "strategy" comes from the Greek word *stratos* (army) and the verb *igoumai* (to lead). Strategy, therefore, is leading the army, presumably toward a final objective: winning the war. The definition implies the existence of a long-term objective and of a leader (strategist or general) who manages the resources of the army toward achieving this long-term objective (strategy management).

The above general definitions can be applied to the level of a business unit (competitive strategy), a diversified multi-unit firm (corporate strategy), the industrial sector of an economy (industrial strategy), or the economy as a whole (national strategy). Important considerations raised in each of these cases are the identification of the long-term objectives, the strategist (principal), the agents, as well as the process of choosing, implementing, and controlling selected strategies. The existing literature on industrial organization, industrial policy, and industrial strategy, and on strategic management, competitive strategy, and corporate strategy, is very much consistent with these general definitions (see Teece 1990 and below). There is, however, no clear consensus about the issues concerning objectives, principles, and agents. Our focus in the rest of this section is on industrial policy, industrial strategy, competitive strategy, and their interrelationships, and on the relationship between these policies on the one hand, and national strategy on the other. Corporate strategy necessarily involves competitive strategy, and it raises special strategic management issues that are of no immediate concern for this chapter. Porter 1987 and Kay 1991 have useful discussions of concepts of corporate strategy.

The fundamental dilemma: industrial policy versus competitive strategy?

The economics literature has typically linked industrial policy to the theory of industrial organization (IO). Traditionally, mainstream or neoclassical IO was concerned with the structure, conduct, and performance of industries, and in particular, the extent to which structure (concentration, barriers to entry) affects performance (e.g. profitability). A central tenet was that departures from competitive structures may be associated with monopoly profits, leading to welfare losses in terms of reductions in consumer surplus. Early neoclassical models of IO, such as limit pricing and generalized oligopoly, confirmed such concerns (Modigliani 1958; Cowling and Waterson 1976). A large empirical literature on such losses also confirmed their existence. Despite huge variations in the estimates of monopoly welfare losses (ranging from 0.1 percent to 50 percent of US GDP), most mainstream economists would accept Scherer's (1980) modest estimate of 6 percent of US GDP.[2]

Under this early view of IO, monopoly is a form of market failure that leads to a breakdown of the first fundamental theorem of welfare economics (that a perfectly competitive economy can allocate resources in a Pareto efficient way). The immediate policy implication was the necessity to regulate monopolies and vehicles of their attainment, such as horizontal mergers. Indeed, despite the efforts of a large political economy literature (see, for example, Grant 1982), the industrial policy implications of neoclassical industrial organization hardly progressed beyond this rather mundane and not too useful statement. Practical industrial policies in the UK, US, and the European Community's Rome Treaty, apparently informed by this theory (discussed further below), were rather passive and very much of the *laissez-faire* view; intervention was called for only where signs of monopoly abuse were apparent. There were dissenting voices as to whether the burden of proof should lie with the state or the firm (see, for example, Cowling 1982), but until the early 1980s there was no fundamental challenge to the perspective as a whole.

Industrial policy as described above represents industrial strategy only in a negative way, namely that it is assumed that firms have a strategy of their own and that the state's role is to support firms in their efforts until they clash with the interests of consumers. Up to this point, the objectives of the firm and the nation-state are symbiotic, so that the strategies of the firm and the state coincide. In this context, industrial policy simply delineates the boundaries of firm strategy so as to avoid structural market failures. Despite this rather limited nature, industrial policy is potentially incompatible with both national and competitive strategies; both relate to the issue of firm size and market power.

The term *competitive strategy* is relatively new, coined by Michael Porter in his 1980 homonymous book. In Porter's words, competitive strategy is about creating competitive advantage in each of the businesses in which a company competes. Accordingly, competitive strategy refers to the level of the business unit. Corporate strategy, on the other hand, refers to the company as a whole. Porter's contribution is firmly based on the theory of IO. However, instead of using IO theory to inform policymakers, he focuses on advising firms.[3] Contributions such as the 5-forces model for the analysis of industry are already to be found in spirit in IO theory; Porter made these notions more workable, more accessible to managers, and more elaborate in a practical way, through, for example, his notion of strategic groups (sets of firms with similar competitive profiles within an industry) and his three generic strategies. Porter has also extended his analysis to internal issues of firms (e.g. value chains), to the competitive advantage of nations, and more recently, even to inner cities (Porter 1990, 1995). However, Porter's competitive strategy need not be compatible with industrial policy. Competitive strategy is explicitly concerned with creating competitive advantages for firms, which often involves acquiring and maintaining monopoly positions through cost advantages, differentiation, focus, and the use of strategic entry barriers.[4] Consequently, a potential incompatibility emerges between conventional industrial policy and industrial strategy, since the former is concerned with controlling the monopoly power that the latter often promotes. To put it bluntly, a neoclassical industrial economist cannot be both an industrial policy advisor *and* a competitive strategy advisor without suffering from a Jekyll and Hyde syndrome.

Solving the dilemma: efficiency of size arguments

One way of solving this dilemma is to question the importance and very existence of monopoly power and welfare losses. Williamson's trade-off model, Demsetz's differential efficiency hypothesis, and Schumpeter's differential innovations hypothesis are important examples of early approaches to untying this knot. All three question the monopoly welfare losses argument and thus the conventional industrial policy implications. Williamson argues that monopolies may have lower costs that offset welfare losses through gains in cost efficiency. Demsetz maintains that large size attained through efficiency advantages is the prize for efficiency-enhancing entrepreneurship; such efficiency gains should be set against any welfare losses due to monopoly power. For Schumpeter, differences in innovative activity lead to large size (in a static version of this hypothesis it is alleged that large firms are more innovative), and therefore gains from innovative activity should be set against any welfare losses. Although the evidence in support of these hypotheses is inconclusive (Pitelis 1991), they do provide theoretical arguments for reducing the incompatibility between industrial policy and competitive strategy. Consequently, competitive strategy can render firms more efficient, in the expectation that efficiency gains would offset any distributional (consumer surplus) losses. In extreme cases, industrial policy could be used as a weapon of last resort.

The above conclusion is also strengthened by the Austrian (and Schumpeterian) focus on potential competition (see, for example, Littlechild 1981). In this view, potential competition can engender competitive behavior even in the presence of large oligopolistic firms, constraining large firms from fully exploiting their efficiency-generated market power and reducing consumer surplus. All in all, potential competition and the three efficiency-based arguments mentioned above provide strong support for large size and establish a compatibility between industrial policy and competitive strategy. The focus on potential competition has reemerged more recently in Baumol's

(1982) contestable markets hypothesis, which maintains that free entry and costless exit can reestablish the competitive norm even in the presence of economies of scale and scope. We will not repeat the large and ongoing debate on contestability and potential competition here, other than to point to an emerging consensus (which includes Baumol himself) to the effect that it would take more than potential competition to establish competitive behavior, and that contestability should be seen as no more than a benchmark (Baumol 1991; see also, *inter alia*, Dixit 1982; Dasgupta 1986).

More recently, compatibility between industrial policy and competitive strategy has been established through the theory of transaction costs, wherein the very existence of firms and their strategies can be explained as an attempt to solve market failures due to transaction costs (costs of obtaining information, negotiating and concluding contracts, and policing and enforcing such contracts). Excessive market transaction costs emerge through the existence of bounded rationality, opportunism, and asset specificity, all of which are attenuated under hierarchies – such as firms. Vertical integration, internal organization (the M-form), conglomerates, and transnationals can all be explained through variants of the transaction costs hypothesis, thus implying that large size can be the efficient solution to, rather than the source of, market failure. Coase (1937) is the father of this perspective, and Williamson (1975) the principal recent contributor. Under the transaction-costs perspective, large firms can again be seen as efficiency-enhancing; thus, one can advise firms to pursue competitive advantage through reductions in market transaction costs (for example, backward integration where suppliers are opportunistic and there exists asset specificity) in the expectation that the efficiency gains thereby generated will offset any consumer surplus losses. Industrial policy can again be used as a weapon of last resort in the absence of contestability (absent in any case in this theory from the very assumption of asset specificity). It follows that mainstream transaction costs theorizing also in part resolves the Jekyll and Hyde syndrome of the industrial economist. However, a problem once again arises from the conceptual and empirical difficulties of the transaction costs perspective, including problems of definition and operationalization (see Pitelis 1993 for detailed critical assessments).

The apparent incompatibilities between neoclassical, IO-based industrial policy and competitive strategy can thus be partly solved by alternative approaches that provide efficiency-based reasons for large size. But such approaches are all beset with conceptual and empirical difficulties. Important among these is that efficiency and market power may be inseparable, whereby the former necessarily leads to the latter. For example, Malcolmson (1983) argues that reductions in transaction costs can be a vehicle for acquiring market power. The argument can similarly be applied to the differential efficiency and innovations hypothesis. Thus, the incompatibility problem reemerges, at least in the absence of contestability, since large firms arising from efficiency-related reasons could still make use of their size to acquire market power through, for example, Porter-type policies or even unfair and illegal practices. In fact, this is exactly what the US Justice Department claimed in alleging that Microsoft "used unfair and illegal practices to maintain its dominant position" (*Financial Times*, 18 July 1994). Put simply, large size is neither necessarily the result nor the cause of market power, but it may be and often is. It is therefore useful to consider alternative ways of addressing the potential incompatibility between industrial policy and competitive strategy. One such way, which focuses on small size, is pursued next.

Solving the dilemma: small firms and competitive strategies

Efficiency-based arguments are not the only way of making industrial policy and competitive strategy compatible. An alternative, based on small rather than large firm size, has acquired interest in recent years. Best (1990) presents an excellent, sympathetic yet critical appraisal of the new literature (which has used such characterizations as the second industrial divide, the new competition, industrial districts, and flexible specialization) which points to a competitive strategy designed to support small size, thus avoiding the drawbacks of giantism.

Although interest in the putative benefits of small size is not new, it has become extremely fashionable recently. Among conventional IO theorists, for example, there is an emerging consensus that the benefits of large size have been exaggerated, and accordingly, the focus on giantism and national champions by national governments and the European Community has been misplaced, leading instead to "sleepy giants" (see Geroski and Jacquemin 1989). Not only are economies of scale not ubiquitous as formerly believed, but large firms are also beset with problems such as bad industrial relations and absenteeism. The literature on the new industrial competition is less conventional, tending to emphasize the advantages of flexibility, innovativeness, hands-on approaches to management, and improved labor relations. All are associated with networks of small, cooperating, customer-oriented firms that have managed to beat the recession in a number of industrial districts in Europe and America.

The success of industrial districts and of the related new approaches to management and entrepreneurship has been hailed by some as the emergence of a new post-Fordist era of flexible specialization and of a more democratic form of running firms. This form succeeds in making better use of the dispersed knowledge of employees and suppliers, thus reducing transaction costs more through trust than through hierarchy (see the contributions in Pyke *et al.* 1990). The empirical validity of these conceptual formulations is not yet clear. For one thing, some of these new approaches have been used or even initiated by large (Japanese) firms. Moreover, it is questionable whether employees of small firms do, in fact, face generally better working conditions. Last, but not least, given the potential ultimate dependence of small firms on large transnationals (TNCs), some flexible arrangements used by TNCs (e.g. outsourcing) can hardly be hailed as more democratic, and are innovative only in that they represent new ways for TNCs to make profits. (For some authors such as Cowling and Sugden [1987], subcontractors fall into the ambit of TNCs and are thus part and parcel of them.)

It is unlikely, in our view, that under free market conditions networks of small firms will succeed in effecting a qualitative change in the nature of industrial organization as we know it, in other words, posing a major challenge to the power of large TNCs. More likely, the tendency will be for small firms to become agents of TNCs as Hymer (1970) predicted. He attributed this change to a desire by TNCs to eliminate hardware (production *per se*) and the difficulties associated with it, and to concentrate instead on the control of software (marketing, brand name, distribution, etc.). This is not to say that small-firm networks are unimportant or that markets should be left to operate freely, far from it. Small-firm development represents a potential challenge and source of competition to TNCs. They are a living proof of the claim that alternatives to economic growth through giantism are feasible; they are also good *per se* because pluralism in IO forms should be welcome for its competition and information-providing qualities. Care should be taken, however, that small-firm networks do not become agents of TNCs, for which the cooperation and support of governmental authorities is required, for example in the provision of infrastructure and legal frameworks facilitating the reduction of transaction costs.

To summarize, the mainstream, monopoly-welfare-losses perspective points to the need for state intervention, in particular industrial policies designed to curb monopoly power that are inconsistent with competitive strategies that encourage the acquisition of monopoly power. Conversely, the efficiency-of-large-size arguments coupled with contestability notions are generally supportive of free market forces; they argue for industrial policies that permit large size and are therefore consistent with competitive strategies that are designed to acquire monopolistic advantages. Finally, the small-firm network approach points to a different form of intervention, one designed to support small firms, consistent with competitive strategies that seek advantages through means other than giantism. The problem with all of these approaches is that they fail to make explicit the model of *national strategy* that they are based upon, as any industrial policy and industrial strategy should be. A clearly articulated national strategy is a necessary precondition for assessing the consistency among industrial policy, industrial strategy, competitive strategy, and national strategy in each approach, and for choosing among the alternative approaches. This requires us to go beyond existing theories and to begin restructuring from some key assumptions, most fundamentally that industrial policies should be an integral part of a more general national strategy for development. The latter, however, needs to be developed from first principles, in particular an analysis of the theory of the state (including its existence, objectives, evolution, and constraints) and its relationship with the private sector (domestic firms, transnationals, markets, and consumers).

THEORY OF STATE AND NOTIONS OF NATIONAL STRATEGY

Industrial strategy is, by definition, part and parcel of the more general national strategy for economic development. In the industrial organization and competitive strategy literature, the issue of a national strategy is nearly always left undiscussed. The implicit assumption is that a national strategy for economic development is directed toward increasing economic growth, and that proposed industrial policies, industrial strategies, and competitive strategies are somehow compatible with it. However, this begs the question of precisely what national strategy is. More importantly, it fails to address the issues of what national strategy ought to be. To address these issues seriously we need a theory that explains the emergence, evolution, functions, and constraints of the state in market economies. Such a theory would help in the formulation of a desirable and feasible national strategy, identification of the conditions under which it can be implemented, and determination of the criteria for compatibility with industrial policies, industrial strategies, and competitive strategies.

There are three major perspectives on the theory of the state: mainstream, "new right," and Marxist. According to the mainstream view, states exist in market economies in order to solve problems of market failure, notably public goods, externalities, and monopolies (see, for example, Stiglitz 1986). This is the standard public economics approach that has more recently been generalized in terms of market transaction costs (Coase 1960; Arrow 1970). According to this perspective, the role of the state is similar to the role that Coase (1937) postulated for the firm – to reduce often-excessive market transaction costs – and its objectives and functions are designed to do just that. The literature does not, however, address possible constraints that arise from the costs of governing which are themselves a form of transaction cost, and which are attributable to bounded rationality, opportunism, and investments in specific assets on the part of both state functionaries and other agents (Williamson 1986). This explains the limits of state activity (i.e. why not central planning) and, correspondingly, the idea that optimal resource allocation is dependent on the optimal institutional mix between the public and private sectors, at least with respect to minimization of transaction costs.

The new right, represented by the public choice and Chicago perspectives, explicitly entertains the possibility of inefficiencies in state intervention due to opportunistic – or, more politely, utility maximizing – behavior by bureaucrats and politicians. In this view, internalities and redundant and rising costs are attributable to utility-maximizing behavior by state functionaries in their pursuit of status, power, and privilege (Friedman 1962; Stigler 1988; Wolf 1979; Mueller 1989). Although the state can emerge spontaneously as a consequence of individuals trying to raise themselves above the anarchy of the market (Hobbesian state of nature), states can be captured by organized interest groups, thus hindering the efficient allocation of resources. Therefore, markets should be left to operate freely, with the state limiting itself to the provision of stable rules of the game, for example in the clear delineation of property rights. The dramatic growth of the state observed in all OECD countries is explained by the mutual interests of utility-maximizing state functionaries on the one hand, and the powerful interest groups (mainly producers and trade unions) who have captured the state on the other (Mueller 1989).

The transaction costs and new right perspectives have been brought together in Douglas North's (1981) attempt to provide a "neoclassical theory of the state." He argues that wealth-maximizing or utility-maximizing rulers exchange sets of services (protection, justice) for revenue. In doing so, states act as discriminating monopolists, tailoring and devising property rights so as to maximize state revenue, subject to the constraint of potential entry by other rulers (other states or parties). The objective is to maximize rents and reduce transaction costs so as to foster maximum output, and thus maximize tax revenues accruing to the ruler. Two separate constraints – existing competition by rivals and transaction costs in state activities – typically tend to produce inefficient property rights. The former implies favoring powerful constituents while transaction costs in metering, policing, and collecting taxes provide incentives to states to grant monopolies. These two constraints give rise to a conflict between a property right structure that produces economic growth and one that maximizes rents, thus accounting for the widespread inefficiency of property rights. North regards this idea as the neoclassical variant of the Marxian notion of the contradictions in the mode of production in which the ownership structure is incompatible with potential gains from existing technological opportunities.

The similarity between the new right and North on the one hand, and the Marxian school on the other, do not end here. Marx himself was one of the first to contemplate a theory of capture, something he considered as an integral part of capitalism due to existing inequalities in production. For Marx, the inherent inequity between workers and capitalists implied a state bias in favor of capitalists. The capitalist capture of the state has been explained by latter-day Marxists in instrumentalist terms, linking state personnel with capital (Miliband 1969) and structural terms that focus on the control of capital over investments (Poulantzas 1969). Moreover, Marxists have explained the autonomous form of the capitalist state, both in terms of the direct control of labor by capital in the production process (thus eliminating the state's need to assume direct control of labor) and in terms of the state's need to support production (for example, through the provision of infrastructure), as a result of the anarchy of the market (Holloway and Picciotto 1978). For the Marxist school, the growth of the state and fiscal crises can be explained in terms of laws of motion, for example the concentration and centralization of capital, declining profit rates, and the consequent class struggle over state expenditures (see, for example, O'Connor 1973).

Both North and Marxian theory may tend to underplay the power of consumers as electors and as a source of tax revenues. Electoral defeats and reductions in rents accruing to the state due to reduced employment levels are further constraints on the behavior of state functionaries, whether they are maximizing their own utility or that of capital. On the other hand, the possibility of capture is an important point of consensus between new right, Marxian, and North's theories. Neither is it totally alien in the conventional neoclassical tradition, especially in regards to the relationship between states and transnationals. For example, the views of Vernon (1971) and Kindleberger (1969) on the limitations of state autonomy due to the locational flexibility of TNCs are well known. Last but not least, the Marxian focus on the need to reduce production costs – already expressed in the conventional neoclassical focus on public goods (Adam Smith 1776) – counterbalances the exclusive reliance of transaction costs theorists on the exchange side.

This review of alternative perspectives on the state permits a generalization of North's theory: the state exists because of excessive private-sector transaction *and* production costs, and it aims to reduce these costs in order to increase output and thus increase revenue for state functionaries. Increased output also helps legitimize income inequities which Marxists claim are inherent in capitalism and which are widely observed empirically anyway. The state is constrained from achieving its objectives by the prospect of capture (inherent for Marxists, arising *ex post* for the new right) which tends to generate inefficient property rights and hinders increases in output. Transaction costs in metering, policing, and enforcing taxes also lead to inefficiency in terms of states granting monopolies. Moreover, governing costs also limit the state's ability to replace the private sector efficiently. This leads to a need for a plurality of institutional forms.[5]

It follows that the aim of the state should be to remove the constraints to reducing private-sector transaction and production costs, most notably the problem of capture by powerful constituents. This points toward the need to establish competitive conditions in product and labor markets. Competition would tend to reduce the power of such constituents.[6] It would, moreover, tend to reduce problems with governing costs, for example those associated with powerful, opportunist, private-sector suppliers of required state services. Competitive conditions, however, should not be limited to the private sector only, but should be extended to the market for government control; namely, within limits, political positions should be contestable. This would provide useful sources of information on possible differences in efficient governing and tend to reduce the costs of government.

The reduction of private-sector transaction and production costs by the state is aimed at providing the conditions for the efficient production of goods and services by the private sector. This introduces the concept of national strategy for growth as the set of state policies intending to reduce private-sector production and transaction costs so as to increase realized output in the form of income. Examples of policies that reduce production costs are investments by the state in infrastructure, education, and skills. Policies that reduce market transaction costs delineate and enforce property rights. The internalization of private-sector activities by the state should be pursued up to the point where an additional transaction or production activity would be produced at equal cost in the private sector. This reinforces the concept of pluralism in institutional forms, i.e. the complementarity between the public and private sectors for the efficient production and allocation of resources.

This notion of national strategy takes the revenue side as given, it being the exclusive prerogative of the private sector. However, the state can affect revenues in addition to production and transaction costs. This can be done by directly undertaking production activities, by directing cost-reducing activities to particular sectors, or by pursuing strategic trade policies. In a world of trade and open economies, growth can be achieved via both domestic and foreign demand, while incomes and rent will be affected positively both through reductions in transaction and production costs *and* through increases in revenues. Strategic trade policies specifically address the revenue enhancing side.[7] It follows that national strategy in open economies should be designed not only to raise productivity by reducing overall production and transaction costs for the economy, but also to influence the revenue side so as to increase the income accruing to the nation and taxes to the state.

The analysis of the state and national strategy provides a crucial starting point for addressing the issue of compatibility and choice between industrial and competitive strategies. In particular, the notion of capture as a potential constraint to developmental policies provides a demarcation criterion for industrial and competitive strategies in reemphasizing the need for competition and for a plurality of organizational and institutional focuses as prerequisites for state autonomy and the exploitation of dispersed knowledge.

COMPATIBILITY OF STRATEGIES: IMPLICATIONS FOR LESS FAVORED COUNTRIES

Historically, industrial policies in the US, UK, and EU have been permissive and even encouraging of large size, despite the lip service that has been paid to curbing abuses of monopoly power (Geroski and Jacquemin 1989; Pitelis 1994). This apparent inconsistency between theory and practice can be explained by a strong regard for growth through international competitiveness. Particularly following Servan-Schreiber's call to arms – his claim that Europe had become technologically dependent on US firms – EU policymakers tended to focus on growth through increased competitiveness, believed to be achievable through giantism. Similar to American-based TNCs, giant European firms could exploit economies of scale and other advantages of size, thus enhancing Europe's export surpluses and stimulating growth. Such advantages were, often implicitly, taken to be important enough to offset any consumer surplus losses associated with giantism.

Japanese industrial policy has not been so different in its focus on large firms. In contrast to Western convictions regarding the ability of free market forces to identify the best sources of international comparative advantage, however, Japanese policymakers have tried explicitly to shape the market through identification of high-return sectors and through provision of selective incentives (Matsumoto 1992). Japan's MITI has been hailed in the literature as a model of industrial strategy designed to create dynamic comparative advantages rather than accepting the imperatives of existing static advantages.

In addition to the problems of large size discussed earlier, focus on giantism reinforces the problem of capture of the state by large producers, tending to hinder a national strategy of reducing transaction costs. In this sense, focus on large size is inconsistent with a national strategy as described in the previous section. Industrial policy and competitive strategy designed to facilitate large size also become inconsistent with national strategy. Moreover, these problems are exacerbated in an era of global production and TNCs. By pursuing the pure logic of private profit maximization, TNCs could exploit their locational flexibility to capture the state, thus increasing transaction costs of governments. This is true even when TNCs emerge in order to reduce market transaction costs, as argued, for example, by Buckley and Casson (1976). Nor is it obvious that the benefits of TNC operations accrue to the host countries. Profits generated abroad can be reinvested abroad or dissipated, at least in part, through transfer pricing. Finally, TNCs are unlikely to alleviate the process of deindustrialization; they may even exacerbate it by fleeing from unattractive, deindustrializing countries. International bidding for the services of TNCs by host governments tends to further the problem of capture with its associated transactional and distributional problems.

Industrial and competitive strategies that focus on the benefits of large size and TNCs tend to facilitate capture of the state by TNCs; consequently, they are incompatible with a national strategy that emphasizes growth through reduced transaction costs. An alternative developmental industrial strategy based on networks of small firms in industrial districts is less liable to exacerbate problems of capture. In this sense, industrial and competitive strategies that promote this approach to economic development are more consistent with a national strategy as described in the previous section. Moreover, this paradigm presupposes closer cooperation between the public sector, including local authorities, and the community. Finally, a small-firm network strategy provides a competitive challenge to the reign of TNCs. These arguments point toward industrial and competitive strategies designed to assist the emergence and success of clusters and industrial districts, ideas that are advocated in this chapter.

The limitations of industrial districts, some of which are mentioned above, should not be ignored. It must be recognized that the export of economic growth to the Third World, especially the dramatic growth of the newly industrialized countries (NICs), has been achieved in part through TNCs. However, even accepting that the often dependent development achieved through TNCs has been good for NICs, it is not self-evident that economic development could not be achieved otherwise, including through industrial districts. The arguably dominant position of TNCs in market economies, and the fact that TNCs are often a *sine qua non* for the emergence and survival of industrial districts (through, for example, demand for small-firm products and services), argue against monolithic approaches to national strategy, and thus industrial and competitive strategies; instead, it argues for institutional pluralism, including competition between alternative institutional forms. Having said this, the dynamics of the system tend to favor cumulative processes that favor the existing giants – TNCs. To avoid the problems associated with this, governments need to pursue strategies designed to support alternatives to TNCs, such as industrial districts, in order to establish consistency between national strategy, industrial strategy, and competitive strategy by avoiding the problem of capture and the problems (transaction costs, distributional) that this generates. For institutional pluralism to be feasible, the market for government itself should, up to a point, become contestable, so that captured state functionaries can be removable.[8]

Our theoretical support for national industrial strategies in favor of networks of small firms is particularly important for small LFCs, where domestic market size might be a constraint for the development of large-scale production and, therefore, locally based TNCs. The industrial development needs of such countries can be addressed by attracting foreign direct investment (FDI) from foreign-based TNCs. However, given the problems associated with exclusively relying on foreign firms,[9] a preferable strategy for LFCs would be the development of networks of small and medium-sized firms, potentially complemented by FDI. It is instructive to note that such a policy is consistent with the experience of the so-called Four Tigers, who simultaneously attempted also to develop domestically based large TNCs (see Pitelis 1994 for more on these).

Despite the apparent positive implications of our analysis for LFC development, there remains a fundamental problem: the very adoption of such policies presupposes extensive state involvement of the "right" type. However, government failure in delineating and enforcing property rights is arguably the very reason why such countries are LFCs to start with (North 1991). Moreover, failure is in itself a reason for excessive state involvement in that it tends to increase the relative costs of transactions relative to governing (high themselves), thus increasing state involvement further. The power of the state in such cases can be high enough actually to stand our previous analysis on its head, namely that the state may capture the private sector. Whether, in such a context, the state will choose to undertake productivity-increasing policies will depend on the incentives and expected payoffs to state functionaries. This will be influenced by complex considerations, including beliefs, culture, and ideology. The outcome is not predetermined and the situation not easily amenable to prescriptions. Consequently, our analysis can be taken only as indicative, but cannot provide hard and fast solutions to LFC development. While we can arguably formulate the fundamental questions, as North (1991) points out, we are not yet capable of delivering the answers. Nonetheless, one normative implication can be solidly derived, namely that steps to improve public-sector efficiency and generally to reduce the relative costs of governing can and should be pursued. It is instructive that improving public-sector efficiency is currently one of the basic pillars of EU policy for competitiveness. Moreover, consensus-building can be a useful prerequisite for progress in this direction.

To summarize, we advocate an industrial strategy of assisting clusters of small and medium-sized enterprises for a complex set of interrelated reasons. These include: problems of state capture by large firms; the need for competition, especially with respect to TNCs; the information- and knowledge-related advantages of a plurality of competing institutional forms; and the advantages of clusters compared to TNCs in developing consensus, trust, and bottom-up properties. We want to emphasize that such advocacy does not derive from any anti-TNC rhetoric, SME romanticism, or *ad hoc* assumptions. Instead, our key assumptions were derived from a metaframework built on the almost self-evident requirement that industrial and competitive strategies should be consistent, both with respect to each other, and in regards to a more general strategy for (inter)national development.

Our discussion has neglected distributional issues arising from the pursuit of national and industrial strategies in market economies. These are important considerations (and closely related to the problem of capture) that have been analyzed elsewhere (Pitelis 1994); it should be recognized that distributional issues need to be explicitly considered in order to achieve feasible, consensus-based strategies for development. Regardless of this, any efficiency-enhancing national strategy targeted to reducing production and transaction costs, and consistent with industrial and competitive strategies, can best be achieved by fostering an environment that favors competitive challenges by small firms to TNCs as well as to state functionaries. In both cases, this is achieved by reducing problems associated with capture. Such a strategy, moreover, seems particularly suited for LFCs, at least on theoretical grounds. Implementation, however, need not be straightforward.

CONCLUSIONS

We have argued that traditional IO-inspired industrial policy is hostile to monopoly power and is thus inconsistent with a competitive strategy that advises firms to achieve monopolistic advantages. Efficiency-based arguments question the existence and/or significance of monopoly power, thus reestablishing consistency between industrial policy, industrial strategy, and competitive strategy.[10] Such arguments and the associated purported positive role of large size on international competitiveness have been responsible for an encouraging stance by Western governments favoring large size. Consistency between industrial policy, industrial strategy, and competitive strategy can also be achieved, however, through a focus on clusters of small firms and industrial districts. A choice between the two by the state presupposes an analysis of the nature, objective, and constraints of the state and its functionaries.

Starting from first principles, we regard the state as an institutional device for the production, allocation of resources, and the division of labor that can reduce transaction and production costs of the private sector. This introduces a static notion of national strategy, one intending to foster increased output and income, and thus taxes for the state. An important constraining factor is the problem of capture, which tends to increase transaction costs and generates inefficient property rights and increased distributional inequities. A large firm-based industrial strategy tends to foster the problem of capture, thus being inconsistent with a national strategy for development. This is particularly true in the case of TNCs. An industrial strategy focusing on clusters of small firms does not suffer from this problem of inconsistency to the same degree, and provides a welcome source of competition to TNCs. These arguments point to the need for institutional pluralism and competition between alternative institutional forms, including, up to a point, competition for state offices. Such pluralism will tend to reduce the problem of capture, increase efficiency, and establish consistency between national, industrial, and competitive strategies. Support for networks of small firms appears most suitable for LFCs, subject, however, to the existence of incentive mechanisms for the implementing agency, the state itself. This is a fundamental issue of concern for political economy requiring further analysis and research.

NOTES

1 An earlier version of this chapter has been presented to an Industrial Economics Study Group at Warwick. I am grateful to the organizers and participants for the invitation and comments. Also to the editors of this volume for useful comments. Errors are mine.

2 Note, however, that in the most recent edition of his book, Scherer himself is reluctant to put an exact figure on welfare losses.

3 For Rumelt *et al.* 1991, Porter's contribution was to shift emphasis from the industry to the firm. However, the main shift in my view is from advising governments to advising firms; focus on industry, for example, is still there in the 5-forces model. It is this shift, moreover, that introduces the incompatibilities mentioned above.

4 The same is true of other competitive strategy approaches; for example, the Boston Consulting Group advises firms to seek market share. In industrial organization, market share is mostly viewed as anticompetitive (Rumelt *et al.* 1991).

5 The analysis here is limited in that it does not attempt to explain the very reason for exchange, the market, production for exchange, the firm (including the TNC),

and the state. Such a more general analysis, which also takes a historical-evolutionary line is found in Pitelis 1991. Our discussion here is consistent with, but not as comprehensive as the analysis there.

6 Competition will not succeed in eliminating constituent power if it is inherent in production. This implies that full realization of potential efficiency may be unattainable in capitalism.

7 Such policies have been used widely by various countries, most recently Japan and the so-called Four Tigers. They have recently received theoretical blessing too, through the new international trade theory (see, for example, Krugman 1986). As Krugman observes, however, such policies may suffer from problems of implementation (identifying strategic sectors) *and* retaliation (see Pitelis 1994 for a more detailed exposition).

8 It is worth noting, however, that too much competition for government positions can lead to excess competition and dissipation of resources, as in the case of the private sector (Best 1990; Pitelis 1994). In this sense, one could advocate "managed" competition for government.

9 Arguments against exclusive reliance on TNCs include: it engenders excessive dependence on potentially mobile TNCs; TNCs tend to use branch-plant operations of low added value; there exists a risk that domestic markets will be dominated by TNCs; and TNCs thwart the development of domestic industry. See Dunning 1992, *inter alia*.

10 Another efficiency-based approach to industrial strategy could involve the identification, development, and exploitation by either the private or public sector of competencies at both the firm and state levels. Such a competence-based perspective on competitive strategy, industrial policy, industrial strategy, and national strategy has most interesting implications on the pursuit of dynamic efficiency through policy but falls beyond the scope of this chapter. On the competence-based view see Penrose 1959 and Foss 1993.

REFERENCES

Arrow, K. (1970) "The organization of economic activity: issues pertinent to the choice of market versus non-market allocation," in R. H. Haveman and J. Margolis (eds) *Public Expenditure and Policy Analysis*, Chicago: Markham.

Baumol, W. (1982) "Contestable markets: an uprising in the theory of industry structure," *American Economic Review* 72: 1–15.

—— (1991) *Perfect Markets and Easy Virtue*, Oxford: Basil Blackwell.

Best, M. (1990) *The New Industrial Competition*, Cambridge: Polity Press.

Buckley, P. J. and Casson, M. (1976) *The Future of Multinational Enterprise*, London: Macmillan.

Coase, R. H. (1937) "The nature of the firm," *Economica* 4: 386–405.

—— (1960) "The problem of social cost," *Journal of Law and Economics* 3, 1: 1–44.

Cowling, K. (1982) *Monopoly Capitalism*, London: Macmillan.

Cowling, K. and Sugden, R. (1987) *Transnational Monopoly Capitalism*, Brighton: Wheatsheaf.

Cowling, K. and Waterson, M. (1976) "Price cost margins and market structure," *Economica* 43: 267–274.

Dasgupta, P. (1986) "Positive freedoms, markets and the welfare state," *Oxford Review of Economic Policy* 2, 2: 25–36.

Dixit, A. (1982) "Recent developments in oligopoly theory," *American Economic Review* 72, 2: 12–17.

Dunning, J. (1992) "The competitive advantage of nations and the activities of transnational corporations," *Transnational Corporations* 1, 2: 135–168.

Foss, J. N. (1993) "Theories of the firm: competence and contractual perspectives," *Journal of Evolutionary Economics* 3: 127–144.

Friedman, M. (1962) *Capitalism and Freedom*, Chicago: University of Chicago Press.

Geroski, P. and Jacquemin, A. (1989) "European industrial policy," in A. Jacquemin and A. Sapir (eds) *The European Internal Market, Trade and Competition*, Oxford: Oxford University Press.

Grant, W. (1982) *The Political Economy of Industrial Policy*, London: Butterworths.

Holloway, J. and Picciotto, S. (1978) *State and Capital: A Marxist Debate*, London: Edward Arnold.

Hymer, S. H. (1976) *The International Operations of National Firms: A Study of Foreign Direct Investment*, Cambridge, MA: MIT Press.

Kay, J. (1991) *Foundations of Corporate Success*, Oxford: Oxford University Press.

Kindleberger, C. P. (1969) *International Business Abroad*, New Haven, CT: Yale University Press.

Krugman, P. R. (1986) "Introduction: new thinking about trade policy," in P. R. Krugman (ed.) *Strategic Trade Policy and the New International Economics*, Cambridge, MA: MIT Press

Littlechild, S. (1981) "Misleading calculations of the cost of monopoly power," *Economic Journal* 91.

Malcolmson, J. (1983) "Efficient labour organisation: incentives, power and the trans-action costs approach," in F. Stephen (ed.) *Firm Organizations and Labour*, London: Macmillan.

Matsumoto, G. (1992) "The work of the ministry of international trade and industry," in K. Cowling and R. Sugden (eds) *Current Issues in Industrial Economic Strategy*, Manchester: Manchester University Press.

Miliband, R. (1969) *The State in Capitalist Society*, London: Quarter Books.

Modigliani, F. (1958) "New developments on the oligopoly front," *Journal of Political Economy* 66: 215–232.

Mueller, D. C. (1989) *Public Choice II. A Revised Edition of Public Choice*, Cambridge: Cambridge University Press.

North, D. C. (1981) *Structure and Change in Economic History*, New York: Norton.

—– (1991) "Institutions," *Journal of Economic Perspectives* 5, 1: 97–112.

O'Connor, J. (1973) *The Fiscal Crisis of the State*, New York: St Martin's Press.

Penrose, E. (1959) *The Theory of the Growth of the Firm*, New York: John Wiley.

Pitelis, C. N. (1991) *Market and Non-Market Hierarchies*, Oxford: Basil Blackwell.

—— (1993) (ed.) *Transaction Costs, Markets and Hierarchies*, Oxford: Basil Blackwell.

—— (1994) "Industrial strategy: for Britain in Europe in the world," *Journal of Economic Studies* 21, 5: 2–92.

Porter, M. E. (1980) *Competitive Strategy*, New York: Free Press.

—— (1987) "From competitive advantage to corporate strategy," *Harvard Business Review* May/June.

—— (1990) *The Competitive Advantage of Nations*, Basingstoke: Macmillan.

—— (1995) "The competitive advantage of the inner city," *Harvard Business Review* May/June: 33–71.

Poulantzas, N. (1969) *Political Power and Social Class*, London: New Left Books.

Pyke F., Becattini, G., and Sengenberger, W. (1990) *Industrial Districts and Inter-Firm Co-Operation in Italy*, Geneva: International Institute for Labour Studies.

Rumelt, R. P. *et al.* (1991) "Strategic management and economics," *Strategic Management Journal* 12: 5–29.

Scherer, F. M. (1980) *Economics of Industrial Structure, Conduct and Performance*, Skokie, IL: Rand McNally.

Smith, A. [1776] (1977) *The Wealth of Nations*, reprint, London: Dent.

Stigler, G. (1988) "The effect of government on economic efficiency," *Business Economics* 23: 7–13.

Stiglitz, J. E. (1986) *Economics of the Public Sector*, New York: Norton.

Teece, D. (1990) "Contributions and impediments of economic analysis to the study of strategic management," in J. W. Frederickson (ed.) *Perspectives on Strategic Management*, New York: Harper and Row.

Vernon, R. (1971) *Sovereignty at Bay*, Harlow: Longman.

Williamson, O. E. (1975) *Markets and Hierarchies*, New York: Free Press.

—— (1986) *Economic Organisation: Firms, Markets and Policy Control*, Brighton: Wheatsheaf.

Wolf, C. (1979) "A theory of non-market behaviour: framework for implementation analysis," *Journal of Law and Economics* 22, 1: 107–140.

7 The regional development potential of inward investment[1]

Ash Amin and John Tomaney

INTRODUCTION

This book advances two central propositions with novel implications for industrial policy. The first is that industrial policies are necessary, but in ways that break with the traditional efficiency-detracting forms of intervention, such as state hand-outs to firms, the protection of target industries, nationalization, or strict regulation of markets. The suggestion is that public policy should focus on the framework conditions of entrepreneurship and competitiveness. This ranges from the quality of infrastructure, labour markets, and knowledge environments, to the supply of business services and institutionalized support for firms. An added implicit suggestion is that, in delivering such support, the state should become one among several institutions of coordination and regulation of business life. These might include trade associations, labor organizations, development agencies, business service centers, and so on. Thus industrial policy is couched in terms of a broadly based infrastructural policy, in the hands of a coordinated set of specialized agencies.

The second proposition is that it is productive systems – industrial districts, clusters, value chains – and not individual companies or nations that compete in global markets. While it is contestable that individual companies do not compete, the proposition is right to suggest that the competitiveness of an individual firm rests on a series of vertical and horizontal linkages that have a direct bearing on the cost and opportunity structure of the firm (Porter 1990; Lazonick 1993). Firms are locked into networks of competition and cooperation with other firms (e.g. suppliers and buyers), as well as ties of institutional association (e.g. trade organizations, professional bodies, clubs, and contact networks), and infrastructural provision (e.g. educational organizations as sources of skills and training, local authorities for business premises, chambers of commerce for market information). The policy implication is that industrial policies should move from being firm-centered, or industry-specific, toward becoming system-centered, seeking purposefully to act upon the networks in which firms find themselves (Storper 1995; Dunning 1993a).

Conceived along these lines, industrial policy can become a tool for stimulating self-sustaining local economic development, if the right clusters and networks are selected. The principle is that support should be given in ways that provide spillover effects to more than just the initial beneficiaries. Firm-centered policies, such as the offer of financial incentives, have for too long ended up as a means of subsidizing individual companies, with little regard to their impact on the host community. A "systemic" industrial policy, in contrast, would seek to intervene in ways that either strengthen local ties (e.g. incentives for local purchasing or interfirm collaboration) or upgrade the local asset base as a means of attracting further investment and entrepreneurship (e.g. a program to offer the highest quality premises, services, skills, and know-how in selected industrial clusters). This is not to argue that industrial policy should become autarkic – in an era of increasing globalization of production and firm networks, this would serve only to divert investment – but rather that it should be conceptualized as a bridge between global economic orientations and local development needs, as a means of building local externalities that help firms to improve global competitiveness or their standing in global networks.

Nowhere is this global–local nexus put more to the test than in the nature of the relationship between TNCs and their host locations. In our age of hypermobility and intensified global competition for investment, how can TNCs be turned into engines for local economic development? What can be done to maximize the local benefits of inward investment? In the case of less favored regions, such as old industrial areas or regions of lagging industrialization, what scope is there for policies seeking to maximize local spillover effects, if investors have no interest in them other than as low-cost locations, and if the challenge of building institutional needs proves to be too great? To what extent are such locations capable of sustaining system-based growth?

This chapter focuses on the development potential of inward investment in the context of less favored regions (LFRs), which historically have tended to attract projects that have either intensified problems of dependent development or have failed to act as growth poles. It asks, on the basis of a survey of new "flagship" projects in a selection of European Union LFRs, whether the quality of inward investment in such regions is changing for the better. It then goes on to consider policy actions that might feasibly be adopted to maximize local spillover effects.

THE CHANGING MULTILOCATIONAL FIRM

Recent literature on business organization and management tends to suggest that the geography of multilocational firms might well be changing. As is well known, the experience of "branch plant" industrialization in LFRs during the 1960s and 1970s has been judged to have fallen short of meeting the original expectation that inward investment could act as a "growth pole." The argument is that, during this period, companies used regional policy incentives to locate either capital-intensive or low-wage "cathedrals in the desert," which offered little to the host economy in the way of skill formation, technology transfer, linkage opportunities, transmission of new managerial and entre-preneurial know-how, and reinvestment of profits. Terms such as "branch plant economy," "dependent development," and "industrialization without growth" were coined to highlight the incorporation of such regions within the global business logic of firms governed from elsewhere – a logic working against any self-governing and self-sustaining regional economic develop-ment (Firn 1975; Massey 1984).

Today, however, there is a perception among researchers that the nature of the multilocational firm might be changing. A distinction has been found between the cost- or price-sensitive company that relocates specific tasks to LFRs for financial incentives and cheap labor, and the "performance" com-pany that derives its competitive advantage from product excellence and seeks locations that can offer qualified personnel and innovation-rich environments (Schoenberger 1991). "Performance" companies are those that operate in rapidly changing, specialized, and demanding segments of a product market. It is said that the acute pressure on such companies, associated with volatil-ity and the changeability of products and technologies, has favored the development of organizational structures and strategies based on integrated manufacture, erosion of traditional divisions between managerial, scientific, and manual functions, and the establishment of closer and more collaborative ties with suppliers (Porter 1990; Mytelka 1991; United Nations 1993; Best 1990; Clarke and Monkhouse 1994).

This distinction at the corporate level is mirrored at the plant or divisional level. The cost-driven company, specializing in large volume, medium-technology goods, continues to be characterized by task-specific plants displaying different levels of functional complexity in different locations – all closely tied into a framework of centralized and hierarchical governance. In contrast, "performance" companies, it is said, appear increasingly to be moving over to product-based, rather than task-based, plant structures for the management of worldwide operations, especially in manufacturing. Overseas plants have responsibility for developing, producing, and marketing particu-lar products, often on the basis of possessing a continental or world product mandate (Howells and Wood 1993). Such plants are of strategic importance within the corporation, and functionally far more complex than the tradi-tional branch plant. The plants have leading roles for particular products or technologies – a responsibility accompanied by up-grading of capabilities across the spectrum of tasks and duties. "Performance" plants appear to work on a cooperative basis with each other and with HQ offices, with the former emphasis on domestic "lead" and overseas "lag" in terms of the division of research and production expertise gradually disappearing (Cusumano and Elenkov 1994). Finally, with the change in plant status comes a devolution of management and decision-making capability, thus allowing local managers and workforces to respond rapidly and successfully to changing circumstances.

The "performance" plant is part of a "heterarchical" system of management (Hedlund 1986; Ohmae 1989; Drucker 1990; Dunning 1993b) that is quite different from the older, centralized, and hierarchical patterns of control within branch plants.

The "performance" plant, operating in markets for ever changing, innovation-intensive and quality goods, possesses a set of distinctive attributes that make it an attractive opportunity for stimulating endogenous development (United Nations 1992; Dunning 1994). Four attributes in particular justify a reexamination of the role of inward investment as a stimulus for self-sustaining local economic development. First, the "performance" plant is likely to incorporate a wider range of functions, thus serving to enhance the skill-base and entrepreneurial qualities of the host region. Positive effects might range from the growth of local R&D to the transfer of state-of-the-art skills and industrial practices into the local labor market. Second, the possession of decision-making authority serves to create a local management committed to the long-term survival of the plant, as well as to secure the transfer of vital entrepreneurial capability into the labor market. Third, the "performance" plant has the potential to stimulate more extensive and qualitatively better local supplier linkages than the traditional branch plant. It requires a wider range of inputs as well as flexible but reliable links with suppliers – conditions that could be secured, at least in part, by physical proximity. Fourth, the strategic position of the "performance" plant within the corporation turns the threat of closure or rationalization, so typical of older branch plants, to a positive opportunity for further expansion.

What is less evident from this new academic literature stressing the rise of "heterarchy," "networking," "vertical disintegration," and "performance-based" competition is whether the "performance" plant has emerged or could emerge in the context of LFRs (Dicken *et al.* 1994). Such regions might, for instance, lack the infrastructure to attract quality-seeking inward investment. Nor is it clear whether "performance" plants are attracted to particular types of region, and if so, whether "best practice" might be transferable to other LFRs via appropriate policy interventions. Finally, it is not self-evident whether improvements in the status of plants in given LFRs, where observed, are the result of the rise of the new organizational forms suggested above, or the outcome of different reasons. It has been observed that certain plants in LFRs gradually acquire and develop research and technical skills, often associated with local problem-solving and adaptation to local markets (Hakansson 1990; Young *et al.* 1993).

The next section addresses this issue by examining the quality of projects considered to be "flagship" investments in a selection of European Community LFRs. It draws upon a study for the Directorate-General for Regional Policy of the European Commission completed in March 1993 (Amin *et al.* 1994). The study was stimulated by a desire on the part of the Commission to explore ways in which the offer of EC regional incentives might be calibrated to the "value added" offered by mobile investments to host regions. It sought to identify the scope for attracting quality-based investments into the LFRs and to outline the policy priorities in order to maximize their economic contribution to the region. The study examined the quality of half a dozen recent "flagship" investments in each region on the basis of the following plant-level indicators: functional complexity and decision-making autonomy; innovation potential; training intensity; quality of labor; local content. The study also appraised the influence of regional incentives and the policies and practices of local development agencies on the quality of investment attracted by the regions.

The section draws upon material from the case studies in Scotland, Ireland, and Portugal. It argues that to date there is little evidence to show that new "performance" plants are being located in the LFRs. Instead, evidence for gradual, evolutionary upgrading of plants is far more significant, related to the offer of "softer" forms of support, than to conditions attached to incentives.

FLAGSHIP INWARD INVESTMENT IN THE LFRs – "PERFORMANCE" PLANTS?

Table 7.1 summarizes the characteristics of companies examined in the three regions. The majority of plants belong to well-known international corporations operating in growing or dynamic markets. The majority of the plants were opened in the course of the 1980s. In all three regions, the investments were considered by local agencies to be among the most prestigious attracted into the region.

Strategic functions and decision-making autonomy

Despite the fanfare in Portugal that has surrounded investments such as those by Ford-VW, Delco-Remi, and Blaupunkt, these prestige projects exhibit a strong bias toward final assembly and packaging activities, and the absence of top and middle order management activities. The plants have limited financial autonomy, while the functions of purchasing, product strategy, sales, marketing, and investment are controlled by divisional or head offices outside Portugal. In addition, senior executives tend to be expatriates showing little long-term commitment to the Portuguese plants.

In Ireland, the tendency appeared to be opposite, with evidence that plants were making gains in both the range of functions and in levels of management autonomy, although none of the plants had marketing or sales departments. Each plant, over a period of time, had been awarded either a continental or world product mandate by its parent company. Although integrated into wider corporate networks, in two cases, plants contained functions of strategic importance to the corporation as a whole. In the case of one engineering plant – Garrett Ireland (owned by Allied Signal) – the original plant had acquired an important foundry which significantly increased the status of the plant in the corporate hierarchy. More generally, there is evidence

Table 7.1 Characteristics of selected "flagship" investments in Portugal, Scotland, and Ireland

Portugal

Investor	Total investment (ECU million)	Total grant (% of total investment)	Training grants (%)	Local content (% of national value added)	Size of plant (No. of employees full capacity)	Main product	Major market	Comments
Auto Europa (Ford VW) est. 1991)	2,700.0	40	90	45	5,000	Multi-purpose vehicle (people carrier)	Europe (US)	Greenfield investment Largest ever FDI project, 95% of units exported. About a third of Portugal's total exports
Delco Remi	56.1	38.6	100	22	550	Electronic ABS braking systems	Worldwide ignition	Greenfield site. World market mandate. Located in tax free zone. Part of global purchasing network
Blaupunkt (Bosch) est. 1990	25.0		0	0	1,500	Car radios	Europe worldwide	Expansion of Grundig site
Gelbi (Stora Group) est. 1967	93.0		95	20	740	Paper	Worldwide (Sweden)	Greenfield site

Table 7.1 Characteristics of selected "flagship" investments in Portugal, Scotland, and Ireland – contd

Scotland

Investor	Total investment (Pounds million)	Total grant (% of total investment)	Local content (% of supplies)	No of jobs	Training spend (Pounds million)	R&D (No. employed)	Main markets	Comments
Caledonian Paper (Finland) est. 1989	215	9	70	430	0.45	40	UK, EC US	Capital-intensive Operates in tandem with other European plants
Health Care International (US) est. 1991[a]	180	16	50	800	3.0		EU	Provision of advanced medical care and research
NEC (Japan) est. 1982	174	20	30	830	2% of payroll	0	EU	High capital intensity (210,000 pounds per job) No R&D
Inmac (US) est. 1987	4	20	35	120		4	EU	World product mandate

Table 7.1 Characteristics of selected "flagship" investments in Portugal, Scotland, and Ireland – *contd*

Ireland

Investor	No. of employees	Products	R&D technical support	Comments
Rhône-Poulanc	60	Semi-solid pharmaceutical products	2–3 Quality control and technical staff	1984 World Product Mandate (WPM) for all semi-solid products (secondary production) and suppositories
Allied Signal (Garrett) est. 1979	345	Foundry and production of automotive turbochargers	9 R&D process development workers	After 1982, WPM or Continental Product Mandate (CPM) for two products, New R&D process development unit, Software development unit (30 employees)
Lotus est. 1982	300	Production of packaged software	20 in UNIX development group	1985 CPM for software packages 1986 "Translation" unit move from UK to Dublin
Yamanouchi	150	Production of bulk pharmaceutical intermediaries (primary production)	5–10 technical division	1986 new product added, New pilot plant and facility, Process development unit

Note: [a] Ceased activity after 1994

of the emergence of an Irish management cadre, which presses for greater decisional autonomy. Typically, the Irish managers are strongly committed to the success of their plant, which often leads to upgrading of the status of the plant over time.

In the Scottish case, the profile of top corporate functions and decision-making autonomy differed according to sector. The electronics sector, which has a large presence in Scotland and has been a target sector for development agencies, was characterized by a limited range of corporate functions and constrained management autonomy. Some plants, however, do appear to have continental or world product mandates. On the other hand, investments in the health care and pulp and paper industries appeared to have an extensive range of corporate functions, including control over marketing and sales activities. They were important sites of decision-making in the global management hierarchy.

Innovation capacity

The Portuguese plants visited were characterized by an absence of, or the presence of only rudimentary, research capabilities. There is evidence that more recent investments have been characterized by relatively higher levels of R&D in terms of numbers employed, but activity remains heavily biased toward process development (engineers rather than scientists).

In Ireland, an internal study by EOLAS, the science and technology agency, suggested that significant increases had occurred in the expenditure of overseas companies on R&D. In addition, Ireland has succeeded in attracting some large-scale research activity. For instance, General Semiconductor has relocated a large R&D center from Arizona to Macroom in County Cork. However, in general the EOLAS survey found that research is process-oriented, although in the companies we visited we found evidence of Irish plants beginning to provide corporate-wide R&D services, especially in IT areas. A case in point was Garrett (Allied Signal) which, after extensive negotiations with its parent, had won a key computing service activity. Indeed, in one important case, that of Lotus, a pool of relatively low-cost graduate computing skills in Ireland had been judged to be a key location factor for the firm. A further feature in Ireland is the apparent growth in links between overseas firms and Irish universities. There is also evidence that the R&D capability of overseas firms in Ireland is beginning to improve, but this improvement has occurred over a long period and has been supported by a range of "soft" policy measures and extra finance provided by the Irish Industrial Development Authority (IDA) and EOLAS.

In Scotland, the picture on R&D was mixed. In the electronics sector, research evidence, confirmed by the plant visits undertaken for this study, indicates low levels of R&D (in terms of expenditure, numbers employed, and type of activity) and tends to confirm the traditional branch-plant character of this sector in Scotland. By contrast, establishments in the medical services and pulp and paper sector that were visited were found to fund relatively high levels of R&D. These two establishments were also characterized by a greater level of plant autonomy in other strategic areas. In the case of Health Care International, a key declared locational attribute was the existence of a pool of (English-speaking) medical graduates and research strengths in Scottish universities. Paradoxically, however, the venture ran aground in 1994 owing to its inability to build sufficient demand from the world's rich for its private medical care.

Training intensity

Cross-national differences in training performance are notoriously difficult to measure, and researchers have found it hard to make meaningful comparisons between regions and investors. Measurement in this survey concentrated on the volume of formal training provided. There was insufficient data available on the quality and effectiveness of training to allow reliable comparisons between the regions.

In Portugal, the level of training was limited (in terms of both budget and training days) and tended to be on-the-job. Given that training effort was heavily supported by public (often European Social Fund) grants, it seems to be the case that large amounts of public funds are being used as a wage-cost subsidy.

Recent reviews of Irish industrial policy (Culliton 1992) have suggested that there is significant room for improvement in the provision of training in Ireland. The Irish authorities do not measure the training performance of overseas plants in the same way as they do R&D performance. However, the plants visited for this study were characterized generally by a high level of training. Particularly important appeared to be initiatives (especially for supervisory grades) related to upgrading toward total quality management systems. The involvement of Regional Technology Colleges in this effort appeared to signal the gradual improvement of the training infrastructure in Ireland.

Although the UK as a whole can be criticized for the failings of its training system, in Scotland there was evidence of a comparatively high level of training at the plants visited, including significant off-the-job training. All plants had relatively large training budgets. The provision of bespoke training packages by Local Enterprise Companies (LECs) for inward investors was a distinctive feature in Scotland. For instance, Dumbartonshire LEC was providing training in specialist medical skills for the investment by Health Care International. For the authorities in Scotland the provision of such packages is a means of offering additional inducements to firms that might otherwise be drawn away by higher levels of direct subsidy available in southern Europe.

Overall, the training demands of firms differed significantly between Portugal and the other two regions. In Ireland and Scotland, awareness of the link between training and quality of investment has led to reorganization of the training system, although the immediate effects of this are as yet unclear.

Quality of labor

Attempts to quantify differences in labor quality are similarly confounded by the difficulties of cross-plant, let alone cross-regional, comparisons, given the absence of uniform measures. Information provided by firms, therefore, had to be supplemented by more qualitative impressions in the survey, in order for comparisons to be made.

The occupational profile of the Portuguese plants was heavily skewed toward semi-skilled assembly work. Also significant was that top management jobs tended to go to expatriates rather than the indigenous population, despite the large size of the Portuguese managerial labor market.

In Ireland, by contrast, there is evidence that some improvement has occurred in the labor profile of overseas plants over time. As noted earlier, in the case of Lotus, the existence of a pool of graduate software skills was a significant locational factor, and the firm had established a 100 strong software development team. In other plants visited, the occupational structure remained skewed toward manual grades, but all had been characterized by steady improvements in the numbers of non-manual (notably technical) staff. In contrast to Portugal, a key feature of the plants – and of Ireland more generally – is the presence of Irish managers in key management positions. This appears to be a key factor in explaining the improving quality of overseas investment in Ireland, as Irish managers fight tenaciously for further rounds of investment for their plants.

In Scotland, the labor profile differed by sector. In electronics, the workforce structure was heavily skewed toward semi-skilled manual occupations. By contrast, in the other sectors, the labor profile was more diverse, in part accounted for by the different nature of the processes and by the wider range of strategic functions attached to each facility. As in Ireland, a significant feature of the Scottish plants was the presence of Scots as managers in key positions..

In general, and despite examples of best practice in Ireland and Scotland, the occupational profile of the plants visited bore more resemblance to the archetypal branch plant than to the "performance" plant.

Local content and supplier linkages

The degree of local supply content is perhaps the most significant indicator of the embeddedness of an investment in its host region. A variety of measures of local content were found to be utilized across the regions. One measure is value added (revenues less expenditure), which, of course, gives no direct measure of the extent of local supplier linkages. In other cases, total expenditure within a region is used as a proxy for local content, but this can include items as wage costs, taxes, and even interest on loans. This measure gives only a limited indication of the scale of local multipliers. The most accurate indicator of quality is the proportion of expenditure on materials and services within a region, although the majority of firms examined were unable (or unwilling) to provide this information. When such information was made available, companies were generally reluctant to give specific information on the value distribution of purchases.

In Portugal, a significant level of local content was achieved by a pulp manufacturer that used locally produced eucalyptus trees. With this exception, the plants surveyed in Portugal were characterized by few local linkages. In some cases, the production process amounted to little more than the assembly and packaging of imported components. Even in the case of the pulp plant, originally it had been agreed to establish a paper plant next to the pulp facility as part of the aid package. However, the company in question had not done so and appeared to have no intention of doing so in the future. The anticipated arrival of AutoEuropa, the biggest investment ever in Portugal, by Ford and VW, has prompted a new concern with local linkages and the setting up of a linkage development initiative. As yet there appears to be little evidence of significant increases in local purchase agreements.

The Irish plants visited for this study generally had low levels of local content. The pharmaceutical plant owned by Rhône Poulenc imported 80 percent of its raw materials from a sister plant in Germany, although the pharmaceutical plant owned by Yamanouchi purchased over 50 percent of its raw materials in Ireland. Garrett (owned by Allied Signal), although occupying a strategically important place in the value chain, made few local purchases. In the case of Lotus' software and disk duplication facility, there was significant local purchasing – software manuals from the Irish printing and packaging industry. Indeed there is evidence that the existence of a printing industry that meets international quality standards (together with graduate software skills) is emerging as a key location factor in Ireland. The IDA operates some local linkage development initiatives that have led to modest improvements in the level of Irish purchases by overseas companies. The IDA conducts a regular "Survey of Irish Economy Expenditures" which indicates some improvement in local purchasing.

In Scotland it was found that local content and local purchasing were limited in the electronics sector. Despite a heavy promotional focus on this sector and a significant concentration of investment in Silicon Glen, research evidence suggests a low level of integration (Turok 1993). The firms investigated in our study had very few forward or backward linkages. By contrast, a pulp and paper plant owned by Caledonian Paper had a very high level of local content (e.g. through purchases of local forestry products and local energy).

Across the regions, the extent of local purchasing was surprisingly disappointing overall. Equally surprising was the degree to which regional development agencies fail to monitor such activity – a notable exception being Ireland.

Summary

Four general observations regarding the quality of recent "flagship" investment in the LFRs can be drawn from the preceding discussion. First, there exist significant variations in the quality of investment between the LFRs. In Ireland and Scotland, examples were found of plants occupying a relatively strategic position in the corporate division of labor and drawing upon local human resources. Though such plants generally continued to lack control over investment and procurement strategy as well as product development capability, they did contain process development capability, scientific, technical, and engineering personnel and staff with higher degrees, a continental or global mandate over given products, and local autonomy over nonstrategic decisions. They were noted for their recruitment of senior personnel from the local labor market, as well as the commitment of local managers to the region, especially in terms of winning intracorporate bids for new investments.

By contrast, in Portugal the definition "flagship" project did not readily extend to describe the qualitative aspects of investments. The establishments were production or assembly-oriented, specializing in tasks often duplicated elsewhere, with limited local R&D capability, skill variability, and management autonomy. Closely integrated into the governance structures and global value chain of their parent organizations, they were found to provide little stimulus to the local supplier, skills, or knowledge base. In many respects, the investments were like traditional branch plants, remote from the text-book "performance" plant.

A second observation is that the improvement to quality in Scotland and especially Ireland has taken place over time and appears to be related to the provision of "aftercare" services and finance to upgrade investment. Third, important variations in the local embeddedness of the investments can be related to sectoral differences. The least embedded investments were so-called "hi-tech" sectors, notably electronics. These investments tended to lack strategic functions and made few local purchases. This was true even in Scotland where some plants were characterized by better labor profiles and product mandates. Finally, the most embedded plants tended to be those that were linked to a genuine (i.e. nonfinancial) locational advantage of the region. This could be the knowledge-base, a skilled workforce, a supply industry, or even a raw material source.

POLICY ISSUES

For the present, the text-book "performance" plant has yet to feature in the context of Europe's LFRs in any significant way (see also Giunta and Martinelli 1995, on Southern Italy). Examples of success do, of course, exist, but they are not representative of major upgrading in the quality of new inward investment in LFRs. One explanation could be the endurance of hierarchical forms of organization and governance within multilocational firms, resulting in the allocation of particular tasks to individual sites. Another reason could be that companies continue to perceive LFRs as locations that lack the infrastructure to support plants that make complex demands on the host economy (CEC 1990).

To recognize this failing, however, is not to suggest that nothing has changed or that nothing can be done to ameliorate the quality of mobile investment in LFRs. The stark difference in quality between Portugal on the one hand, and Scotland and Ireland on the other hand, is, in itself, revealing. The least industrialized regions of the EU such as Portugal generally have a less developed skills' base, less advanced training opportunities, poor supplier networks and limited institutional capacity. They are thus less able to support the needs of knowledge-intensive and supply-rich investment. These regions continue to offer cost incentives, notably low industrial wage levels and lucrative financial incentives (Camagni 1992; Nam et al. 1991). The longer term risk they run is to remain trapped in attracting only low-grade branch-plant activities: a specialization that fails to stimulate endogenous development.

In the case of regions such as Ireland and Scotland, which have pursued a more coordinated and strategic approach toward inward investment, there are clear signs of upgrading in the quality of investment. Evidence can be found of plants that possess a product mandate, some product and process development capability, functional heterogeneity, and middle management and scientific capability. On the other hand, and despite the efforts of agencies established explicitly for the purpose, the record of even the best quality projects has been modest in terms of, first, their stimulus to local linkage formation (notably the purchase of high value-added products and services from indigenous companies) and, second, the transfer of technology via links with local firms and research establishments (Turok 1993; Culliton 1992; O'Malley et al. 1992). It is in the areas of skill formation and entrepreneurial capability that benefits can be said to have accrued to the host region, rather than in the areas of innovation and local linkage formation.

The question that has to be asked is what are the factors that have contributed to the upgrading of inward investment? In our analysis, three factors in particular stand out in importance. The first is an emphasis by development agencies on generic upgrading of the physical, human, and communications infrastructure. This includes a commitment to industry training initiatives, investment in higher education, upgrading of transport and communications networks, and the offer of high-quality amenities. In attempting to offer a rich supply-side milieu, these regions display a long-term commitment to "performance"-based entrepreneurship and, in so doing, offer a good reason to investors for procuring their higher value-added inputs from within the region.

The second factor is the presence of institutions such as Scottish Enterprise and the IDA which are committed to a proactive, selective, quality-conscious, and coordinated approach toward inward investment. These are agencies that have developed long-term strategies to encourage particular industrial

Table 7.2 Elements of "good" institutional practice toward mobile investment

- Identification of a small number of strategic sectors in order to promote clustering and the build-up of related agglomeration economies, building where possible on existing industrial strengths.
- One-stop provision of incentives and other forms of assistance in order to facilitate the speed of transactions.
- Understanding the needs of firms establishing a relationship of trust with them and support for local managers in their attempts to upgrade the status of the plant (financial and technical).
- Sector-specific research to identify strengths and weaknesses in the region's resource base of relevance to mobile investors.
- "After-care" support to match investor needs to regional strengths.
- Provision of financial and other incentives to potential suppliers to upgrade product quality and delivery practices.
- Provision of indirect support in the form of infrastructural improvements that can help secure a firm within a region, and also improve the wider supply side characteristics of the region (infrastructure, telecoms supply, generic skills training, etc).
- Regular monitoring of the purchasing, R&D and training performance of investors.

clusters, by seeking out and satisfying selected international firms in targeted sectors. Where sector strategies have been based upon building on existing local industrial strengths, the offer of "one-stop" packages to investors by institutions that have both detailed knowledge of a region's assets and the power to mobilize other regional agencies appears to have helped to attract new investors to Europe who are more open to suggestion concerning the quality and availability of diverse local factor inputs. In addition, the commitment to a targeted strategy has built into it the principle of selectivity, although in practice, quality expectations have often been relaxed when investors have threatened to take the investment elsewhere. Thus, it is not institutional capacity in its own right, but the pursuit of a particular regional strategy that is of significance, and this is of relevance to regions that stop at simply creating narrowly focused institutions of economic development (Dicken and Tickell 1992; Amin and Thrift 1994).

The third, and perhaps more significant, factor has been *in situ* upgrading of plants over a period of time. Achievements such as broadening of a product range, attainment of a product mandate, investment in new research facilities, and expansion of functions are the result of annual improvements in plant performance and the efforts of local managers (usually of indigenous origin) to win new resources and new responsibilities from central management. While the initiative for *in situ* upgrading comes from local managers, the offer of "after-care" support from local development agencies appears to play a significant role in securing success (see also Young and Hood 1995). "After-care" support might include a number of "soft" incentives, such as the offer of help for new recruitment and training targets; the provision and preparation of new premises and communications infrastructure; link-up with potential suppliers, who in turn are assisted to upgrade product quality and delivery; and assistance with reducing red-tape in dealing with government and other public sector bodies. Thus, such support serves not only to improve plant competitiveness, but also to strengthen the hand of local managers in negotiations with the parent firm.

The elements of "good" institutional practice leading up to and after an investment that appear to have had an impact on quality are summarized in Table 7.2. These, together with consistent investment across the spectrum of supply-side infrastructure, appear to be key factors in influencing the regional development potential of inward investment.

Policy choices

The most obvious policy implication of the preceding discussion is that, despite the absence of any noticeable transition toward the location of new "performance" plants in LFRs, the pursuit of maximizing "quality" from investors is a worthwhile objective within LFRs. In light of intensified trade-off and competition between LFRs in the trail of European corporate restructuring post-1992 (see Ramsay 1995), regions will have to look for ways that help in rooting investments within the locality. It is an objective, however, that implies forms of intervention and practices that go well beyond simple adjustments to the financial incentives on offer under European and national regional policy.

This said, there remains some scope for calibrating regional incentives to the quality of mobile investment. It could be argued that the poor quality of projects in countries such as Portugal is, in part, the result of the ability of investors to obtain disproportionately high levels of funding. Thus, a case can be made for cutting back, across Europe, on current levels of regional subsidy (automatic and discretionary) in order to reduce the pursuit of short-term, cost-based, investment projects by regions. The level at which ceilings should be set for different LFRs is clearly a matter of careful consideration, because of the fine balance between ensuring that investors are not kept away, and minimizing interregional competition on the basis of the size of incentive packages (Allen *et al.* 1989). To reduce incentives to the point of discouraging investment from low-cost regions is clearly problematic.

In addition, there is a case for regions to take steps to secure good-quality investments in the first instance, via tying discretionary awards to agreed quality targets. It is important, however, that realistic targets are established for different types of LFR. In institutionally more "advanced" regions like Scotland and Ireland, awards might be weighted in favor of rewarding promising spin-offs in the research and supplies linkage potential of inward investment, while in less "advanced" regions like Portugal, the weighting might be biased toward criteria such as task multiplicity, local decision-making autonomy, and skill formation. Without such a regionalization of policy expectations, the current practice by investors and development agencies to ignore unachievable quality targets set down on paper will not alter.

Ultimately, however, policy changes that exceed the modalities of financial incentives are required. Our study has made it clear that the most common route to plant upgrading in LFRs has been incremental change among existing investments. This suggests the need for policy reforms in the direction of "after-care" support, covering at least three areas. First, discretionary awards should be made available in the course of the life of an investment, when plans to upgrade the status of a plant are being considered by a company. Second, and for the same reason, the significance of "softer" forms of support, such as assistance for training courses, linkage programs, access to local research institutes, and so on, should not be underestimated. What is important, however, is to ensure that such support is sought for genuine upgrading ventures rather than as a means to help investors reduce operating costs. Third, such direct support should be accompanied by investment aimed at upgrading the general infrastructure of a region (notably communications, education and training, research capability, and industrial premises). But, here too, it is important that regional agencies seek to match local strengths to the profile of inward investors. Just as inward investment strategies might focus on particular industrial clusters, wider regional "infrastructure" programs should focus on improving particular sectoral, labor market, or educational strengths within a region. Otherwise the task of constructing a link between inward investment and indigenous needs will remain a distant prospect.

Thus, real success is likely to rest on building strategic local institutional capability. Such capability would require both a proactive approach to inward investment as well as its integration with a broader, longer term, regional development strategy. It is a capability that simultaneously has a sense of the desirability of regional specialization around existing indigenous strengths in an increasingly competitive "open" Europe, and a sense of the advantages of an integrated local economy "thick" with local interconnections. This is something that requires long-term vision, persistence, innovative development agencies, and coordinated inter-institutional behavior. It may turn out that the difference between those European regions that can and those that cannot embark upon a development path based on attracting and retaining good-quality inward investment will lie in their ability to develop such institutional capacity.

This observation takes us back full circle to the two propositions at the start of this chapter: the desirability of a multi-institutional governance model centered around a strategic or "developmental" state; and a systems-based industrial strategy. This chapter has tried to outline the bare bones of an inward investment policy designed to forge a mutually reinforcing relationship between mobile projects and the host region. The policy approach centers around careful disbursement of locational incentives, consideration of mobile projects within a framework of regional industrial policies designed to promote clusters of interrelated firms and sectors, and general upgrading of the quality of the supply environment.

The key question, however, is whether LFRs possess the means to implement such a strategy. Only too often, the common feature among LFRs is that of public authorities and public agencies that lack strategic vision and that pursue sectarian interests, often in favor of the most powerful local economic and political lobbies. In addition, private interests tend to be either fragmented or dominated by large firms or local business mavericks. Finally, there is often a notable absence or underdevelopment of intermediate associations contributing to the formation of skills, know-how, education, and informational networks of indigenous benefit. In brief, the institutions of collective representation, interest-coordination, and local orientation are lacking. This should not be surprising, since institutional distortion or absence is one of the defining features of LFRs.

Herein lies the paradox of the new industrial policy. While its integrative nature undoubtedly raises the prospect for cumulative regional development, its institutional requirements might elude those regions most in need of such an approach to local economic development.

NOTES

1 This chapter is a slightly amended version of a chapter in a book edited by the authors on prospects for regional cohesion in Europe (Amin and Tomaney 1995).

REFERENCES

Allen, K., Yuill, D., and J. Bachtler (1989) "Requirements for an effective regional policy," in L. Albrechts, F. Moulaert, P. Roberts, and E. Swyngedouw (eds) *Regional Policy at a Crossroads*, London: Jessica Kingsley.

Amin, A. and Thrift, N. (1994) "Living in the global," in A. Amin and N. Thrift (eds) *Globalization, Institutions and Regional Development in Europe*, Oxford: Oxford University Press.

Amin, A. and Tomaney, J. (1995) "The regional development potential of inward investment in the less favoured regions of the European Community," in A. Amin and J. Tomaney (eds) *Behind The Myth of European Union: Prospects for Cohesion*, London: Routledge.

Amin, A., Bradley, D., Howells, J., Tomaney, J., and Gentle, C. (1994) "Regional incentives and the quality of mobile investment in the less favoured regions of the EC," *Progress in Planning* 41, 1: 1–112.

Best, M. (1990) *The New Competition*, Cambridge: Polity Press.

Camagni, R. (1992) "Development scenarios and policy guidelines for the lagging regions in the 1990s," *Regional Studies* 26, 4: 361–374.

CEC (1990) *An Empirical Assessment of Factors Shaping Regional Competitiveness in Problem Regions*, Brussels: Commission of the European Communities.

Clarke, T. and Monkhouse, E. (1994) *Rethinking the Company*, London: Pitman.

Culliton, J. (1992) *A Time for Change: Industrial Policy for the 1990s* (Report of the Industrial Policy Review Group), Dublin: Stationery Office.

Cusumano, M. and Elenkov, D. (1994) "Linking international technology transfer with strategy and management: a literature commentary," *Research Policy* 23: 195–215.

Dicken, P. and Tickell, A. (1992) "Competitors or collaborators? The structure of inward investment promotion in Northern England," *Regional Studies* 26: 99–106.

Dicken, P., Forsgren, M. and Malmberg, A. (1994) "The local embeddedness of transnational corporations," in A. Amin and N. Thrift (eds) *Globalization, Institutions and Regional Development in Europe*, Oxford: Oxford University Press.

Dunning, J. H. (1993a) "Globalisation: the challenge for national economic regimes," Department of Economics, University of Reading, Mimeographed.

—— (1993b) *The Globalisation of Business*, London: Routledge.

—— (1994) "Globalisation, economic restructuring and development," Department of Economics, University of Reading, Mimeographed.

Drucker, P. E. (1990) "The emerging theory of manufacturing," *Harvard Business Review* May–June: 94–102.

Firn, J. (1975) "External control and regional development," *Environment and Planning A*, 7: 393–414.

Giunta, A. and Martinelli, F. (1995) "The impact of post-Fordist corporate restructuring in a peripheral region: the Mezzogiorno of Italy," in A. Amin and J. Tomaney (eds) *Behind the Myth of European Union: Prospects for Cohesion*, London: Routledge.

Hakansson, H. (1990) "International decentralisation of R&D – the organizational challenges," in C. A. Bartlett, Y. Doz, and G. Hedlund (eds) *Managing the Global Firm*, London: Routledge.

Hedlund, G. (1986) "The hypermodern MNC – a heterarchy," *Human Resource Management* 25: 9–35.

Howells, J. and Wood, M. (1993) *The Globalisation of Production and Technology*, London: Belhaven.

Lazonick, W. (1993) "Industry clusters versus global webs: organisational possibilities in the American economy," *Structural Change and Economic Dynamics* 4: 1–24.

Massey, D. (1984) *Spatial Divisions of Labour*, London: Macmillan.

Mytelka, L. (1991) *Strategic Partnerships and the World Economy*, London: Pinter.

Nam, C., Russ, H., and Herb, G. (1991) *The Effect of 1992 and Associated Legislation on the Less Favoured Regions of the Community*, Report to the European Parliament Institut für Wirschaftsforschung, Frankfurt.

Ohmae, K. (1989) "Managing in a borderless world," *Harvard Business Review* May–June: 152–161.

O'Malley, E. *et al.* (1992) *The Impact of the Industrial Development Agencies*, (Report of Economic and Social Research Institute to the Industrial Policy Review Group), Dublin: ESRI.

Porter, M. (1990) *The Competitive Advantage of Nations*, New York: Free Press.

Ramsay, H. (1995) "*Le défi Européen:* multinational restructuring, labour and EU policy," in A. Amin and J. Tomaney (eds) *Behind the Myth of European Union: Prospects for Cohesion*, London: Routledge.

Schoenberger, E. (1991) *U.S. Investments in the United Kingdom: Tendencies, Prospects and Strategies*, Report for the County Durham Development Company, Durham.

Stanworth, J. and Gray, C. (eds) (1992) *Bolton 20 Years On*, London: Paul Chapman.

Storper, M. (1995) "Territorial economies in a global economy: what possibilities for middle-income countries and their regions?," *Review of International Political Economy* 2, 3: 394–424.

Turok, I. (1993) "Inward investment and local linkages: how deeply embedded is 'Silicon Glen'?," *Regional Studies* 27, 5: 401–417.

United Nations (1992) *World Investment Report 1992: Transnational Corporations as Engines of Growth*, New York: UN Transnational Corporations and Management Division.

—— (1993) *World Investment Report: Transnational Corporations and Integrated International Production*, New York: United Nations.

Young, S., Hood, N. and Peters, E. (1993) "Multinational enterprises and regional economic development," *Regional Studies* 28, 7: 657–677.

Young, S. and Hood, N. (1995) "Attracting, managing and developing inward invest-ment in the Single Market," in A. Amin and J. Tomaney (eds) *Behind the Myth of European Union: Prospects for Cohesion*, London: Routledge.

Part III

Case studies

8 Learning, innovation, and industrial policy
Some lessons from Korea

Lynn Krieger Mytelka[1]

INTRODUCTION

Korea is a prototype of the newly industrialized economy, yet in a number of important respects its development path does not conform to the myths that have grown up around the policies and practices that allegedly led to the emergence of the newly industrializing countries (NICs) and which today continue to inform debates about the role of the market and of the state, the kind of macroeconomic environment needed for growth, and the importance of specialization in production and trade. Nor has Korean industrial development consisted mainly of "rapid movement along prevailing production functions" with few gains in efficiency, as some accumulation theorists have argued (see, for example, Krugman 1994; Young 1993; Kim and Lau 1994). To understand better the factors that have contributed to the process of industrial catch-up in Korea, and more importantly to its sustainability, one must look elsewhere than to these conventional approaches.

This chapter thus proceeds from the assumption now common among innovation theorists that catching up and keeping up involve not only capital accumulation, that is investment, but the building of technological capabilities at the firm level. Recent studies, moreover, have shown that to sustain the competitiveness of individual firms, a wide array of domestic linkages between users and producers and between the knowledge-producing sector (universities and R&D institutions) and the goods and services-producing sectors of an economy are required (Freeman 1988; Lundvall 1992; Nelson 1993). I extend these arguments to suggest that "keeping up" in Korea has involved a continuous process of learning not only at the firm level but also within government as it learns and unlearns past habits and practices with respect to public policy.

Learning to innovate, however, is neither a passive nor an automatic process. It requires conscious and sustained effort by both firms and governments. Three broad sets of factors interact in shaping the extent to which firms are willing and able to invest in the acquisition and diffusion of productivity-enhancing technological and organization innovations. These are policy dynamics – that is, the interaction between policies and the behavior of targeted actors – market forces,[2] and the traditional habits and practices of firms. Collectively they constitute what elsewhere I have called an incentive system.[3]

This chapter traces the changes in Korea's policies and in the practices of its firms. By paying particular attention to two industrial sectors – textiles and clothing, and telecommunications – this chapter is able to capture the way in which Korea has been able to adapt to the growing knowledge intensity of production and the globalization of an innovation-based mode of competition across all industries.

MOVING TOWARD EXPORT MANUFACTURING

Among the Four Tigers, Korea stands out, since it is neither a small city-state nor an island country, but a country with 44 million people and a per capita income in 1995 of $10,000, which places it at about 75 percent of the average income among OECD countries (OECD 1997: 1). In 1950, however, its per capita income was approximately $355 and, like Taiwan, it was initially dependent upon a massive inflow of American foreign aid. But once this diminished in the late 1950s and early 1960s, Korea's principal source of investment capital came not from foreign direct investment (FDI), as in Singapore, Brazil, Chile, or Argentina, but from loans contracted by the state. In adopting this development path, the military government of General Park Chung Hee took inspiration from Japan, where General Park had been trained. This choice would subsequently facilitate the close relationship that developed between the state and large Korean-owned conglomerates known as chaebols, again reminiscent of Japanese practices. But it would be an over-simplification to describe these choices as purely imitative. Rather, they represented a combination of emulation and adaptation that involves a continuous process of learning and innovation.

In 1961, for example, the year in which the Park Chung Hee regime came to power, iron ore, tungsten, raw silk, anthracite, and fish accounted for over 48 percent of Korea's exports (Sakong 1993: 232). But Korea was not a resource-rich country like Chile, Mexico, and Argentina, where agricultural products, oil, and copper were and remain major export commodities. The resource constraint was accompanied by a demand constraint that set it apart from countries such as India, Indonesia, Mexico, and Brazil. The population was small and the people were poor, but largely as a result of the introduction of new technology in agriculture by the Japanese during the colonial era, and land reform imposed by the Americans in the immediate post-Second World War period (Cumings 1987), Korea was characterized by a distribution of household income that was among the most equitable in the developing world. While this reduced social tensions and facilitated the emergence of a domestic consensus around the need for rapid growth in manufacturing, it also meant that Korean producers could not count on the pull of domestic demand as an engine of growth. Export promotion was thus an early strategic choice, and by 1970 textiles and garments alone accounted for 41 percent of Korea's exports, with plywood and wigs in second and third place. Five years later, the latter two were replaced by electronics and steel products.

The speed with which Korea was transformed into an exporter of manufactured goods and the rapid diversification of its manufactured exports were not the result of market forces – domestic markets in the 1970s were highly concentrated, wages remained low, keeping domestic market pull weak, and the macroeconomic environment with its high rate of inflation, balance of payments deficits, and won devaluations was not propitious to risky undertakings. Instead, they were very much a function of specific policy initiatives taken under the Third (1972–1976) and Fourth (1977–1981) Development plans and a vision of the development process that sustained the commitment to policy directions whose fruits would be born only in the longer term.

In explaining Korea's export success, most studies took as their point of departure the macroeconomic policies and the reforms of the trade and exchange rate regimes that were said to have put Korea on the path toward liberalization, both at home and in export markets. Four reforms are generally given prominence in this connection:

1 guaranteed free access to imported raw materials and intermediate inputs for exporters, which began in 1959;
2 automatic and rapid access to export-financing;
3 access to bank loans for working capital; and
4 periodic devaluations, the first two of which took place in 1961 and 1964.[4]

To these were added a number of tax incentives and price reductions on such inputs as electricity to stimulate exports further, and a purely Korean innovation, the domestic letter of credit through which domestic suppliers of exporting firms and the domestic suppliers of these domestic suppliers had equal access to duty-free imported inputs and to financing (Rhee *et al.* 1984: 12). By reducing market distortions, such policies were expected to generate quasi-automatically an investment climate in which "private domestic investment and rapidly growing human capital . . . [can act as] . . . the principal engines of growth" (World Bank 1993: 5).

There is no doubt that this set of policies reduced the bias between exports and sales in the domestic market, thereby creating an environment more propitious for exports. But they, in themselves, did not give rise to exports, nor were they directed at a liberalization of the domestic economy.[5] To the contrary, given its relative autonomy[6] from domestic social forces and its support by the military, the state under Park Chung Hee and his successors, Chun Doo Hwan and Rho Tae Woo, centralized economic policymaking in a new institution, the Economic Planning Board, and in technocrats close to the Blue House.[7] More importantly, it designed a series of financial, investment, and tariff policies to accompany these trade promotion measures.

Primarily through its control over the inflow of FDI and selective credit mechanisms, for example, the state was able to preserve economic space for the emergence of privately owned domestic firms. In contrast to the situation in most of the developing world, FDI thus played a relatively small role in Korean development. Over the period 1962–1979, for example, FDI contributed an average of only 1.2 percent to gross domestic capital formation, and its effect was limited to only a few sectors – chemicals and petrochemicals in the 1970s, electronics and transportation equipment in the 1980s (Koo and Bark 1989). Much of this investment, moreover, was in joint ventures and only 32 percent of cumulative FDI in 1978 consisted of wholly foreign-owned companies (Westphal *et al.* 1979: 368). Not until the foreign Capital Investment Act was revised in December 1984 did the investment process become more transparent. Even then FDI in Korea lags far behind that in comparable countries such as Taiwan.[8] Moreover, by the late 1980s the large diversified firms known as chaebols had become powerful economic forces both at home and abroad.[9] This was particularly true in the telecommunications industry, as will be shown below.

With its control over the domestic banking system, over the inflow of foreign capital which accounted for a high percentage of the corporate borrowing in Korea, and over interest rates in the formal banking sector, the Korean government could exercise considerable influence over private firms by rationing longer term domestic and foreign loans (Rhee *et al.* 1984: 14). Very high debt-to-equity ratios in these companies then meant that domestic firms were constrained to return to the banks for loans, thus giving the banks considerable leverage over them.[10] The continuous policy dialogue between the state and the chaebols that emerged during the 1970s would subsequently shape the very nature of these firms, their growth strategies, and their relationship to each other and to their subcontractors, as will be shown below.

Over nearly a quarter of a century Park Chung Hee and his successors used these financial levers to combine "vigorous export expansion in highly labor-intensive products, and selective import substitution in capital-intensive intermediate products and consumer durables" (Westphal 1979: 233).[11] This was particularly important during the 1960s when, as several studies have shown, export production remained less profitable than production for the domestic market and many exporters would have been operating at a loss without government subsidies (Amsden 1989, 1992; Hamilton 1986: 44; Kim Seung Hee 1970: 99; Lim 1981: 44–45).[12] Government was thus obliged to exercise considerable coercive power over business in the form of tax penalties, loss of import licenses, and access to credit during the 1960s and 1970s in order to achieve its export targets. But in exchange it offered subsidies and tax concessions, erected barriers to imports, thus protecting the domestic market, and granted exclusive import rights to manufacturing firms.[13] Indeed, during the 1970s and 1980s, imports of textiles, automobiles, refrigerators, television sets, VCRs, and other consumer durables were virtually prohibited until such time as they could be produced locally.

Lastly, trade promotion was accompanied by policies to induce diversification of the productive structure. As privileged industrial partners of the state, the emerging chaebols were well placed to take advantage of the shift toward chemicals and heavy industries promoted under the Third Five Year Plan (1972–1976). Legislation was adopted to attract Japanese chemical and petrochemical companies, then in the process of internationalizing, and loans were granted to large Korean companies to encourage their entry into these new industrial activities as licensers and joint venture partners. By the end of the Third Five Year Plan, the textile industry had become wholly integrated from petrochemicals through synthetic fibers, to spinning, weaving, dyeing, finishing, and apparel manufacture. Similarly, the Electronics Industry Promotion Law of 1969, which made electronics a strategic export industry, and later sectoral promotional measures under the Fourth Five Year Plan (1977–1981), induced a number of the larger chaebols to move into this new industry. Over the 1970s, these firms broadened their product range to include not only simple products such as radios, but black and white and later color television sets, both of which made use of locally manufactured components and picture tubes by the end of the 1970s (Bloom 1992: 29). As in the case of textiles and clothing, they developed the technological capabilities required for large-volume production of standardized products. Shipbuilding, steel, and automobile production were also encouraged by sector-specific policies over the 1970s and 1980s.

CONTRADICTIONS IN THE KOREAN GROWTH MODEL

Despite the positive impact of Korean policies on industrial growth and manufacturing exports during the 1960s and 1970s, there were also inherent weaknesses in this strategy, particularly in the way it conditioned the habits and practices of Korean firms with respect to production and innovation. First, within the protected domestic market a handful of the largest chaebols became dominant, thus diminishing the importance of price competition[14] and narrowing still further a domestic market whose growth was slowed by the very low wages that prevailed throughout most of the 1960s and 1970s. Well into the 1980s, therefore, the domestic market played only a minor role in stimulating innovation within the textiles and clothing and the electronics industries, and both remained highly vulnerable to fluctuations in international prices and tastes, as well as to a host of other international market and nonmarket forces.[15]

Second, although backward linkages to intermediate production developed, linkages to the machinery-building industry remained weak, and the more a downstream sector exported, the more it tended to rely on imported machinery. This would later become a serious disadvantage in developing own-brand products in the electronics industry.

Third, to meet export targets, large firms relied heavily on overseas subcontracting and later on Original Equipment Manufacturing (OEM) relationships to the detriment of product innovation. This delayed the emergence of in-house R&D and encouraged the use of domestic subcontracting as a means to maintain competitiveness through low-wage production. As competition rose from neighboring low-wage countries, this practice would subsequently erode Korea's competitiveness in textiles and clothing.

Fourth, coupled with their role as OEM producers, the practice of growth through diversification also diminished the demand for technology generated by the local science and technology community. Although the Korean government

> aggressively recruited overseas-trained Korean scientists and engineers to establish a public research institute in 1966 as an integrated technical center to meet industry's technological needs . . . there was no demand from industries for the kind of expertise the institute could offer, while the latter lacked the manufacturing know-how that would enable them to solve teething problems of the former in the early years.[16]
>
> (Kim and Dahlman 1992: 445)

The lack of demand for research scientists and engineers similarly affected the education system. Korea's strength traditionally lay in its well-developed middle and vocational school system and the early development of engineering training. But its universities were not research-oriented, and when enrollment ratios were pushed higher in the early 1980s, the tendency for all universities to become "primarily undergraduate teaching-oriented rather than graduate research-oriented" increased (Kim and Dahlman 1992: 446). Not until the very end of that decade does one begin to see links developing between the universities and industry.

By the end of the 1970s the Korean model underwent its first shock as income gaps widened[17] and the economy – shaken by two oil price increases – began to succumb to debt, inflation, and balance of payments problems. GNP fell 6 percent in 1980, corruption became more apparent, and quiescence to exploitation gave way to

> vastly enhanced opposition power deployed around Kim Dae Jung . . . [drawing its] support from textile workers, small businesses and firms with national rather than international interests in his native southwestern Cholla region, which . . . had been left out of much of the growth of the previous fifteen years. Major urban insurrections occurred in the southeastern cities of Pusan and Masan in the autumn of 1979. Some 700 labor strikes were recorded in 1979–80. . . . In May, hundreds of thousands of students and common people flooded the streets of Seoul, leading to martial law, which in turn touched off a province-wide rebellion in South Cholla.
>
> (Cumings 1987: 79–80)

In 1979, President Park was assassinated and replaced by General Chun Doo Hwan who outlawed strikes and negotiated a $4 billion package of loans and credits from Japan. Despite the repression, social unrest continued throughout the 1980s and was accompanied by mounting domestic pressure on Chun Doo Hwan and his successor Rho Tae Woo to democratize the political system, attend to "regional disparities in economic development . . . and the perception of inequitable income distribution" (Koo and Bark 1989: 15), and rein in the chaebols whose "economic power and its resultant monopolistic abuses (e.g. creating scarcities, price gouging and ruining smaller competitors)" (Kim and Dahlman 1992: 446) had become an object of domestic contention.

With regard to the former, the 1980s were decisive, and political pressures culminated in the 1987 Declaration of Democratization and the December 1992 election of Kim Young-Sam, the first nonmilitary candidate to the presidency since Park Chung Hee took power in 1961. With regard to the latter, however, as Korean export growth accelerated toward the middle of the decade and its balance of trade moved into surplus, international pressure for greater market access, notably from the United States, Korea's major export market, intensified. Stimulating innovation in Korean industry was thus essential to its continued export success, especially in the electronics industry; yet pursuing sector-specific policies would conflict with external demands for market liberalization. In an attempt to respond simultaneously to pressures for liberalization and for domestic innovation, in a major policy shift, the Korean government abandoned its traditional sector-specific policies for a more functional set of policy instruments. The Industrial Development Law of 1985 thus replaced directed credits by subsidies for R&D and changed its performance criteria from the promotion of capacity expansion for exports to productivity growth. The new legislation also put greater emphasis on promoting joint R&D between government laboratories and private firms, particularly in the electronics industry. The results of these policies were initially negative. Complacency reigned amongst large conglomerates for whom a protected home market and the market power they wielded provided few incentives to change traditional habits and practices.

Thus, well into the 1980s, a convincing argument could still be made that, lacking both the dynamic pull of domestic market demand and the push of domestically generated technology, Korea was embarked on a path of dependent development (Evans 1979). Events of the 1980s, however, showed that the bases had been laid for a response to political and economic crises through change, and that learning was taking place not only at the level of the firm but also amongst those making public policy in Korea. The textile and clothing and the telecommunications industries illustrate this process.

LEARNING FROM PAST MISTAKES: THE TEXTILE AND CLOTHING INDUSTRIES

In 1975, the chaebol's role in exports and their relationship to domestic subcontractors were strengthened by two policy changes. First, the Korean government switched its export promotion policies from the duty-free import of inputs used to produce export goods, to a tariff rebate or drawback system under which tariffs are paid on these imports and a portion are rebated at the time of export. The new system had both positive and negative consequences for domestic industrial structure and linkages. On the one hand, it further encouraged the use of domestically produced inputs because the formula for calculating the drawback tended to "overcompensate or undercompensate for duties and indirect taxes paid on inputs used in export production by an individual producer, depending upon whether that producer purchases relatively more or less of his input from domestic producers than the industry as a whole" (Westphal 1979: 267). On the other hand, it put a burden on smaller firms which now had to finance customs duties on imported inputs from the time of import until after the finished goods were exported and the rebates were paid. For small Korean firms this was a major disincentive to direct exporting.

Second, the Korean General Trading Companies, modeled on the Japanese trading houses and tied to dominant industrial groups, were given legal status (Haggard and Moon 1983: 1967) and, in a move to streamline the administration of export incentives, the government "provided additional incentives for establishing large trading companies which produce and export on their own account or act as exporting agents for smaller enterprises" (Westphal 1979: 268–269). In this context, the shift to a rebate system accelerated the use of domestic subcontracting in which exports by smaller firms were intermediated by the large trading companies. Between 1980 and 1986 the number of small and medium-sized enterprises (SMEs) in Korea rose from 29,775 to 48,883, and the share of those engaged in subcontracting increased from 30 to 43 percent (Lee 1988: 35).

In line with the inducements offered in the Third and Fourth (1977–1981) Development plans, larger textile and clothing firms began to diversify production outside of textiles and clothing, a practice that would accelerate in the 1980s. Real growth rates of output and investment in the industry thus declined in the late 1970s and early 1980s (Mytelka and Ernst 1996). During this period, however, textiles and clothing remained Korea's principal export earner, and debt service payments as a share of exports were high as a result of earlier borrowing. Somewhat belatedly, therefore, the government set up a textile and clothing modernization fund under the Fifth Development Plan (1982–1986). But firms were already convinced that textiles and clothing were a sunset industry and the fund remained underutilized. At the end of the Fifth Plan period only 11 percent of the looms installed in Korea were shuttleless looms, whereas the equivalent figure in Taiwan was 27 percent and in Hong Kong 25 percent (ITMF 1986: 14). Between 1980 and 1987, moreover, Taiwan overtook Korea as a textile exporter (GATT 1989: 66).

As competition intensified, the hierarchical relationship that developed between the chaebols and their subcontractors thus became increasingly more exploitative, in the sense that profits were squeezed, and by the early 1980s wages of production workers in the smaller firms (those with 30 or less workers) were averaging only about 76 percent of those in larger firms (those with over 500 workers) (Koo 1984: 1032). The pressure on SME subcontractors increased further over the 1980s as the low-wage based comparative advantage of Korean manufacturers eroded once the heavy and chemical industries absorbed much of the excess labor, bidding wages up,[18] and lower-wage countries in Southeast Asia became attractive sites for simple assembly operations. The difficulties this posed for SMEs is reflected in the annual surveys of small and medium-sized enterprises carried out by the Ministry of Commerce and Industry which showed that the share of firms citing pressure on delivery prices as a serious problem rose from 31 percent in 1981 to 40 percent in 1986.

In response to these pressures and to the liberalization of outward FDI that took place in the mid-1980s, many of the large chaebols began to move production abroad. Between 1986–1987 and 1990–1992, outward FDI in the textile and clothing industry rose from $46 to $331 million.[19] As the chaebols abandoned in-house manufacturing activities, however, they were less able to serve as transmitters of "best practice" to their subcontractors. In the aggregate, Korea's comparative advantage in clothing exports thus began to erode. But this concealed the emergence of independent small and medium-sized clothing manufacturers as innovative exporters. Moreover, as a support to the clothing industry and as an activity on its own, Korea had considerable potential for increasing the knowledge-intensity of production in the textile sector, as Germany, Japan, and later Taiwan had done. New policies, for example, could have been designed over the 1980s to build upon Korea's strong base in dyeing and finishing, to add value to garment production through enhanced design capabilities, and to induce petrochemical firms to undertake the R&D needed to compete with new fibers and fabrics being developed by producers in Japan and Taiwan. Yet in the first two instances this would have obliged the Korean government to learn new habits of interaction with industry, since the more innovative firms in both sectors were small and medium-sized enterprises, and in the third instance it would have required policymakers to rethink the "functional" policy orientation adopted in 1986 or to develop creative policies within this new context. By the very end of that decade signs of a major change in government's policymaking habits and practices had begun to appear.

In the case of the small and medium-sized printing and dyeing companies who worked as subcontractors to the larger yarn, fabric, and apparel companies, the 1980s were a period of severe profit squeeze as the chaebol's export competitiveness eroded and they increased pressure on their subcontractors to reduce prices. Although a few of these firms tried to move out on their own, seeking clients elsewhere in Asia, for most this was not feasible since it would have required an expansion of capacity, and the waste treatment plants then serving the 111 dyeing firms in Taegu and the 63 in Banwol were too small to handle an increase in activity. A lack of financing, moreover, prevented these SMEs from investing in newer equipment that was less polluting. Subsequently, within the context of the Industrial Development Law of 1986, a three-year rationalization program (1989–1991) was put in place with a view to restoring the competitiveness of declining industries. Financing now became available to dyeing and printing firms, thus enabling them to expand production and contribute to the development of higher value-added textile products. Two new research and training institutes, partially funded by the state, were also set up in 1990 under this program – the Korea Sewing Science Research Institute, whose mandate was to develop new sewing technology, including ways to improve the organization of production and to provide training programs for SMEs in the apparel industry; and the Korea Academy of Industrial Technology, designed to work with small and medium-sized enterprises to improve their technological capabilities.[20] As the government recognized the advantages that Korea still possessed in the textile industry, new policies were also designed to encourage investment in the upstream petrochemical industry. One of the more innovative policies was to change the rules of the competitive game by opening the industry to new Korean investors. Although new entrants were smaller chaebols, their presence served to stimulate the development of competition based on innovation as well as price (Chesnais and Kim 1996). R&D expenditures by petrochemical firms, which were barely 1 percent of sales in 1988, doubled to 2.1 percent in 1990 and have remained at this level (Chesnais and Kim 1996). By the 1990s, Korean textile manufacturers had regained international competitiveness, increasing their share of world textile exports, and had pulled ahead of arch-rival, Taiwan, amongst the world's top ten textile exporters.

STIMULATING INNOVATION IN THE TELECOMMUNICATIONS EQUIPMENT INDUSTRY

Early in the 1980s the Ministry of Communications (MOC) determined that the licenses Samsung and Goldstar had respectively concluded with ITT and AT&T for the production of digital switches for the domestic market were far too costly, given the growing importance of telecommunications in industrial competitiveness in this period.[21] With an eye to the way in which indigenous telecommunications technology had been developed in Japan, notably the relationship between Nippon Telegraph and Telephone (NTT) and its four-firm "Den Den" family of suppliers,[22] and wielding its procurement leverage once again,[23] the Korean government prodded several of the chaebols into collaborating with the public sector Electronics Technology Research Institute (ETRI)[24] in the development of what became known as the TDX family of switches.

In 1985 the first small digital switches were commercialized locally, and some 200 engineers from ETRI working with 500 engineers from Samsung, Goldstar, Daewoo, and Otelco[25] were involved in developing larger, more sophisticated switches. Core technology, however, remained the preserve of ETRI, and the relationship of ETRI to the chaebols was closer to that of principal to agent than to that of partners. Since the firms did not master all of the technology involved in digital switching, and as the Korea Telecommunications Authority did not reward more dynamic firms with larger market shares, there was little incentive for these four firms to innovate.

By the end of the 1980s, when the larger TDX 10 switch was under development, the companies had thus settled into a comfortable pattern. Telecommunications accounted for only a small share of the overall business of these chaebols – 5 percent in the case of Samsung and Goldstar, 20 percent in the case of Daewoo – but it had become a kind of cash cow, providing a stable market for which production could be planned ahead and into which highly subsidized technology would flow. In the early 1990s, however, the rate of new lines in Korea peaked. For the firms, growth would thus have to come either from taking market share away from one of the other four firms manufacturing the TDX family of switches or through exports. The former, however, continued to be discouraged by Korea Telecom which allocated roughly equal market shares to each of the four companies and used its purchasing power to push prices lower, a process consistent with the historical practices of the firms in becoming efficient mass producers in other industrial sectors. ETRI, moreover, had embarked on a number of longer term research projects in the newer ATM and cellular switching and needed to share costs and manpower with the firms. Collaborative work on a standard product was also favored by Korea Telecom, both to avoid the problem of having to deal with many different kinds of switches, but also because they did not wish to be dependent upon only one or two big chaebols for digital exchanges. Exporting thus appeared to be the only option for the more innovative of the telecommunications equipment manufacturers.

Pressure to export also came from demands by the United States that Korea open its domestic telecommunications market to imports. The Korean government successfully resisted opening the domestic market to imports of central office switches until 1993, at which point domestic firms were better able to compete on their own terrain. Over the intervening years, however, the government moved to help these firms begin to export by setting up Korea Telecom International to prospect for markets and negotiate with potential client governments and by providing financing through the Economic Development Cooperation Fund for sales to Third World countries.

One of the key problems the chaebols faced in going abroad, however, was that Korea Telecom, like NTT in Japan, had set its specifications too high. Central office switches were thus overengineered, making them too costly for export. The cost of producing switches to that standard had initially been borne by the state through subsidized R&D, but to be price competitive abroad these firms would have to cut their costs. One way to do this was to strip down the TDX and target markets in the developing world. But, as competition had intensified globally by this time, Korean firms were obliged to compete in export markets not only by providing cheaper "solutions," but also by innovating to add the new features already incorporated in rival switching systems.[26] This required considerably higher expenditures on R&D,

both to reverse engineer the TDX switches and to accelerate the introduction of new functions. It also required closer links between marketing and R&D than had been practiced in these firms in the past. Within Samsung and Goldstar (now the LG Group) this link was forged in the 1990s and both firms began to develop their own versions of the TDX switching system, to invest more heavily in telecommunications R&D, to export, and to establish assembly plants in potentially large markets such as China.

New government policies on the demand side have also strengthened the innovative potential of the telecommunications equipment industry. To some extent these policies reflect a growing awareness of the need to establish closer linkages between supplier and client firms within Korea as a means to stimulate innovation. Privatization in the telecommunications operating sector has been one means of cementing this link. The contrast between the first moves toward privatization and more recent efforts is illustrative. When Korea Telecom ended its long-standing monopoly over international telecommunications services in 1991 and the Ministry of Communications designated the Data Communications Corporation (DACOM) as a competing carrier, DACOM purchased its switches from Northern Telecom and AT&T, and linkages to local suppliers were weak. But three years later the decision to end the Korea Mobile Telecommunications Corporation's (KMTC) monopoly and begin to privatize led to quite a different approach. The Sunkyong Group, Korea's thirteenth largest chaebol, was allowed to move into telecommunications by purchasing 23 percent of KMTC in January 1994;[27] six months later the Ministry of Communications designated a consortium led by POSCO as the second mobile phone company.[28] The new consortium counts among its share holders: POSCO, which holds a 15 percent share and will manage the company; Kolon, a large textile and chemical conglomerate with 14 percent; Samsung, Goldstar, Daewoo, and Hyundai, which are involved in developing the CDMA (code division multiple access) switching system with ETRI, each of which will have 3 percent of the shares; and some 300 small and large domestic equipment suppliers (Kim C. T. 1994: 22). The earlier practice of diversification has thus served as the basis for designing a new response to the growing domestic demand for better telecommunications services and increased pressure from abroad for opening the domestic market.

CONCLUSIONS

Historical analysis shows that governments and enterprises interact in shaping the policy dynamics, market forces, and traditional habits and practices of target firms that collectively constitute a nation's incentive system.[29] For example, through an impressive array of policy instruments, governments can affect firm-level innovation strategies either directly through tax credits or subsidies for the purchase of equipment or R&D, or indirectly through their impact on the macroeconomic environment, on factor markets, demand-structure, patterns of competition, labor, and other practices. However, as the Korean case shows, what matters is less the policies themselves than the policy dynamics that result from the impact of specific policies on particular types of economic actors. Different actors, in contexts shaped by different incentive systems, will react differently to policies that, for all intents and purposes, appear identical. Moreover, policies that at one point in time might stimulate innovative behavior may, at a later date, given changes in other policies or in market dynamics, discourage innovation. To be effective, policies must take these changes into consideration. This suggests that just as firms are called upon to be continuously innovative, governments, too, must engage in an on-going learning process.

Not all incentive systems are conducive to learning and innovation. An incentive system stimulates innovation and thus indirectly contributes to sustainable industrial development if

- by constraining rent-seeking strategies of economic actors it raises the economy's investable surplus;
- it insures that a high proportion of these resources is invested in productive capacity and the formation of technological capabilities within the national territory;
- it guides investment into industries and toward the building of technological capabilities that are important for the economy's ability to sustain higher wages in the future; and
- it gradually proceeds to expose these investments to international competitive pressure.

Korea's incentive system and the interaction between policymakers and producers that shaped it have changed considerably over time, but on balance they have moved in the direction suggested by this ideal type. Of most interest to less favored regions of Europe are the most recent shifts in policies and the policy dynamics to which they have given rise. For the most part, these were provoked by a combination of three factors: pressures for market-opening in line with Korea's ambitions to join the OECD and play the role of industrialized country within the new World Trade Organization; weaknesses in Korea's export sector as export growth rates averaged less than 6 percent in the early 1990s and the balance of trade was once again in deficit; and the growing difficulties in managing an economy dominated by a few large chaebols.[30]

Ten years after it had weathered its first crisis, the Korean model was thus under pressure once again. This time, however, the competitive game had radically changed and cheaper wages could no longer restore Korean competitiveness. High interest rates and a tight credit policy introduced to dampen inflation, moreover, were cutting into domestic consumption and driving up the bankruptcy rate. Confidence among Korea's business executives was sagging,[31] multiple efforts undertaken to bring the chaebols under control had largely proved ineffective,[32] and attempts to reduce the power of the chaebols seemed to have given way to a tactical alliance between the state and the chaebols to push through the internationalization of the Korean economy.[33] But this had been accompanied by stronger and more innovative policy instruments that have renewed the state's ability to steer the process of change as the textile and telecommunications industries have illustrated.

These policies included greater attention to the promotion of R&D and to linkages between public-sector R&D, training activities, and private-sector firms, and between suppliers and clients within the productive sector. Thus a domestic system of innovation is slowly being created in Korea. Korean textiles compete increasingly on the basis of innovation, and increased R&D has been reflected in the share of gross expenditures on R&D (GERD) in gross domestic product (GDP), rising rates of patenting activity by Korean firms,[34] and in the world class ranking of its semiconductor industry. They also included the careful sequencing and selective use of competition and tariff policies to restructure markets and encourage the kind of competition that promotes innovation and sustains competitiveness. The telecommunications industry provides a useful example of these policies, their sequencing, and the policy dynamics that were generated.

As shown above, state procurement policies through Korea Telecom provided a guaranteed market for domestic telecommunications equipment suppliers. During the catch-up phase and into the keeping-up phase, Korean telecommunications firms were also the privileged recipients of digital switching technology developed by a public-sector research institution. Despite the development of in-house technological capabilities, largely derivative of government pressure to participate in joint research on digital switching, complacency rather than innovativeness characterized the traditional habits and practices of Korea's telecommunications firms throughout the 1980s. In terms of global prices or product design and functionality, their output was not internationally competitive and none of these firms exported.

What broke these traditional habits and practices was the particular type and sequencing of policy reforms and the growing conviction that policy reform would not be reversed. Tariff reductions, however, were introduced very slowly and only after considerable domestic restructuring of industry had taken place. In fact, reforms in Korea were first aimed at transforming both the ownership structure and the regulatory environment of the telecommunications industry. The way privatization took place also strengthened locally owned firms, and not until policy reforms had begun to stimulate these firms to look for new ways of competing was the market opened to foreign competition. Even then, trade liberalization was a gradual process stretching over four years, with firms informed in advance of the products that would be liberalized. In the telecommunications industry, where international competitiveness required the development of a vastly more elaborate marketing structure capable of working with a host of corporate and institutional users across a wide range of countries, sustained support in the form of public-sector R&D and export-marketing assistance was a major asset for Korean firms. Korean firms thus had both the time and the resources needed to adjust.

The introduction of competition into the domestic market has the added advantage of putting the chaebols on the defensive and strengthening the state's ability to finance SME development. In 1993, for example, President Kim Young-Sam prohibited the use of aliases in banking transactions and secured the agreement of Korean chaebols to reduce the period of paying on promissory notes – a major contributing factor to the liquidity problem faced by small businesses. In addition to these new transparency requirements in the banking sector, since 1995 multiple charges of corruption have been laid against family members of the major chaebols and public officials.[35] While the relationship between the state and the "first tier" chaebols will undoubtedly remain conflictual, the emergence of "second tier" chaebols – firms that have diversified and assumed chaebol status more recently – suggests that competition amongst chaebols is likely to increase in the future. Widening of the chaebol sector, along with the further growth of innovative SMEs, could thus open new possibilities for alliance formation between the state and industry that further discourages rent-seeking and stimulates a process of continuous innovation in the future.

NOTES

1 Professor, Carleton University (Ottawa) and CEREM-Forum, University Paris-X (Nanterre). email: 100334.1406 at Compuserve.com
2 These include factor costs, industrial structure, as well as the size and sophistication of demand.
3 These concepts were first developed in Ernst *et al.* (1996).
4 The devaluations assured that high rates of domestic inflation relative to world inflation rates would not be translated into an anti-export overvalued exchange rate.
5 Nor did they contribute, as Korea's double-digit inflation illustrates, to the kind of macroeconomic stability that allegedly favored industrialization in late industrializers such as Taiwan and Thailand. Moreover, to offset the savings–investment gap caused by the government's policy of controlled interest rates and subsidized credit during the Third Five-Year Plan which favored the heavy and chemical industries, Korea borrowed heavily on international capital markets and its debt service payments as a share of exports remained high throughout the 1970s and 1980s. In contrast to Latin America, however, much of this debt was used to diversify into new industrial sectors, to purchase capital goods and intermediate inputs for these new manufacturing activities, and to induce and coerce these firms into exporting.
6 Haggard and Cheng define this relative autonomy to mean "that the activities of autonomously organized social and political groups are limited and that these groups lack effective access to centers of decision-making power within the state structure. Where corporatist channels do exist, they tend to be state-controlled rather than societal" (1987: 101). As Amsden noted, "the Korean state was able to consolidate its power in the 1960s because of the weakness of the social classes. Workers were a small percentage of the population, capitalists were dependent on state largesse, the aristocracy was dissolved by land reform and the peasantry was

atomized into smallholders" (1989: 52). See also Cumings 1987, Hamilton 1986, and Koo 1987.

7   The Blue House is the presidential mansion. For a more detailed discussion of the state in Korea see Haggard and Moon 1983, Jones and Sakong 1980, Luedde-Neurath 1986, and Enos 1984.

8   According to figures in UNCTAD's World Investment Report for 1993, average annual FDI inflows were roughly similar for Korea and Taiwan in the period 1983–1988 ($387 for the former and $448 million for the latter), and rose in both countries thereafter but far more rapidly in Taiwan. In the 1989–1991 period, Korea received $863 million in FDI inflows as compared to $1,402 in Taiwan, and in 1992–1994, $379 million as compared with $1,049 million. FDI thus continues to play a relatively minor role in the Korean economy.

9   In 1985 the top ten Korean chaebols ranked as follows among the Fortune 500: Samsung Group (23), Hyundai (25), Lucky Goldstar (43), Daewoo (49), Sunkyong (67), Ssangyong (137), Korea Explosives (180), Hyosung (204), Pohang Iron and Steel (206), and Doosan (412) (*Fortune* August 4, 1986, pp 181–197 and p. 203).

10   In addition, the state could reward well-managed companies with new licenses to expand or to enter new sectors, could refuse to bail out poorly managed firms in healthy industries, and allow better-managed firms to take them over (Amsden 1989).

11   Similarly, Luedde-Neurath (1986) demonstrates that the liberalization of the 1963–1964 period, to which many neoclassical economists had earlier attributed the Korean "miracle," concealed an intricate system of import controls that protected the domestic market.

12   Amsden, for example, argues, that "as late industrialization has unfolded, it has become clear . . . that low wages are no match for the higher productivity of more industrialized countries . . . governments have to intervene and deliberately distort prices to stimulate investment and trade. Otherwise industrialization won't germinate" (1992: 53).

13   Thus, brewers could import beer, and spinners but not weavers could import yarn.

14   Many prices were also set by the Economic Planning Board.

15   These nonmarket forces included changes in the mode of competition from one based on price to one based also on quality and innovation, the growing use of antidumping charges, and changes to the multifibre agreement that increased its restrictiveness.

16   The Korea Institute of Science and Technology (KIST) was set up in 1966 as a multidisciplinary industrial research institute. When the lack of research within industry and the small scale of KIST resulted in little increase in R&D activity, the government took actions to strengthen the R&D system through legislation, such as the Law for the Promotion of Industrial Technology Development (1973, 1977) and the establishment of a number of public industrial research institutes in the mid-1970s, such as the Korea Institute for Electronics Technology (KIET) which later became the Electronics Technology Research Institute (ETRI) and as such played a major role in the development of digital switching in the telecommunications industry. In the textile industry, the Korea Textile Inspection and Testing Institute was set up in 1969 mainly for the cotton-spinning industry.

17   The Gini coefficient, which measures income inequality, declined from 0.45 to 0.33 between 1960 and 1970 and then rose again to 0.39 by 1980. Similarly the income share of the bottom 40 percent of the population, which had risen to 19.6 percent in 1970, fell to 16.1 percent in 1980, while the share of the top 20 percent of the population rose from 41.6 percent in 1970 to 45.4 percent in 1980. Much of the increase in income inequality comes from wage inequality in the manufacturing sector. Koo argues that this was due to four sets of policies that influenced the pattern of income distribution during the 1970s: policies that (1) favored big business,

(2) controlled the labor movement, (3) involved inflationary financing, and (4) led to regressive taxation (Koo 1984: 1030, 1032).

18 Pressure on wages also came from the Middle East boom which "drained the most energetic able-bodied men from the labor force in unprecedented numbers. According to data from the Ministry of Labor, between 1977 and 1979 roughly 292,600 male workers migrated overseas, equaling almost 27 percent of the male manufacturing work force" (Amsden 1989: 100).

19 Unpublished data from the Korean Federation of Textile Industries.

20 This is based on interviews with senior staff at the Ministry for Trade and Industry and the Korea Federation of Textile Industries in February 1993.

21 Material for this case study is drawn from Mytelka 1996c.

22 The "Den Den" family of suppliers consisted of: NEC, Fujitsu, Hitachi, and Oki (Fransman 1990: 14).

23 The Korean government's procurement leverage involved the promise of a guaranteed market but the threat that only firms that collaborated in the national research program would be permitted to sell switches based on foreign technology in the domestic market – a technique already used in the textile industry, cf. fn. 17.

24 ETRI was under the Ministry of Science and Technology from 1985 to 1992 and then became an affiliated research institute of the MOC.

25 Otelco was a joint venture with Ericsson of Sweden.

26 Automated billing systems, call forwarding and other such features had become standard in systems provided by global competitors such as AT&T, Ericsson, Alcatel, Siemens, and Northern Telecom.

27 Mainly active in textiles and chemicals, Sunkyong's affiliate, Taehan Telecom, will be in charge of the cellular phone project and they expect to invest heavily in upgrading KMTC's service (Kim, C. T. 1994: 22).

28 POSCO, 35 percent state owned, was primarily a steel producer.

29 See, for example, Polanyi 1944, Landes 1969, Mowery and Rosenberg 1989, and Wade 1990.

30 "Out of 39,000 firms registered in the manufacturing sector, the 1 percent which belong to the top chaebols account for 50 percent of manufacturing shipments (1994) and 30 percent of manufacturing value added (1990)" (Chaponnière 1996). Exports of the seven largest general trading companies, all chaebols, totaled $57 million, 48 percent of Korea's exports in 1995 (*Korea Economic Weekly*, January 29, 1996).

31 The annual survey conducted by Asian business showed that confidence among Korean business executives had fallen from an index score of 71 in 1989 to a low of 62 in April 1992 (*Asian Business*, June 1992: 35).

32 A Fair Trade Act, for example, included a prohibition against unfair cartel practices and mutual investment among the chaebols' affiliate companies, set ceilings on the flow of credits to chaebols, and regulated their vertical and horizontal integration (Kim and Dahlman 1992: 446).

33 The Samsung group seems to have been particularly successful in winning over the new government. It has been repeatedly praised by President Kim Young-Sam as a role model for the modernization of the public administration, and the Blue House is reportedly sending its staff for training at Samsung's private management institute (*Financial Times*, February 23, 1994: 13).

34 In 1992, GERD as a percent of GDP was 2.3 percent in Korea as compared with 1.3 percent in Italy, 0.6 percent in Greece, 0.9 percent in Spain, 1.1 percent in Ireland, 2.4 percent in France, 2.5 percent in Germany, 2.9 percent in Japan, 2.7 percent in the US, and 3.1 in Sweden; while the percent of GERD performed by business in Korea in that year was 69 percent, placing it at the level of Germany (67 percent), Japan (66 percent), Sweden (70 percent), and the US (72 percent). The number of US patents held by Koreans more than doubled between 1990 and 1993, rising from 224 to 765, placing it ahead of small European countries and less

favored regions such as The Netherlands, Sweden, Spain, Greece, and Ireland but behind Taiwan (1,186), Italy (1,244), France (2,809), and Germany (6,588) (OECD 1997: 105–107).
35 These included against the Head of Hyundai and two former Presidents, Rho Tae Woo and Chun Doo Hwan.

REFERENCES

Amsden, A. H. (1989) *Asia's Next Giant South Korea and Late Industrialization*, New York: Oxford University Press.

—— (1992) "Theory of government intervention in late industrialization," in L. Putterman and D. Rueschemeyer (eds) *State and Market in Development Synergy or Rivalry?*, Boulder, CO: Lynne Rienner.

Amsden, A. H. and Kim, L. (1986) "A technological perspective on the general machinery industry in the Republic of Korea," in M. Fransman (ed.) *Machinery and Economic Development*, London: Macmillan.

Bark, T. (1991) *Anti-Dumping Restrictions Against Korean Exports: Major Focus on Consumer Electronic Products*, Seoul: Korea Institute for International Economic Policy.

Bloom, M. (1992) *Technological Change in the Korean Electronics Industry*, Paris: OECD.

Chaponnière, J. (1996) "Democracy and the reform of Korean INC," Paper presented at the Conference on Changing Consumer Behavior and Life Style in Asia: Relevance of the Western Model, February 9–10, Fontainebgleau: INSEAD Euro-Asia Center.

Chesnais, F. and Kim, H. (1996) "Petrochemicals in Brazil and Korea," in L. Mytelka (ed.) *Competition, Innovation and Competitiveness in Developing Countries*, Paris: OECD.

Clark, C. and Chan, S. (eds) (1992) *The Evolving Pacific Basin in the Global Political Economy: Domestic and International Linkages*, Boulder, CO: Lynne Reiner.

Cumings, B. (1987) "The origins and development of the northeast Asian political economy: industrial sectors, product cycles, and political consequences," in F. C. Deyo (ed.) *The Political Economy of the New Asian Industrialism*, Ithaca, NY: Cornell University Press.

EIAK (1992) "Electronic Industry of Korea," Seoul: Electronics Industries Association of Korea.

Edquist, C. and Jacobsson, S. (1987) "The integrated circuit industries of India and the Republic of Korea in an international techno-economic context," *Industry and Development* 21: 1–62.

Enos, J. (1984) "Government intervention in the transfer of technology in the case of South Korea," *IDS Bulletin*, 15, 2: 26–31.

Enos, J. and Park, W. H. (1988) *The Adoption and Diffusion of Imported Technology: The Case of Korea*, London: Croom Helm.

Ernst, D. and O'Connor, D. (1992) *Competing in the Electronics Industry. The Experience of Newly Industrializing Economies*, Paris: OECD Development Center Studies.

Ernst, D., Mytelka, L., and Ganiatsos, T. (eds) (1996) *Technological Capabilities and Export Success: Case Studies from Asia*, London: Routledge.

Evans, P. (1979) *Dependent Development: The Alliance of Multinational, State, and Local Capital in Brazil*, Princeton, NJ: Princeton University Press.

—— (1995) *Embedded Autonomy: States and Industrial Transformation*, Princeton, NJ: Princeton University Press.

Fransman, M. (1990) *The Market and Beyond: Cooperation and Competition in Information Technology in the Japanese System*, Cambridge: Cambridge University Press.

Freeman, C. (1988) "Japan: A new national system of innovation," in G. Dosi, C. Freeman, D. Nelson, G. Silverberg, and L. Soete (eds) *Technical Change and Economic Theory*, London: Pinter.

GATT (1989) *International Trade 88–89 Vol. 2*, Geneva: GATT.

Gershenkron, A. (1962) *Economic Backwardness in Historical Perspective*, Cambridge, MA: Harvard University Press.

—— (1968) *Continuity in History and other Essays*, Cambridge, MA: Harvard University Press.

Haggard, S. and Cheng, T. (1987) "State and foreign capital in the East Asian NICs," in F. C. Deyo (ed.) *The Political Economy of the New Asian Industrialism*, Ithaca, NY: Cornell University Press.

Haggard, S. and Moon, C. (1983) "The South Korean state in the international economy: liberal, dependent or mercantile?," in J. G. Ruggie (ed.) *The Antinomies of Interdependence: National Welfare and the International Division of Labor*, New York: Columbia University Press.

Hamilton, C. (1986) *Capitalist Industrialization in Korea*, Boulder, CO: Westview Press.

Hobday, M. (1995) *Innovation in East Asia: The Challenge to Japan*, London: Edward Elgar.

Horie, Y. (1965) "Modern entrepreneurship in Meiji Japan," in W. M. Lockwood (ed.) *The State and Economic Enterprise in Japan*, Princeton, NJ: Princeton University Press.

ITMF (1986) *International Textile Machinery Shipment Statistics Vol. 9*, Zurich: International Textile Manufacturers Federation.

Jones, L. and Sakong, I. (1980) *Government, Business and Entrepreneurship in Economic Development: The Korean Case*, Cambridge, MA: Harvard University Press.

Kim, C. T. (1994) "Picking teams," *Economic Report* (Korea) 9, 4: 22–23.

Kim, J. H. (1991) "Korea: market adjustment in declining industries, government assistance in troubled industries," in H. Patrick with L. Meissner (eds) *Pacific Basin Industries in Distress: Structural Adjustment and Trade Policy in the Nine Industrialized Economies*, New York: Columbia University Press.

Kim, J. I. and Lau, L. J. (1994) "The sources of economic growth in the East Asian newly industrialized countries," *Journal of Japanese and International Economics*, 8, 3: 235–271.

Kim, L. (1993) "Korea's national system for industrial innovation," in R. Nelson (ed.) *National Innovation Systems: A Comparative Analysis*, New York: Oxford University Press.

Kim, L. and Dahlman, C. J. (1992) "Technology policy for industrialization: an integrative framework and Korea's experience," *Research Policy* 21: 437–452.

Kim, Seung Hee (1970) *Foreign Capital for Economic Development: A Korean Case Study*, New York: Praeger.

Kom, Y. (1995) "Industrial policy for technological learning: a hypothesis and Korean evidence," Working Paper No. 201, The Hague: Institute of Social Studies.

Koo, B. H. and Bark, T. (1989) "Recent macroeconomic performance and industrial structural adjustment in Korea," Korea Development Institute Working Paper, No. 8924, Seoul.

Koo, H. (1984) "The political economy of income distribution in South Korea: the impact of the state's industrialization policies," *World Development* 12: 1029–1037.

—— (1987) "The interplay of state, social class, and world system in East Asian development: the cases of Korea and Taiwan," in F. C. Deyo (ed.) *The Political Economy of the New Asian Industrialism*, Ithaca, NY: Cornell University Press.

Krugman, P. (1994) "The myth of Asia's miracle," *Foreign Affairs* December: 62–78.

Landes, S. (1969) *The Unbound Prometheus*, Cambridge: Cambridge University Press.

Lee, C. H. (1994) "Korea's direct foreign investment in Southeast Asia," *ASEAN Economic Bulletin* 10, 3: 280–296.

Lee, K. U. (1988) "The relationships between small or medium firms and large firms in Korea," Korea Development Institute Working Paper, No. 8814, Seoul.

Lim, Y. (1981) "Government policy and private enterprise: Korean experience in industrialization," Institute of East Asian Studies, Korea Research Monograph no. 6, Berkeley, CA: University of California.

Lim, Y. (1995) "Industrial policy for technological learning: a hypothesis and Korean evidence," Working Paper, The Hague: Institute of Social Studies.

Luedde-Neurath, R. (1986) *Import Controls and Export-oriented Development: A Reassessment of the South Korean Case*, Boulder, CO: Westview Press.

Lundvall, B. (ed.) (1992) *National Systems of Innovation: Towards a Theory of Innovation and Interactive Learning*, London: Pinter.

Mowery, D. and Rosenberg, N. (1989) *Technology and the Pursuit of Economic Growth*, Cambridge: Cambridge University Press.

Mytelka, L. (1982) "In search of a partner: the state and the textile industry in France," in S. Cohen and P. Gourevitch (eds) *France in a Troubled World Economy*, London: Butterworth.

—— (1991) "Crisis, technological change and the strategic alliance," in L. Mytelka (ed.) *Strategic Partnerships and the World Economy*, London: Pinter.

—— (1996a) "Competition, innovation and competitiveness: a framework for analysis," in L. Mytelka (ed.) *Competition, Innovation and Competitiveness in Developing Countries*, Paris: OECD.

—— (1996b) "Competition policies and innovation practices: how the two relate," in L. Mytelka (ed.) *Competition, Innovation and Competitiveness in Developing Countries*, Paris: OECD.

—— (1996c) "Telecommunications equipment manufacturing in Brazil and Korea," in L. Mytelka (ed.) *Competition, Innovation and Competitiveness in Developing Countries*, Paris: OECD.

Mytelka, L. and Ernst, D. (1996) "Catching up, keeping up and getting ahead: the Korean model under pressure," in D. Ernst, L. Mytelka, and T. Ganiatsos (eds) *Technological Capabilities and Export Success: Case Studies from Asia*, London: Routledge.

Nelson, R. (ed.) (1993) *National Innovation Systems: A Comparative Analysis*, New York: Oxford University Press.

OECD (1997) *Reviews of National Science and Technology Policy: Korea Part II: Examiners Report*, Doc. No. DSTI/STP (95) 15 (November 12), Paris: OECD.

Polyani, K. (1944) *The Great Transformation*, Boston: Beacon Press.

Rhee, S. (1987) "Policy reforms of the 1980s and industrial adjustments in Korean economy," Korea Development Institute Working Paper, No. 8708, Seoul.

Rhee, Y. W., Ross-Larson, B., and Pursell, G. (1984) *Korea's Competitive Edge: Managing the Entry into World Markets*, Baltimore: Johns Hopkins University Press.

Sakong, I. (1993) "Korea in the world economy," Washington, DC: Institute for International Economics.

Scott, A. J. and Storper, M. (1992) "Industrialization and regional development," in M. Storper and A. Scott (eds) *Pathways to Industrialization and Regional Development*, London and New York: Routledge.

Stiglitz, J. E. (1987) "Learning to learn, localized learning and technological progress," in P. Dasgupta and P. Stoneman (eds) *Economic Policy and Technological Performance*, Cambridge: Cambridge University Press.

UNCTAD (1978) "Case studies in the transfer of technology: policies for transfer and development of technology in pre-war Japan (1868–1937)," Doc. No. TD/B/C.6/26, Geneva: UNCTAD.

Wade, R. (1990) *Governing the Market: Economic Theory and the Role of Government in East Asian Industrialization*, Princeton, NJ: Princeton University Press.

Westphal, L. (1979) "Manufacturing," in P. Hasan and D. C. Rao (eds) *Korea Policy Issues for Long-Term Development*, Baltimore: Johns Hopkins University Press.

Westphal, L., Rhee, Y. W., and Pursell, G. (1979) "Foreign influences on Korean industrial development," Oxford Bulletin of Economics and Statistics 42, 4, November.

Woo, J. (1991) *Race to the Swift State and Finance in Korean Industrialization*, New York: Columbia University Press.

World Bank (1993) *The East Asian Miracle,* Washington, DC: IBRD.

Young, A. (1993) "The tyranny of numbers: confronting the statistical realities of the East Asian growth enterprise," Cambridge, MA: MIT, Sloan School, July.

9   Industrial policy for catching up

The case of Taiwan

J. R. Chaponnière and Marc Lautier

INTRODUCTION

The economic development of Taiwan – from a poverty stricken country in 1950 to one of today's high-income countries – is a spectacular success story. A small (21 million inhabitants) and diplomatically isolated island, it has become the twelfth trading nation. These economic achievements have fueled the rise of a rights-conscious middle class which contributed to the smooth transition toward democracy and the first direct presidential election ever held in a Chinese state in 1996.

Unitary explanations of such a broad transformation are always hazardous. Among the most important factors are the initial conditions, the dynamism of the private sector, and, last but not least, the strategic orientation of the industrial policy. After a rapid introduction to Taiwan's economic development, this chapter focuses on this last issue. The second section deals with the strategic choices of the Taiwanese industrial policy; the third section presents the main institutions in charge of designing and implementing these choices, after which two specific sectoral experiences are studied in the final section.

ECONOMIC DEVELOPMENT AND THE CONTEXT OF INDUSTRIAL POLICY

Economic development

Between 1951 and 1995, the average economic growth was 8.7 percent and income per capita increased sixtyfold to reach US$12,000. During these 45 years, the economy never experienced a setback. The share of exports in GNP rose from 10 percent to 56 percent (1986). In the last ten years this ratio declined again to 43 percent (1995) due to the dynamism of the domestic market. Taiwan started to develop a trade surplus in the early 1970s and accumulated huge foreign exchange reserves that stand second only to those of Japan in the world.

The spectacular export growth should not lead one to forget the equally remarkable record of factor accumulation. The high level of domestic savings has financed a considerable investment effort. The constant price investment to GDP ratio was around 10 percent in 1950 and grew steadily to 27 percent in 1975, after which it fluctuated around 20 percent. The importance of foreign aid declined in the 1960s but the inflow of FDI played a rather modest role.[1] After 1986, Taiwan became a substantial capital exporter itself and, according to the Central Bank, it was the eleventh largest foreign investor between 1986 and 1993.[2]

One remarkable characteristic of Taiwan is its balanced income distribution, which has resulted from the Land Reform implemented in the 1950s, as well as the very dynamic job creation process in manufacturing industry.

The government of Taiwan has followed cautious macroeconomic management. The Kuomintang administration heeded the lessons of the huge inflationary period of the 1930s in mainland China and implemented, in the late 1940s, a stringent stabilization program. Starting in the 1950s, it chose to pursue a policy of positive real interest rates, rather unusual at that time. Along with tight money, the government followed a conservative budgetary policy with a budget surplus for all but one year between 1965 and 1995. This conservative macroeconomic policy resulted in high domestic savings, low domestic inflation, and 30 years of stability of the NT$; its appreciation since 1987 has been the result of international pressure.

The banking system, which is controlled by the state, has often been criticized for being too conservative. The Bank of Communication, whose role is that of a development bank, assumes a rather low profile; it handles policy loans in the same way as normal lending (Cheng 1994).

As a result of this conservative macroeconomic policy, planners were largely deprived of two instruments of industrial policy: the control over credit and budgetary allocations for development purposes (Park 1990). To promote industrial development, Taiwan relied primarily on fiscal incentives that were periodically revamped to favor new sectors and activities. While the use of credit allocation usually favors big firms with good credit ratings or closeness to the government, as in the case of Korea, in Taiwan fiscal incentives were extended to any firm, and this greatly contributed to Taiwan's specific industrial structure (see below).

Industrial transformation

Taiwan has undergone one of the most compressed industrial transformations in East Asia. In terms of value added, the ratio of light to heavy industries fell from 4 to 1 in 15 years while the same evolution took 25 years in Japan (Wanatabe 1985). The evolution of the export mix illustrates this diversification, as the share of traditional industries (food-processing, textiles, rubber, and plastics) declined from 45 percent to 20 percent (1970–1995), while that of electronics and machinery industries rose from 15 percent to 38 percent.

The dynamism of the manufacturing sector spearheaded this development. In 1970, manufacturing products accounted for over 80 percent of total exports and over 90 percent since 1980. Manufacturing experienced a double digit growth rate and its share of GDP grew from 17 percent (1952) to a maximum of 39 percent in 1986 and then declined to 29 percent (1995).

During the 1960s, exports increased at a phenomenal rate as Taiwan became a successful exporter of labor-intensive products. In the early 1970s, the accumulation of foreign exchange provided capital for the Ten National Construction Projects (electric power, telecommunications, and transportation utilities) and allowed public owned enterprises (POEs) to invest extensively in petrochemical, iron, and steel. After a relative slowdown in the early 1980s, the second half of that decade was extremely dynamic. The main change came from the transformation of the East Asian economic environment. In the immediate post-Plaza period (1985), the trade tensions between Japan and the United States were extended to Taiwan (and Korea), as these countries exploited their advantages by not following Japan in reevaluating their currencies against the dollar. Voluntary export restraints (VERs) and non-tariff barriers restricted Taiwan access to the US market, and the Taiwanese government was pressured to open its domestic market and to allow its currency to float.

Besides this, the average manufacturing wage rose from US$200 in 1980 to US$800 in 1990 and US$1,200 in 1995. These considerable changes prompted companies to relocate some of their manufacturing activities in lower cost countries and to change their trade patterns. Strategies previously pursued, particularly the primary reliance on exports for the American market, were no longer viable. The share of OECD markets rapidly diminished in Taiwanese exports. China and the rest of South East Asia gained in significance as Taiwanese firms relocated some of their activities in neighboring countries. But in the meantime new firms emerged in higher value-added activities.

Initial conditions

To put the country's economic development in a historical perspective, it should be noted that although Taiwan was a poor country in the late 1950s, its social indicators placed it in a different rank from what per capita income figures predicted. Thus according to an index of socio-economic indicators computed by Adelman and Morris (1967), Taiwan was close to Cyprus which was characterized by a nominal per capita income three times higher.[3] The school enrolment ratio was satisfactory and the literacy rate in Taiwan was higher than that of most developing countries.

Between 1895 and 1945, the incorporation of Taiwan into the Japanese empire was accomplished through a process of conservation and restructuring of the indigenous socio-economic system. This incorporation involved the specialization of agricultural production (rice, sugar) in order to cover new cash expenses such as taxes and debts. Japan transformed the island into its agricultural appendage, but this rural development laid the ground for Taiwan's industrialization. Even if food-processing was the dominant activity, local demand stimulated the growth of the chemical industry as well as light industries, and in the thirties the Japanese chose to locate selected heavy industries on the island.[4] Average industrial growth was 5 percent between 1911 and 1938 (Mizoguchi 1979), and in 1940 Taiwan was the most industrialized of the Chinese provinces. During the colonial period primary education generalized and, by 1943, 71 percent of the 7 to 14 years old age group attended primary school.

Industrial capacity was destroyed during the war, but the destiny of Taiwan changed with the arrival of the Chinese Nationalist or Kuomintang (KMT). Between 1949 and 1951, around 2 million soldiers and civilians fled from mainland China and added to the population of 6 million. This large influx saddled the island with a bureaucracy and an army of continental size, but it also brought in an educated workforce that replaced Japanese technicians and administrators. Thus by 1951, industrial output reached the pre-war level, despite the withdrawal of the Japanese. At the outbreak of the Korean war (1949), Taiwan benefited from a geostrategic rent and received assistance well above that of other developing countries. International aid financed 40 percent of the gross domestic investment during the 1950s. This assistance was instrumental in launching the Land Reform, which laid the ground for the equal income distribution.[5] Barro and Lee (1993) have provided additional evidence of the importance of initial conditions as they have measured that, among the different sources of Taiwanese growth between 1965 and 1985, the biggest contribution came from "the net convergence effect," which illustrates the fact that Taiwan had low initial per capita GDP levels but high levels of human capital per worker.

Industrial structure

Interactions between change in industrial policy and industrial organization are often strong in developing economies. In comparison with the experiences of most of the industrialized countries, notably the other fast growing Asian economies (Japan, Korea), the most distinctive feature of Taiwan's industrial structure is the predominance of small and medium enterprises (SMEs), even if the role of large enterprises should not be underestimated. The regional balance of industrial production throughout the country is partly due to the early development of agro-industries, but also to the rapid development of infrastructure and a political willingness to limit urban concentration. Among the 145,000 manufacturing enterprises, 98.7 percent are small and medium-sized and they accounted for 68 percent of manufacturing employment and 65 percent of exports in 1985.[6]

The overall industrial concentration is low by international standards: the

100 largest companies accounted for 21 percent of the manufacturing sales in 1970 and 22 percent in 1980 (Chou 1988). On a sectoral basis patterns differ significantly, as for instance in intermediate and capital-intensive activities (steel, chemical), in which the country-leading business groups are strongly committed (Nan Ya Plastic, China Steel, Formosa group, etc.). Several of these large companies are publicly owned.[7]

The actual feature differs sharply with the initial phase of Taiwan's development. In 1949, public-owned enterprises (POEs) accounted for two-thirds of the industry, and the large enterprises share remained high (56 percent) in the early 1960s.[8] The state's strong direct commitment in manufacturing activities was due to two main reasons: the colonial legacy and the first development strategy. The Chinese nationalist government took over the Japanese enterprises and was operating them after their consolidation into 22 large public corporations in 1946. Taiwan's economy was thus dominated by POEs, and their role remained important in the 1960s as they became a strategic tool to reduce import dependence in upstream industries. POEs still enjoy a monopoly position in a few capital-intensive intermediate products industries, but their contribution to manufacturing output has decreased dramatically (10 percent in 1994).

For ideological and political reasons, the government was reluctant to promote large private enterprises. Having dismantled the indigenous landlord class through a land reform in the first half of the 1950s, the KMT regime avoided the formation of a powerful entrepreneur. Private enterprises were offered neither generous incentives nor preferential access to credit. The difference between Taiwan and Korea can be illustrated in the case of the promotion of the large trading companies. In the two countries, the Japanese Sogo Soshas played a very important role in channelling exports in the 1960s and the government wished to limit this dependence. In Korea, the government gave credit privileges to the general trading companies (GTCs) which were the trading arms of the chaebols. In Taiwan, the government tried to promote large trading companies (LTCs) independent of the large industrial firms. While the GTCs flourished and their growth fostered industrial concentration in Korea,[9] Taiwanese LTCs were a failure. Nevertheless, a few Taiwanese entrepreneurs succeeded in establishing large business groups in the 1960s. They often enjoyed strong political connections and privileges (Numazaki 1991), and they benefited from the production and import barriers raised on the domestic market.

Beside this political context, the dynamism of private entrepreneurs has been the main determinant of industrial organization changes since the 1950s, from a POEs-dominated economic structure to the predominance of private SMEs. Ho (1980) compared the annual growth rate of manufacturing employment by size of plants in Taiwan and Korea from 1954 to 1971. While in Korea the largest firms were the fastest growing ones, in Taiwan the intermediate category, i.e. firms between 100 and 500 workers, were the most dynamic and achieved a growth rate of about double the industry average. From 1966 to 1986, the employment share of Taiwanese SMEs in manufacturing kept growing, from 43 percent to 68 percent (Chou 1992).

Taiwan's model of "diffuse industrialization" (Chaponnière and Jolly 1989) is based on a very dynamic SMEs demography, and industry spillover is an essential component of the country's economic growth. This specific business structure cannot be considered as the result of a deliberate policy aiming at the promotion of SMEs. It is rather rooted in Chinese tradition and culture. In a country where the social cost of failure is relatively low, workers are usually keen to take any opportunity to set up their own workshop or company. As the Chinese proverb has it: "Better the head of a chicken than the tail of a cow".[10] State investment in upstream industries (chemical, steel) generated external economies and helped reduce barriers to entry for small manufacturers in final goods.

But the growth differential may also be explained by differences in market orientations. While the largest companies, including POEs, focused on domestic sales,[11] SMEs were mainly export-oriented. The small and medium-sized private sector accounted for 65 to 70 percent of manufacturing exports in the 1980s, and SMEs exported on average 71 percent of their output in 1985. SMEs' heavy reliance on export sales resulted from the structure of the domestic market which was dominated by large companies, often backed by government privileges (import licenses, government contracts). SMEs were therefore bound to export in order to grow. While big GTCs were of little importance in Taiwan's development, independent traders have proliferated since the 1960s, extending access to foreign markets for small-volume manufacturers (Levy 1987). Japanese trading companies and foreign importers widely contributed to the development of SMEs export sales. In some cases access to industrialized markets has been supplied through subcontracting for export-oriented FDI (Schive 1990).

Furthermore, from a financial point of view, Taiwanese SMEs have a significant advantage in engaging in export rather than in domestic sales. On the domestic market a firm must deal with the fact that the normal business practice is a three months' payment term. By contrast, if SMEs engage in export sales, their working capital will be much lower, since a foreign Letter of Credit (L/C) can be liquidated in a local bank (San Gee 1994). This incentive has been critical for firms that have received little "institutional credit" (Ho 1980), until recently.

To sum up, entry barriers have been lower and profit margins higher in export activities. The relatively low cost of entry on export markets has reinforced industry spillover. Several studies (Chaponnière and Fouquin 1989; Lautier 1994; Levy and Kuo 1987) have documented the abilities of Taiwanese SMEs to strengthen their competitiveness and to adapt themselves quickly to changes in international demand and supply.

This specific pattern of industrial organization has undoubtedly contributed to productivity growth and to speeding-up industrial restructuring. The traditional dichotomy, between inward-looking large private companies on the one hand and POEs and export-oriented SMEs on the other, has been reduced due to changes in the competitive environment both on the domestic and exports markets. The contribution of large firms increases now in exports sectors (see p. 242 on electronics), while a growing number of SMEs are now able to compete successfully with sophisticated imports in the domestic market (see p. 244 on machine tools). In any case, the export competitiveness of the small-sized private sector cannot be isolated from that of the large companies who have always been critical of upstream inputs suppliers.

IMPLEMENTING INDUSTRIAL POLICY

The first account of industrial development in Taiwan emphasized the role of macroeconomic policy, as well as the reforms that allowed exporters to obtain their inputs at world prices. Manufacturing development did undoubtedly benefit both from the economic (as well as political) stability and the export orientation. However, the market paradigm does not tell the whole story.

The state implemented an industrial policy that aimed at promoting certain sectors and fostering international competitiveness, by affecting investment, production, and trade decisions of private firms. Its basic framework was laid out early. The country's industrial catching-up trajectory was already defined in the 1965–1968 Plan:

> For further development, stress must be laid on basic heavy industries (such as chemicals, wood pulp, petrochemical intermediates, and large-scale integrated steel production) instead of end-product manufacturing or processing. Industrial development in the long run must be centred on export products that have high income elasticity and low transportation cost. And around these products there should be development of both forward and backward industries, so that both specialization and complementarity may be achieved in the interest of Taiwan's economy.[12]

While the industrial policy was more supportive than interventionist, it was not as orthodox as it has often been presented. Among its main components are industrial targeting, management of foreign trade, promotion of intra-industry linkages, and technology policy.

Industrial targeting

Taiwan did practice industrial targeting and its "picking the winners" policy speeded up the development of several sectors, starting from textile in the 1960s to semiconductor and aerospace in the 1980s and 1990s. The sequence of the state intervention shows that it did not wait for the erosion of comparative advantages but tried to anticipate it. However, industrial targeting has been much more diluted than in Korea.

The basic philosophy underlying the government strategy was that an economy will undergo certain stages of development, and at each stage there are certain key industries (integrated steel mill, large shipyards, petrochemical plants) that through various linkages will bring about the development of the entire economy. This strategy assumes that government officials know what those key industries are and what policy measures should be adopted to develop them. Furthermore, they have to share their vision with private entrepreneurs. By and large, state intervention has been more vigorous in capital and technology-intensive sectors, such as iron and steel, petrochemical or semiconductors, than in labor-intensive sectors (garment, electronics assembly).

In the case of the textile industry, the state entrusted some selected enterprises with the task of transforming the raw material that it sold to them, and bought back the finished products. Thus by following a strategy similar to the "putting out" practiced by the English nineteenth-century merchants, it spared firms the difficulties of buying raw materials, ensuring working capital or dealing with marketing problems.[13] After some years of "cocooning," those firms were able to face international competition.

The efforts to promote heavy industry were frustrating as local entrepreneurs were unable or unwilling to make large investments. Thus Taiwan's heavy and chemical industrialization drive was on a much smaller scale than that of Korea. It aimed at deepening the industrial base and supplying intermediate goods to downstream industries rather than attempting to turn heavy and petrochemical firms into the backbone of export industries. In the 1950s, the first plastics plant was built under government supervision and handed to a private entrepreneur upon completion (Wade 1990). In the petrochemical industry, the capital-intensive and lower margin portion of the upper stream was assigned to Chinese Petroleum Corp, a government-owned company, while the most profitable intermediate and downstream plants were granted to the private sector.

In the early 1970s, the government warned private entrepreneurs against the dangers of overspecialization in labor-intensive products and urged them to enter into more technology-intensive activities. These warnings were ignored and the incentives were too low to promote significant private investment in high technology. In 1982 a sectoral policy was adopted that aimed at identifying and promoting strategic sectors in order to speed up the industry restructuring process. Preferential fiscal measures and financial state incentives were offered to high-tech sectors. Later the Six Year Development Plan (1991–1996) selected ten "star industries" whose development was considered essential for future industrial success: telecommunications, information technology, consumer electronics, semiconductors, precision machinery and automation, aerospace, advanced materials, specialty chemicals and pharmaceuticals, medical and health care, pollution control.[14] According to San (1994), the definition of strategic sectors was based on the same two high–two large–two low principle: industries targeted are high in technology and value-added intensity, large in market potential and industrial linkages, and low in energy consumption and pollution.

These interventions had a moderate effect on relative prices. When an intervention did cause prices to deviate from the market levels (because of quotas or tariffs), the government intervened a second time to counterbalance the distortion. Thus, industrial targeting contributed strongly to industrial modernization. But policies were more supportive than dirigist, and did not lock the private sector, especially the SMEs, into a sectorally narrow development path.

Management of foreign trade

Taiwan is a very open economy. The share of imports in domestic demand has been over 40 percent since the early 1970s. Exports have risen even faster, contributing to 50–55 percent of GNP in the 1980s. But, while this trade performance can easily be described, the explanation of this success is not so obvious.

In line with the traditional comparative advantage theory, the most influential analysis of Taiwanese (and East Asian) development emphasizes the crucial shift from import substitution to export promotion in the early 1960s. During the 1950s, international assistance allowed Taiwan to follow an import substitution strategy that ran out of steam at the end of the decade. The shift from an import-substitution to an export-promotion strategy took place gradually between 1955 and 1962. A system of import duty and commodity tax rebate was introduced in 1955. In 1956, manufacturers were authorized to retain up to 80 percent of the foreign exchange they earned from exports and to use it to finance their import needs. The multiple exchange rate system was unified between 1958 and 1961 and the difference between the official exchange rate and the market price of foreign currency was insignificant by 1960. These measures removed the bias against exports and created highly profitable labor-intensive exports opportunities that led private firms to invest. This initiated a virtuous circle of trade-driven growth that has extended over three decades (World Bank 1993).

This standard presentation of Taiwan's trade regime has been challenged by several arguments which emphasised that the "free-trade thesis" does not explain how the export expansion induced economic growth and what made it possible. The challengers have focused on two main issues: the role of the state in trade performance and the causality between growth and exports. Wade (1990) has comprehensively demolished the view that Taiwan's trade policies became suddenly noninterventionist in the early 1960s. Noting that the growth of exports that accounted for 10 percent of GDP in 1960 had less impact than the increase of domestic investment, Rodrik (1995) has suggested that the sequence may have been the reverse. Export orientation did enable economic growth but the reason for growth must be traced back to reasons why it became profitable to invest. The important turning point was the Nineteen Points Reform (1960) which signaled a major shift in government attitude toward investment. It simplified administrative procedures and offered very generous tax incentives to investors. Thus local firms exported because they had chosen to invest and had to finance their import of capital goods. In line with this argument, Bradford (1993) has explained the East Asian development experience from a growth-driven trade rather than from a trade-driven growth perspective.

Whatever the sequence between exports and investment may have been, a distinctive feature of Taiwan's development strategy is the integration of its trade policy within the industrial policy. According to Wanatabe (1985), Taiwan's (and Korea's) strength lies in the combination between import substitution and export promotion which, by allowing an enlargement of the domestic market for intermediates products, made investments in upstream industries feasible.

The Taiwanese policy has been far less protectionist than in most developing countries, but the government has not been neutral in the transformation process of trade specialization. The state has actively contributed to building up new comparative advantages through the promotion of certain industries. This objective has gradually replaced the initially pure mercantilist orientation of the trade policy framework.[15]

The adoption of an export-oriented strategy was not accompanied by a parallel import liberalization. The establishment of export-processing zones, as well as the implementation of the rebate system, did allow export-oriented firms to import their inputs rather freely, but domestic-oriented firms did not enjoy the same status. The average tariff rate decreased from 47 percent (1955) to 31 percent (1980), and more rapidly under international pressure after the mid-1980s.[16] But this general trend masks the fact that the tariff structure was precisely differentiated by product. As Chou (1988) points out, while the general degree of protection decreased, protective functions were maintained. Even if nontariff barriers such as import licences and local content ratio were less extensively used than in other Asian countries, they did play a rather significant role. While the ratio of controlled and prohibited import items decreased very rapidly in the 1970s, the permissible list contained products that were not freely imported. A would-be importer was required to furnish a letter from the relevant industrial association attesting that the domestic suppliers cannot meet his term on price, quality, or delivery (Wade 1990). However, it should be stressed that protectionist measures were sometimes unnecessary since technical capabilities and domestic competition were high enough to lower the price of local products below that of imports. The government also used international prices to discipline the price-setting of domestic suppliers, and the threat of allowing imports was often sufficient to hold domestic producers' prices near international levels.

On the export side, the rebate tax system was an important export incentive, but additional measures were implemented to create a positive discrimination in favor of export sales and to foster the trade competitiveness of the industry. Macroeconomic management in particular has strongly contributed to export expansion. The devaluation of the currency by about 60 percent in 1958 and the stability of the exchange rate until 1986, combined with a very cautious wage policy, made labor-intensive and simple-processed products very competitive on foreign markets.

More targeted measures have included preferential loans, export–import links, establishment of export processing zones (EPZs), and export assistance. A special export loan program was initiated in 1957. Favorable interest rates for export-financing existed until their complete abolition in 1992 (OECD 1993). Under this scheme, a firm was entitled to preferential credits according to its previous year's export sales and its planned export sales for the current year. While the benefit of such loans to exporters was considerable, it has never been as important as in South Korea, and the Taiwanese government progressively cut back the volume of such credits and the interest rate margin.[17] Otherwise, the government has promoted exports by using firms' export performance as a basic criterion for judging import applications. In a context of strict government control of foreign exchange, exporters were also entitled to manage relatively freely their foreign exchange surplus. The strongest tax and administrative privileges were given to firms in the EPZs.[18]

Following Japanese practices, the government has also helped exports by developing marketing assistance and product quality inspection. The China External Trade Development Council (CETRA) was set up as a semi-public institution in 1970 to supply domestic firms with the international marketing expertise they were lacking. Through its overseas offices network, CETRA carries out detailed market research, finds out import agents, organizes trade fairs, etc. Export quality inspection has been strengthened since the early 1950s in order to transform a negative externality, i.e. the penalizing low-quality reputation of Taiwanese producers, into a competitive asset.[19] As much as 800 inspectors were active in export quality control. According to Wade (1990: 144), factories under the minimum quality level were not allowed to export.

While exports financed only 58 percent of imports in 1952, they climbed to US$110 billion in 1995. Taiwan enjoys one of the largest trade surplus in the world. The rapid appreciation of the NT$ since 1986 has sped up the industrial restructuring process toward more technology-intensive sectors, but exports keep growing. Taiwan's industry has become highly internationalized and the pursuit of its growth depends mostly on firms' performances on foreign markets. This may explain government compliance with free trade principles at the present time. Taiwan's reform of its tariff and nontariff barriers is now opening the domestic market to increased competition from imports. The government's current plan, set up for the country's accession to the WTO, implemented a negative import list system in 1994.[20]

Intra-industry linkages promotion

Except in a few rare cases, such as the textile industry in the 1960s, industrial policy neglected the SMEs sector up to the 1980s. But emphasis has gradually been put on the improvement of the intra-industry division of labor and on sustaining the SMEs sector since the 1980s. The technology policy was a key component in this process (see below), though other means were used as well. Manufacturing structures have been strengthened through a mix of horizontal and vertical policy measures that have aimed at promoting interfirms linkages and at filling intra-industrial gaps in terms of critical components and specific resources.

Domestic linkages development has been promoted by state-led investments in upstream industries (see above). At the intra-industry level, local content ratio, tax incentives, and promotion of subcontracting have been used to encourage linkages. Minimum local content measures have strongly favored backward linkages in a few targeted industries (motor vehicles, electronics). The design of the implementation scheme has strongly favored the parts and components sector manufacturing efficiency. In the case of the automobile industry, for instance, each carmaker must buy a number of locally made components to be chosen from a list edited by the Ministry of Economic Affairs (MOEA). The list has regularly increased, and so did the number of components to be localized. The clever point in this localization scheme is to let buyers define their procurement policy themselves. The local content criteria incites them to purchase parts from the most efficient domestics producers. The main consequence of such behavior is therefore to strengthen the comparative advantage of the auto parts industry.[21]

Since the 1980s, Taiwanese policymakers have also tried to modernize the industry structure by promoting the development of subcontracting relationships following the Japanese pattern. The Center Satellite Factories (CSF) program seeks to organize and integrate subcontractors around a core firm in order to upgrade their management and technological capabilities. To benefit from the CSF scheme, manufacturers are required to have at least ten satellite plants and to meet certain other financial and management standards. The advantage for a firm in associating itself with a CSF system is that it can receive a lot of financial, manpower training, and technical engineering assistance from government agencies (San Gee 1994). Intra-industry specialization has also been fostered by components standardization plans launched by government-sponsored agencies in cooperation with industrial associations (automobile, machine tool, electronics).

Component targeting has been another method of strengthening intra-industrial structures. Three main programs have been launched by the IDB in the last decade: the "Development of New Industrial Products program" (DNIP) in 1984, the "Development Targeted Leading Products program" (DTLP) in 1991, and the "Development of Critical Components and Products program" (DCCP) in 1992. While they are basically designed as

R&D promotion programs, their major concerns are in fact to encourage product range upgrading in certain industries and to reduce trade deficit with Japan. Targeted products/components therefore include those that have a pivotal position among the industries, a high market potential, or for which Taiwan's industry is heavily dependant on Japanese imports.[22] A stronger emphasis has been gradually put on critical components development in the electro-mechanical industries. Private firms engaged in new products/components development may apply for several advantages in terms of state subsidies (as much as 50 percent of the development cost),[23] low interest loans, research support, and other administrative privileges. The implementation of these programs involves a detailed screening of industries' weaknesses and market potentials. This process is led by the IDB, in close cooperation with the private sector (industrial associations) and research institutions.[24]

The leading firm strategy has also been used by the government at the intrasectoral level, to strengthen industry structures when the private sector is reluctant to invest in the development and production of targeted components. State direct involvement has been "downward-pull" in the sense that it aimed at complementing an existing production network. This sequence explains why most of these projects succeed and why, when they fail, the main cause of failure is the opposition of downstream private firms (see below).

The government also took a number of steps to enhance the business capabilities of SMEs. In Taiwan as elsewhere, and even if financial institutions are established with the aim to support them, SMEs have difficulties in borrowing from the financial market and have raised funds from the curb markets.[25] To support SMEs, in 1981 the Ministry of Economic Affairs set up a special system of guidance and assistance at the core of which stood the Medium and Small Business Administration, which coordinates the efforts of related support organizations:

- financing assistance
- accounting assistance
- management and technological assistance
- marketing assistance from CETRA

Nevertheless, government direct intervention in the SMEs sector has been relatively modest, compared to the importance of these enterprises in Taiwan. But industrial policy has never been strongly biased toward large firms. As Schive (1993) points out, Taiwanese policies in favor of large firms have not worked seriously against SMEs, and policies influencing resource allocation (tax incentives, credit control, use of public enterprises) have been applied with a high degree of self-restraint. Staley and Morse (1965: 273) noted that "Part of the process of industrial development is growth of cost-conscious specialization among firms." While in Taiwan the state has not led this specialization process, it has significantly contributed to its achievement by promoting intra-industry linkage and externalities developments, which resulted in lowering entry cost in the manufacturing sector and extending business opportunities for medium-sized producers.

Technology policy

The swift diversification of Taiwan's industrial structure is a clear illustration of its rapid technological development. During the 1960s and the 1970s, the technology policy was clearly related to the trade and investment policies. However, since then the provision of subsidized technology inputs and the organization of collective technology programs by research institutes have become its main components. Nevertheless, Taiwan's recent technology policy cannot be considered as horizontal or nonselective, because not only industry targeting but also product (and component) targeting have remained important (cf. the DTLP and DCCP programs).

Before the implementation of this institutional technology policy, technology diffusion within Taiwanese industry was mainly based on informal means of transfer. Questioned in 1985 on the origin of their technologies, over 60 percent of a sample of 4,226 firms answered that they were the results of their own research (Hou and San Gee 1993). In 1992, a similar survey found that 71 percent of small firms and 68 percent of large firms had developed their technology by themselves (Kao 1994). In many cases these technological developments were the results of reverse-engineering, as the purchase of foreign goods has been the main channel of technology imports. Even if they are very crude, the comparison between the cumulative amount of capital goods imports and FDI is illustrative enough. From 1952 to 1994, Taiwan imported US$125 billion of capital goods, while the cumulative amount of FDI was US$22 billion. While Taiwan did protect its domestic industry, Taiwanese firms had no difficulty in importing modern manufacturing equipment.

Modern machinery imports have contributed to industrial technological upgrading. Its exposure to world quality standards was also transmitted to export firms through original equipment manufacturing (OEM) contracts, and to the whole economy through export firms' demands for intermediate inputs. OEM and, more recently, original design manufacturing (ODM)[26] are important exports channels and in many cases these contracts have been critical for the acquisition of technology.[27]

FDI inflows did not play a very significant role in the financing of investment in Taiwan, but they had a more important role than licensing for the transfer of technology. The priorities of the Council of Investments went successively to light industry, heavy industry (in the 1970s), and capital as well as technology-intensive activities (in the 1980s). Even though the state did not impose local participation, preference was all the same given to joint ventures, and up to 1985 foreign investors had to respect trade-related investment measures such as local integration and technology transfer conditions.

Research policy has been on the government agenda since the 1950s: a national plan for long-range scientific development was promulgated in 1959 and the Council on Long-range Scientific Development (latter renamed the National Science Council) was established to implement these guidelines. But the state's direct commitment in technology issues became only significant in the 1970s, when it established industrial research institutes and the Hsinchu Science Park.

One of the shortcomings of Taiwan's specific industrial structure is that most enterprises do not have sufficient human resources to engage in R&D activities. This is why the government funded a large number of industrial research institutes. Through these institutions and R&D incentives, the state has financed over 50 percent of R&D since 1980.[28] The main economic functions of these institutes are to undertake research programs, to develop new products and technologies, and to transfer the results to private firms. They are both research institutions and technology diffusion centers. They can also assist firms on specific R&D projects on a contract basis (see below). The Industrial Technology Research Institute (ITRI), created in 1973, is the largest of them and, since its creation, it has played a very active role in the country's technological development. Taiwan's "national system of innovation" is now based on an efficient division of labor in R&D between research institutes and private firms (see below).

The Hsinchu Science Park is another important component of the high-tech drive. In order to offer further incentives to firms willing to invest in high-tech products and to attract the Taiwanese who were working in the US, the government announced its intention to build a Science Park in the late 1970s. Since its opening in 1980, the Park has attracted over 150 firms and 40,000 employees, mostly in electronics, and its production reached US$4.8 billion in 1994. It has been administrated by the National Science Council on the model of Stanford Science Park. Among the incentives that are offered is a government start-up capital of up to 49 percent of the equity. The first company to apply for an entry in the Park was United Microelectronics Corporation (UMC), a spin-off from ERSO that was made of the team that had developed the integrated circuit (IC) technology in Taiwan. UMC is now at the leading edge of the IC technology and one of the few firms that has developed a microprocessor rival to Intel. It has been followed by several other local IC companies and by design houses. ITRI was instrumental in disseminating IC design technology (see below).

THE KEY INSTITUTIONS

The East Asian economic development has been strongly dependant on the cooperation between the state bureaucracy and private entrepreneurs. While each of these countries has built its own pattern, they have shown a common ability to articulate efficiently firms' profit-seeking behaviors with government developmental goals. Particularly important in the case of the industrial policy is the institutional arrangement that links the different actors of the industrialization process. In Taiwan, three sets of organizations were involved in the design and implementation of industrial policies: the state through its administrations responsible for economic affairs (CEPD, MOEA), the semi-public or intermediates institutions, often created upon state initiative but in which state's direct control varies (POEs, industrial associations, research institutes), and finally the private sector. This section deals with the two first components of this framework. Their interactions with the private sector will be studied in the final section.

The state's economic administration

Johnson (1987) has documented the role of "authoritarian" states and of the bureaucratic elite in the success of East Asian economic development. The main advantages he identifies are the political stability over the long term and state autonomy from political influence. In Taiwan, the KMT, which had a long practice of concentrating all powers, could rely on author-itarian means to put down any challenges to its domination. It inherited the Japanese centralized administrative structure, and among the Chinese who fled mainland China there were a large number of skilled administrators who could fill the void left by the departure of the Japanese. Afterwards, the KMT electoral strength has been based on excellent records in rural areas and its large financial assets, which have allowed it to remain completely independent from big business for electoral funds.

The Taiwanese state's economic intervention has been mainly conducted through two key institutions, the CEPD and the MOEA. The Council for Economic Planning Development (CEPD) began as the Council on United States Aid (CUSA) in 1948. It was then responsible for economic planning and resources allocation. It became an economic coordination council in 1963 (the CIECD), and lost its influence. In 1978, the Taiwanese govern-ment, inspired by the example of the Korean Economic Planning Board, decided to strengthen the planning agency functions, which was renamed as the CEPD. But, whereas the CEPD enjoys direct links with the Prime Minister's office, it has never gained the status of a superministry. In contrast to the Korean EPB, the CEPD does not control the budget and has no direct administrative authority. It is staffed with over 300 professionals, whose responsibilities cover the formulation of development plans, the analysis of the current economic situation, and the evaluation of POEs' investment pro-jects. They are also used to perform arbitration functions between the different ministries. The CEPD is therefore only an advisory body, albeit a very influential one. Whereas the planning council partly lost its authority, more power was given to the Ministry of Economic Affairs (MOEA). The MOEA is responsible for planning industrial development. Within the MOEA, the Industrial Development Bureau (IDB) is more directly in charge of industrial policy. It transforms CEPD's recommendations into sectoral plans. Measures resulting from industrial policy (fiscal incentives, subsidies, controls, protection, prices) are elaborated at this level. MOEA's prerogatives also include trade policy (through the Board of Foreign Trade) and foreign investment promotion. The Industrial Development and Investment Center and the Joint Industrial Investment Service Center attract foreign investment, while the Investment Commission screens all proposals. The core members of the Investment Commission are representative of the CEPD and the Ministry of Finance; the other representatives are brought in according to the type of proposals being considered.[29] But the IDB is the key agency within the Ministry. It influences the trade policy through its recommendations to the Board of Foreign Trade on industrial matters, and the foreign investment decisions are influenced in the same manner. The IDB is also the more interventionist economic body. It has been the main source of pressure for protectionism within the government, often in opposition to the CEPD and the Ministry of Finance's more liberal orientations (Fransman 1986; Wade 1990).

Intermediate institutions

While fairly close ties exist between the state (and the KMT) and some large private groups established by mainlanders, the main intermediaries between the state and the firms are the state enterprises (POEs), the industrial associations, and the R&D centers.

A surprisingly large share of the industry is still accounted for by state-owned enterprises. The government has frequently used this tool to establish new upstream industries and then either hands the factories over to selected private entrepreneurs or runs them as public enterprises.

During the 1950s, POEs accounted for half of the industrial output – an embarrassing figure for a country that denounced the massive appropriation of production means in the People's Republic of China. The drop in this percentage from 56 percent (1952) to 20 percent (1970) and 10 percent (1994) reflects not the withdrawal of the state but the vitality of the private sector. Officially launched in the late 1980s, the privatization program has not made much progress and POEs still dominate such sectors as refining (Chinese Petroleum Co), iron and steel (China Steel), and engineering (BES engineering). They enjoy a monopoly position in those sectors deemed strategic, but this position has been rather supportive and they have made use of their monopoly power to support downstream private enterprises. Thus, in order not to handicap exporters of plastic products, Chinese Petroleum Co based its price of ethylene on the average European and American price, while the synthetic rubber price was based on the standard price of natural rubber in Singapore.[30] Even recently, the government still relies on POEs in order to strengthen a given sector, as in the case of the promotion of the electronic industry in the 1980s[31] and of the aviation industry in the 1990s.

Among the numerous industrial research centers established by the state, ITRI is the most important. It has a staff of 5,800 people (1992), of which 42 percent hold a Master's or Ph.D degree. ITRI is made up of several laboratories as the Metal Industry Research Laboratory (MIRL) and the Electronics Research Scientific Organisation (ERSO). Several of the critical innovations that have spearheaded the emergence of Taiwan's integrated circuit industry have come from within the ERSO laboratory. Among the other research centers are the Institute of Information Industry, Food Industry Research and Development Institute, and China Textile Institute.

These research centers help to bridge lack of R&D efforts by most local firms. They act as a go-between for the domestic industry and the international state of the art. They buy foreign technologies which they then sublicense to firms, thus eliminating price-raising competition between firms for the same technology. In the 1990s, they have fostered the formation of technology alliances which allowed the industry to move rapidly toward leading edge products. While some ambitious projects (software standardization, motor) had disappointing results, others such as the notebook (see below) were successful. ITRI did also contribute to the technological upgrading of the industry through its turnover in human capital: a large number of its engineers and technicians ended up working in local companies or establishing their own business.

The industrial associations have also played a strategic role in Taiwan's industrialization. Their existence sheds light on the mechanisms by which the state can intervene in a highly competitive market economy in which SMEs are predominant. As early as the 1950s, the government promoted the creation of industrial associations in order to regulate production and to promote exports (Alam 1989). In the 1960s, subsidies to exporters were tied to export targets administered by industrial associations. During the 1970s, 30 percent of the imports had to be approved by the IDB or by an industrial association. Their intervention in exports intensified later when they took charge of managing VER quotas, and distributed export shares to their members. Industrial associations contributed also to improve local integration by attracting the attention of the IDB on a weak point in a given sector (the case of the dye sector for example) and by helping it to find investors. The strengthening of these associations is still one of the objectives of the IDB which assists them in conducting surveys and collecting data. Overall, industrial associations that define themselves as intermediaries between the government and the private sector and not as industry lobbies had a significant influence on industrial policy choices (targeting, research program).

The Taiwan Textile Federation is the most powerful industrial association. It was established in 1975, as an umbrella for the 18 textile associations created in the 1950s, in order to negotiate export quotas with Europe and the United States. Over 2,000 manufacturing firms belong to the TFT.[32] It became involved in export promotion and the gathering of commercial data; furthermore TFT established a design cell in order to assist the enterprises.

SECTORAL EXPERIENCES

Electronics

The Taiwanese electronics industry is characterized by its rather low profile on the world scene, as only a handful of domestic firms have become well-known brand names. However, this image is rather misleading since Taiwanese electronics exports amount to US$30 billions (1995) which is as much as Korea's. The island ranks third in the world information industry and fourth for integrated circuits, and it occupies a leading position in several niches such as monitors, keyboards, motherboards, and scanners. This contrast is explained by the "smaller is better" approach followed by the Taiwanese. The industry has maintained a small-scale approach. There are over 3,600 firms and thousands of exporters, while the three largest firms account for only 6 percent of total production.[33] Taiwanese firms engaged in cut throat competition have proved to be astonishingly adaptable to changes in world demand.

The industry started in the late 1940s when local firms began to assemble radios using imported parts from Japan. While the industry took advantage of the import restrictions on finished products, it was limited by the extent of the domestic market. This constraint disappeared in the 1960s. The combination of the incentives offered to investors (Nineteen Points Reform) and to exporters and the efforts made by the administration to attract foreign firms, launched a new dynamic for the electronics industry. Although FDI has played a rather modest role in the overall economy, its contribution to the growth of the electronics industry should not be underestimated. US firms started to invest in 1964 to make simple products and components for exports, while Japanese companies invested in joint ventures for the domestic market. In the 1960s, foreign firms were attracted by fiscal incentives and low labor cost. In the following decade, Taiwan became more selective and encouraged FDI that could introduce new technologies rather than labor-intensive operations in the country.[34]

If FDI investments was the catalyst, it was the dynamism of local firms, and mostly SMEs, that allowed Taiwan's electronics industry to go beyond the status of a foreign enclave and become a broad-based industrial sector. Among the reasons for this achievement there is the market awareness of small local companies that were very rapid to propose their services to foreign firms as soon as they had invested in Taiwan. As time passed, a growing number of these local firms were established by former technicians of the foreign-owned firms. They were able to win export orders from foreign buyers. While SMEs exploited the export opportunities, the larger firms – Tatung Teco – diversified from the electrical electronics industry.

By the mid-1970s, after 15 years of 25 percent average annual growth rate, electronics had become the second largest export industry. It was highly praised as an employment and a foreign exchange provider, but it was not considered as a strategic industry. The main industrial policy measure was local content requirements applied to both material goods and intangibles. The local content requirement demonstrates that the industry was still mainly an assembly operation.

A consensus was progressively reached among representatives of industry, government, and academics that the government should support the initial development of a high-tech industry. Due to its development potential and broad interindustry interdependence, the semiconductor industry was selected as a target industry and, within it, the IC technology was selected as the one to develop. At that time there was no local experience or knowledge in that field. A Technology Advisory Committee was set up and the ITRI was chosen to establish a pilot plant. The TAC chose to purchase the mature 7 micron technology from RCA after visiting several other IC firms. In 1974, the ERSO was established by ITRI to promote the necessary technology transfer, and in 1977 the first IC were produced. Since then, there has been continuous investment in IC technology, and process technology was upgraded to 1 micron and submicron.

By 1987, there were 30 design houses that had to use the services of foundries in Japan or the US. The next critical step was the establishment by the government and Philips of the Taiwan Semi Conductor Manufacturer Company. Philips transferred the static random access technology to the joint venture which was staffed by 200 personnel from ERSO and located in Hsinchu. It has now become one of the first companies to offer foundry only services (fabrication with no design), making it the most competitive foundry firm in the world.[35]

Taiwanese small firms – pop and mom shops – were among the first to seize the opportunities created by the diffusion of the PC in the early 1980s. The growth of ACER, from a start-up in 1976 to a US$5.8 billion power-house in 1995, led the development of the industry.[36] Among the other key actors there are the established firms of consumer electronics and hundreds of small firms specializing in peripheral products. The industry also benefited from early governmental support. In 1979, the Executive Yuan promulgated the Science and Technology Development program which identified infor-mation technology system as a key area and recommended the establishment of the Institute for Information Industry (III). The CEPED developed a ten year plan to promote the production as well as the diffusion of computers. The targets were based on the assumption that Taiwan could secure 2 percent of the world market by 1989. Forty-two products were considered strategic. The ITRI was contracted out for the implementation of the strategy and the Institute for Information Industry was in charge of promoting the domestic use of computers and the development of computer systems. This objective was more than fulfilled: Taiwan is now the third largest producer of IT prod-ucts and this segment has become the most important within Taiwan's electronics industry.

Since the 1980s the government has opted to work in closer cooperation with the private sector and to strengthen the efforts of firms that are already engaged in the semiconductor industry. This has been the case of the sub-micron project (US$270 million) to develop the next generation of chips. The state exercised pressure on private firms to develop a public–private project targeting not only integrated circuits but also work station and TVHD. The 1991–1995 National Science Council plan (US$503 million) gave a high priority to the development of integrated circuits, liquid crystal display, and DRAM in order to reduce the trade deficit with Japan for components.

Contrary to what has sometimes been written (Mody 1989), Taiwan's flexible industrial system has not proved to be a hindrance to its entry into higher technology segments. Indeed, Taiwan IT production is far ahead of that of Korea. Technology alliances organized by industrial research centers in close collaboration with industrial associations allowed firms to pool resources together in order to develop new products. They have had mixed results over the years.. The notebook consortium is a good example of such cooperative projects. It was initiated by a review of world trends in the computer market by ERSO and the Taiwan Computer Association which concluded that the world market for the "notebook computer" would develop rapidly and that if Taiwanese firms were not able to enter this new niche, they would be marginalized. Thirty enterprises joined the alliance to develop a prototype. Each subcommittee, followed by a researcher of ERSO, was in charge of the resolution of a specific technical problem of the notebook manufacturing process. Drawing from their conclusions, ERSO was able to develop a prototype that was then given to the members. Then, each enterprise developed its own notebook and competed with the others in the market.[37] The notebook project was highly successful, since 30 percent of the units sold in the world are now "Made in Taiwan." However, other similar attempts were less successful.

Machine tools

The Taiwanese machine tool industry is one of the most competitive in the world. Taiwan is now the sixth largest machine tools exporter and the seventh producer. No other producing country has enjoyed such a high growth rate in the two last decades. The industry output has grown from US$11 million in 1970 to more than US$1.1 billion in 1994. While Taiwan accounted for 0.9 percent of the world output in 1980, its share reached 3.8 percent in 1994.

We will briefly examine here the development trajectory of the machine tool industry, and how the industrial policy has contributed to this achievement. The Taiwanese SMEs' successful shift to the new product technology, based on numerical control (NC), in the early 1980s is a turning point in this sequence. It explains why the industry export growth path has been maintained and even consolidated since then.

Taiwanese machine tool enterprises typically originated in small workshops that either repaired old machinery or produced custom-made for the needs of local industry. Imitation of a few imported products rapidly allowed Taiwanese producers to supply simple, general-purpose machine tools (lathes). They soon engaged in export sales because of the relatively intense domestic competition at this time[38] and the small size of the domestic market. The outward orientation was fostered by the Vietnam war which created a boom in the neighboring countries. Export to Southeast Asia was therefore the first step of the industry into the world market. Taiwanese firms concentrated their productions on cost-competitive general-purpose machine tools, which gained a growing reputation on the international market. The USA emerged as their major foreign customer in the late 1970s. Later on the implementation of a voluntary export restraint (VER) agreement between the USA and Taiwan induced machine tools firms to orient their sales to Western Europe, which became their main export market in 1990. When Western Europe entered into a recession they moved again, to the dynamic Chinese market (PRC) which accounted for a third of their foreign sales in 1993 (Lautier 1994).

Export flexibility and marketing ability explain why Taiwan machine tool exports (and production) have grown much faster than international demand. However, the growing competitiveness of Taiwanese products in advanced countries is also based on rapid technical improvements. Imitation, reverse-engineering, and emulation were initially the key components of the technological development process. Fransman (1986) defined it as a frontier-following strategy, very attentive to modifications of the international state of the art but focusing on close followership rather than pure innovation. In her survey of nine Taiwanese machine tools builders, Amsden (1985) showed that almost all of them, whether large or small, had acquired their initial know-how through copying or reverse-engineering. Japan has been the major source of imports (63 percent in 1993), and hence of reverse-engineered technology. However, Taiwanese manufacturers have gradually built a strong expertise in mechanical process and product improvement. They did not merely copy the foreign models, but also modified their designs and reduced production costs.[39] While licensing and FDI have never been an important source of technology flow, technical guidance was provided by foreign purchasers and overseas agents. Most of these knowledge transfers have not been contract-based but rather informal. Tsai (1992) called this stage "the period of self dependence", because technological development was relatively self-dependent in the 1960s and 1970s.

Government support of the machine tools industry was not considerable before its recent developments (Amsden 1985; Jacobsson 1986; Tsai 1992; authors' interviews). There has been no government-owned machine tools manufacturer in Taiwan, and the last attempt to create a large-scale government-supported company failed. CEPD and IDB planned to set up a holding company for the industry around 1984, with shares held by a government bank and a foreign firm (Wade 1990). The domestic makers should have specialized in line with this new industrial giant, . . . but they refused to cooperate with this project.[40]

The machine tools firms have been active in using export-related incentives,[41] but these measures were not specifically directed to this industry. Despite a few protectionist measures, the domestic machine tools market was open to foreign products early.[42] But the state's involvement in the machine tool industry increased in the early 1980s when private firms had to cope with a new technological paradigm.

The development and the application of computer numerical control (CNC), based on microprocessor technology, opened the way for a new type of machine tools, of which the main expressions have been NC lathes and machining centers (MC).[43] Japanese firms dominated this growing segment of the world market early. While the largest Taiwanese makers had become experienced in reverse-engineering, machine design, and mechanical technologies, they lacked the electronics capabilities that are critical in the NC machine tools field. Furthermore, Taiwanese firms were too small to internalize the development process of such a complex product.[44]

State-sponsored research institutes assistance became critical at this juncture. The main technical support came initially from the Metal Industries Research Laboratories (MIRL) of ITRI. Around two-thirds of MIRL's budget comes from the government. The laboratory launched an NC machine tool project in the early 1980s. It developed NC lathes and machining centers prototypes, and transferred them – on a non exclusive basis – to private manufacturers. Since then, NC machine tool production has increased rapidly, and by 1991 Taiwan accounted for more than 3 percent of NC lathes and MC world output. Design and diffusion of new models of machine tools have been the most important contribution of MIRL to the upgrading of the Taiwanese industry. Because of the growing importance of flexible manufacturing systems (FMS) in international demand, the government commissioned MIRL to carry out a two-year FMS technology development program (1992–1994). MIRL has also produced some precision components and established a component standardization system.

While the diffusion of targeted products, supported by government funds, is one side of the cooperation between MIRL and the machine tool manufacturers, MIRL also works on a contract basis for private firms, on specific research projects, problem-solving, standard-setting, etc. MIRL has become a "high-tech" subcontractor that undertakes specific projects for the private sector and completes firms' design teams. Another of its economic functions is to spread R&D risks and costs. According to industry surveys (Lautier 1994; San Gee 1994), MIRL has become the most important technological services supplier for Taiwanese machine tool firms (much more than their own R&D departments).

While MIRL's interventions focus on product development, another technological institution, the Precision Machinery research and development

Center (PMC), cooperates with machine tool firms on product improvement. A previous organization, CMD, was established in 1983 by 14 of the largest machine tools firms, and partly subsidized by the IDB. This small body (15 employees) was mainly devoted to quality control and machine tools testing. Its most valuable achievement has been to set up a product evaluation and assessment system, based on Japanese standards. In 1993, CMD was merged with a newly created organization, PMC, cofunded by the machine tools industry association (TAMI) and the government (50/50). The role of the new institution is more ambitious and its size bigger.[45] PMC undertakes two kind of activities, backwards and forwards. First, it carries on with machine tools testing and quality control, because firms do not have in-house facilities. Machine tool manufacturers also request PMC assistance to comply with foreign standards (aerospace standards, ISO norm, etc.). Second, PMC provides technical services for product improvements: testing of a modified function; assistance in key-components evaluation; development of specific CNC applications and software, etc. The new commitment on product improvement and testing (rather than on product development) illustrates the current technical weakness of the Taiwanese machine tool industry in the international competition.

Government support in the machine tools industry, as in several others cases, has been industry-pull rather than government-push. The only important assistance given by the state to the machine tools industry was the provision of technological resources at low cost through MIRL and PMC.[46] Government support came late in the industry history, but its timing was judicious. It helped private firms to cope with the new technological paradigm barriers and successfully develop their NC machine tool exports.

CONCLUSION

The analysis of the role of industrial policy in Taiwan's economic development tells a more ambiguous story than in the case of Korea or even Japan.

In the 1980s, Taiwan dominated the world market in industries such as toys, footwear, or sport-related products (bicycles, tennis rackets, etc.). Most of those sectors, for which Taiwan's "revealed comparative advantages" were high, were not officially targeted by industrial policy. But, at the same time, Taiwanese industry became highly competitive in several high-tech sectors (electronics, NC machine tools, etc.). In the mid-1990s, electronics and machinery have become the island's leading exports sectors. The industrial policy has actively intervened in this industrial transformation process.

However, government intervention has not focused on "sunrise" industries. Empirical investigations (Smith 1995) reveal that the incentive structure was aimed more at sustaining losers than picking winners. The winners exhibited a lower rate of effective assistance and subsidy and the major recipients of subsidies were textiles and other low-tech industries.

The government has done more than passively adjust Taiwan's economy to changes in comparative advantages. The early shift from import substitution to export orientation did not bring the government protective stance to an end. The deepening of the industrial structure and the promotion of new sectors was not a response to but an anticipation of the changes of Taiwan's comparative advantages. As the industry enters into leading edge technologies, the technology policy has become the main component of the industrial policy, and by this way the government still intervenes actively to push the international competitiveness of key industries, as in the semiconductors or aerospace cases.

In addition, the policy framework has avoided creating a bias in favor of large enterprises. On the contrary, the development of state-led upstream industries and the growing density of SME support organizations have contributed to upgrade Taiwanese SMEs' competitive advantages on international markets. The combination of the private-sector dynamism with a supportive rather than dirigist government has built up a very efficient industrial system that is based on a highly developed division of labor at the intersectoral, intrasectoral, and functional (R&D, marketing) levels.

NOTES

1 In the 1970s, foreign invested firms (including export processing zones) accounted for less than 10 percent of the manufacturing value added.
2 With a cumulative amount of US$23 billion of direct investment abroad. However, this figure underestimates the extent of Taiwan's internationalization. According to host country figures, the Investment Cooperation Commitee evaluates that Taiwan's cumulative investment in South East Asia is US$48 billion, one half in China where Taiwan is the second largest foreign investor.
3 The indicator of socio-economic development included the extent of dualism, urbanization, importance of the indigenous middle class, social mobility, literacy, mass communication, cultural and ethnic homogeneity, fertility, sense of national unity, etc.
4 Thus in 1938, the apparent consumption of cement was larger in Taiwan than in Greece, Portugal, and Spain (CEMBUREAU 1995).
5 The export orientation of the 1960s may also be considered as an indirect consequence of the US aid, because it was the prospect of its end that first convinced the government of the need to earn foreign exchange.
6 Sources: *Statistics of Small and Medium Business in Taiwan ROC*, MOEA 1987 and Chou 1992. According to the 1982 definition, any enterprises meeting one of the following criteria is an SME: A paid-in capital of less than NT$40 million and total assets under NT$120 million for manufacturing, processing or handicraft industry; mining enterprises with a paid-in capital under NT$40 million; and annual sales revenues under NT$40 million for exporters/importers.
7 Among the 100 largest manufacturing companies, only 15 were publicly owned in 1982 but they accounted for 58 percent of the total turnover of these 100 leading firms (Chou 1988). Ever since, these figures have not significantly decreased, despite the government's official commitment to privatization (see OECD 1993).
8 Amsden and Singh 1994. They define large enterprises as those with more than 500 employees.

9 According to a recent evaluation (*The Economist* July 6, 1996), the four leading GTC account for almost 60 percent of total exports, and the cumulative sales of the four largest chaebols represent more than 80 percent of the GDP in South Korea.

10 Quoted in Fransman 1986.

11 According to Chou, in Taiwan the scale on which the enterprise operates is negatively related to the export/production ratio and export contribution. Export concentration is indeed quite low: the 100 largest firms accounted for only 20 percent of the country's total exports in the early 1980s.

12 CIED, *Fourth four-year plan for economic development 1965–1968*, 1965; quoted in Wade 1990.

13 Li K.T, "The growth of private industry in free China," *Industry of Free China*, 12 n°6 (December 1959); quoted in Alam 1989.

14 Target definition is the result of a synthethis of researches made by international consultants (IMD Little, Dataquest etc.) and local research institutes, as well as of advice given by the chairmen of large multinationals that participate in technical consulting groups established by the state, and of industrial associations feedbacks.

15 In the early 1950s, foreign exchange saving was the most important motive for import control. As the balance of payments improved, this mercantilist stance has declined, but not disappeared.

16 In 1992, the average rate of nominal duty was 6.52 percent (and trade weighted average 5.77 percent). See: *Position paper of Taiwan/ROC in relation to its negotiation for accession to the GATT*, 30/6/94, BOFT, Taipei.

17 The proportion of export loans to total loans dropped from 6.3 percent in 1972 to 2.3 percent in 1979. At the end of 1977, total export credits amounted to only 2.9 percent of the previous twelve months' exports, while in South Korea at the same time the figure stood at 12.3 percent. By 1981, export credits as a portion of total bank loans had fallen to 2.1 percent. For a complete presentation of these export-promotion measures, see Wade 1990: 139–148.

18 In 1966, Taiwan was the first developing country to build an export processing zone (Kaoshiung followed by Taichung and Nantze) which offered a whole range of support facilities and reglementations to ease investment procedures. EPZ success should not be overemphasized, since at their peak in 1988 they employed 3 percent of manufacturing employees and accounted for 6 percent of manufacturing exports. They have played a less important role than joint ventures.

19 The government and CETRA have begun to market quality products under a special "It is very well made in Taiwan" international campaign in order to promote Taiwan's image as a center of manufacturing excellence. Stringent tests are applied before individual products can be sold with this label.

20 In 1990 there were two categories of imported products: 241 products were "controled," and 8,770 were "permissibles," of which 2,858 require prior application, and 688 of these need specific approval from the Board Of Foreign Trade (BOFT/MOEA).

21 Indeed, the Taiwanese autopart industry has become quite competitive. According to the industry association (TTVMA), exports reached US$1.6 billion in 1993.

22 One of the major reasons for Taiwan's trade deficit with Japan is the heavy reliance on Japan for intermediate products and components. Around one-third of Taiwan's imports come from Japan (but 10 percent of its exports are directed to Japan). Japan's share of Taiwan's imports is particularly high for machinery and electrical equipments (45 percent) and electronic components (41 percent) (ratio based on 1993 data).

23 From 1991 to 1993, of the 123 applications to the DTLP program, the total development expenses were NT$11.5 billion, of which two-thirds were supported by the government.

24 The DCCP program has listed 22 critical products and 44 critical components. The latter list includes, for instance, liquid crystal display, machine tool spindles, or bicycle brake systems. The 66 products/components list was established by the IDB after discussion with the industrial associations. These critical components were classified in three categories according to their level of feasibility. For each of these categories, special funds were established.

25 Bank loans extended to SMEs accounted for no more than 30 percent of the total in the late 1970s (see Yen 1984).

26 Under an ODM arrangement, a Taiwan firm is contracted by a third party such as a retail chain to design as well as to build a product for a specified market niche.

27 According to Kao (1994), OEM contracts accounted for 23 percent of large firms' sales, and 30 percent for small firms, while ODM contracts accounted for 22 percent in both cases (based on 1991 data).

28 R&D total expenditures represent over 2 percent of GNP in 1994.

29 The commission meets once a fortnight and is empowered to bargain with foreign investors on technical and financial issues.

30 Author's interview in 1993.

31 In 1985, it took the initiative to create a joint venture in order to build a silicon foundry (see below).

32 And 6,000 trading and other services companies. The smallest pay NT$300 per month.

33 The turnover of the largest firm, Acer, is equivalent to 25 percent of Samsung's Electronics turnover.

34 Electronics has been a prime target for foreign investors and, by the end of 1995, their aggregate value amounted to US$5.8 billion scattered over 1,000 projects. Matsushita, Sanyo, and Philips are among the largest investors.

35 It plans to invest US$1 billion to build a foundry in the USA.

36 Even if there are a very large number of players, the sector is relatively concentrated by Taiwanese standards, as ten manufacturers account for 80 percent of the total output.

37 Interviews.

38 By 1961, of the 38 machine tools companies, only 14 had been in operation for more than five years (Amsden 1977).

39 Foreign models have remained the main source of product change. Taiwanese firms' entry into NC machine tools manufacturing in the early 1980s had been preceded by a surge in the imports of these items. In a similar way, several makers have recently taken advantage of the Japanese discount policies, and have bought up-to-date flexible manufacturing systems (FMC and FMS).

40 A similar governmental failure occurred around 1982 in the automobile industry. The government wanted to concentrate the industry and to set-up a "big auto plant." It planned to establish a joint venture with Toyota and China Steel. This project faced a strong opposition from the local car-makers.

41 See above. For more on the use of export incentives and the import–export link in the machine tool industry, see Desai and Lautier forthcoming.

42 The share of imported machine tools in apparent consumption was above 60 percent in the 1970s. It has been reduced since the 1980s and evolves now in the 45–55 percent range. Official tariffs on machine tools imports have decreased from 13 percent in 1971 to around 5 percent in 1992. The current tariffs structure on machine tools is now based on a distinction between conventional products, which enjoy a 5 percent rate, and NC products, with a 10 percent rate.

43 The machining center is the first machine specifically designed around the concept of numerical control. Traditionally, parts were mobile and moved from one machine tool to the next; in a machining center the part is fixed and the tool heads are mobile.

44 There are no machine tools firms with more than 1,000 employees in Taiwan. Only two firms have more than 500 employees.
45 In 1994, PMC had a staff of 66 people, of which 58 were engineers and technicians.
46 While machine tools have not been included in the DTLP program, launched in 1991, the DCCP program (1992) has targeted some machine tools items (NC injection moulding machines, spindles, linear guides, CNC controllers). But they have not had a high priority, according to the hierarchy of the IDB list.

REFERENCES

Adelman, M. and Morris, C. (1967) *Society, Politics and Economic Development: A Quantitative Approach*, Baltimore: Johns Hopkins University Press.

Alam, S. (1989) *Government and Markets in Economic Development Strategies: Lessons from Korea, Taiwan and Japan*, New York: Praeger.

Amsden, A. H. (1977) "The division of labor is limited by the type of market: the case of the Taiwanese machine tool industry," *World Development* 5, 3: 217–233.

—— (1985) "The division of labour is limited by the rate of growth of the market: the Taiwan machine tool industry in the 1970s," *Cambridge Journal of Economics* 9: 271–284.

Amsden, A. H. and Singh, A. (1994) "Concurrence dirigée et efficacité dynamique en Asie: Japon, Corée du Sud, Taiwan," *Revue Tiers Monde* 35, 139: 643–659.

Barro, R. J. and Lee, J. W. (1993) "Losers and winners in economic growth," NBER Working Papers, No. 4341, Cambridge, MA.

Bradford, C. I. (1993) "From trade-driven growth to growth-driven trade: reappraising the East Asian development experience," Paris: OECD.

CEMBUREAU (1995) *Cement Statistics*, Brussels: CEMBUREAU.

Chaponnière, J. R. (1993) "Entrepreneurs, state and networks," in Proceedings of the seminar on entrepreneurship and socio-economic transformation in Thailand and South-East Asia, Chulalongkorn University, Bangkok.

Chaponnière, J. R. and Fouquin, M. (1989) "Technological change and the electronic sector: perspective and policy options for Taiwan," Research report of the OECD Development Centre.

Chaponnière, J. R. and Jolly, D. (1989) "Le modèle Taiwanais," in J. L. Maurer and P. Regnier, *La Nouvelle Asie Industrielle*, PUF.

Cheng, T. (1994) "Guarding the commanding heights: the state as banker in Taiwan," in S. Haggard, C. Lee, and S. Maxfield (eds) *Politics of Finance*, Ithaca, NY: Cornell University Press.

Chou, T. C. (1992) "The experience of SME's development in Taiwan: high export-contribution and export-intensity," *Rivista Internazionale di Science Economiche e Commerciali* 39 (December).

Chou, T. C. (1988) "The evolution of market structure in Taiwan," *Rivista Internazionale di Science Economiche e Commerciali* 35 (February).

Desai, A. V. and Lautier, M. (forthcoming) "Machine tool industries in India and Chinese Taipei: a comparison," in L. K. Mytelka (ed.) *Competition, Innovation and Competitiveness in Developing Countries*, Paris: OECD.

Fransman, M. (1986) "International competitiveness, technical change and the state: the machine tool industry in Taiwan and Japan," *World Development* 14, 12: 1375–1396.

Galenson, W. (ed.) (1979) *Economic Growth and Structural Change in Taiwan*, Ithaca, NY: Cornell University Press.

Gold, T. (1986) *State and Society in the Taiwan Miracle*, New York: Sharpe.

Ho, S. (1980) "Small-scale enterprises in Korea and Taiwan," World Bank Staff Working Paper, No. 384 (April).

Ho, S. (1978) *Economic Development of Taiwan (1850–1970)*, New Haven, CO: Yale University Press.

Hou, C. M. and San Gee (1993) "National systems supporting technical advance in industry: the case of Taiwan," in R. R. Nelson (ed.) *National Innovation Systems: A Comparative Analysis*, Oxford: Oxford University Press.

Jacobsson, S. (1986) *Electronics and Industrial Policy: The Case of Computer Controlled Lathes*, London: Allen and Unwin.

Johnson, C. (1987) "Political institutions and economic performance: the government–business relationship in Japan, South Korea and Taiwan," in F. C. Deyo (ed.) *The Political Economy of the New Asian Industrialism*, Ithaca, NY: Cornell University Press.

Kao, C. (1994) "The development of small and medium sized enterprises in the Republic of China," *Industry of Free China* (March).

Lautier, M. (1993) "The growth of the automobile industry in Asia: the state's role in promoting domestic entrepreneurs," in Proceedings of the seminar on entrepreneurship and socio-economic transformation in Thailand and South-East Asia, Chulalongkorn University, Bangkok.

—— (1994) "Competition, innovation and competitiveness in Taiwan's machine tool industry," Research report, OECD Development Centre.

Levy, B. (1987) "Export intermediation and the structure of industry in Korea and Taiwan," Korea Development Institute Working Paper, No. 8717 (December).

—— (1991) "Transactions costs, the size of firms and industrial policy: lessons from a comparative case study of the footwear industry in Korea and Taiwan," *Journal of Development Economics* 34.

Levy, B. and Kuo, W. J. (1987) "The strategic orientations of firms and the performance of Korea and Taiwan in frontier industries: lessons from comparative case studies of keyboard and personal computer assembly," Korea Development Institute Working Paper, No. 8719 (December).

Mizoguchi, T. (1979) "Economic growth of Korea and Taiwan under the Japanese occupation," *Hitotsubashi Journal of Economics* June.

Mody, A. (1989) "Institutions and dynamic comparative advantage: electronics industry in South Korea and Taiwan," The World Bank Industry and Energy Department Industries Series Paper, No. 9.

Numazaki, I. (1991) "The role of personal networks in the making of Taiwan's guanxiqiye," in G. Hamilton (ed.) *Business Networks and Economic Development in East and Southeast Asia*, Hong Kong: Hong Kong University Press.

OECD (1993) "Tendances récentes et mesures de politique industrielle dans les nouvelles économies industrielles d'Asie," in *Politiques Industrielles dans les Pays de L'OCDE*, OECD.

Park, Y. C. (1990) "Development lessons from Asia: the role of government in South Korea and Taiwan," *American Economic Review* 80, 2: 118–122.

Rodrik, D. (1995) "Getting interventions right: how South Korea and Taiwan grew rich," *Economic Policy*.

San Gee (1988) "The status and an evaluation of the electronics industry in Taiwan," Report for the OECD Development Centre.

—— (1994) "Interactions between research institutions and firms in Taiwan manufacturing industry," Chung Hua Institution for Economic Research, Mimeographed.

Schive, C. (1990) "Linkages: do foreign firms buy locally in Taiwan?," *Asian Economic Journal* March: 1–15.

—— (1993) "Small and medium enterprises," in the ROC Small and Medium Enterprise White Paper, MOEA.

Smith, H. (1995) "Industrial policy in East Asia," *Asian Pacific Economic Litterature* 9, 1: 230–255.

Staley, E. and Morse, R. (1965) *Modern Small Industry for Developing Countries*, New York: McGraw-Hill.

Tsai, S. D. (1992) "The development of Taiwan's machine tool industry," in N. T. Wang (ed.) *Taiwan Enterprises in Global Perspectives*, New York: Sharpe.

Wade, R. (1990) *Governing the Market: Economic Theory and the Role of Government in East Asian Industrialization*, Princeton, NJ: Princeton University Press.

Wanatabe, T. (1985) "Economic development in Korea: lessons and challenges," in T. Shishido and R. Sato (eds) *Economic Policy and Development: New Perspectives*, London: Auburn House.

World Bank (1993) *The East Asian Miracle: Economic Growth and Public Policy*, Oxford: Oxford University Press.

Yen, G. L. (1984) "Industrial policies as they relate to SMBs: a financial perspective," Joint conference on the industrial policies of the Republic of China and the Republic of Korea, Chung Hua Institution for Economic Research, December.

10 Industrial policy in Ireland and the problem of late development

Eoin O'Malley

INTRODUCTION

When the Irish Free State (later the Republic of Ireland) was established in the early 1920s, it had a very small industrial sector. According to the Census of Industrial Production of 1926, just 56,400 people, or less than 5 percent of the labor force, were employed in manufacturing. The Census of Population for the same year indicated a higher figure of 9 percent of the labor force being engaged in manufacturing, but either way these are small percentages. By comparison, about 25 percent or more of the labor force was engaged in manufacturing in other small European countries, such as Denmark, Sweden, Belgium and The Netherlands, at around that time. Almost half of Irish manufacturing employment and three-quarters of manufacturing gross output was concentrated in the food and drink sectors in the 1920s. Thus, other sectors of industry were of little significance for the economy.

Clearly, therefore, when Ireland began as an independent state it was a latecomer to industrialization relative to many other European countries. Since that time, Irish industry has grown considerably and the proportion of total employment that is in industry now is much more similar to Denmark, The Netherlands, or Sweden. In some important respects, however, the nature of Ireland's relatively late industrialization has been rather different from that of earlier developers, and the structure of industry in Ireland today differs from that of more advanced economies. There have also been certain similarities to the experience of developing countries or newly industrializing countries outside Europe. Thus, up to the present, it is instructive to regard Ireland as a latecomer country as regards the experience of its industry and the nature of its industrial policy.

PHASES OF INDUSTRIAL GROWTH

The 1920s

In the first decade of Irish independence in the 1920s, economic policy was predominantly passive and orthodox, with a basic reliance on free trade and market forces. It was argued that a policy of free international trade was important for the sake of agricultural and food exports, which were the key earners of foreign exchange for the economy at that time. In addition, policy in the 1920s looked primarily to growth of agricultural production to stimulate the development of the economy. Within this context, there was rather little in the way of an explicit industrial policy in the 1920s.

The administrations of the 1920s did give consideration to the use of protection against imports as a means to encourage industry, and, in fact, formal structures were established to assess the merits of protection and to canvass the opinions of industrialists on this matter (see Girvin 1989: Chapter 2). But, given a primary emphasis on the objective of developing export agriculture and the need to keep costs competitive, only a rather small number of protective tariffs were approved as a result of this process, with the objective of increasing employment in certain selected industries.

There was a modest increase in industrial employment in the 1920s. Employment in transportable goods industries[1] increased from 61,300 in 1926 to 67,900 in 1929, with a slight decline to 66,500 in 1931 (Kennedy 1971: Table 2.2). This increase occurred particularly in the newly protected industries. Lyons (1976: 601) says that over 100 new factories had opened in the protected industries by 1930. And data presented by Girvin (1989: Table 3.4) indicate that employment in the protected sectors of industry increased by almost 8,000 from the year of introduction of the relevant tariffs up to 1927.

The protectionist phase: 1930s–1950s

Following the general election in 1932, there was a change of government which brought about significant changes in economic and industrial policy. This ushered in the first phase of substantial industrial growth in the 1930s and 1940s. A major change in industrial policy was the introduction of a much stronger and more wide-ranging policy of protection against imports. In addition, restrictions were introduced on foreign ownership of new manufacturing ventures and a number of new state-owned enterprises were established.

The objective of the protectionist policy was stated to be the development of national self-sufficiency. Whereas the limited experimenting with tariffs in the 1920s might be interpreted as support for infant industries that would have the potential to develop a real competitive advantage over time, this could hardly be said of protectionist policy after 1932 (O'Grada 1994: Chapter 16), for the policy was applied in a rather indiscriminate fashion, and there was generally little sign of a longer term concern to have the protected infant industries develop to a competitive maturity (Kennedy *et al.* 1988: Chapters 2 and 11). Rather, the primary focus was on having more Irish people employed in Ireland producing goods required by the domestic market.

Following the introduction of strong protectionist policies, industrial employment (in transportable goods, see footnote 1) increased from 66,500 in 1931 to 103,200 in 1938 (Kennedy 1971: Table 2.2).[2] This growth was interrupted by the difficulty of importing fuel and material inputs during the Second World War, but industrial employment stood at 116,300 by 1946 and it then increased further to 148,000 by 1951.

This experience of considerable growth in industrial employment beginning during the international depression of the 1930s was rather unusual among Western European countries. But it corresponds quite well with the contemporary experience of some of the less developed countries (e.g. Argentina, Brazil, Chile, and Mexico) which were independent at the time and resorted to protection during the depression, thereby facilitating a process of import-substituting industrialization. By 1951, 15 percent of total employment in Ireland was in manufacturing. This was distinctly higher than in the 1920s but was still little more than half the level of many Western European countries, although it was comparable to some Latin American countries such as Mexico and Brazil (Furtado 1976: Chapter 11).

The main emphasis in industrial expansion had been on consumer goods and certain technically mature intermediate products, with only a very limited range of capital goods or technically advanced industries in general. The pattern of industrial growth had been fairly typical of what is commonly called the "easy" stage of import-substitution in developing countries. It appears that protection helps to overcome the difficulties faced by new or small firms in a late industrializing country when competing with larger and stronger established foreign competitors, in the home market at least, in the more technically mature and less complex types of industry. But in Ireland there was little progress in developing the more technologically demanding or highly skill-intensive activities.

There was also very little development of industrial exports, as the protected industries relied very heavily on the home market. In 1929, 45 percent of industrial output had been exported, while the figure for industries other than food, drink, and tobacco was 27 percent. But by 1951, only 16 percent of industrial output was exported and, if food, drink, and tobacco are excluded, the figure was just 6 percent for the rest of manufacturing (O'Malley 1989: Chapter 4). Thus, protection probably fostered growth in industrial employment for a couple of decades, but it did not generate progress in breaking into open competition with advanced industrial countries.

Against the background of a general failure to develop competitive exporting industries, the phase of protectionist expansion of Irish industry eventually ran into a crisis in the 1950s. There was virtually no further increase in manufacturing employment between 1951 and 1958. Since this occurred while the large agricultural labor force continued to decline in accordance with a long-established trend, the total labor force declined quite rapidly and emigration rose to exceptionally high levels.

The difficulties of the 1950s were basically due to the emergence of a chronic balance of payments constraint. This arose partly from the near exhaustion of the easy stage of import-substituting industrialization, which meant that there was little further replacement of imports by new domestic production. At the same time, imports of goods that had not been replaced by domestic production, including many of the materials and capital goods required to sustain production, had to continue to grow as long as the economy was growing. Thus the cost of imports of goods that had not been substituted by domestic production eventually grew to exceed the cost of all imports before the process of import-substitution began. Since there was a continuing failure to achieve adequate growth of exports, serious balance of trade deficits became inevitable, leading to recurring balance of payments problems and prolonged recession in the 1950s (O'Malley 1989: Chapter 4). Arguably, the balance of payments constraint on further growth could have been eased for a time in the 1950s by using the country's external reserves and by foreign borrowing to finance more expansionary fiscal policies (Kennedy *et al.* 1988: Chapter 3), but ultimately the balance of payments was going to be a major constraint in the absence of more significant export growth.

Thus, Ireland in the 1950s experienced a fairly typical conclusion to a process of import-substituting industrialization, in which rather indiscriminate protectionism was the main policy instrument used. Other late developing countries using the same approach commonly ran into a similar problem eventually with a balance of payments constraint on further growth, although many of them went through the sequence rather later than Ireland, since they only acquired the independence necessary to adopt protection in the 1950s or 1960s.

Outward-looking policies: late 1950s to 1980s

In view of the difficulties experienced in Ireland in the 1950s, a number of related and quite fundamental changes in industrial policy were introduced. A more outward-looking approach evolved in the 1950s and the 1960s. This meant that the emphasis shifted to developing industrial exports, and new tax concessions and grants were introduced to encourage and assist firms to develop production for export markets. In addition, active steps began to be taken to seek out and attract foreign firms to produce in Ireland for export markets. And finally, the protectionist measures against imports were gradually dismantled, opening up the home market to more direct foreign competition.

Such a switch from an inward-looking to an outward-looking strategy for industrialization has since been at least partially followed by quite a large number of developing countries that ran into problems similar to those experienced by Ireland in the 1950s. However, while many of them adopted the goal of export promotion and sought to attract foreign firms as one means of achieving that aim, until quite recently not many went as far as Ireland did in entering into full free trade arrangements with major advanced industrial countries.

The general change in Ireland's strategy for industrial development in the 1950s and 1960s reflected a growing acceptance of the need to develop industries that would be internationally competitive. International competitiveness became an objective of industrial policy, although the ultimate purpose of this was generally still stated to be creation of employment and reduction of emigration. This view of the objectives of industrial policy – international competitiveness in order to enhance employment – gradually became established and has remained in place up to the 1990s.[3]

A number of factors combined to bring about the change in the orientation of industrial development strategy. For one thing, there was an obvious motivation for some sort of policy change arising from the economic crisis of the 1950s, and this motivation was heightened by an awareness of the more favorable situation in other countries. The 1950s was not generally a period of international recession or slow growth. Furthermore, the need to develop exports at least, whatever the desirability of removing protection, was clear from the nature of the crisis of the 1950s. In addition, the new strategy was geared to take advantage of newly emerging opportunities – both to secure more satisfactory export markets for the country's important agricultural sector, and to attract export-oriented FDI, which was a phenomenon that first became significant in the world economy in the 1950s. Apart from some positive attractions of the new policy, from the late 1950s onwards it was increasingly felt that there would be some necessity to follow the UK into the EEC or whatever international free trade arrangements might emerge involving the UK, in view of Ireland's overwhelming dependence on the British market for exports.

The reorientation of industrial policy towards a more outward-looking approach was an evolutionary process that took some time.[4] In 1952, the Industrial Development Authority (IDA) was given the task of seeking to attract foreign industries to Ireland, although this activity was at that time still subject to certain legal restrictions. In 1952, also, the government established Coras Trachtala (the Irish Export Board), a promotional and advisory body, to assist firms attempting to develop exports. During the 1950s, in a number of stages, a scheme of financial grants was introduced to support capital investment in new and expanding industries. The investment grants scheme encouraged the development of export-orientation in industry, since grant-aided firms were required to be internationally competitive and to have favorable growth prospects; in practice this usually meant that only export-oriented firms qualified (McAleese 1971: Chapter 2).

Export development was further encouraged by major changes in taxation of industrial profits in 1956 and 1958. After these changes, no tax was charged on manufacturing profits earned from increases in export sales over the 1956 level. This tax relief meant that there was no tax on profits arising from all exports of firms starting up after 1956, including new foreign-owned establishments. New investment by foreign firms in export-oriented industry was further encouraged by the removal of existing legal restrictions on foreign ownership after 1958.

Following the measures outlined above, the main elements of the policy package to promote exports and to encourage FDI for that purpose were in place by the end of the 1950s. Further changes in the incentives and supports for industry over the next two decades tended to strengthen this general approach, rather than changing it radically. Such later changes in financial supports included the introduction of grants to support R&D and training of workers. Also, since the 1970s, firms involved in internationally traded services have been eligible for industrial policy supports.

In the area of tax policy, the tax relief on export profits remained in place during the 1960s and 1970s. But in the 1980s it was replaced by a new low rate of corporate profit tax of just 10 percent for all manufacturing industries (not only exporters) and for certain internationally traded services. A number of observers in the 1970s and early 1980s concluded that the Irish package of tax and grant incentives for investment in industry and in exports particularly was one of the most attractive available in Europe; and they concluded that the efforts to market Ireland as a location for export-oriented foreign industries were also among the most effective (O'Malley 1989: Chapter 5).

The process of dismantling protection and returning to free trade began in 1963 and 1964 with minor reductions of all tariffs. This was followed in 1965 by the signing of the Anglo-Irish Free Trade Area agreement, which removed the few UK tariffs on Irish manufactured products and the more severe British restrictions on imports of Irish agricultural products and foods. In return, Ireland was to remove protection against imports of British manufactured products by ten annual reductions of 10 percent each. When Ireland and the UK, together with Denmark, joined the EEC in 1973, Ireland agreed to remove protection against other EEC-manufactured products by five annual tariff cuts of 20 percent each. To prepare for freer trade, the government set up structures in the 1960s to encourage firms in each industry to specialize more, to consider mergers, and to cooperate in areas such as purchasing materials and marketing – all with a view to improving economies of scale and hence competitiveness. "Adaptation grants" were also made available to help meet the costs of necessary structural change, and such grants were eventually paid to most of Irish industry.

Under the new outward-looking strategy, industrial growth picked up considerably in the 1960s and 1970s compared with the 1950s. Whereas manufacturing output grew by just 1.7 percent per annum in 1951–1958, it increased to 6.7 percent per annum in 1958–1973 and 5.1 percent per annum in 1973–1979. The average annual rate of growth of manufacturing employment increased from just 0.2 percent in 1951–1958 to 2.4 percent in 1958–1973 and 0.8 percent in 1973–1979.[5] This phase of industrialization was characterized by particularly rapid growth of exports. Whereas just 19 percent of manufacturing output was exported in 1960 (only marginally higher than the figure of 16 percent in 1951), this rose to 41 percent in 1978 and further to 64 percent by 1988. This trend helped to ease the balance of payments difficulties that had caused major problems in the 1950s, and thus it facilitated overall growth of the economy.

In the 1980s, however, worrying new trends emerged, even though the indicators may have appeared somewhat ambiguous at first sight. Manufacturing employment reached its peak level in 1979 and then declined by as much as one-fifth between 1979 and 1987. Conversely, during most of this period, industrial output continued to grow quite strongly, often at about the highest rate of any OECD country. The roots of these apparently paradoxical developments lie in the major structural changes that had been occurring in Irish industry and in the differing experience and performance of Irish indigenous and foreign-owned multinational firms.

IRISH INDIGENOUS INDUSTRY

Even during the 1960s and 1970s, Irish industrial performance had a significant weak spot. It was new investment by foreign-owned multinational companies that made the major contribution to the growth of industrial employment, output, and exports, while native Irish-owned or indigenous industry did not fare so well. Indigenous industry was apparently not able to take much advantage of the new incentives and opportunities to export, while at the same time it was quite rapidly losing market share to competing imports in the home market as the protectionist measures were dismantled after the mid-1960s.

In this context, there was no employment growth in indigenous industry between the mid-1960s and the end of the 1970s, and then in the 1980s its employment fell sharply by 27 percent in just seven years. It is very likely that by the mid-1980s employment in indigenous industry was lower than at any time since the 1940s. Essentially, what happened was that indigenous industry was just about able to maintain its overall employment level while domestic demand was growing sufficiently strongly in the late 1960s and the 1970s to compensate for the loss of market share to competing imports. But when domestic demand weakened considerably in the 1980s for a variety of reasons, its employment slumped.[6]

Within indigenous industry, however, some sectors fared relatively well. These mostly involved either basic processing of local primary products such as food, or else sheltered or nontraded activities which have a significant degree of natural protection against distant competitors and do not usually enter much into international trade. Such activities can be sheltered in the local market by high transport costs for low-value products (e.g. concrete products, cement, packaging materials), whilst others can be sheltered because of a need for local knowledge or close contact with customers (e.g. printing, publishing, and engineering or other activities that involve an element of on-site installation). While indigenous firms in such activities were able to grow and to increase in relative importance, other more internationally traded activities declined.

A second structural change within indigenous industry was a particularly rapid decline among the larger firms in the more internationally traded activities, while there were generally increasing numbers of small firms. It seems that the larger firms were generally engaged in activities in which there are significant economies of scale, hence their own relatively large size by Irish standards. But they were generally not large enough to match still larger and longer established foreign competitors under free trade, so that they were at a disadvantage due to inferior economies of scale and this hastened their decline.

At the same time, smaller firms, which would generally have been engaged in activities in which economies of scale are less important, increased in numbers. In fact, the rate of establishment of new small native industrial firms in the 1970s, in relation to the size of indigenous industry, was similar to the USA and Canada in the 1950s and 1960s, and about 40 percent greater than in the United Kingdom in the late 1960s and early 1970s (O'Farrell and Crouchley 1984). Nevertheless, total indigenous manufacturing employment scarcely changed in the 1970s due to the simultaneous decline of larger firms. Later on, the establishment of many new small firms meant that the total number of indigenous manufacturing companies changed little during the substantial fall in employment of 1980–1987, when there were many closures of existing firms.

Irish indigenous industry was relatively lacking in large-scale enterprises by the 1980s, and there was generally little indigenous activity in those sectors in which economies of scale are most important and which are consequently dominated by large firms in more advanced European economies. For example, there were seven (NACE 2-digit) sectors in each of which large firms employing over 500 people accounted for more than 70 percent of the sector's employment in West Germany, France, the UK, and Italy in the mid-1980s.[7] These seven sectors accounted for 40 percent of manufacturing employment in the EC, but they accounted for only 12 percent of employment in Irish indigenous manufacturing in 1987.

The existence of significant economies of scale, and the consequent presence of large established firms in a range of important industries in the advanced industrial countries, can be seen as presenting a significant barrier to the development of such industries by new or small firms in a relatively late developing country that trades freely with the advanced countries. For they generally lack the resources that would be required to enter into competition on a competitive scale of production, or to survive a period of initial loss-making while building up to an adequate market share to support a competitive scale of production. Of course, a basic purpose of protection was to make it possible for Irish industries to get established by shutting out overwhelming competition from larger and stronger firms already existing elsewhere. This succeeded to some degree but, in many cases, with a rather small protected market, the Irish firms did not attain a scale of operation that was adequate to match foreign competitors following the return to free trade.

While the existence of economies of scale and large established competitors has presented a barrier to the development of Irish indigenous industry in a range of important sectors, there are also some other significant types of barriers to entry arising from the strength of established competitors elsewhere.[8] For example, it can be very difficult for new or small indigenous firms in a late industrializing country to match the technological capabilities already developed by companies in advanced economies in sectors where technology is of key importance. Similarly, if strong marketing is a key requirement for an industry, the established marketing strength of existing firms presents an important entry barrier for new or small firms.

In addition, the advantages of external economies, which are enjoyed by firms in existing industrial centers or districts, can represent a further obstacle to the development of newcomers in late industrializing countries. Such external economies consist mainly of the advantages of close contact with related firms, specialist suppliers and services, supportive institutions, pools of specialized labor skills, and perhaps a large local market. These types of advantages, in some form, are commonly reflected in the existence of large, and often specialized, industrial towns and geographically concentrated (or at least adjacent) clusters of related industries. If advantages of external economies are important in an industry, it may well be relatively easy for many new firms to emerge and grow within existing locations of that industry; at the same time, however, this is a good deal less likely to happen in late industrializing countries that do not have strong industrial centers or districts and would have to compete with the existing industries.

It is likely that such barriers or obstacles to the development of latecomers comprise a substantial part of the explanation for the relatively poor performance of Irish indigenous industry; many other potential explanations do not appear to be very convincing. For example, the record of a very high rate of start-ups of new small firms suggests that there was not a marked lack of entrepreneurial initiative. The problem was rather that new start-up industries were generally restricted to small-scale activities, while larger firms declined. Also, as is outlined below, many foreign multinational companies found the Irish economic environment quite attractive and have operated successfully in it. This suggests that there can scarcely have been crippling defects in factors such as the quality of the labor force, labor costs, the transport and communications infrastructure, the tax system, or the political and bureaucratic system.

It is likely that the general quality of native management skills left something to be desired, but it nevertheless seems clear that there was at least a certain amount of good quality managerial talent available, for most of the foreign-owned multinational companies in Ireland have been content to recruit their local management from within the country. Also, many of the larger Irish firms, including those in naturally sheltered or nontraded types of business, have engaged successfully in international markets in the form of taking over foreign firms and becoming multinational companies.

FOREIGN-OWNED INDUSTRY IN IRELAND

The main source of industrial growth in Ireland after the end of the 1950s was new investment by foreign-owned multinational companies that chose Ireland as a site in which to produce for export markets. At first, until about the end of the 1960s, most of this was production of technologically mature and often labor-intensive products such as clothing, footwear, textiles, plastic products, and light engineering. As Vernon (1966) observed at around that time, mature industries such as these, with standardized products, were most capable of being located in industrially undeveloped countries because they did not depend on close contact with the specialized technologists, skills, suppliers, and services found in advanced industrial centers. And since they were generally quite labor-intensive, they had a motivation to move to relatively low-wage locations. The international dispersal of such industries occurred quite early in relatively low-wage countries on the periphery of the developed world, such as Puerto Rico and Ireland. Then, from about the mid-1960s, such mobile transnational industries increasingly went to poorer, less developed countries with much lower wages.

Apart from the attraction of relatively low wage costs by Western European standards, Irish government policy, since the 1950s, had explicitly sought to attract FDI in industries that would produce for export markets. To this end, investment grants were offered and taxation on profits arising from new industrial exports was eliminated, which probably did much to enhance the motivation for foreign investment in production for export markets. The development of foreign-owned export industries was also facilitated by the shift to free trade policies and the removal of restrictions on foreign ownership of new industrial firms.

From about the late 1960s, foreign investment in Ireland increasingly involved newer, more technologically advanced products, such as electrical and electronic products, machinery, pharmaceuticals, and medical instruments and equipment, again primarily for export. Typically, however, these industries involved only certain stages of production which were usually not the most demanding on local technological inputs, skills, and high-quality suppliers.

Again there is some parallel here with the type of mobile industry that has been able to go to less developed countries since the late 1960s (see Helleiner 1973). But the industries going to Ireland include some more highly skilled activities, particularly in electronics and pharmaceuticals, even if they have usually lacked the key technological functions of the firm, such as R&D, or other key business functions. Thus the electronics industry in Ireland employs a significantly higher proportion of engineers and technicians than in Singapore or Hong Kong, but a significantly lower proportion than in the

USA or UK, while the industry in Ireland does much less R&D in relation to sales than in the USA or UK (see O'Malley 1989: Chapter 7).

While export-oriented foreign investment in Ireland after the late 1950s can be regarded as having been motivated, at first, mainly by relatively low wage costs, tax concessions, and grants, there has been the further significant attraction of assured access to the large EC market, since Ireland joined the EC in 1973. For many foreign investors since that time, the first decision was to choose a location within the EC, and then they chose Ireland as a suitable base for penetrating EC markets. Thus, Ireland's main competitors in attracting such industries have usually been other Western European countries rather than low-wage developing countries. Within that context, Ireland has remained competitive on wage costs relative to most Western European countries, with the major additional attraction of very low taxes on industrial profits, as well as grants for industrial investment. In addition, the Industrial Development Authority (IDA) was doing an effective job in marketing Ireland as a location for expanding multinational companies that would be likely to be considering a new European production base. At the same time, the Irish education system managed to produce a good supply of people with certain key types of qualifications at times when these were in strong demand for some rapidly growing industries internationally, for example electronics, pharmaceuticals, and, more recently, software. More generally, the fact that the Irish labor force is English-speaking has been a further attraction for many overseas investors, particularly those from the USA.

The importance of access to the EC market in attracting export-oriented foreign investment can be seen in the fact that, since Ireland joined the EC in 1973, an increased proportion of the exports of foreign firms have come from companies of non-EC origin (especially US companies) that have been selling increasingly into the EC market. In 1974, 58 percent of exports of grant-assisted foreign-owned manufacturing firms came from firms of non-EC origin (McAleese 1977: 34). But by 1993, 83 percent of exports of foreign manufacturing firms came from non-EC firms (Central Statistics Office 1997). And in 1974, just 23 percent of exports of grant-assisted foreign industry went to EC countries other than the UK (with 39 percent going to the UK). But by 1993, 50 percent of exports of foreign industry went to EC countries other than the UK (with 23 percent going to the UK).

The new export-oriented foreign-owned firms contributed substantially to industrial growth. By 1993, foreign firms came to account for 44 percent of manufacturing employment, 58 percent of manufacturing output, and 77 percent of manufactured exports (Central Statistics Office 1997). Much of the employment concerned has been relatively well paid by Irish standards. McAleese and Foley (1991) show that average earnings per person engaged were 11 percent higher in foreign-owned firms than in Irish-owned firms in 1983, rising to 20 percent higher by 1987. This was partly because foreign-owned firms are more concentrated in sectors with relatively high pay rates, but it was also the case that average wages and salaries per person were higher in foreign-owned firms than in Irish-owned firms in 17 out of 26 industrial sectors in 1985.

While employment in foreign-owned manufacturing grew almost continuously in the 1960s and 1970s, it reached a peak at 88,400 in 1980 and then fell continuously to 78,700 by 1987. While this was a distinctly lower rate of decline than in the indigenous sector, it still amounted to a cumulative decline of 11 percent over seven consecutive years.

The output of foreign-owned firms continued to grow quite strongly, even while their employment was declining, for much of the 1980s. But a problem as regards the contribution of such growth to the Irish economy was that most of the growth occurred at very high rates in a small number of predominantly foreign-owned sectors that had relatively low levels of linkages with the local economy. Thus virtually all of the growth of industrial output in the period 1980–1987 can be attributed to five sectors – pharmaceuticals, office and data processing machinery, electrical engineering, instrument engineering, and other foods – while all other sectors combined had virtually no growth (Baker 1988). These sectors import a high proportion of their inputs and expatriate very substantial profits, so that data on their output can give a rather misleading impression of their contribution to the economy.

What matters from the point of view of the Irish economy is not simply the value of output of foreign firms, but rather how much of that value is retained in Ireland in the form of payments of wages and taxes and purchases of Irish-made goods and services as inputs. It has been found that such "Irish economy expenditures" are a considerably lower proportion of the value of output in foreign-owned industry than in indigenous industry, and this is especially true of the five high-growth sectors of the 1980s mentioned above.[9] Thus, although there was quite high growth of output in foreign-owned industry in 1980–1987, this does not reverse the impression, arising from its falling employment, that its contribution to domestic economic growth weakened in that period compared with the 1960s and 1970s.

Part of the reason for this weaker performance of foreign-owned industry in most of the 1980s was a reduction of inflows of new foreign investment after 1981.[10] This, in turn, partly reflected the fact that new US investment in Europe was declining or stagnating for much of the 1980s. In addition, there was increasingly intense competition from other European countries that were trying more actively to attract mobile industries because they were experiencing persistent unemployment.

Apart from the slowing down of new foreign investment in Ireland in the early 1980s, it had also emerged that the longer established foreign firms already in Ireland tended to decline in employment eventually, after an initial period of employment growth. This pattern was already established during the 1970s. For example, employment in foreign-owned manufacturing firms established before 1969 fell by 12 percent between 1973 and 1980, while overall industrial employment was increasing at the fastest rate of any EC country. This meant that overall growth of employment in foreign industry was being sustained only by the continuing inflow of new first-time foreign investors. With the passage of time, the overall trend of employment in foreign-owned industry was being increasingly affected by the large stock of relatively old plants with declining employment, so that an ever greater inflow of new first-time investors would have been needed to maintain a given growth rate. By the early 1980s, when new foreign investment was reduced, the result was employment decline in most branches of foreign-owned industry and in the foreign sector as a whole.

With employment declining in foreign-owned industry, there was continuous decline in total industrial employment until 1987. At the same time, unemployment was rising from 7 percent of the labor force in 1980 to almost 18 percent in 1987, and there was substantial emigration as well. Already in the early 1980s the Telesis (1982) report to the National Economic and Social Council (NESC) had made a number of criticisms of the practice of relying so heavily on foreign investment, and this point was largely taken on board by the NESC (1982). The events that followed tended to give weight to the view that more had to be done to develop a stronger indigenous sector, since heavy reliance on foreign industry was no longer producing the sort of results that it had for the previous two decades. In this context, there was a growing feeling that there was a need for some significant revisions to industrial policy.

INDUSTRIAL POLICY DEVELOPMENTS SINCE THE MID-1980s

Beginning in the mid-1980s, a number of changes were made in industrial policy. These changes did not transform the nature of policy as radically as the switch to comprehensive protectionism in the 1930s or the switch to an outward-looking strategy in the late 1950s and 1960s. Irish industrial development strategy certainly remained outward-looking in the sense outlined earlier. But within the broad parameters of that strategy there were changes of emphasis and policy instruments that arguably defined the beginning of a distinctive phase of policy.

Shifts in policy objectives

The basic objective of industrial policy remained as it was, namely the development of an internationally competitive industrial sector that would make the maximum contribution to employment growth and higher living standards. And policy remained committed to free trade (within the context of EU membership), promotion of exporting or internationally trading industries, and an active approach to attracting FDI. In these respects there has been no change from the objectives and approach of the 1960s and 1970s. But some of the more specific aims of policy have changed since the early 1980s.

In particular, since the White Paper on *Industrial Policy* (1984), there has been an increased emphasis in official policy statements on the aim of developing Irish indigenous industry. This arose, not from a rejection of foreign-owned industry, but more from a recognition that there were limits to the benefits that could be expected from foreign investment and that the relatively poor long-term performance of indigenous industry called for a greater focus on addressing that problem.

More specifically, policy statements since 1984 have referred to a need for policy towards indigenous industry to be somewhat more selective, aiming to develop larger and stronger firms by building on those with a reasonable track record, rather than assisting a great many start-ups and very small firms indiscriminately. Policy was intended to become more selective, too, in the sense of concentrating state supports and incentives more on correcting specific areas of disadvantage or weakness that would be common in indigenous firms (but not so common in foreign-owned firms), such as technological capability, export-marketing, and management skills. It was intended to shift expenditures on industrial policy from supporting capital investment towards improving technology, export-marketing, and management (*Industrial Policy* 1984: Chapters 1 and 5; Department of Industry and Commerce 1987: Chapter 2).

Another prominent theme in statements of industrial policy objectives after the early 1980s, in a context of mounting concern about the growing public debt at that time, was a strong emphasis on the need to make spending on industrial development more cost-effective so as to obtain better value for money. And a further notable element in statements of policy objectives after the early 1980s was the objective of not only attracting foreign enterprises to produce in Ireland, but also aiming to strengthen their linkages or their degree of integration with the Irish economy. This means aiming to have them purchase more of their inputs from Irish sources and to carry out in Ireland functions such as R&D and marketing, so as to increase the share of their value added that is retained in Ireland and to generate greater technical spillovers.

Changes in policy measures

The introduction of policy changes in pursuit of the objectives mentioned above was in some respects rather hesitant and gradual, and indeed there was some questioning about the real strength of commitment to the objectives. For example, in 1992, the Industrial Policy Review Group (1992: 67) recognized that greater efforts had been undertaken by then to promote indigenous industry, but still considered that there had not been a full commitment to this process. The Group called for a more decisive shift in the focus of policy towards developing indigenous industry, and this objective has since been reemphasized. However, even going back to the mid-1980s, there were quite a number of relevant policy changes, of an incremental rather than a radical nature, introduced over a period of some years.[11]

For example, the Company Development Programme was introduced in 1984. This involves staff of state development agencies with a range of expertise working with selected indigenous companies that have potential for significant growth and a firm commitment to achieving it. The aim is to help companies analyze their competitive position and prepare strategic development plans that can be implemented with the support of a range of state assistance. In addition, the National Linkage Programme commenced in 1985 with the aim of further developing selected indigenous subsuppliers of components, particularly to the foreign multinational companies, in order to strengthen local purchasing linkages. The role of the state agencies in these programs is not to dictate development plans to the companies involved. Rather their role is more to act as catalysts, sharing opinions and expertise, acting as information-brokers, and making suggestions on how they can assist a company's long-term development through their range of financial supports and services.

After the mid-1980s, efforts were made to award capital investment grants more selectively to firms that would have the best prospects for growth in international markets in order to concentrate resources somewhat more on building larger and stronger firms. Thus the group of existing firms (i.e. excluding new start-ups) that were awarded grant assistance in 1984 employed 25,900 people, whereas the existing firms that were awarded grant assistance in 1990 were a considerably smaller group employing 13,200 people (O'Malley *et al.* 1992: Chapter 3). Significantly, the award of such grants was increasingly made dependent on firms having prepared overall company development plans. With a view to obtaining better value for state expenditure, the average rate of capital grant was reduced after 1986, performance-related targets were applied as conditions for payment of grants, and a shift began towards the use of repayable forms of financial support such as equity financing rather than capital grants. Given these constraints, together with a more selective focusing on relatively promising indigenous firms, the share of the industrial policy budget going to support capital investment declined from 61 percent in 1985 to 47 percent in 1992.

In this context, there was a shift in emphasis towards "soft" measures other than capital grants. From 1985, a range of new initiatives were introduced to strengthen the export-marketing capabilities of Irish firms, and the share of the industrial policy budget going to support marketing increased from 10.9 percent in 1985 to 16.6 percent in 1992. Assistance to improve marketing was redirected from short-term operational support towards developing companies' long-term potential. And this support for marketing was focused more selectively on indigenous firms. Science and technology policies for industry were also reorganized considerably after the mid-1980s, and new technology policy measures were introduced such as technology acquisition grants, subsidized technology audits of firms, and subsidized placement of graduates and experienced technologists in firms. The share of the industrial policy budget going to science and technology measures increased from 11.1 percent in 1985 to 20.9 percent in 1992.

Among other new measures introduced since the mid-1980s, there are management development grants to strengthen the quality of management in indigenous firms and to assist with recruitment of managers with necessary skills. In addition, the Mentor Programme provides experienced business people as temporary advisers to help companies to overcome obstacles to growth. There is also a program that assists indigenous firms to develop new business opportunities involving alliances and partnership arrangements with overseas companies.

These policy changes were accompanied by substantial reorganization of the institutional arrangements for implementing policy. In particular, administrative responsibility for promoting indigenous industry was separated from the task of encouraging FDI so as to ensure that there would be a body of state agency staff giving their full attention to the indigenous sector.[12]

Another type of initiative since the mid-1980s has been the formulation of sectoral development strategies or plans for a number of selected sectors. The purpose of such strategies is to identify development opportunities, and to help to focus the support of state agencies on building on areas of actual or potential competitive advantage and on correcting identified weaknesses. Related to this, an important recommendation of the Industrial Policy Review Group (1992) was that policy should focus on developing groups of related industries or clusters; this recommendation was influenced by the work of Porter (1990). There has been some discussion among those responsible for formulating and implementing Irish industrial policy about the merits of developing policy along these lines, but efforts to do so are in a preliminary stage as yet.

While policies to develop Irish indigenous industry have changed quite significantly since the early 1980s, there has been less extensive change in policies for foreign-owned industry. As was mentioned above, the National Linkage Programme was introduced in 1985 in order to further develop indigenous subsuppliers of components, particularly to the foreign multinational companies, with a view to strengthening the local purchasing linkages of the multinationals. This Programme focuses on the indigenous subsuppliers as much as on the foreign firms. Apart from this, IDA Ireland would now be more conscious than formerly of the desirability of attracting foreign firms that would establish key business functions in Ireland such as R&D or marketing, rather than production alone. For this tends to make such companies more committed to continuing and expanding in the country, and it can generate beneficial spillovers for other firms. To this end, IDA has flexibility to negotiate the rate of grant assistance it offers to foreign investors. Thus, the rate of grant assistance offered to a project can be made to depend on factors such as the expected level of linkages with Irish suppliers and the type and quality of business functions that it is proposed to locate in Ireland, as well as the amount and quality of employment and the proposed location of the project.

Industrial performance after the mid-1980s

Manufacturing employment in Ireland had declined by as much as one-fifth between 1979 and 1987. After that, however, it grew by 13 percent in the period 1988–1996. An increase in new foreign investment, leading to employment growth in foreign-owned industry after 1987, was quite a large part of the reason for this recovery. However, there was also a noticeable improvement in Irish indigenous industry. Employment in indigenous manufacturing had declined by 27 percent between 1980 and 1987, but it scarcely declined any further in 1988, and then increased by over 6 percent between 1988 and 1996 (Forfas Employment Survey). This was quite a modest increase but it represented a distinct improvement over previous experience. It was also a relatively strong performance by international standards, since manufacturing employment in the EU and the OECD declined in the same period.

An important aspect of the long-term weakness of indigenous industry had been its failure to make much progress in developing exports. *Census of Industrial Production* (CIP) data show that 26.6 percent of the output of indigenous manufacturing was exported in 1986, which indicates little or no change from estimates of about 26 or 27 percent in 1973 and 1976 (O'Malley 1989: Chapter 6). However, the CIP data show an increase to 33.4 percent in 1990 and 35.3 percent in 1993. The value of indigenous manufacturing exports, in current dollar terms, increased by an average of 11.1 percent per year in the period 1986–1993, compared with an average annual increase of 8.4 percent for the manufacturing exports of the European Union, also valued in current dollars.[13] Furthermore, in 1986 as much as 55 percent of the exports of Irish indigenous industry went to a single market, the UK, with just 17 percent going to the rest of the EU. But there was considerable diversification in the destination of indigenous exports after that, with 44 percent going to the UK and 28 percent going to the rest of the EU by 1993.

Thus, the export performance of Irish indigenous industry after 1986 was relatively strong by European standards and quite unprecedented in indigenous industry's own experience. The employment performance of indigenous industry after 1988 was also a good deal better than previous experience, and relatively strong by international standards, although there was not very strong employment growth in absolute terms. These improved trends in indigenous industry are probably not sufficiently strong or sufficiently long established to show that indigenous industry is on a new long-term growth path. But there is at least some indication here that the policies introduced since the mid-1980s to give a new impetus to the development of a stronger, internationally competitive indigenous sector have been meeting with some success.

CONCLUSIONS

Ireland began life as an independent state in the 1920s with very little industry. In that respect it differed from most Western European countries and had something in common with many late-developing countries that have aimed to develop industry in this century starting from a negligible base. Much of the discussion about industrial development strategy for less developed or newly industrializing countries has concerned the merits and disadvantages of an inward-looking strategy of import-substituting industrialization as compared to an outward-looking strategy of export-led industrialization. Ireland has attempted versions of both of these approaches at different times.

Ireland's experience with the inward-looking or protectionist strategy in the 1930s–1950s was ultimately unsatisfactory, since it culminated in almost a decade of virtual stagnation. The key failure was the lack of development of exports, since the policy of protection did not result in development of internationally competitive industries. It is worth noting, however, that before introducing the protectionist strategy, Ireland had previous long experience of a predominantly free trade *laissez-faire* approach, both as part of the UK and as an independent state in the 1920s. This approach had not fostered industrial development. Against this background, it seems likely that the introduction of the protectionist strategy did have the effect of encouraging and facilitating growth of industrial output and employment. But this effect was ultimately not sustained. The protectionist policy was not accompanied by any significant attempt to ensure that protected infant industries would develop to a competitive maturity, and so the protected industries tended to remain inefficient and uncompetitive in international markets.

Under the outward-looking strategy introduced in Ireland from the late 1950s, there was considerable improvement in growth rates of industrial output, exports, and employment compared with the 1950s. However, a distinctive feature of this performance was that it relied very heavily on foreign-owned multinational companies. Up to the mid-1980s at least, the strategy was not a success as regards the performance of indigenous industry. Thus, Ireland's fairly strong industrial growth in the 1960s to early 1980s was basically due to the fact that an exceptionally large proportion of the available mobile export-oriented FDI was attracted into what is a rather small economy. Since such internationally mobile investment occurs on only a limited scale worldwide, relative to the size of all the less developed or newly industrializing countries, this was an exceptional experience that could not be readily repeated by many other such countries.

It seems unlikely that the poor performance of Irish indigenous industry at that time could be attributed simply to serious defects in the general economic environment, such as an inadequate infrastructure, a low-quality labor force, or a misguided tax system. Numerous foreign multinational firms were finding the Irish economic environment quite tolerable and reasonably conducive to successful operation at the same time as indigenous industry was experiencing great difficulties. There was also no great lack of a spirit of indigenous enterprise, in the sense of a scarcity of people who were willing to start up and run industrial companies. The problem was more that new indigenous firms generally remained small while larger existing Irish firms tended to decline.

It seems reasonable to conclude that the form of outward-looking strategy applied in the late 1950s to mid-1980s proved inadequate as a means of developing indigenous industry, despite the existence of general economic conditions that were not seriously unfavorable. To a considerable extent, this can be explained by the prevalence in many industries of barriers to entry – arising from the strengths of established competitors – that confront new or small indigenous firms in a late industrializing country such as Ireland. For example, the existence of significant economies of scale, and the consequent presence of large established firms in many important sectors in advanced economies, presents a barrier to the development of such industries by new or small indigenous firms in a late developing country that trades freely with advanced economies. It can also be difficult for new or small indigenous firms in a late industrializing country to match the already existing technological strength of firms in advanced economies in sectors where technology is of key importance. Similarly, if strong marketing is a key requirement for an industry, the established marketing strength of existing firms presents an important entry barrier for new or small firms. In addition, the competitive advantages arising from external economies, which are enjoyed by firms in existing, often specialized, industrial centers or districts, can represent a further obstacle to the development of newcomers in late industrializing countries that would have to compete with the existing industries.

If the existence of these various types of barriers to entry represents a significant part of the explanation of the difficulties of Irish indigenous industry under free trade policies, then at least some of the developments in Irish industrial policy since the mid-1980s look like appropriate responses. The present policy approach involves focusing assistance somewhat more selectively on relatively promising firms, so as to develop larger and stronger indigenous firms with relatively good growth prospects, rather than aiding a great many firms indiscriminately. It also involves focusing assistance more on specific areas such as technological capability and export-marketing (which are often areas in which relatively late developing industry faces some disadvantages), rather than just general support for investments. And there has been some debate about the merits of fostering the development of groups of related industries which could be expected to generate mutually supportive advantages for each of the industries concerned.

While retaining a commitment to free trade, a liberal and encouraging approach to FDI and an emphasis on the need for competitiveness in international markets, the present policy approach to assisting indigenous development does involve somewhat selective intervention in the operation of market forces. However, the intention is not to resist those forces indefinitely, as with the former protectionist policy. Rather the aim is ultimately to provide indigenous industry with the characteristics and strengths required to survive and grow in a competitive environment. Since about 1987, the results seem to have been fairly encouraging, although this is quite a short period on which to judge the effectiveness of an industrial development strategy.

NOTES

1 "Transportable Goods" industries are almost the same as total manufacturing, except that they include a few thousand jobs in mining.

2 These figures probably overstate the rate of growth of employment to some extent since the Census of Industrial Production increased its coverage in this period. Nevertheless, it is clear that there was substantial expansion in industrial employment at this time; see Daly 1988, Johnson 1988, and Girvin 1989: Chapter 4, pp 108–111.

3 For example, the Department of Industry and Commerce (1990: 15), in setting out the objectives of policy, said: "The primary objective of industrial policy is to promote the development of a strong internationally competitive industrial and international services sector in Ireland which will make the maximum contribution to employment growth and higher living standards."

4 Further details on the changes in policy measures which are outlined very briefly here can be found in O'Malley 1989: Chapter 5.

5 The source for these data is the *Census of Industrial Production*.

6 See O'Malley 1989: Chapter 6 for details on these and other developments discussed in this section.

7 The seven sectors concerned are motor vehicles, other means of transport, chemical industry, man-made fibers industry, production and preliminary processing of metals, office & data processing machinery, and electrical engineering. The source of data on industry size structures is Eurostat, *Structure and Activity of Industry: Data by Size of Enterprises–1984*.

8 See Porter 1980: Chapter 1 for a review of the principal types of barriers to entry that can occur in different industries.

9 Data on this were collected annually after 1983 by the IDA in its Irish economy expenditures survey. Irish economy expenditures of foreign-owned nonfood manufacturing grew at just two-thirds of the rate of growth of its gross output in 1983–1987, because of the fact that nearly all of the growth of its output occurred in sectors with particularly low levels of Irish economy expenditures in relation to sales.

10 See O'Malley 1989: Chapter 7 for details on this and other developments discussed in this section.

11 The relevant policy changes are summarized rather briefly here. Further details can be found in official documents such as *Industrial Policy* 1984, and Department of Industry and Commerce 1987 and 1990. Details on the package of industrial policies existing now can be found in the *Operational Programme for Industrial Development 1994–1999*.

12 This was done first in 1988 by means of an internal reorganization within the Industrial Development Authority (IDA), which involved the establishment of separate divisions for the promotion of indigenous and overseas industry. Since 1993, there have been separate agencies for these two functions – the Industrial Development Agency of Ireland (or IDA Ireland) for overseas industry, and Forbairt for indigenous industry.

13 The data on the EU's manufacturing exports are from the OECD's *Historical Statistics*; they include SITC categories 0, 1 and 5–9.

REFERENCES

Baker, T. J. (1988) "Industrial output and wage costs 1980–87," *Quarterly Economic Commentary* October, Dublin: The Economic and Social Research Institute.

Central Statistics Office (1993) "Census of Industrial Production 1990," Dublin: Stationery Office.

—— (1997) "Census of Industrial Production 1993," Dublin: Stationery Office.
Daly, M. E. (1988) "The employment gains from industrial protection in the Irish Free State during the 1930s: a note," *Irish Economic and Social History* 15: 71–75.
Department of Industry and Commerce (1987) *Review of Industrial Performance 1986*, Dublin: Stationery Office.
—— (1990) *Review of Industrial Performance 1990*, Dublin: Stationery Office.
Furtado, C. (1976) *Economic Development of Latin America: Historical Background and Contemporary Problems*, Cambridge: Cambridge University Press.
Girvin, B. (1989) *Between Two Worlds: Politics and Economy in Independent Ireland*, Dublin: Gill and Macmillan.
Helleiner, G. K. (1973) "Manufactured exports from the less developed countries and multinational firms," *Economic Journal* 83, 329: 21–47.
Industrial Policy (1984) Government White Paper, Dublin: Stationery Office.
Industrial Policy Review Group (1992) *A Time for Change: Industrial Policy for the 1990s*, Dublin: Stationery Office.
Johnson, D. (1988) "Reply," *Irish Economic and Social History* 15: 76–80.
Kennedy, K. A. (1971) *Productivity and Industrial Growth: The Irish Experience*, Oxford: Clarendon Press.
Kennedy, K. A., Giblin, T., and McHugh, D. (1988) *The Economic Development of Ireland in the Twentieth Century*, London and New York: Routledge.
Lyons, F. S. L. (1976) *Ireland Since the Famine*, London: Fontana.
McAleese, D. (1971) *Import Demand, Protection and the Effects of Trade Liberalisation on the Irish Economy*, Ph.D. thesis, Johns Hopkins University.
—— (1977) *A Profile of Grant-Aided Industry in Ireland*, Dublin: Industrial Development Authority.
McAleese, D. and Foley, A. (1991) "The role of overseas industry in industrial development," in A. Foley and D. McAleese (eds) *Overseas Industry in Ireland*, Dublin: Gill and Macmillan.
National Economic and Social Council (1982) *Policies for Industrial Development: Conclusions and Recommendations*, NESC Report, No. 66, Dublin: NESC.
O'Farrell, P. N. and Crouchley, R. (1984) "An industrial and spatial analysis of new firm formation in Ireland," *Regional Studies* 18, 3: 221–236.
O'Grada, C. (1994) *Ireland: A New Economic History 1780–1939*, Oxford: Clarendon Press.
O'Malley, E. (1989) *Industry and Economic Development: The Challenge for the Latecomer*, Dublin: Gill and Macmillan.
O'Malley, E., Kennedy, K. A., and O'Donnell, R. (1992) *The Impact of the Industrial Development Agencies*, Report to the Industrial Policy Review Group, Dublin: Stationery Office.
Operational Programme for Industrial Development 1994–1999 (1994) Dublin: Stationery Office.
Porter, M. E. (1980) *Competitive Strategy: Techniques for Analysing Industries and Competitors*, New York: Free Press.
—— (1990) *The Competitive Advantage of Nations*, London and Basingstoke: Macmillan.
Telesis Consultancy Group (1982) "A review of industrial policy," NESC Report, No. 64, Dublin: NESC.
Vernon, R. (1966). "International investment and international trade in the product cycle," *Quarterly Journal of Economics* 80, 2: 190–207.

11 Promoting coordination at regional level

The case of Northern Greece[1]

Lena J. Tsipouri

INTRODUCTION

This chapter examines the process and the dynamics of an effort to promote collective action at the subnational level. Unlike the previous case studies, it does not address industrial policy in one country treated as a homogenous territory.[2] Its aim is to identify the extent to which regions are able to distinguish themselves from their neighbors by better utilizing the opportunities offered in a national context so that they can establish the foundations of a sustainable economic system. The question we address is whether, in the absence of established regional autonomy, it is possible (or likely) for particular areas to trigger a process of changing conventions and informal rules leading to improved economic results, even when the region is subject to the same formal rules, incentives, opportunities, and threats as the rest of the country.

In this context we examine the process and the dynamics of recent initiatives to promote industrial policy in Northern Greece, a region that is more industrialized than most of the rest of the country, representing the second largest manufacturing agglomeration after the Athens area. Using the ideas developed in this book regarding learning and coordination, we examine the extent to which the introduction of regional policies and programs have affected behavioral rules in Northern Greece differently from the rest of the country. We investigate regional differences in the reaction of agents to emerging opportunities by trying to identify whether agents responded rapidly, coherently, and collectively in an effort to build up a community spirit, promote self-help, and adopt new types of infrastructure leading to increased collective efficiency. The question is whether they have succeeded in reversing a longstanding industrial culture of mistrust and individualism.

The national context was not favorable. Greece is one of the so-called cohesion countries, notably countries that need to catch up with EU-average, no matter which indicators are taken as a measure (with the exception of unemployment). Despite remarkable rates of growth in earlier periods, the economy has been in near stagnation for the last two decades. The combination of high import penetration (associated with the accession of the country to the EU in 1981), a rapid decrease in direct and indirect protectionism, and political instability in the late 1980s fostered deindustrialization triggered by the inability to cope with the relative increase in factor costs.[3] Industrial policy in Greece was absent or inefficient in recent decades, while investments were characterized by individual economic rationale without any sign of a common socio-cultural identity leading to collective action. In this context it is not surprising that the Greek manufacturing sector – whose growth was based on a cheap-labor advantage – was by and large unable to turn into a learning system, capable of adjusting to changes in its environment and assuring sustainable development. This situation engendered defeatism, continuous deterioration in the effectiveness of the public administration, and increased uncertainty to a greater extent than in the other less favored member states of the EU.

This environment explains why new opportunities were sorely needed in Greece. To some extent these opportunities presented themselves in the late 1980s when the European Union decided to accompany the creation of the Single European Market with a massive transfer of funds to the less favored regions of the Union, in order to strengthen their infrastructure and allow them to compete on better terms with their trading partners. This exercise took the form of two consecutive Community Support Framework programs (CSF), which were individually designed for each member state, earmarking large sums to be transferred for enhancing development in regions with GDP per head lower than 75 percent of EU average. The allocation of these funds is determined by plans drafted in agreement between EU and national authorities. Greece, like Portugal and Ireland, was eligible for development aid throughout its territory.[4] While this presented a major opportunity for modernization, it nevertheless created certain tensions between the public and the private sector, and between the state and the regions, as to how these funds should be best absorbed. After long negotiations it was decided to incorporate both a national development plan and regional development plans tailored to the needs of each region into the CSF; the former was to be designed by national authorities and cover state priorities, such as infrastructure, energy, technology, and education; under the latter component, the 13 regions of the country were to adopt regional operational programs reflecting local priorities and proposed actions. As there is no tradition of regional autonomy in the country, this unique opportunity encountered the serious problem of managerial weakness in regional capabilities to implement such an ambitious program at subnational level.

During the period under study, from the late 1980s until the present, two additional opportunities, arising out of changing political and economic conditions, complemented the introduction of new financial support from the EU. The first was the alleviation of the wage/productivity burden, following the partially successful implementation of stabilization policies.[5] The second was the opening of the Balkan market in the early 1990s. However, while all of these opportunities should be expected to affect national and regional economic structures, productivity, and profitability, it is still too soon to compare the effects accurately and usefully.

Instead, our study focuses on the reactions and behavioral evolution of collective agents. We argue that a new pattern of trust and infrastructure developed, beginning in Central Macedonia – the core of the geographical focus of this chapter – and spread to a wider area. Despite the very centralized nature of the Greek administration, agents in Central Macedonia successfully distinguished themselves in a short period of time by becoming active components of the modernization process and shaping both concrete actions and informal rules that influenced the design of regional industrial policy. We observed the creation of partnerships, which started timidly when financial incentives were first offered and grew rapidly into sustainable alliances, willing and able to promote local industrial strategy along modern principles even in the absence of formal autonomy. It remains to be seen whether this attitude can be sustained without financial incentives and whether in the next decade Northern Greece becomes a winner in terms of regional development. Building trust-based relationships is one key element of this approach; the creation of relevant, well-utilized infrastructure is the other.

We begin by briefly describing Greek economic and industrial policy, followed by an examination of the position and role of Central Macedonia and Northern Greece in this context. The following section describes the initiatives taken in response to the opportunities offered, initially in the core and then in the extended region. We compare initiatives undertaken in Northern Greece with those that are part of the national plans, and contrast the absence of similar initiatives in other regions of Greece. Finally, we attempt to draw some general conclusions regarding the lessons to be learned from this differentiated behavior, focusing on its origins, the process, and the likelihood of success under the current circumstances.

ECONOMIC AND INDUSTRIAL POLICY IN GREECE

In the last decade Greece has had the lowest per capita income, the lowest productivity, the highest inflation rate, and one of the highest public debts in the European Union. Only unemployment was traditionally lower than in most other member states, but even this grew rapidly in the last two years. Despite the fact that by international standards Greece is rich and one of the most prosperous latecomers, compared to the EU or OECD average it is poor. An historical perspective demonstrates that over the 160 years of independent statehood, phases of economic growth have been few and far apart. For most of its historical existence, modern Greece has been in a state of economic stagnation, even crisis. The small size of the internal market has disadvantaged investment in "heavy" or "intermediate" industrial sectors, skewing actual activities towards light manufacturing, labor-intensive industries, and small-firm organization (Thomadakis 1996).

Economic historians have offered a variety of explanations for Greece's inability to exploit its episodic – and at times substantial – growth and to develop a manufacturing sector capable of being a source of sustainable wealth creation; these have included: a lack of capital (Zolotas 1926), the inadequacy of human resources (Dertilis 1984), and the deficiency of the internal market combined with the fragmentation of production (Chatziiossif 1993). Economic and sociological analyses also point to the role of the state and industrial culture: the state was unable to proceed with public investment in manufacturing or to regulate the economy with a long-term vision of collective profit, while the country's industrial culture failed to foster modern managerial resources. Technology management in particular, which would have allowed firms to adjust to new circumstances and sustain their temporary competitive edges, was for the most part absent during the post-war years. An alliance developed between a timid and inefficient (or even impotent and corrupt) public administration and private manufacturing firms that exhibited short-termist patterns of behavior, resulting in what Stavros Thomadakis calls the "politicization of the economy" (1996), a situation well known to many latecomers.[6]

The Greek economy has remained in a situation of quasi-permanent crisis since the 1970s. The industrial character of the crisis is reflected by declining investment and production in modern manufacturing and a relative increase in traditional sectors. The danger of deindustrialization is apparent in the emergence of services as the major growth pole of the economy, while the industrial sector's position in the international division of labor deteriorates (Giannitsis 1985). The already apparent crisis was aggravated in the early 1980s by the accession of Greece to the European Community (as the EU was called at the time) which led to increased import penetration without compensating export opportunities. Compared to both newly industrializing countries (NICs) and southern Europe, industrial competitiveness has been eroding over a protracted period of time (Giannitsis 1984). The very low number of start-ups – compared both to the EU average and to the other two small less favored member states (Commission of the EU 1995) – suggests that restructuring is unlikely to succeed. In response to this situation, economic policy was concentrated on stabilization in the form of a series of austerity programs aimed at improving wage/productivity ratios, the results of which were only partially successful (Alogoskoufis 1993).

Vaitsos and Giannitsis (1987) have documented the inability of the manufacturing sector to adapt to technological changes. They suggest that the most important limitation to overcoming these problems is that Greek industry does not demonstrate the necessary mechanisms and productive specialization to enable it to identify potential areas of dynamism and develop capabilities there. More recently, in a systematic effort to identify the use of technological sources in Greek industry, Giannitsis and Mavri (1993) concluded that international technological and productive restructuring has had a devastating effect on Greek industry. Although some segments of the industrial sector that survived the changes became more competitive, serious conditions of uncertainty were introduced and technologies of a monopolistic character were adopted. Overall, the Greek economy was not prepared to accumulate technological knowledge and skills as required in order to participate effectively in a massive technology transfer. Innovative performance was very limited, concentrated in traditional industrial sectors, and only few timid steps may be observed lately in the adoption of the value of intangible investments.

During this same period, and for as long as it could afford this position, the state's role was limited to a strongly protectionist policy. Protectionism was a substitute for industrial policy, while the state refused or was unable to participate in the design of a coherent long-term structural policy, with clear targets, consistent programming, and definite and transparent rules of the game (Mitsos 1989). Neither did capital and money markets support industry. Bank loans were the only means of financing manufacturing investment and operating capital. But the criteria used excluded many SMEs from the system, while the bigger and established companies had easy access to loans, often more than their needs could justify. Bank participation in the shareholding capital of the large companies further distorted competition. The international crisis during the 1970s, aggravated by the withdrawal or nonrenewal of inward investment which had previously spurred the growth episode of the 1960s, contributed to a severe and persistent crisis (Xanthakis 1989).

Gradual integration into the European market formally ended the projectionist period. The reaction of the Greek state was to increase capital incentives, in particular through generous investment grants, and to impose a transfer of large indebted companies to a state holding. The latter measure produced a further deterioration in the climate of confidence between state authorities and big industry – confidence was already nonexistent with respect to SMEs – and despite the increased capital incentives, investment reached its lowest level in the 1980s. The end of this period was marked by an improvement in international demand and the decision of the EU to substantially increase its regional aid to create the necessary infrastructure and productive mechanisms in the less productive regions of the union. The trans-European regional aid program was received with great relief in Greece, but the program's vague design and administrative inefficiencies resulted in a low absorption of EU funds by industry. The mechanisms adopted for the EU aid did not differ substantially from those applicable to previous national intervention programs; the Community Support Framework only facilitated an increase in the order of magnitude. This experience forced the public authorities to proceed to a more proactive industrial policy design resulting in the Operational Program for Industry (OPI) which included four major subprograms (infrastructure, support for private investment, modernization of companies, and SME support). In all these areas, modern methods for linking aid with business plans and new systems of management were announced, but overall absorption rates remained very limited.

The moderate achievements of the macroeconomic stabilization programs, economic growth in Greece's main trade partners, and the massive transfer of EU regional aid did change, to some extent, the structure of manufacturing industry. A high price was paid in terms of increased unemployment and business failures, but manufacturing enterprises that survived are now, on average, more competitive than in the 1980s. Despite this slight improvement in domestic competitiveness, globalization has had, on balance, a negative effect in Greece, due to a wave of MNC withdrawals from the country that were not compensated by any major new investments.[7]

After the accumulated problems of the 1970s and 1980s, the 1990s have been notable for three new opportunities:

1 reaping the advantages of the partial achievements of stabilization;
2 exploiting new export markets and the Balkan market in particular; and
3 increased transfer of funds for infrastructure and training.

In summary, the high level of uncertainty that tends to dominate less favored markets in general has increased considerably in Greece since the last growth episode of the 1960s. The implication of this with regard to informal rules was a lack of community spirit within the public and private sectors. Labor relations ranged from hostile to mediocre. No socio-cultural identity or trust relationships were built up. Profits were reinvested for capacity expansion rather than innovation. Investment decisions were based only on short-term economic rationale,[8] and even very high incentives were insufficient to trigger new growth, both because of the uncertainty and the politicization of the economy. The long lasting lack of trust relations prevented the application of classical instruments of industrial policy, such as the management of public purchases, when other member states were using them. Elsewhere – as reported in the literature on the learning economy and successful implementation of industrial districts – local entrepreneurial associations and local governments typically create specialized service centers, strengthen infrastructure, and launch initiatives for supporting the industrial sector (see Rabellotti 1995 and Brisco 1990). This was not the case in Greece, however, where the concept of collective efficiency leading to competitive advantage deriving from local externalities and joint action has been notoriously absent (Schmitz 1990), with the sole exception of the controversial case of Kastoria.[9] The effort in the mid-1980s to create state-induced research associations ended with many of the inefficient ones being abolished after a decade, and with many of the remainder working under suboptimal conditions and unable to play a leverage role. Similarly, employers' associations acted solely as lobbying groups.[10] Efforts to supplement the absence of trust by overregulation were observed in many cases; these resulted in highly bureaucratic procedures for any type of subsidy, tight price controls for over a decade, and procurement regulations that ultimately proved to delay modernization instead of protecting the state. The regulatory environment was confusing and the rules of the game were not always respected.[11]

The situation we have described above can be characterized as one where informal rules were governed by mistrust. At the same time, formal rules established to substitute for the disappearing informal rules were ineffective and increased transaction costs.

NORTHERN GREECE: ECONOMIC AND INSTITUTIONAL ENVIRONMENT

Northern Greece is composed of two geographical areas: Macedonia and Thrace. Macedonia is a large region dominated by Thessaloniki, the second biggest city in Greece, with relatively important manufacturing activities. Thrace is a small, poor region on the Turkish and Bulgarian border that, despite generous incentives, suffers from political instability and very low economic performance. Administratively, the two geographical areas are composed of three (artificially created) regions: Central Macedonia (home to Thessaloniki), Western Macedonia, and Eastern Macedonia/Thrace. The efforts and activities to promote collective efficiency originated in Central Macedonia, the most prosperous of the three regions, and spread to the wider geographical area beyond regional administrative links.

The economic environment

According to the 1991 population census, 20 percent of national industrial employment is concentrated in the region of Central Macedonia, with the Prefecture of Thessaloniki accounting for 63 percent. Outside of the Thessaloniki Prefecture, agriculture is extremely important, with a high potential for expansion in selected areas. Macedonia is well above the Greek average in manufacturing share, accounting for 23 percent of total Greek industrial output but only 13 percent and 11 percent in trade and services respectively.[12] Comparative data suggest very solid industrial activity compared to the rest of Greece. Industrial enterprises in Macedonia perform well above the Greek average in terms of employment, sales, and profit (see Table 11.1).

Table 11.1 Industrial performance

	Greece %	Macedonia %
Industrial employment as a share of total nonprimary-sector employment (1991)	46.7	81.3
Growth in industrial turnover (1990–91)	13.5	19.7
Change in net profit (1990–91)	–37.2	+38.2
Share of local companies earning profits (1991)	74.4	77.3

Source: ICAP, Research on Macedonian Enterprises, Thessaloniki 1992

The most important Macedonian manufacturing sectors are clothing and footwear, food and beverages, wood and furniture, and tobacco; these sectors' regional share of manufacturing employment is higher than the national average. As in the rest of Greece, the manufacturing sector is composed almost exclusively of SMEs with an average of 6.5 employees per firm, and with most enterprises seriously in need of improving their productivity, technological capabilities, and modern management techniques (RTP 1996).

Despite the sound manufacturing record relative to national standards, Macedonian firms are similar to enterprises in the rest of the country with regard to modern industrial organization. Lean production and quality control systems have been adopted only to a very limited extent by large firms. For example, the region accounts for only 9 percent of the country's ISO 9000 certified enterprises (RTP 1996: 30). Technology infrastructure is limited with respect to industry-driven technology transfer agencies, even though it is well above average in terms of institutions of higher education. Virtually none of the research associations promoted by the state and the Organization for Small and Medium Sized Enterprises in the mid-1980s was established in Northern Greece. A single technology park – composed of a highly skilled institute and an incubator – is struggling to create an identity, and no Business Innovation Centres (BICs) are operational. However, efforts to supplement this gap are now being undertaken, as the next section will demonstrate.

In contrast to Macedonia, Thrace is extremely underdeveloped. Political instability has diminished economic activity, despite a long-standing policy of very high financial incentives. A border region with a strong Muslim minority and a region receiving political refugees of Greek origin from the Commonwealth of Independent States, Thrace has seen its manufacturing activities diminishing constantly, despite very low labor costs.

The institutional environment

Before we turn to the detailed analysis of the strategy and the process, it is important to explain the regional institutional environment. The degree of regional autonomy in Northern Greece was limited as in other Greek regions. Nonetheless, several layers of administration could be distinguished:

1 The Ministry of Northern Greece was created in recognition of the importance of the area, but its authority remained limited since it depended on the central government for its financial resources.

2 In response to the need for regional administration, the country was later divided into 13 artificially[13] created Regional Authorities, including Central Macedonia, Western Macedonia, and Eastern Macedonia and Thrace. The General Secretaries of the regions are political appointees of the central government, although it was foreseen that they would be elected at a later stage.

3 The administrative regions are further divided into prefectures. Prefects were elected for the first time only in the mid-1990s. Budget procedures remain centralized, and despite ongoing plans and efforts on the part of the EU, regional authorities do not have independent budgets or funds.

As a consequence of this structure, regional authorities have very limited negotiating power. Regional authorities evaluate and approve proposals presented by local agents, but they must then recommend projects to the national authorities to assure financial support. Prefectures are responsible for the implementation of work, while city councils are responsible for town-planning. Prefectures, composed of local agents of the national ministries, have budgets for studies and for the implementation of public works. Decisions for the absorption of these resources are taken by the council of each prefecture.

Overall, the public administration has no autonomous status, and freedom of action increases gradually at the various subregional levels. Combined with the general inefficiency of the public sector, no initiatives for changing conventions could be expected. But in parallel with the public administration, collective interests are organized at and represented by two types of bodies, with or without state aid:

1 *Semi-public associations*: Chambers of Commerce and Industry exist in all three regions; there is also a Chamber of Small and Medium Sized Enterprises in Thessaloniki. Their administration is composed of civil servants and their board is elected from among companies. Their original function was to issue licenses and supervise contacts between their members and the state. Traditionally, their lobbying power has been limited, often depending on the personalities of board members rather than on statutory rights. Their role increased after the accession of the country to the EU, as Community funds and initiatives gave them the opportunity to apply for and implement information exchange activities (of the Euro-Info-Centre type, hosting BICs, etc.)

2 *Lobbies*: Two influential voluntary lobbying bodies were created on the initiative of local producers without any state interference, each extending to all three regions of Northern Greece. The Federation of Industries of Northern Greece (hereafter referred to as the Federation), initially representing the larger of local enterprises, later expanded to include SMEs and even very small companies. The Federation is fully autonomous, accountable only to its own general assembly, and depends financially on the participation fees of its members,. The second lobby, the Federation of Exporters of Northern Greece, is generally organized along similar lines.

The Federation played a central role in the effort to promote the idea of regional industrial policy, as described in the following section. It is noteworthy that although the rest of Greek industry is organized into sectoral and regional associations, all represented in the Federation of Greek Industries located in Athens, the industries of Northern Greece do not participate in the

national federation, instead maintaining an independent lobbying and negotiating voice in their dealings with public authorities. As the Greek Federation
is the main partner of the Greek government and trade union discussions, it
may be assumed that the intense efforts of the Federation of Northern Greek
Industries to promote a structural policy were not independent from its need
to find a role for itself.

Three factors ultimately combined to motivate local agents to shape a
strategic vision of economic development: the region's relatively high industrial concentration, particularly in Thessaloniki; the limited existing
infrastructure; and the locational advantages due to the proximity of the
Balkan market.[14] With this as a base, we next describe and then analyze the
initially gradual but ultimately accelerating process by which regional agents,
who originally ignored and mistrusted one another, managed to create an all-
encompassing and effective regional alliance.

NEW STRATEGIES FOR REGIONAL INTERVENTION

This section describes the development and implementation of regional
industrial policy in Northern Greece. It demonstrates how targets and activities grew more ambitious over time, and how accumulated past experiences
influenced and determined further developments. The components and
sequence described here perfectly illustrate the process of institutional learning, and will be used as the basis for a thematic and stylized presentation of
this concept in the next section.

Throughout this presentation, it becomes clear that the driving force
behind this change in industrial cultural was the Federation of Industries of
Northern Greece, which took the initiative to mobilize resources for acting
and learning when the EU funding opportunities appeared.[15] This lobbying
body realized that given the lack of administrative capabilities at the national
and regional levels, a detailed examination of the needs of local industry
could lead them to an original formulation of ways to meet those needs, thus
facilitating the design of local industrial policy in accord with the priorities of
the manufacturing sector. More than that, since local industry would consequently then be able to absorb development funds more rapidly than other
economic sectors or regions that lacked solid preparatory ground, it might
end up with additional funds to those originally foreseen.[16]

The interventions described here contributed to the process of institutional
learning in two ways:

- by distinguishing the institutions of Northern Greece from those in other
  parts of the country; and
- by using past experiences to influence future actions and trigger new initiatives or adjustments in local industrial policy.

Interventions that did not play a substantial role in the differentiation of the
region from the rest of the country are not considered here; these include a

variety of small projects and other activities supported by the EU, such as Euro-Info-Centers and VALUE Relay Centers. Similarly, many regions and companies demonstrated satisfactory performance in terms of isolated promotion actions and individual economic rationale (for example, research institutions in Crete and the BIC in Larissa); but only in Northern Greece does one observe regionally distinct synergies and continuous collective actions covering a wide number of interactions.

One of the earliest important activities was the creation of the *Center for Entrepreneurial and Cultural Development*. In the early 1990s both the European Commission and the Greek government realized that the absorption of regional aid was hampered by the national government's inability to manage an operation of that size. The Commission then strongly promoted the idea of permitting private nonprofit organizations to administer whole programs or measures.[17] This shift towards private sector mobilization would not only have allowed collective interest groups to cooperate with the state to determine how best to exploit the resources of the European Regional Development Fund (ERDF) and the European Social Fund, but it would also have given them an opportunity to participate in the design of industrial strategy at the national, regional, or sectoral level. Although this strategic planning role was welcomed by the most active associations, it never materialized. Whether in order to assure proper financial management, or because state authorities were unwilling to give up their central power, the law that finally passed through the Greek Parliament conceived a different type of organization – an administrator rather than a strategy promoter.[18] While eligible organizations were to be selected by means of calls for proposals, the law and the presidential decree that established the rules of the game introduced a heavy bureaucratic structure with state intervention at every stage of implementation.[19] The Ministry of National Economy was to strongly influence both selection criteria and evaluation.[20] The intermediary was downgraded to a simple administrator, using its skills to follow up grants and managing payments. Two private nonprofit companies were created for this purpose, one by the Greek Federation of Industries and one by the Northern Greek Federation. Each was selected under autonomous calls to administer a number of public programs.

Very little remained from the original effort to change the informal rules whereby collective bodies would actively learn and influence strategy. While the formal rules changed (private nonprofit organizations were now eligible to manage EU regional aid), the conventions remained the same. The state fully maintained its power by creating more accountable but not autonomous partners. The logic was to create a new cash administration. There was no provision under which private companies could learn and adjust in response to the programs they would administer, let alone ultimately be able to design industrial strategy. Consequently, on this point one could not differentiate between the north and the rest of the country; the same opportunities were grasped in the same way. But as a result in Northern Greece, industrialists initiated a persistent search for alternative solutions to meet their original goal.

In 1992 the Federation took a first step towards collective learning by launching and financing the *Strategic Plan for the Development of Macedonia and Thrace* (BCS 1994). This study, jointly and equally financed by the Interreg[21] Community Initiative and the Federation, strongly influenced the design of the National Operational Program for Industry and the Regional Operational Programs for Macedonia and Thrace under the second Community Support Framework (1994–1999). The plan was unique because it was a strategic program suggested by collective industrial interests. Furthermore, the Federation itself took a very active part at a very high level in trying to guide the consultants who implemented it. A steering committee composed of, *inter alia*, the chairman and two vice-chairmen of the Federation, guided and supported the consultants in their work, and was generally acknowledged to have demonstrated a much more active role than the usual rubber-stamping steering committees. Such a study is relatively inexpensive and would have been within the capabilities of and affordable to any industrial lobby, other regional federations, sectoral industrial associations, and certainly the national federation.

But such actions simply did not happen elsewhere. Instead, operational programs tended to be elaborated by consultants following open calls for proposals by the public administration that evaluated the proposals and funded the studies. Although the interests of industry were communicated to the consultants, and the position of the manufacturing sector duly conveyed to national authorities, their voice was only one among others in the design of the proposed intervention. Consequently, their input was minor in comparison to the well-documented contributions of industrialists in Northern Greece. There, the program started with a complete analysis of regional strengths, weaknesses, opportunities, and threats; it then proceeded with a set of well-articulated and documented measures that could be implemented, either within national or regional frameworks, or through other options, such as the Community initiatives. The Northern Greece program indeed gave a head-start to the region and established a reputation for the local industrial federation; in the following years the Federation tried to exploit all opportunities available to implement the totality of the proposals included in the study. The benefit was substantial. The study not only directly and considerably influenced the creation of the regional operational plan (as was its original aim); but it also enhanced the reputation of Central Macedonia as an attractive area for other interventions, both by national and EU authorities. The 50 percent subsidy from Interreg was only a minor incentive in monetary terms, but it was a crucial factor for changing routines, such as convincing the board that such a study could have multiple positive feedbacks, with considerable payoffs relative to the resources committed. Given the positive results achieved thus far, it now seems that conventions have changed; collectivities should not expect state authorities to undertake national or regional planning, but should instead be proactive. Undoubtedly, financial issues should not present a problem in the future, since the mobilization of resources can be solved in several ways, as is described later in this section. But it was unthinkable back in the 1980s that an industrial federation board would have accepted such an approach.

The region's enhanced reputation began to pay off when the European Commission – impressed by the moderate but above average achievements, the commitment, and the documented positions – decided to use Central Macedonia as a pilot region. The Brussels administration was preparing new pilot initiatives that were to be generalized with open calls for tenders under Article 10 of ERDF regulations. The regions for the pilot actions were to be selected all over Europe by agreement between the Commission and the member states. Two pilot actions were initiated at the time, one related to technology policy and the other dealing with the Information Society. The Commission suggested Central Macedonia for both initiatives and the Greek government approved the choice. In addition to the direct benefits of the pilot actions described below, this further enhanced the reputation of Central Macedonia because in no other member state was one region selected for both initiatives. Eventually, Northern Greece came to be recognized even by the national administration as an outstanding region.

The first pilot initiative was the *Regional Technology Program*, which was initiated in four Northern European regions and immediately expanded to four regions in the south. The aim of the program was to strengthen the endogenous technological capabilities of the selected regions and, through consensus-building, to pave the way for a long-term coherent policy involving all relevant agents. The model of management structure used in this initiative was unique in the region; it consisted of a steering committee composed of high-level officials and designed to oversee and approve the direction of the program, while the management unit was composed of researchers and consultants.[22] The public sector was virtually absent in daily management. Delays and friction between public and private interests were noted initially, but they were overcome during the course of events. The consensus-building strategy identified cooperative mechanisms in many areas of common interest, and as a result a good partnership was created. An analysis of the framework of regional technological development was followed by an elaboration of a local strategy; this forged a common vision and resulted in a technology promotion program approved by all local agents. The EU evaluated the Central Macedonian regional technology program as being very successful by European standards. By Greek standards the program had two additional important merits: first, it was the reputation of selected agents that was used to broaden the local partnership; and second, it was the first time an autonomous, transparent, and accountable (not formal) organization was created. Its main disadvantage, the lack of active involvement of the regional authorities in daily management, served as a lesson that was corrected in the initiative described next. Following the philosophy of geographical diffusion of successful programs, an effort is under way to replicate the RTP experience in Western Macedonia.

The other pilot project directly funded by the Commission of the EU was the *Interregional Information Society Initiative*. Six European regions participated in the program, which was established in 1994 to promote universal access to the opportunities and advantages of the Information Society, with a view to generating new employment opportunities, improving the quality of life, and addressing the challenges of structural adjustment and sustainable development. The real aim of the initiative was to help regions prepare the ground by creating strategies, action plans, and feasibility studies, all totally financed by the EU outside of national aid quotas. The expectation was that if and when national finance would be made available, Information Society activities could then be coherently and successfully implemented. The institutional design was similar to that of the technology initiative described above. A steering committee, a regional Information Society unit, and thematic working groups were created, mobilizing all regional agents, this time with a strong commitment on the part of the regional authority, as well as from the local scientific community. Despite the difficult economic situation, Greek academics, both inside and outside the country, have excellent skills that are valuable for basic research and for partnerships with foreign leading edge industries, but which tend to be largely underutilized at local level (as is common in less favored countries). The substantial funds absorbed by the various research teams had created a local know-how that was exploited mostly for publications or transnational collaborations (Tsipouri and Xanthakis 1994). The structure of this initiative provided an opportunity to apply academic knowledge to the benefit of regional development planning. By EU standards, as in the previous case, the overall targets seem to have been achieved. This case thus shows evidence of learning from experience, in particular because for the first time the local administration actively and successfully joined the challenge. The "imposed" coordination fell upon very fertile ground, unploughed by a regional Information Society strategy, but mature enough to benefit from the creation of discussion forums that led to a consensus strategy, no doubt with limitations, but unique in the Greek environment.

The next step was the most ambitious. The failure of the original targets of the private industrial funds management led, as suggested earlier, to an effort to find new ways to conceive and implement an industrial strategy. Experience from the state's approach in the private-nonprofit funds case showed that the federations did not have the power to change formal rules. Consequently, an alliance solution was elaborated, whereby Northern Greek industrialists could share a new vision with other relevant local bodies, trying at the same time to identify new opportunities for financing the initiative. A formal autonomous enterprise was established, the *Association for the Development of Private Infrastructure*. It included not only the regional

Industrial Federation, but also the regional Exporter Federation, the three regional Chambers of Commerce and Industry, the SME Chamber of Thessaloniki, the public agency for SME support, and the regional trade union center – in short, everybody who would be interested in contributing to such a vision. Financial resources were targeted in the form of a direct *Global Grant* from the EU.

The Global Grant is a particular provision in the EU procedure that had not been applied in Greece before.[23] The main idea is that an intermediary organization can receive funds directly (with the EU contribution being subtracted from the total national quota) and manage them according to specific priority orientations agreed to in advance. This means that national authorities see their policy-making power reduced. The new company wanted the direct grant in order to avoid the double administration that had resulted from the original administrative and policy-oriented procedures in the transfer of power from the national authorities to private-nonprofit companies (e.g. the case of the Center for Entrepreneurial and Cultural Development).[24] More importantly, the independent financing was a way of getting a chance to adopt an independent policy and influence state interventions so that a real strategy can ultimately emerge. Again, this was not an easy task, as the Northern Greek agencies had to fight their way through the state bureaucracy. In many cases they had to create formal rules *ex nihilo*, since no precedent existed for the state to transfer part of its rights (to manage EU funds) to a nonpublic organization. The discussions created a strong informal alliance between the local partners and the EU administration, which liked the idea of the grant because of its originality. It was aimed at equal cofinancing of private infrastructures necessary to meet the regional development objectives set by the first strategic plan, modified as necessary by the recent experiences and the gaps left by regional planning. The program of 30 million ECU is one of the larger Global Grants awarded by the EU. Implementation of the program had not yet begun when this chapter was written, but it appears that the major barriers have been overcome and investment can begin. This particular action, which took a long time to materialize, shows that it is possible to increase coordination and include a wide variety of agents once a positive reputation is earned, and past successes promise positive outcomes in the future. It also suggests that by learning from past experiences, obstacles that blocked previous efforts can be overcome. Thus, agents become more ambitious as time goes by and as the new conventions take root.

Along the same lines, the *Inter-Balkan and Black Sea Center* was created as an observatory to identify opportunities and support Greek investors and exporters in the Balkans and neighboring countries. This time financial resources came from the national budget. The initiative was taken by the collective bodies, but the alliance was fully financed by the public investment budget. A majority position for the public agents was required in order to assure the necessary funding; however, this was balanced by important veto and safeguarding clauses added to the statute, to assure minimal direct political intervention, which past experience had indicated could occur at any moment and level of decision-making.

The final activity described in detail refers to the extension of efforts to include Thrace. The benefits of coordination and learning created a new momentum that permitted the expansion of activities beyond the core region of Central Macedonia to its poorer neighbor, Thrace. Since there was no direct public funding opportunity at the moment, a sponsor was found – an investment fund of local shareholders – and a study similar to the one done earlier for Macedonia was commissioned: the *Strategic Plan: Competitive Advantages of Thrace* (BCS 1996). Because the regional operational program of Thrace had already been established, the study included an evaluation of the effectiveness of public policy in the region, as well as an appraisal of the characteristics of the international economic environment, identification of necessary interventions, and a strategy for demonstration and exploitation of the competitive advantages of Thrace. The objectives were thus slightly different from those of the Macedonian study. On one hand, the Thrace plan sought to push coordination beyond the subregion to make the new conventions attractive for agents in neighboring regions. But, perhaps more importantly, the study seemed to indicate that because of the region's enhanced reputation, previous successes, and partnerships, local forces felt strong enough not only to point out solutions but also to criticize the efficiency of government policies. This last point suggests that the Northern Greek partnerships now consider themselves equal partners in discussions with the national government.

An increasing number of initiatives for additional activities are now under way. In our view they constitute the result of new routines. Their nature does not differ from similar initiatives actually thriving throughout the country. These include:

- the creation of local research associations, such as an institute for textiles and an institute for food and beverages;
- a National Institute of Metrology located in Thessaloniki (although this institute seems to suffer from old conventions and inefficiencies of the public administration);
- an information and service network in neighboring regions outside of Central Macedonia;
- the functioning of off-shore companies in the financial sector; and
- continuous education of managers from the Balkan countries in Greek educational establishments.

What differentiates these from similar initiatives in other regions is their local concentration, coherence, and partnership management, with emphasis on the creation of transparent, autonomous, and accountable procedures.

We have no indication of how effective all these initiatives will ultimately be. For our purposes it is important to review what has been accomplished until now, in a way that will permit us to evaluate whether anything has changed, and, if so, how and why.

APPRAISING EFFORTS TO CHANGE CONVENTIONS

This chapter began with a description of recent Greek economic history, emphasizing the stop-and-go character of industrial development and growth, and hence the failure to establish the foundations for sustainable development. The Greek economy can be characterized as having suffered from missed opportunities, in particular during the 1970s and 1980s, engendering a steady deterioration in confidence among economic agents. This increased uncertainty and had the effect of consolidating informal rules that brought the country's manufacturing system into long-lasting difficulties. Northern Greece was no exception to this pattern of intermittent growth and accompanying negative climate for industrial development.

A reversal of this difficult situation began in the 1990s as a consequence of declining factor costs, expanding markets, and new finance opportunities. Although these conditions applied throughout Greece, they were exploited most coherently in Northern Greece, where, as the initiatives analyzed above suggest, they enabled agents to go beyond fragmented measures in an effort to create an industrial strategy. Initiatives undertaken by the collective bodies of industrial interests in Central Macedonia initiated a process that is slowly reducing uncertainty, and which is expanding geographically and becoming increasingly ambitious. This process occurred as a direct consequence of gradual learning and adjusting.

If the future bears out our conclusions, the development of an effective regional industrial strategy in Northern Greece can serve as a valuable lesson. In this section we attempt to generalize the lessons of that experience, and to develop a stylized approach to understanding regional industrial policy. The main issues that we address are:

- the factors that distinguished Northern Greece – and Central Macedonia in particular – from the rest of the country, enabling that particular region to formulate a coherent collective reaction to opportunities, in contrast to the fragmented and individual reactions elsewhere;
- the process that contributed to the success of these initial efforts, particularly the strategy of the agents involved and way in which they overcame the barriers they encountered; and finally
- the achievements in changing current conventions and, more importantly, the sustainability of these changes once current opportunities fade away.

Conditions triggering change

Many reasons can be suggested as to why the North grasped opportunities better than to the rest of the country. We offer four explanations: the prior existence of a critical mass of industrial activities; the absence of even rudimentary technological infrastructure; the proximity to newly emerging markets; and conjectural and personal elements.

The first condition that contributed to the openness of Northern industrialists to collaborative approaches to regional policy was the existence of a *critical mass of manufacturing activity*. The heart of the region, where the conventions first began to change, was already among the most industrialized and profitable areas in the country. Central Macedonia ranked second only to Athens in terms of industrial output, but well ahead of the rest of Greece; in other regions – like Thessaly in Central Greece – where efforts were made to revitalize industry, manufacturing activities were too limited to provide the necessary support for change. But in the north, the relative weight of manufacturing – as compared to tourism or agriculture – reinforced the industrial character of regional development programs.

A very poor regional infrastructure base relative to industrial concentration established the second condition favorable to regional coordination in the north. With respect to infrastructure and other services supporting manufacturing, Northern Greece was quite disadvantaged compared to Athens. In addition to being the heart of industrial and technological activities in the country, the Athens area was also always the center for conventional (hard) and technology (soft) infrastructure. Further, the national ministries managing incentives were concentrated in Athens, and the entire country was served from there. This was also the case with academic activity, which was traditionally located in Athens; when technology policy emerged for the first time in Greece in the mid-1980s, Athens was home to three of the five newly created active research associations, and a fourth was close by. The only technological resources in Northern Greece were the University of Thessaloniki, a technical college, and a university in Thrace that was established 20 years ago with law and medical departments. In other words, the *gap between needs and opportunities* was strongest in Northern Greece.

Geography is a third reason why Central Macedonia took a proactive approach to industrial policy. The Balkan market is so close that small companies (sometimes quite opportunistically) could more easily profit from it. Thus, the opportunity afforded by the opening of the Balkan markets was more pronounced than in the rest of the country. However, the other side of this opportunity was the threat that Northern Greece's predominantly traditional manufacturing activities could relocate to Bulgaria, where labor cost differentials and Phare program incentives are both substantial. Thus, this combination of geography-based threats and opportunities gave Central Macedonia *stronger market messages* than in the rest of the country.[25]

The last, but surely not least important reason is related to *cyclical and personal factors*. Following a decade of open and barely concealed hostility between private industry and the state, the Greek government formally introduced a cooperative and consensus-seeking policy. Restoring confidence is a long-term process, however, and this gesture was taken up with various degrees of caution by individual industrialists and local or sectoral lobbies. In Northern Greece, however, agents responded to the challenge immediately, persistently, and with growing momentum, beginning with well-documented and concrete suggestions. The dedication of the local Federation board members since the late 1980s and their decision to increase the budget in order to employ the necessary human resources, in advance of any concrete results, can be seen as an indicator of personal commitment, quite distinct from the usual positions taken by lobbies elsewhere in Greece. Similarly, semi-public bodies and selected public servants joined the appeal for a regional partnership in an effective and sometimes enthusiastic way. At that stage, the process of change was still quite fragile, and the resistance or opposition of individuals would have been able to halt the process in its infancy.

Process and barriers to change

The process described here spanned about ten years, beginning at a point where agents in the region independently pursued their own targets and interests, and ultimately arriving at a point where most regional agents managed to build alliances with the goal of achieving collective efficiency. A level of trust has been built up and expectations have risen; consequently, one may argue that uncertainty has been reduced.

Our analysis shows that learning by interaction occurred and informal rules were modified: a slow, not very ambitious start on the part of an individual agent, with scattered and unrelated actions; a number of motivating factors may induce the specific responses, including: the presentation of specific opportunities; urgent pressure resulting from new threats to competitive position; or possibly a vision on the part of an agent struggling for a more favorable identity or improved regional, national, or international position. In the case of Northern Greece, the agent was the Federation of Industries; the impetus was a combination of opportunities and a desire to be differentiated from the national Federation of Greek Industries; and the fragmented actions were the development plan of Macedonia and the creation of the first non-profit organization.

These first scattered initiatives may encounter important barriers (financial, internal conflicts of power, external pressures, etc.) that ultimately discourage the pioneer and return him to the initial situation. The initial reputation is important and so are the reactions of other agents or authorities to novel initiatives. Some initiatives may be perceived as coming prematurely, and be met with hostility from other agents who combine to oppose the change; conversely, when change is proposed in a more mature environment where the modernization gap is strongly felt, then individual agents may try to resist it in an effort to defend their own status, while others will support the differentiated initiatives. Opposition by public authorities, especially at high levels, is another possible hurdle, but alternatively, strong commitment from those officials can be a source of important support. Exogenous sources of support can also be important tools to help to alleviate barriers.

In the Greek case the pioneering industrialists encountered a variety of barriers, particularly at the level of the national administration. Examples included the management of structural funds in the first effort to promote regional strategy and the lack of flexibility of national rules. But on the positive side, they benefited from a mature situation, a national government (but not administration) that took their initiatives seriously, and exogenous support from the European Commission which took particular interest in their case. Equally important, the strong top-level commitment on the part of the regional industrial federation helped to overcome resistance from other agents. Indeed, resistance to change seems more often insurmountable at the level of daily practice than at decision-making level. Thus, although enemies were made in the national administration and at regional level, the positive reputation earned by the innovating agents allowed them to gain important allies.[26]

The way in which agents respond to these obstacles and the reactions of others is critical. Institutional learning represents a positive reaction, with the objectives of improving efficiency in the future and creating a vision on which to base further actions. When the reaction to initial barriers is positive, then a more ambitious plan can follow, where visions and strategies take the place of the exploitation of individual opportunities. In this case incentives do not initiate actions, but goals are set and incentives to meet them are sought. This new round is characterized by a search for new opportunities, alliances, and partnerships. This is what happened in Northern Greece. The first hesitant steps, consisting of studies and design of new infrastructure tailored to national incentives gave way to planning wider infrastructure initiatives in alliance with regional agents, which were designed from the very beginning as autonomous and accountable organizations most likely to achieve collective efficiency. The alliances created a new momentum and diminished the internal skepticism of the public authorities. Support was also sought from the local academic sector. The regional technology planning and the strategy for the Information Society reflect the effort to design a vision, while the conception of the Global Grant and the Inter-Balkan and Black Sea Center demonstrate the idea of collective infrastructure according to a new way of thinking. Past learning and interaction with the public authorities in the initial phase taught valuable lessons.

In Northern Greece, innovators learned to become more ambitious and take advantage of the need for change that was being expressed throughout the economy and society. Consequently, this process can be repeated, setting even more ambitious targets, broader alliances, and new initiatives. In the case of Northern Greece, this is represented by the extension of efforts from the core to the periphery of the region.

Anticipating the sustainability of change

The process we have described suggests that in Northern Greece the climate of mistrust has been at least temporarily reversed. In the course of gradually increasing ambitions and concrete successes, local agents reached a consensus that did not exist previously. As a result, conventions are gradually changing, although formal rules remain largely unchanged.

The description of the efforts undertaken demonstrates that many self-help initiatives are in the process of being implemented or planned. Unlike previous efforts in Greece, they are based on a satisfactory degree of local consensus, with private-sector agents playing an important role. The new institutions are designed to be autonomously managed but fully accountable, avoiding the burden of public bureaucracy.

At this point it is too early to evaluate the impact of these changes using quantifiable regional development indicators. Most of the initiatives already implemented are of too modest a scale to substantially affect industrial competitiveness and economic growth. The major projects, the Global Grant and the Inter-Balkan and Black Sea Center, are approved but not operational. The next challenge is to build on this momentum of change and trust-building, over a reasonable time horizon. Once the initial opportunities have faded away, can the planned initiatives continue to create and improve collective efficiency, leading to continued and more rapid regional development in Northern Greece? Ultimately, we will be able to confirm the significance of this model of gradual change of conventions only if the institutional changes are sustained and quantitative analysis proves positive economic results.

There is no doubt that important steps remain to be taken before real success in terms of productivity and competitiveness is achieved. But this case demonstrates that conventions can begin to change in the medium term even in an initially unfavorable environment. If adequately designed and with strong messages, these changes may be brought about even more rapidly than previous research has suggested.

NOTES

1 I want to thank Stavros Thomadakis for very constructive comments on an early version of this chapter. I also want to thank Mr Tassos Alexandridis and Mr Jiannis Stavrou very much for their support and advice in identifying relevant sources and clarifying facts for me, which could not be found in the literature. I should also state that the author of this chapter was born, lives, and works in Southern Greece. As a consequence, I hope that the positive examples stated will not be misunderstood to reflect local patriotism.
2 The term "subnational" refers to regions within a country, and it is in this sense that we use the terms "region" and "regional."
3 The government was politically stable during the 1980s but went through a period of hostility against manufacturing profits and high salary increases that deteriorated wage productivity and led to an austerity program in favor of stabilization; the end of the 1980s was characterized by three consecutive elections within one year; and the government at the beginning of the 1990s had a one-vote majority.

4 Recently, stronger incentives were designed for the most depressed areas within the country, but this does not affect the period we are studying.
5 According to the International Competitiveness Report of the Davos Forum, Greece has been competing with Turkey for last place throughout the last decade.
6 Afonso Fleury (1995) identifies exactly the same problem for Brazil when he suggests that instead of investing in technological capabilities, firms channeled their efforts into political lobbies aimed at negotiating taxes and subsidies.
7 See, for instance, the weekly newspaper *To Vima*, August 4, 1996.
8 On the other hand, a historic review demonstrates that in earlier periods investments took into consideration national or collective interests in Greece (Chatziiossif 1993). This suggests that conventions deteriorated in the post-war years.
9 Kastoria, a prefecture in Western Macedonia, was a classical industrial district specializing in fur production and trade, particularly famous for the very skilled work in sewing fur parts together; the local industry was not able to adjust to new international conditions (new machinery and globalization of both production and trade) and saw its competitive advantage erode very rapidly.
10 This has been explained by Hubert Schmitz (1995), who suggests that high differentiation renders collective action more difficult.
11 Surveys of the barriers to direct foreign investment rate the unstable regulatory framework as one of the major hurdles for multinationals. In Greece, it is often stated that the only law necessary to stabilize the economic environment would be one requiring compliance with existing laws.
12 The service sector in Greece is characterized by a high share of banking, insurance, and public administration, while modern high-tech services are very limited.
13 Artificial here means that the EU and the Greek government decided to split the country administratively into regions able to submit coherent development plans.
14 The Balkan market presents a most important opportunity for Northern Greece, since Thessaloniki is closer (by highway) to Sophia than to Athens.
15 It is not yet clear whether learning or action came first, but it appears that action based on intuition and previous knowledge of Federation members preceded institutional learning. What is important though, is that in Northern Greece learning did emerge and accelerate, while elsewhere, fragmented action failed to trigger institutional learning.
16 The process of the distribution of the CSF foresees internal shifts of funds when areas or sectors are unable to implement what was initially approved.
17 The design role was kept in the hands of public authorities, since measures are adopted under the famous partnership principle that was originally conceived by the state and then approved by the EU.
18 It is worth mentioning that although a Christian-Democratic government was in power at the time, the law did not receive a majority the first time it was presented in Parliament. Strong EU and party political pressure were exercised to have an amended version voted on a few months later. The explanation given in the press at the time related to the reluctance of the public sector to grant management authority of EU funds to the private sector (even if nonprofit).
19 Law 1961/91 and presidential decree 114/82 set up the rules on how the Ministry of National Economy could entrust the management of EU funds to nonpublic bodies.
20 Four out of six representatives in the regulatory committee were appointed by the Ministry, one by the EU, and one only by the implementing organization.
21 One of the ERDF Initiatives that offer financial support in areas selected by the Commission, independently of the CSFs.
22 The steering committee included the Minister of Northern Greece, the General Secretary of the Regional Authority, the Chairman of the Federation, and most other relevant agents.

23 The Global Grant has been mainly used by Spain, France, and Italy (typical beneficiaries being regional authorities, ANVAR, and the Confindustria), with the classical promotion of grants aimed at improving return of investment for SMEs or venture capital type support.

24 The company was formally created in April 1995, with a 12 member board, the chairmanship alternating between the Federation of Industries of Northern Greece and the Federation of Exporters. A regional assembly meeting twice a year is the supreme authority and an investment committee is responsible to the board for selecting investment proposals.

25 In the Hirschmannian sense the amplification of market messages is the best way to trigger economic development.

26 In the sense of "no prophet in his own country," people in Central Macedonia claim that their reputation is better outside than inside the region.

REFERENCES

Alogoskoufis, G. (1993) "Growth, inflation rate and balance of payments in Greece: the long term role of economic policy," in G. Alogoskoufis *et al. Macroeconomic Management and the Blocking of Development*, Athens: Gutenberg.

BCS (1994) *Strategic Plan for the Development of Macedonia and Thrace: Industry as an Engine for Development*, A report submitted to the Federation of Industries of Northern Greece, Thessaloniki, Mimeographed.

—— (1996) *Strategic Plan: Competitive Advantages of Thrace*, A report submitted to the Federation of Industries of Northern Greece, Thessaloniki, Mimeographed.

Brisco, S. (1990) "The idea of the industrial district: its genesis," in F. Pyke, G. Becattini, and W. Sengenberger (eds) *Industrial Districts and the Inter-firm Cooperation in Italy*, Geneva: International Institute of Labor Studies.

Chatziiossif, C. (1993) *The Old Moon: Industry in the Greek Economy*, Athens: Themelio.

Commission of the EU (1995) *Observatory of SMEs*, Luxembourg: Publication Office of the EU.

Dertilis, G. (1984) *Greek Economy and Industrial Revolution*, Athens: Exandas.

Fleury, A. (1995) "Quality and productivity in the competitive strategies of Brazilian industrial enterprises," *World Development* 23, 1: 78.

Giannitsis, T. (1984), *International Specialization and Division of Labour between Greece and Newly Industrializing Countries*, Athens: KEPE.

—— (1985) *The Greek Industry, Development and Crisis*, Athens: Gutenberg.

Giannitsis, T. and Mavri, D. (1993) *Technological Structures and Technology Transfer in Greek Manufacturing*, Athens: Gutenberg.

Kevin, M. (1996) "The evaluation of the IRIS initiative in Central Macedonia," Cardiff University, A report submitted to the Commission of the EU, DG XVI, Mimeographed.

Mitsos, A. (1989) *The Greek Industry in the International Market*, Athens: Themelio.

Rabellotti, R. (1995) "Is there an 'Industrial District Model'? Footwear districts in Italy and Mexico compared," *World Development* 23, 1: 29–41.

RTP of Central Macedonia (1996) *Interim Report* (April), Mimeographed.

Schmitz, H. (1990) "Small firms and flexible specialization in developing countries," *Labor and Society* 15, 3: 257–285.

—— (1995) "Small shoemakers and Fordist giants: tale of a supercluster," *World Development* 23, 1: 9–28.

Sugden, R., Pitelis, C., and Tsipouri, L. (1996) "Outward investment, international competitiveness and industrial development," in P. Devine, Y. Katsoulakos, and R. Sugden (eds) *Competitiveness, Subsidiarity and Industrial Policy*, London and New York: Routledge.

Thomadakis, S. B. (1996) "Greek economic performance: puzzles, prospects and requirements," *XXXXX* 30: 2–3.

—— (1997) "The Greek economy: performance, expectations and paradoxes," in A. T. Graham and K. Nikolaides (eds), *The Greek Paradox: Promise versus Performance*, Cambridge, MA: MIT Press.

Tsipouri, L. and Xanthakis, M. (1994) "Impact of the EU R&D policies in the Greek RTD policy," Center of Financial Studies, University of Athens, Mimeographed.

Vaitsos, K. and Giannitsis, T. (1987) *Technological Transformation and Economic Development*, Athens: Gutenberg.

Xanthakis, M. (1989) *The Crisis of Greek Manufacturing and the State Intervention*, Athens: Papazissis.

Zolotas, X. (1926) *Greece in the Phase of Industrialization*, Athens: Eleftheroudakis.

12 Inward investment in Central and Eastern Europe

The compatibility of objectives and the need for an industrial strategy

David Bailey, Roger Sugden, and Rachael Thomas[1]

INTRODUCTION

Following the demise of state socialism in Central and Eastern Europe from 1989, a glut of literature has emerged dealing with the region's transition to a market-based economy and advising on how best to achieve the metamorphosis. Much commentary has stressed the importance of integrating the region into the global economy, emphasizing the view that investment by foreign transnationals could play a significant role in assisting these late-comers to develop. For example, the EBRD in its 1995 *Transition Report* states, "foreign direct investment and partnership can carry great benefits in providing market skills, management, technology and finance, as well as effective corporate governance." In line with this, many countries in the region established agencies to "woo" transnational investors. Furthermore, stress was laid on the initial attraction of all and any investment, rather than the effective utilization of investment for the appropriate economic development of the domestic economy.

That the region needed to make a transition from the centrally administered economies of state socialism is not disputed in this chapter. Instead, the discussion focuses on whether policy towards inward investment has been appropriate for assisting governments to achieve their objectives. It appears that in some overall sense governments have desired a free market economy. However, in the face of transnational activities, what would it mean to have such a free market system? Would the introduction of such a system have repercussions for the specific objectives governments have set themselves? Even if such a system would be preferable to the one it replaced, might governments be able to pursue more imaginative policies with yet higher benefits? These are the sorts of questions that will be considered in this chapter. In doing so we consider the differing motives of both inward investors and host governments in the region, and the compatibility of these objectives.

This chapter is an extension, in the context of the specific case of Central and Eastern Europe, of the corporate versus industrial strategy issue discussed more widely and more generally by Cowling and Sugden (1993, 1994). We explore the differences between strategies for industrial development conceived by and in the interests of strategic decision-makers within large transnational corporations on the one hand, and strategies devised by and in the interests of a wider set of agents in the community on the other.

A traditional economic view of issues of industrial development is the industrial policy approach rooted in the concept of market failure. According to Sawyer (1992), "the role of government can . . . be seen as the correction of 'market failure', either through the implementation of perfect competition or through the regulation of prices, profit rates, etc." A crude and simple form of this argument is as follows: in theory a complete set of perfectly competitive markets yields Pareto efficient outcomes; in practice a market system may not be characterized by omnipresent perfect competition, hence it may not yield efficient outcomes; thus the role of government is to correct for this failure by introducing perfect competition or by alleviating the consequences of imperfect competition. This is an industrial policy analysis centered on markets and an analysis that we will argue is consistent with policies adopted by Central and East European governments in seeking inward investors. In devising their policies, Central and East European governments have naturally looked to the West for assistance. However, this brings with it two sets of problems. First, there is a question mark as to whether Western-style policies are adequate to correct for such market failures as the existence of monopolies. Second, the application of Western-style policies in the East may not be appropriate given the region's inheritance, such as the severe monopoly problems left over from state planning.

In contrast, Cowling and Sugden (1993) center their analysis on the concept of strategic decision-making. Their basic reasoning is as follows:

- Modern free market economies are dominated by large, transnational corporations;
- these global giants formulate and implement corporate strategies to further their own objectives;
- these objectives may cut across the wider interests of various agents in different economies;
- one consequence of the complete freedom that corporations have to pursue their own strategies is the development of free market economies characterized by inherent deficiencies, including problems of product market monopolization, distorted technological change, subverted international trade, and unemployment;
- the response to these deficiencies should be a recognition that strategic planning of industrial activity plays a key role in industrial development and that it must be a core element of government economic policy;
- such strategic planning is in many respects diametrically opposite to the sort of central planning that used to characterize the economies of Central and Eastern Europe.

In other words, it is suggested that governments should focus on ways in which entire communities could pursue their own objectives by formulating and implementing their own strategies, rather than leaving the strategic planning of industrial activity to the global giants. Assuming that a government acts only in the interests of the community it serves and that there are no problems of agency (not an unproblematic assumption, as Cowling and Sugden observe), one interpretation of this suggestion is that a government should pursue community interests by formulating and implementing its own industrial strategy, rather than consigning economic development to the dictates of corporate strategies. Our analysis can be seen as an exploration of this possibility. More specifically, we focus on why an industrial strategy may be advisable, as against a consideration of possible components of that strategy.

The body of the chapter is essentially a review of earlier literature concerned with the role of foreign investment in Central and Eastern Europe. The review is not meant to be comprehensive; our interest is in raising some useful ideas and thoughts, rather than in providing a detailed and up-to-date survey of the literature. The first and second sections discuss, respectively, the motives of transnationals investing in the region and the objectives of governments pursuing such investors. The aim is to draw a picture encompassing transnationals and governments generally, which is not to deny that there will be exceptions for particular firms and particular countries at specific points in time; we attempt to cut through such details, although examples are given to illustrate particular points. The compatibility between transnational motives and government objectives is the subject of the third section, and it is here in particular that we attempt to differentiate between corporate and industrial strategies. Some general conclusions are drawn in the final section.

CORPORATE STRATEGIES: THE OBJECTIVES OF TRANSNATIONALS INVESTING IN CENTRAL AND EASTERN EUROPE

While the motives for transnational investments have been well documented,[2] Radice (1993) suggests two principal motives specific to Central and Eastern Europe that have generally influenced transnational investment in the region, namely market share and low labor costs. Both motives were exhibited by General Electric's investment in the Hungarian light bulb manufacturer Tungsram:

> General Electric (GE) acquired 50 percent of Tungsram who already had 7 percent of the West European market. As much as 70 percent of Tungsram's annual share of this market was shipped to the West from its Hungarian factories where the cost of producing light bulbs was reported to be 30 percent less than in Western Europe – due in part to the fact that wages were one-tenth of those paid in the US. Added to GE's 2 percent share before the acquisition, this gave GE 9 percent of the market, making it third amongst its West European competitors.
>
> (*Business Week*, July 30, 1990)

Related to this is the suggestion that, in entering the market, an investor may desire to preempt competitors by being a first-mover and acquiring a dominant position.

Market share

The prospect of gaining market share has been suggested as a primary objective for investment in the Central and East European region due to both the maturing state of most Western markets and the potential of reaching 420 million Central and East European consumers. Hamilton and Adjubei (1991) suggest that "the growth potential and prospects for sales are huge . . . bucking the trend of Western markets." Given the region's historical emphasis on heavy industry and the shortages resulting from the collapse of the CMEA,[3] some investors perceive a potential outlet for almost any product or service. Marketing costs are slight compared to the intensity felt in oligopolistic Western markets, and the weakness of indigenous industry in the face of transnational resources has helped to secure high market shares for foreign investors in many industries. Dunning (1994) suggests that the potential for transnational investment is nearly infinite, with opportunities existing in various sectors from consumer goods and business services to industrial equipment. The rush by Western tobacco transnationals to the East is a particularly vivid example. In the West, such firms face stagnating demand amidst increasing health worries and restrictions on advertising, while in the East there awaits an enormous market (already larger than that in the US or Western Europe) with market entry facilitated through the privatization process. For example, Philip Morris paid $400 million for its stake in Tabak, the Czech state cigarette monopoly, giving it 80 percent of the Czech market; the firm has also acquired several other cigarette producers in the region (*The Economist*, August 21, 1993).

Additionally, the relative backwardness of the region's industry in even the most basic consumer and durable goods suggested that transnationals did not even have to produce world-class products in order to gain market share. Lines of production whose life cycle had long since expired, or whose production was no longer deemed profitable in Western markets, could be effectively transferred to Central and Eastern Europe. Examples of this include car manufacturer Renault moving production of its obsolescent Renault 5 model to Yugoslavia (before the civil war started) and Rover assembling the aged Maestro model in Bulgaria. One benefit for transnationals arising from the backwardness of Central and East European manufacturing has been that maturing or obsolete lines of production – so-called cash cows – could be profitably milked in the new markets of the region. Host governments, eager to soak up foreign investment, permitted technically backward investment to take place, consequently limiting the region's ability to achieve long-term development due to the reliance on imports of outdated technology.[4]

While certain industries in some Central and East European countries might be attractive to transnational investors in their own right, the size of the region as a whole and its proximity to the rest of the European Union must also be considered as motives for investment. It would be misleading to talk of Central and Eastern Europe as a single market, and since the demise of the CMEA in 1991 there has been a distinct lack of common mechanisms linking the countries. Dobosiewicz (1992) notes that many transnationals have been investing in one country as a springboard to penetrate neighboring countries: "the common view is held that it is easier to export to East European countries from within the region than from outside it." This is confirmed by the results of surveys of foreign investors, nearly all of whom stress access to domestic and regional markets as the key attraction (see EBRD 1994 for summaries of different surveys).

It has been suggested that transnationals following such a strategy seek to establish market share quickly, without incurring much risk or having to establish physical investment in every country they enter. Hence, the development of distribution networks, warehousing facilities, and wholesaling has become common practice as a means of exploring or entering neighboring markets,[5] and many investments made in the region merely involve the marketing and distribution of products imported from transnationals' other plants. For example, Jolly (1994) cites the case of SmithKline Beecham, the major transnational pharmaceutical company, which considered the costs of investing in Poland to be amongst the lowest in the world. Hence nine new foreign brands were being promoted in Poland alongside Central and East European brands in 1992, although usage was only two-thirds that of the UK. SmithKline Beecham's first priority was apparently to establish its distribution channels before setting up a manufacturing plant for its Aquafresh brand.[6]

One repercussion of the use of distribution networks was that transnationals had easy access to market share without making any initial physical investment in manufacturing assets, hence possibly denying a country employment and development benefits.[7] Marton (1993) suggests that transnationals "designed strategies that reduce their exposure whilst permitting them to capture maximum market share." Tertiary investments offered little in terms of technology or production, therefore there was insufficient opportunity for the host country to learn best-practice methods or transfer technology.

In the aggregate, transnationals seeking to establish market share across the entire region appeared to have had little incentive to establish manufacturing facilities in each country. Indeed, given the centripetalism that Cowling and Sugden (1994) argue is inherent in transnational-led economic development, it seems unlikely that manufacturing facilities would be equitably distributed across the region. Instead, certain cities or countries would be favored over others and used to supply Central and East European countries.[8] Therefore it is implied that actual spin-off benefits derived from transnational investment would at best be limited in geographical terms and may serve to reinforce existing regional disparities.[9]

Drawing on this, it can be argued that insofar as there has been free trade, a transnational's global strategy removes the necessity for manufacturing in Central and Eastern Europe *per se*. With international manufacturing operations, the Central and East European market can be supplied from any manufacturing site outside the region, using distribution networks to maximize market coverage. Where local manufacturing has taken place, this has been determined as part of the transnational's corporate strategy to gain advantage over its rivals and obtain maximum global power.

Attempting to gain such an advantage over rivals is a motivation for market entry by transnationals in the first place. While the region's market is potentially enormous, Marton (1993) recognizes that "in several product areas, the relatively small size of the (national) market can only sustain a few enterprises . . . [hence] . . . transnationals have invested in local manufacture in order to preempt the market from a competing transnational." The most obvious route is through the purchase of state monopolies. However, *greenfield investments* are also often similarly oriented; for example, Marton (1993) refers to Suzuki's and GM's greenfield investments in Hungary, in part designed to deter competitors' entry, and similar oligopolistic behavior in the publishing sector.

Further illustration of the nature of incoming transnationals' rent-seeking behavior is given by their success in negotiating packages of assistance from governments that seem to guarantee them continued dominant positions into the future. Trade policy in particular has been subverted toward such goals, despite the provisions of the Europe Agreements with the Visegrad countries reducing the scope for trade protection. For example, Poland raised its tariff on imported new cars from 15 percent to 35 percent in 1991, reportedly because GM made this a condition of its $75 million investment in FSO (see EBRD 1994).

Indeed, negotiators for incoming transnationals looking to acquire assets know that they are in a strong bargaining position because of the desire of host governments to raise cash through asset sales. The soft budget constraint may thus be replaced by a rent-seeking society where political positioning and effective lobbying can substitute for economic adjustment (EBRD 1994). The capture of aspects of governments' industrial policies by transnationals may therefore thwart other government goals such as fostering competition (see below).

Labor costs

Shifting the focus from market share to take a broader view of transnationals' objectives, a second motive for entering Central and Eastern Europe has been the pool of cheap, well-educated labor; Eastern Europe appears to be ideally suited for setting up the production of labor intensive goods when to produce such goods in the high wage countries of the West is no longer profitable (Donges and Wieners 1994). In this regard the transnationals' focus is squarely on using the region's cheap labor markets to create a global strategic advantage over other transnationals and, in doing so, increasing market power in other regions. Again, this view is supported by survey evidence which report that low labor costs are important for investors, although much less so than market access (see EBRD 1994: Table 9.4). For example, Triplex Lloyd has taken a 50 percent stake in a castings plant in the Czech Republic, hoping that low labor costs will enable it to compete with Southeast Asian firms that have captured the lower end of the castings market in Western Europe (Merrit 1991).

In line with this, Radice (1994) suggests that Central and Eastern Europe could be a strategic base for European or world markets in labor-intensive operations, "investment being primarily export oriented and aimed at supplying Western markets." Central and Eastern Europe, Radice implies, should follow the development path pursued by the Southeast Asian region; given that wage levels in Central and Eastern Europe are as low as 10 percent of European Union levels,[10] and that the region was historically linked to manufacturing (albeit often using obsolete technology), he suggests that one possible future advantage lies in labor-intensive niche markets such as component manufacture and investment goods.

Thus, it has been suggested that while a transnational might seek to obtain competitive advantage in Central and East European markets by securing market share, a global strategic advantage might be gained through utilizing the region's low labor costs. Generalizing more widely, it may also be argued that while both market share and cheap labor provide impetus to the investment decision, it is unlikely that any investment will be undertaken without ascertaining how the strategic position of the firm is affected. Whichever motive presides, the underlying purpose of any investment will be to enhance the strategic position and hence global power of the firm.

Consequently, Central and East European governments should perceive locally based affiliates as only one component of a transnational's global strategy. As such, "Western . . . multinationals are unlikely to treat their East European affiliates as stand alone ventures, but to treat them as part and parcel of a Pan-European or even international network of activities" (Dunning 1993). The functional and organizational strategies of East European investments are dictated by the interests of foreign investing firms; therefore, while local affiliates are practically guaranteed to contribute to the enhancement of the transnational's global position – assuming accurate assessments by the transnational – their contribution to the advancement of the host country's interests is far less assured. This suggests that transnational affiliates in individual countries need not produce sizeable returns,[11] utilize high-technology production, or generate exports if these are secured elsewhere. Hence, the relationship between inward investment and accrued benefits becomes less assured. For example, Ford's $80 million investment in

Hungary was not expected to yield the company any significant direct return in Hungary; the attraction lay in the prospect of supplies of cheap parts for its plants in Western Europe and in making those plants more competitive (Dobosiewicz 1992).[12]

LACK OF GOVERNMENT STRATEGIES: THE OBJECTIVES OF CENTRAL AND EAST EUROPEAN GOVERNMENTS SEEKING FOREIGN INVESTMENT

Given the issues facing Central and Eastern Europe – the deteriorating capital stock, the need to rebuild infrastructure, and the intention to move from central administration to a market-based economy – government objectives in seeking foreign investment are extensive.[13] Against this background, the objectives discussed below represent an attempt to generalize some of the more evident motives, while recognizing that the significance attached to each will differ among governments, and that more specific objectives exist in different countries (e.g. a desire to raise revenue through privatization sales to foreign investors or the desire to generate employment).

Technology transfer and modernization

Technology transfer has long been a motivating factor for attracting foreign investment, not least because of the slow rate of technological development of the region, and thus its impact on industry and the wider economy. Central and East European governments have recognized that in opening up the region to foreign competition, the relative technological backwardness of the region has automatically handicapped the ability of domestic industry to compete. Given the apparent historical inability of the state, or even of a growing private sector, to mobilize capital effectively and to establish a domestic technology base, one view has been that foreign investors are needed. However, the alternative of using foreign investors alongside indigenous or government organizations to engender development has not been so readily considered.[14] It is perhaps salutary to bear in mind Inzelt's (1994) finding that, "foreign companies, in taking over Hungarian firms, tend to cut back R&D expenditure, and to centralize all basic R&D activity in their main, Western, locations, leaving their Hungarian research workers to do purely routine work."[15]

Radice (1993) articulates the standard view that "trade competitiveness is seen to depend on the acquisition of the latest technologies which in turn are owned by transnationals," suggesting that a transnational presence is necessary to secure the latest technologies for domestic development. Cantwell (1994) takes the view that the pace of product innovation and technological development originating all over the world has necessitated international linkages due to the high cost of innovation and short product cycles, the argument being that "nationalistic isolation is a recipe for economic backwardness."

Transnationals are thus seen as vehicles for integration into the global (and particularly the European) economy. Whether or not governments understand the likely effects of such linkages is a different matter. For example, many transnationals' operations (including joint ventures) in Hungary are little more than "screwdriver" operations (Okolicsanyi 1993), such as GM's Opel Astra plant which simply assembles complete knock-down kits imported from Western Europe (Ettlie 1993). Not surprisingly, it has been reported that Hungary's pattern of trade has shifted toward one similar to that of the poorer EU nations in Southern Europe, importing semi-finished products that are processed or assembled and then reexported (Okolicsanyi 1993).

Moreover, the needs of the region have grown beyond technical and capital infusion; in order to make the successful transition to a competitive economy and with a view to developing export markets, governments have hoped (rather than ensured) that modern techniques ranging from managerial and marketing skills to production methods would accompany the transfer of technology.[16] Merrit (1991) supports this approach, drawing on the example of Southeast Asia's so-called Four Tigers, which he sees as having successfully utilized Western technology in order to industrialize and become competitive in the world market. Yet Merrit's "imported industrialization," courtesy of the "transnational package," naively suggests that development and foreign investment are linked inseparably. He fails to recognize the proactive strategy of Asian governments that used foreign technology to empower domestic industry, sometimes heavily curtailing foreign direct investment (FDI) so as to give domestic firms time to develop, as in South Korea's case.

Both Radice and Cantwell suggest that without the involvement of transnational firms, at least with respect to technology and modernization, Central and Eastern Europe cannot hope to compete with other nations. It has thus been suggested that while foreign involvement might be an integral part of economic development, in no way should it be implied that foreign investment is a crucial qualification;[17] countries such as Japan have, in the past, sustained rapid development with little foreign investment but with substantial foreign involvement coordinated by the government.[18] Along these lines, Cantwell (1994) argues that given the lack of infrastructure, the absence of a locally competitive environment, and the weakness of indigenous companies, FDI may not be the ideal means by which to industrialize. Following the example of Japan, he suggests that a more effective and controlled means of acquiring technology and know-how may be through the use of joint ventures.

While genuine joint ventures offer a more controlled means of acquiring technology, Dobosiewicz (1992) emphasizes the need for mechanisms to ensure that governments have some degree of control over the quality of technology that is acquired. He infers that while technology transferred might be more modern than previously used, and hence might reduce the development lag between countries, "it is not a long-run solution as the lag still exists."[19] The lag would be reduced or surmounted only if the technology imported was planned or controlled to meet some wider government strategy and was of a quality that domestic entrepreneurs were able to utilize to build sustainable competitive advantage. Dunning (1994) notes the strategy followed by Japan as a singular example,[20] where the technology imported and licensed throughout the 1950–1960s was targeted and specific, not a Western cast-off. By utilizing and further developing imported or licensed technology, Japan's domestic industry was able to compete on the world market. It is clear that Japan did not succeed by inward investment alone.[21]

The Japanese industrial modernization experience yields two lessons for Central and Eastern Europe: first, industrialization was not directly the result of foreign involvement *per se* – instead it was partly attributable to the type of involvement that took place; second, inward investment was used by domestic entrepreneurs to the advantage of indigenous industry.

While Central and Eastern Europe might learn from the Japanese example, caution must be exercised when comparing modernization experiences from other regions or countries. For example, the quantity and quality of entrepreneurs who adapt imported technology and know-how in order to become competitive in domestic and international markets cannot be taken as given in Central and Eastern Europe.[22] Radice (1994) takes the view that Central and Eastern Europe "lacks not only capital but capitalist entrepreneurs,"[23] and suggests that the success of Central and Eastern Europe in utilizing foreign investment to industrialize depends on the development of an entrepreneurial culture. Given the overhang of 50 years of central administration, it seems unlikely that the number of entrepreneurs needed is merely waiting in the wings. Hence, it is suggested that while arbitrary uncoordinated investment might not achieve government objectives of technology transfer or modernization, neither is domestic industry capable of realizing this objective without the use of transnational involvement.

Competition and the introduction of market forces

It has also been suggested by Central and East European governments that foreign investment can be a means of introducing greater competition into their domestic economies. Traditionally, Central and East European industry has been very concentrated due to the monopolies and informal cartels created by state-owned industry. Low productivity, overmanning, and inferior quality have all been tolerated through the system of central administration. Dobosiewicz (1992) notes that by acting as role models for indigenous companies, transnationals' "superior efficiency, productivity and profitability creates a potent 'demonstration effect';" this forces domestic firms to emulate transnational standards in order to remain in business, and implies that they must evolve over time to compete with transnationals for domestic market share.

Foreign investment has thus been perceived as a means through which favorable market forces might be introduced, assuming that superior efficiency, productivity, and profitability is achievable for indigenous industry.

On the other hand, indigenous industries could be "overwhelmed by superior technology, quality or marketing" (Radice 1994) and fail to reach such standards, so that introducing rival producers into the region consequently displaces domestic firms from the market. Although Radice suggests that domestic producers might survive in the long term by imitation, and input suppliers might develop to meet the investors' requirements, he implies that it is generally misguided to assume that transnationals would induce favorable competition with indigenous firms.

In contrast to this, Merrit (1991) suggests that the ethos of "only the strong survive" has been "in aggregate no bad thing" for the restructuring of the region's economies, arguing that "better and more efficient producers drive out the bad." However, it is worth noting that Merrit takes little account of where market restructuring takes place, or of the aggregate effect on regional development. The introduction of transnational firms into the domestic economy can have repercussions for both large- and small-scale indigenous firms, although the anticipated restructuring would have more serious repercussions for the latter. The inherited post-Communist private sector consisted of a large number of small firms, arguably few of which could survive against the resources of the transnationals. However, alongside the private sector are huge state-owned giants, comprising 80 percent of most Central and East European economies; whether remaining under state ownership or transferred to the private sector, by virtue of their size and resources few of these enterprises would be forced to leave the market when faced with transnational competition. Hence, the impact on large industry is likely to be less sizeable. The introduction of transnational investment into the Central and East European economies could thus result in changes in the structure of industry, though whether these changes would be the result of the intended competition between firms is less clear. Small-scale industry could be swallowed by foreign transnationals or could be forced to leave the market by transnational activity, increasing the region's emphasis on large firms as the basis for its economic development.

What has tended to happen is that many small firms in the region have entered into joint ventures with West European firms (which in the process have become transnationals), with the latter usually the dominant partners and increasingly able to influence decision-making (see Wang 1993). This is a potential problem because the objectives of foreign and domestic firms entering joint ventures differ, as a survey by Deloitte Touche Ross International has suggested (EBRD 1994). Foreign firms look for market knowledge and access along with tax advantages, whereas domestic firms seek new capital, technology, products, and training. These differing objectives may not coincide, especially if the Western partner can dominate strategic decision-making, as increasingly seems the case. Hence, there is a question mark over the compatibility not only between transnational and government objectives (which we explore below), but also between the objectives of transnationals and domestic firms. Given both this imbalance of power and the congruence between the interests of government and domestic firms in issues such as technology transfer and new product development, this suggests a positive role for government intervention in support of the objectives of domestic firms. Consequently, while there is a strategy triangle among transnationals, governments, and domestic firms, the interests of indigenous enterprises ought to be considered as an important subset of the broader community interest[24] that Central and East European governments should be pursuing as part of their industrial strategy.[25]

Ellman (1992) suggests that "the development of a large number of medium and small enterprises will be an important part of the structural change process . . . [given that] . . . the traditional absence of both foreign competition and the possibility of entry of domestic competitors, creates a monopolist's dream." However, the extreme monopolization of industry in the Communist era has made the transition to a competitive market economy very difficult; as a result, the market forces injected into the economy by foreign investment might serve only to reinforce the existing oligopolistic structure of the domestic economy.

Privatization

At the forefront of the transition process to a free market economy has been the eagerness of most Central and East European governments to introduce widespread privatization programs, aimed at reducing the level of involvement of the state as an owner, from approximately 80–90 percent to 20–30 percent (Alter and Wehrle 1993). It has been suggested that "without converting a substantial part of state property of productive assets into private ownership, the market economy cannot emerge" (Donges and Wieners 1994).

Dobosiewicz (1992) identifies what he perceives to be a vital role for foreign investment in the process,[26] and in doing so suggests the existence of a feedback relationship between privatization and foreign investment. He first asserts that foreign investment creates greater momentum in the privatization process by supplying the capital necessary to purchase enterprises. Then he claims that privatization itself creates more normal market conditions, attracting additional foreign investors who would otherwise be reluctant to enter state-dominated industry.[27]

With regards to the role of foreign investment in supplying capital to the market, Hunya (1992) argues that "privatization projects in Central and Eastern Europe must rely to a large extent on foreign capital because internal savings comprise only a small part of the value of assets to be privatised and governments do not want to wait until domestic capital accumulates." In order to assess the need for foreign investment, it is useful to distinguish between the different types of privatization. While the sale of land and small- to medium-sized enterprises (SMEs) has been sizeable, with the majority of transfers taking place at the domestic level, domestic capital has been less forthcoming in the privatization of large firms. Given the fundamental lack of funds and management experience, it appears that domestic entrepreneurs have also been reluctant to accept the risks inherent in large-scale privatization.

If the objective of any Central and East European government was to retain domestic ownership (although to the best of our knowledge this has not been argued by any of the governments themselves), the small-scale privatization achieved thus far might be regarded as successful since domestic ownership was prevalent. Given this success in the SME sector, a potential solution to the problem of privatizing large-scale firms might be found by spinning off smaller enterprises in order to facilitate domestic sales. However, the undue emphasis placed on large firms as a principal engine of regional growth and development has led to the rejection of such proposals.[28] Consequently, the role for foreign investors in large-scale privatization has been elevated.[29]

Direct sale to foreign investors has caused much debate and concern amongst the population, chiefly "that in the absence of domestic sources of finance, foreigners will acquire a large part of industry at fire-sale prices" (Hamilton and Adjubei 1991). This echoes fears of foreign economic domination expressed in other regions in the past. However, public opinion does not appear to have influenced government policy. For example, in 1990 the Hungarian Department of Industry issued guidelines on "How to buy a company in 100 days." These were targeted directly at foreign interests, and selected 20 large enterprises whose sale to foreign investors was seen to be a high priority. The government stated that it was open to offers for all and any of the 10,000 concerns on the state's privatization list (Merrit 1991). Central and East European governments have thus been quick to switch their attention to outside investors for large privatizations, but in doing so they have tended to ignore the potential of alternative privatization schemes that could have been utilized to encourage domestic democratic ownership.

The criteria by which governments have assessed the impact of sales to foreign investors have been somewhat narrow, with governments assessing only the immediate gain from the large influx of capital (which is not surprising given the worsening fiscal positions of many governments in the region). Privatization schemes have lacked coherent purpose or strategy other than to achieve widespread, speedy transfers of ownership, with relatively little consideration having been given to the economic consequences of the wholesale transfer of large enterprises to foreign concerns.[30] Governments have tended not to recognize or guard against the influence that foreign ownership of such capital might bring to bear on the economy.

Dobosiewicz's second argument for privatization is that it may encourage further foreign investment by speeding up the transformation to a market economy. However, the assumption that the existence of free market forces must attract foreign investment is questionable. Given that the majority of privatization programs originated from 1991, evidence that foreign investment preceded this date (albeit on a small scale) would suggest that encouraging competition between firms through privatization was not an imperative for foreign investment to take place.

Furthermore, evidence (Hunya 1992; McMillan 1993) suggests that the largest purchases by foreign investors have been in sectors where the state monopoly has been the highest (e.g. automobile-manufacturing, cigarette production, and electronics). Rather than moving to a system where competition results in reduced market share, privatization of large firms has enabled transnationals to buy an automatic oligopolistic market share. Radice (1994) suggests that "even if governments are anxious to develop competitive market structures, it is clear that the attraction of a significant if not dominant market share is important to foreign companies," a corporate objective that we explored earlier.

A prime example of a transnational seeking a dominant position is the Volkswagen (VW) acquisition of Czech auto manufacturer Skoda in 1991. Skoda was deemed strategically important by VW, representing over 70 percent of automobile sales in the Czech Republic. VW acquired 31 percent of Skoda in 1991, with an option to acquire a further 40 percent by 1995. Plans were made to expand its dealer distribution networks within the region in order to increase Skoda's sales in Czech and other Central and East European markets (Dobosiewicz 1992). Furthermore, VW made maintenance of high tariffs on car imports to the Czech Republic a condition of its investment, thus enabling it to raise Skoda's prices by 15 percent in real terms between 1991 and 1993 (EBRD 1994).

There are numerous other examples of transnationals acquiring dominant positions. For example, in Hungary the vegetable oil industry was purchased by a foreign buyer as a single entity, with a state-owned monopoly simply becoming a foreign monopoly (OECD 1994). Governments would thus appear to have been naive in assuming that an increase of foreign investment in privatization was solely, if at all, due to the attractiveness of instituting so-called free market forces, and in presuming that the result of market forces would be an increase in the level of competition between firms.

COMPATIBILITY OF OBJECTIVES: THE NEED FOR AN INDUSTRIAL STRATEGY

The example of privatization illustrates how Central and East European governments, in their eagerness to rely on foreign investment as a complete economic development package, have misconstrued the degree of compatibility between government and transnational objectives. Having explored these objectives in the previous two sections, we now raise the question: can transnationals, pursuing their own objectives, achieve the outcomes that governments desire? Answering this question effectively leads us to the corporate versus industrial strategy issue raised and explored in greater theoretical and empirical detail by Cowling and Sugden (1993, 1994).

The specific governmental objectives that have been discussed – technology transfer and modernization, competition and the introduction of market forces, and privatization – may be reduced to essentially one element: the desire to introduce a free market system and create a more efficient economy, for example by introducing competition between firms. The role of transnationals in this process has been likened to "a battering ram beating down the many obstacles to the introduction of the free market economy" (Merrit 1991). However, what constitutes a free market economy and how this corresponds with government expectations is less clear; for example, if a sluggish central administration is replaced by a market system, will firms compete for market share and the economy become more efficient?

We have suggested that transnationals pursue their objectives of gaining market share and seeking low labor costs with the overall aim of achieving market monopolization in both Central and East European and global markets; this suggestion is consistent with the general arguments advanced, *inter alia*, by Kalecki (1971), Baran and Sweezy (1966), and Cowling (1982). The economic transformation occurring in Central and Eastern Europe offers transnationals the promise of realizing this monopolization goal, an opportunity that they have grasped as illustrated by their involvement in the privatization process and in their use of distribution channels.

Consider first the privatization issue. While identified as a means of introducing new capital flows into the region, privatization has also, and more importantly, been advocated as a means of introducing free market forces in the economy. If evaluated solely at this level, the Central and East European privatization programs might be presumed a success; since sizeable inflows of capital have accompanied the sale of large state-owned firms in areas such as car manufacture, and public ownership rights have been transferred to the private sector, a free market system might be said to have emerged. However, given that the introduction of greater competition between firms was deemed an important objective, the way in which transnationals have responded to the privatization process brings this underlying presumption into question. In reality, transnationals entered the region with the aim of achieving monopoly positions. Consequently, rather than encouraging increased competition as intended, privatization may well have reduced levels of competition. The sale of large, publicly owned, and monopolistic enterprises to transnationals does not necessarily imply an increase in competition, other things being equal. Furthermore, to the extent that privatization forces smaller indigenous producers from the market (or subsumed within transnationals' own structures), levels of competition are likely to be reduced rather than increased. Any restructuring that took place as the result of sales of large firms to transnational interests might usually be identified as a necessary signal of the free market driving out its temporary inefficiencies. Yet if the aim of a free market system is to allocate resources efficiently through competition between firms, reducing the number of firms that are competing calls into question the nature of the market system being established.

If privatization in Central and Eastern Europe is, therefore, simply the transfer of market power from public and domestic to private and foreign hands, and if the market system was indeed manipulated by transnational actors, caution should be exercised in other areas of foreign investment. The distinction between the transnational motive of market monopolization and the governmental objective of introducing a free market system becomes even clearer by extending the privatization hypothesis to the transnational practice of using distribution channels to gain market access. Distribution channels, warehousing facilities, and wholesaling were identified as a means for transnationals to enter new markets quickly and at least cost. While in themselves they can introduce new capital to the region and even take the form of physical investment, the benefits to be derived from their establishment are outweighed by the threat they pose to domestic development. Any action by transnationals that threatens to create a monopoly of domestic markets should be judged with caution by domestic industry and governments of the region. The global operations of a transnational enables manufacturing to be confined to one country within the region, or even removed from the region entirely, whichever the transnational judges to be strategically advantageous, while extensive distribution networks enable markets to be accessed and monopolized through imports.

Both privatization and the use of distribution channels illustrate the transnational corporate strategy of achieving product market monopolization by manipulating favorable circumstances for the achievement of their own ends. Transnationals pursuing such a corporate strategy do not satisfy the government agenda of increasing competition between firms. Thus, the attainment of government objectives becomes subservient to transnational interest. On this count, governments have had little to gain from wooing transnationals, unless processes exist to ensure that the self-interest of transnationals can be harnessed to lead to the fulfillment of government objectives. In other words, unless governments can design appropriate industrial strategies with their objectives clearly laid out and with consequent roles for transnational investment clearly identified (e.g. in terms of technology transfer, contribution to the competitive environment, etc.), "any industrialization taking place is purely incidental to the [transnational's] main objective" (Evans 1979).

Governments that welcome inward investment as an important element of a competitive market system expect to yield the alleged benefits heralded by other supposed free market economies. Yet when considering the distorted market system that results from transnationals pursing their own objectives, the relation between a free market system and the perceived benefits becomes questionable. Theoretically, in a free market system where actors pursue their own interests, the invisible hand of the market leads to an efficient allocation of resources.[31] Neoclassical economics has honed the argument, suggesting that an economy will be Pareto efficient if it comprises actors who pursue their own interests in a system of complete and perfect competition. Hence it is perhaps unsurprising that Central and East European governments have found the notion of the invisible hand so appealing. It is entirely consistent with the traditional view of economists basing industrial policy on the concept of market failure. However, there is a long line of literature systematically arguing that, in fact, free market systems are generally characterized by inherent deficiencies (see Kalecki 1971; Baran and Sweezy 1966; and Cowling 1982; see also other contributions to the monopoly capitalism literature, especially Steindl 1952; Braverman 1974; Friedman 1977; and Cowling and Sugden 1987, 1994). Moreover, the foregoing discussion of the Central and East European experience illustrates that transnationals proactively remove themselves from the rigors of perfect competition by, for example, pursuing a corporate strategy of market monopolization. In doing so the assumption that a market system will yield a Pareto efficient outcome is severely undermined. While such corporate strategies might result in overall *private efficiency* within the global operations of transnationals, governments playing host to such affiliates will not successfully achieve the objectives of the societies they represent; put another way, governments end up supporting *social inefficiency* for the benefit of the transnational, to the detriment of indigenous industrial development.

If the attainment of desirable outcomes was not predetermined by the application of a free market system in this instance, then it becomes necessary to examine the implications for the pursuit and attainment of government objectives more widely. To this end, it is perhaps revealing to use the discussion of technology transfer and modernization from pp. 306–308 as a further example of an objective for governments seeking foreign investment. Again, the disparity between the objectives of governments and those of transnationals illustrates how a distorted market system will not automatically lead to a desirable outcome for governments.

The Central and East European market, unarguably, has been in need of modernization from physical plant and infrastructure to management techniques and best-practice methods. To this end, governments have pursued transnational packages as a means to bypass economic evolution and to move to a more modern, efficient economy. As a means to achieve this, Central and Eastern Europe has utilized its low-wage advantage to attract transnational investments in the hope of stimulating technology transfer and modernization of industry.

Consider, however, transnational investments motivated by cheap labor. By manipulating this competitive edge and using the region as a base for simple, labor-intensive operations, transnationals have been able to obtain a competitive advantage over their rivals. In response, Central and Eastern Europe might have attracted transnational investment on the basis of offering a cheap site for labor-intensive exports. The two sets of objectives initially appear compatible: Central and Eastern Europe offering cheap labor that transnationals wanted, and transnationals possessing the technology and know-how that Central and Eastern Europe needed. However, under a free market system distorted by transnational activity, corporate aims supersede the objectives outlined by governments. While the policies of Central and East European governments have generally ensured that essentially any investment has been welcomed and accommodated, regardless of the technology base it delivered, governments have done little to secure the transfers of technology and modernization that they desire. Given that Central and Eastern Europe attracts low-technology, labor-intensive operations by virtue of its low-cost labor force, it is not clear how this contributes to the modernization objective if the technology used in such investments is, by definition, simple, especially when through the siting of assembly operations little technology or skills transfer is likely to occur anyway. Alongside this, the use of distribution channels and warehousing by transnationals as a means of reaching markets without investing in manufacturing indicates the possibility that in some cases essentially no technology is imported as part of the transnational package.

Governmental actions in the region would appear to suggest that the achievement of transnational objectives has been a prerequisite to domestic development and to the achievement of their domestic goals; yet we have argued that government objectives of modernization and technology transfer are not necessarily attainable through the uncoordinated activities of transnationals. It therefore cannot be presumed that the market – or any other – system serves government development needs simply through transnationals pursuing their own agendas. Under previous policy, there was no means of ensuring that government objectives would be met in the face of transnational investment. Having stated objectives, it would appear, has not been enough.

Looking at the Southeast Asian miracle, proactive government strategies for the use of transnational investment emerge as pivotal to the success of that region; objectives were stated, but a government strategy provided directed means of controlling how transnational activity influenced an economy with a view to cultivating indigenous industrial strength. On this basis, the supposition that Central and Eastern Europe could use foreign involvement in order to achieve economic development cannot be rejected. However, an obsession with transnational investment *per se* ignores the potential for using transnational activity to engender the development of indigenous industry. In effect, domestic enterprise has been relegated to the back seat as the development of the economy has been contracted out to transnational corporations.

The policy of contracting out peripheral activities in order to concentrate on core operations is accepted practice in designing corporate strategies,[32] providing firms with greater opportunity to focus on determining their core concerns, freed of the minutiae of day-to-day operations. However, the policy that has been pursued in Central and Eastern Europe of essentially contracting out *the entirety* of its future development in an uncontrolled fashion is thoroughly questionable. While contracting out or using transnationals to aid development in specific areas, such as technology or infrastructure, might be acceptable or even essential, the practice of pursuing investment as the complete solution would be tantamount to a firm handing over *all* operations to outside contractors and yet still expecting to retain a key decision-making capacity!

The danger inherent in the government policies found in Central and Eastern Europe becomes apparent when realizing that strategic decision-making power has been relinquished via the contracting-out process to organizations whose interests may not coincide with those of the government. From this situation, the ability of future governments to make decisions to determine the evolution of their own economies has been eroded, as the strategies being followed have been those of the transnational corporations, and not of the government. As we have illustrated, transnationals seek to achieve private objectives in pursuing corporate strategies, and these strategies make little contribution to the achievement of government objectives. In the absence of its own coherent industrial strategy, governments lack direction through which to assess or oversee transnational investment and to ensure that such investment yields domestic objectives. Hence, while foreign investment could be used to aid the development of Central and East European countries, governments of the region find themselves being used to further the development of transnational corporations.

CONCLUSION

The principal focus of this chapter has been to identify and explain both the motives of transnationals investing in Central and Eastern Europe and the objectives of governments in attracting such investment. The objectives of transnationals are basically the pursuit of new markets, increased market share, and low-cost production, all with the goal of increasing profitability. Government objectives have the common aim of making Central and East European industry competitive by Western standards: through the modernization of industry, the creation of market systems, and the transfer of state-owned enterprises into private hands. Central and Eastern Europe governments hope that indigenous industry will develop to become efficient, more marketable, and ultimately internationally competitive. However, it is conceivable that the policies pursued by Central and East European governments have in fact weakened rather than strengthened indigenous industry.

The central argument in this chapter is that governments in Central and Eastern Europe have objectives reducible to the key aim of creating a free market system and hence a more efficient economy; that in these free market systems the pursuit of transnational corporate strategies implies private but not social efficiency, hence achievement of transnational objectives rather than government objectives; and that, faced with this conflict, governments would be well advised to design and pursue industrial strategies that use inward investment in furtherance of their objectives rather than those of corporations.

The region is giving away both decision-making power and the potential to determine its own future development. This suggests that using transnationals to develop particular activities or industries that need Western technology or know-how could best be achieved as part of a coherent industrial strategy. Problematic though it might be to achieve this in Central and Eastern Europe, particularly given the acute political difficulties and the region's history of economic mismanagement, we suggest that strategic decision-making power should remain in the hands of the government and should not be entrusted to transnational firms.

NOTES

1 The authors would like to thank David Parker and Stan Siebert for helpful comments. An earlier version of this chapter was presented at the Workshop on Foreign Direct Investment from (Less Favored Countries of) the European Union to (Less Favored Countries of) the CEECs, Cambridge, 1995; we are grateful to participants for discussion.

2 See Dunning 1994 for a comprehensive discussion of the motivation behind transnational investment and host government justification in pursuing such investment.

3 According to Blanchard *et al.* (1991), the Council for Mutual Economic Assistance (CMEA) was responsible for facilitating and coordinating intraregional trade in Central and Eastern Europe and the former USSR, and accounted for the bulk of the region's trade.

4 It has to be noted that in some cases state-of-the-art technology is being transferred; for example, Guardian Industries brought on stream the first float glass production facility in the East, having completely refitted the factory it acquired as part of its Hungarian affiliate.

5 See Pitelis *et al.* 1994 for a discussion of investment in warehousing and distribution facilities as a means of securing markets in neighboring countries.

6 Using the example of Poland, Kozminski (1992) suggests that "an important condition for the growth of enterprises (be they native, foreign or joint ventures) operating on the Polish market is the early restructuring of the distribution system."

7 There is a question mark over this issue: a common form of entry by transnationals in new markets is often through initial distribution outlets for its imports, before moving on to joint ventures, licensing, and perhaps finally, direct manufacturing activity. One might argue that it is sometimes simply too early to observe the latter sort of activity in Central and Eastern Europe.

8 One influencing factor Merrit (1991) suggests is that "circles of political instability" have contributed to the favoring of the so-called Visegrad group (the Czech Republic, Hungary, Poland, and Slovakia) for transnational investors, as they represented least political or economic risk. The resulting favoritism, Merrit argues, served to reinforce the existing disparity between regions and the likelihood of political or economic tension.

9 This is assuming there are any significant spin-off benefits. It is worth noting that despite Hungary attracting between one-third and a half of all investment flows to the region, the role of FDI in Hungary's transition has been limited (see Bailey 1995).

10 See Table 9.6 in EBRD 1994 for details of labor costs in different Central and East European countries.

11 Wang (1993) acknowledges that "foreign firms on the whole, were prepared to accept a lower rate of profit in order to pursue their global investment strategy in Eastern Europe, aimed at the longer term prospects of enlarged markets."

12 See also the discussion in Naujoks and Schmidt 1994 of transnational's subcontracting arrangements with production units in Central and Eastern Europe. It is argued that policymakers in the region bemoaned the fact that such arrangements implied a downgrading of subcontractors' production activity, although Naujoks and Schmidt do not share this pessimism.

13 For a discussion of changes in the region since the mid-1940s, useful starting points include: Blanchard *et al*. 1991; Centre for Economic Policy Research 1992; Dobosiewicz 1992; Hunya 1992; and Lavigne 1995.

14 While foreign involvement via joint ventures has been evident in the Central and East European region, the balance of power between foreign investor and domestic counterpart in such ventures has rarely been equal, and the consequences of foreign involvement have been effectively similar to where the foreign firm has acted alone; thus all forms of foreign involvement have been generally lumped together and discussed as "foreign investment" in this chapter.

15 See also Bailey 1995 on the Hungarian experience more generally.

16 Yet Marton (1993) suggests that, "several transnationals in Hungary produce standardised, relatively low technology products . . . mostly for Western export markets. In these cases the initial investment requirement is low, and the fast and high returns make Hungary an attractive location." There is little suggestion of a broader range of skills being transferred.

17 Kozminski (1992) also suggests that in the case of Poland, "equity ties are a must . . . Poland cannot be just a passive 'customer' for foreign investors", but alongside this "no Polish company can attain a global competitive position 'single handed'."

18 It is not claimed that foreign investment should be avoided in all situations; involvement in certain sectors under certain circumstances and in different ways has proven successful in many developing countries. See Ellman 1992, Evans 1979, and Wade 1990 for discussions of how foreign investment aided the development of Brazil and the Southeast Asian region.

19 Marton (1993) recognizes that "transnationals have reduced the initial investment necessary for local production by importing used equipment from their home country or from other foreign affiliates."

20 For further discussion of the development strategy taken by Japan see Dunning 1993 and Cantwell 1994.

21 See also Bailey *et al*. 1994 for details on the Japanese case, and Teranishi 1994 for a discussion of lessons from Japan for change in Central and Eastern Europe.

22 Wade (1990) emphasizes the role played by domestic entrepreneurs and industries in creating sustained development and industrialization in the Southeast Asian region.

23 In the light of government objectives to introduce market systems into the economy, Radice assumes that this necessitated the development of a capitalist system.

24 This "strategy triangle" between transnationals, domestic firms, and governments, and its significance for the latter's strategy, is an area for future research to clarify and develop.

25 However, governments are not trusted to do this in a region where state power has been so abused. An examination of the feasibility of such an industrial strategy in the region is beyond the scope of this chapter but should also be identified as an area for future research.

26 Dobosiewicz's assertion is well founded, given that "most transnationals that entered the country for local manufacture acquired assets and production facilities through the privatisation of state owned enterprises" (Marton 1993).

27 Dobosiewicz, however, fails to interpret the so-called normal market conditions so alluring to transnational investors, and, in fact, the opposite may have occurred, with FDI taking place to prevent entry by rivals.

28 Only in Rumania have large state firms been broken up into smaller units to encourage domestic sale.

29 Radice (1994) argues that "the massive asset transfers [of foreign investors] overshadow the organic growth of the small business," hinting at the significant role that small indigenous industry has had to play, a point consistently neglected by Central and East European governments.

30 Contradictions can arise when governments try to pursue several objectives with only one economic instrument – in this case privatization. This suggests that other instruments are needed if several objectives (e.g. technology transfer, greater competition) are to be realized, again pointing to the need for strategic planning by governments in the region.
31 Adam Smith's analogy of an "invisible hand" has been at the forefront of the concept of private enterprise, whereby the entrepreneur, "intends only his own gain, and he is in this . . . led by an invisible hand to promote an end which was no part of his intention. Nor is it always the worse for the society that it was no part of it. By pursuing his own interest he frequently promotes that of society more effectually than when he really intends to promote it" (Smith 1950). Marris and Mueller (1980) observe: "few would disagree that Adam Smith's invisible hand theorem is the heart of the economist's *Weltanschaung*. Ask whether trade barriers should be lowered, the spread of multinational corporations restrained, oil prices deregulated, cartels dissolved, or more fundamentally, whether a market-based capitalist system is economically superior to a state-run socialist system, and economists almost certainly will begin to answer the question by trying to apply the theorem."
32 Contracting out is big business in the West; initially based around the "buying in" of components from outside suppliers for use in manufacturing, contracting out now extends to entire processes within manufacturing as a whole. More recently, the contracting out of noncore service activities has become a fundamental concern for large organizations in order to concentrate on value-added activities; hence contracts now range from information technology and distribution to catering, cleaning, and security.

REFERENCES

Alter, R. and Wehrle, F. (1993) "Foreign direct investment," *Intereconomics* (May/June).
Bailey, D. (1995) "Transnationals and the transition: the role of foreign direct investment in Hungary's economic transformation," Occasional Papers in Industrial Strategy, No. 32, Research Centre for Industrial Strategy, University of Birmingham.
Bailey, D., Harte, G., and Sugden, R. (1994) *Transnationals and Governments: Recent Policies in Japan, France, Germany, the United States and Britain*, London: Routledge.
Baran, P. M. and Sweezy, P. M. (1966) *Monopoly Capital*, Harmondsworth: Penguin.
Blanchard, O., Dornbusch, R., Krugman, P., Layard, R., and Summers, L. (1991) *Reform in Eastern Europe*, Cambridge, MA: MIT Press.
Braverman, L. (1974) *Labour and Monopoly Capital: The Degradation of Work in the Twentieth Century*, New York: Monthly Review Press.
Cantwell, J. (1994) "The internationalisation of business and the economic development of Poland and Eastern Europe," University of Reading Discussion Papers in International Investment and Business Studies, No. 180, Reading.
Centre for Economic Policy Research (1992) *Monitoring European Integration: The Impact of Eastern Europe*, London: Centre for Economic Policy Research.
Cowling, K. (1982) *Monopoly Capitalism*, London: Macmillan.
Cowling, K. and Sugden, R. (1987) *Transnational Monopoly Capitalism*, Brighton: Wheatsheaf.
—— (1993) "Industrial strategy: a missing link in British economic policy," *Oxford Review of Economic Policy* 19.
—— (1994) *Beyond Capitalism: Towards a New World Economic Order*, London: Pinter.

Dobosiewicz, Z. (1992) *Foreign Investment in Eastern Europe*, London: Routledge.
Donges, J. B. and Wieners, J. (1994) "Foreign investment in the transformation process of Eastern Europe," *The International Trade Journal* 8, 2.
Dunning, J. H. (1993) "The prospects for foreign direct investment in Central and Eastern Europe," University of Reading Department of Economics Discussion Papers in International Investment and Business Studies, No. 155, Reading.
—— (1994) "Globalisation, economic restructuring and development," University of Reading Discussion Papers in International Investment and Business Studies, No. 187, Reading.
EBRD (1994) *Transition Report*, London: EBRD.
—— (1995) *Transition Report*, London: EBRD.
Ellman, M. (1992) "General aspects of transition," in M. Ellman, E. T. Gardar, and G. Kolodko (eds) *Economic Transition in Eastern Europe*, Oxford: Blackwell.
Ettlie, J. E. (1993) "Issues and analyses: the emergence of manufacturing in Hungary," *Production* August: 34.
Evans, P. (1979) *Dependent Development: The Alliance of Multinational, State and Local Capital in Brazil*, Princeton, NJ: Princeton University Press.
Friedman, A. L. (1977) *Industry and Labour: Class Struggle at Work and Monopoly Capitalism*, London: Macmillan.
Hamilton, G. and Adjubei, Y. (1991) "Analysing the first wave of foreign direct investment to the countries of Eastern Europe 1987–1990" in M. Schenk *et al.* (eds) *New Dimensions in East–West Business Relations*, New York: Verlag.
Hunya, G. (1992) "Foreign direct investment and privatisation in Central and Eastern Europe," *Communist Economies and Economic Transformation* 4, 4.
Inzelt, A. (1994) "Privatisation and innovation in Hungary: first experiences," *Economic Systems* 18, 2.
Jolly, A. (1994) "Business development in Eastern Europe," in *Eastern Europe and the Commonwealth of Independent States*, London: Europa.
Kalecki, M. (1971) *Dynamics of the Capitalist Economy*, Cambridge: Cambridge University Press.
Kozminski, A. (1992) "The main issues of industrial policy for Poland," *Communist Economies and Economic Transformation* 4, 2.
Lavigne, M. (1995) *The Economics of Transition: From Socialist Economy to Market Economy*, Basingstoke: Macmillan.
Marris, R. and Mueller, D. C. (1980) "The corporation, competition and the invisible hand," *Journal of Economic Literature* 18 (March).
Marton, K. (1993) "Foreign direct investment in Hungary," *Transnational Corporations* 2, 1: 111–134.
McMillan, C. H. (1986) "Trends in direct investment and the transfer of technology," in B. Csikos-Nagy and D. G. Young (eds) *East–West Economic Relations in a Changing Global Environment*, London: IEA/Macmillan.
—— (1993) "The role of foreign direct investment in the transition from planned to market economies," *Transnational Corporations* 2, 3: 97–126.
Merrit, M. (1991) *Eastern Europe and the USSR*, London: Kogan Page.
Naujoks, P. and Schmidt, K. (1994) "Outward processing in Central and East European transition countries: issues and results from German statistics," Kiel Working Paper, No. 631, Kiel Institute of World Economics.
OECD (1994) *International Direct Investment Statistics Yearbook*, Paris: OECD.
Okolicsanyi, K. (1993) "Hungary's foreign trade in transition," *RFE/RL Research Report* 2, 29: 32–36.
Pitelis, C., Tsipouri, L., and Sugden, R. (1994) "Outward investment, international competitiveness and industrial development: the case of Greece," Occasional Papers in Industrial Strategy, No. 23, Research Centre for Industrial Strategy, University of Birmingham.

Radice, H. (1993) "Global integration, national disintegration? Foreign capital in the reconstitution of capitalism in Central and Eastern Europe," School of Business and Economic Studies Discussion Paper, University of Leeds.

—— (1994) "Organising markets in Central and Eastern Europe: competition, governance and the role of foreign capital," School of Business and Economic Studies Discussion Paper, University of Leeds.

Sawyer, M. C. (1992) "On the theory of industrial policy," in K. Cowling and R. Sugden (eds) *Current Issues in Industrial Economic Strategy*, Manchester: Manchester University Press.

Smith, A. (1950) *An Inquiry Into the Nature and Causes of the Wealth of Nations*, London: Methuen.

Steindl, J. (1952) *Maturity and Stagnation in American Capitalism*, Oxford: Oxford University Press.

Teranishi, J. (1994) "Economic recovery, growth and policies: gradualism in the Japanese context," *Economic Policy* 19 (Supplement).

Wade, R. (1990) *Governing the Market: Economic Theory and the Role of Government in East Asian Industrialization*, Princeton: Princeton University Press.

Wang, Z. Q. (1993) "Foreign investment in Hungary: A survey of experience and prospects," *Communist Economies and Economic Transformation* 5, 2.

Index

Abramovitz, M. 78, 90
ACER 243
adaptation (through networking) 95
adaptation grants 259
Adelman, M. 226
Adjubei, Y. 302, 311
adjustment modes (of integrating economies) 108–13
after-care services 193, 195–6, 197
aid 227, 295; regional (to Greece) 276, 279–80, 285, 287–9, 294–5
Airbus 23, 35
Alam, S. 241
Allied Signal 185, 188, 189, 192
Alogoskoufis, G. 278
Alter, R. 310
Amin, A. 120, 122, 184, 195
Amsden, A. H. 206, 245
Analogue Devices 144–5
analogy, failures of (between countries) 79–82, 83, 99
Anglo-Irish Free Trade Area 259
anti-agglomeration effect 84–6, 90, 99
Aoki, M. 31
Arrow, K. 170
Asanuma, B. 31
assessment, strategic 32–7
asset specificity 167, 170
Association for the Development of Private Infrastructure 288–9
AT&T 212, 214
atomistic reactions by enterprises (to international competition) 109–10
authoritarianism/autonomy 119–20, 239
Auto Europa 186, 192

Baker, T. J. 265
balance of payments (Ireland) 257, 260

banking sector 120; Korea 206, 217; Taiwan 225
Baran, P. M. 313, 315
Bardhan, Pranab 119–20
bargaining process 56–8
Bark, T. 206, 209
Barreto, J. 55
Barro, R. J. 227
Baumol, W. 166–7
BCS 286, 290
behavioural theory (of firm) 141
Bellak, C. 41, 44, 46, 49, 55, 57, 58, 67, 71
BES engineering 240
Best, M. 111, 168, 183
Blaupunkt 185, 186
Bloom, M. 207
Blue House (Korea) 205
Board of Foreign Trade (Taiwan) 240
Borensztein, E. 49
bounded rationality 167, 170
Bradford, C. I. 233
branch plants 21, 182–3
Braverman, H. 315
Brisco, S. 280
Buckley, P. J. 174
budget constraints 132, 304
Business Innovation Centres (BICs) 282, 285
'business plan' approaches 82
business reactions, collective (to international competition) 110–11
Business Week 301

C-R transactions 18
Caledonian Paper (Finland) 187, 192
Camagni, R. 194
Cantwell, J. A. 41, 44, 47–8, 50–2, 54, 62, 67, 69–71, 306, 307